NVC
Nonverbal
Communication
Studies and Applications
Third Edition

□   □   □

Mark L. Hickson III
University of Alabama, Birmingham

Don W. Stacks
University of Miami at Coral Gables

WCB Brown & Benchmark
P U B L I S H E R S

Madison, Wisconsin•Dubuque, Iowa•Indianapolis, Indiana
Melbourne, Australia•Oxford, England

Book Team

Editor *Stan Stoga*
Developmental Editor *Roger Wolkoff*
Production Editor *Deborah Donner*

WCB Brown & Benchmark

A Division of Wm. C. Brown Communications, Inc.

Vice President and General Manager *Thomas E. Doran*
Executive Managing Editor *Ed Bartell*
Executive Editor *Edgar J. Laube*
Director of Marketing *Kathy Law Laube*
National Sales Manager *Eric Ziegler*
Marketing Manager *Carla Aspelmeier*

Advertising Manager *Jodi Rymer*
Managing Editor, Production *Colleen A. Yonda*
Manager of Visuals and Design *Faye M. Schilling*
Production Editorial Manager *Vickie Putman Caughron*
Publishing Services Manager *Karen J. Slaght*
Permissions/Records Manager *Connie Allendorf*

Wm. C. Brown Communications, Inc.

Chairman Emeritus *Wm. C. Brown*
Chairman and Chief Executive Officer *Mark C. Falb*
President and Chief Operating Officer *G. Franklin Lewis*
Corporate Vice President, Operations *Beverly Kolz*
Corporate Vice President, President of WCB Manufacturing *Roger Meyer*

Cover design and chapter openers by John Rokusek

Copyedited by *Marilyn Frey*

Library of Congress Catalog Card Number: 92–70166

ISBN 0–697–12925–X

Printed in the United States of America by Wm. C. Brown Communications, Inc.,
2460 Kerper Boulevard, Dubuque, IA 52001

10 9 8 7 6 5 4 3 2

Contents

□   □   □

Preface

□   □   □

The third edition of *NVC: Nonverbal Communication Studies and Applications* is the result of almost 18 years of study and research by the authors, their teachers, and their students. The first edition of the book, we believe, broke important new ground in the study of nonverbal communication, both in the theoretical perspectives taken and in its approach to treating nonverbal communication as an area of study. The first edition reflected the interactions of nonverbal communication as representative of biological and sociopsychological functions. In the biological area, relatively new theory and research on brain hemisphere differences—hemispheric style—became an important aspect of our study. Regarding the sociopsychological factors, we stressed much more fully the *sociological* influence on nonverbal communication than was discussed in most texts. Even though nonverbal communication is a psychological phenomenon, we noted that it is also a sociological phenomenon.

The second edition of *NVC* reflected the advances in research during the years between the publishing of the first and second editions. Advancements came both in the theoretical awareness of nonverbal messages and in the methodologies used to study those messages. We are indebted to the many people who adopted the first and second editions and communicated new ideas, research, and applications. Many of the changes found in this edition come from those comments and suggestions. The third edition continues to reflect *both* the sociopsychological and the biological functions found in our nonverbal communication. We believe more firmly than ever that both perspectives must be included to fully understand the impact that nonverbal communication has on our lives. We also maintain a strong sociological focus in this text; nonverbal communication, although strongly psychological in nature, is more than individual and group differences; it reflects the culture and subculture of the communicator. We hope our treatment has maintained a balance between biological and sociopsychological functions, as well as between sociological and psychological emphases.

The book maintains the tripartite division of the previous editions. Some changes, however, were indicated both by personal use and by comments from adopters. In Section 1, ''Introduction,'' we introduce the reader to both the theory *and* the method. This section is important in that we use some terminology that is somewhat different from dictionary definitions and from other nonverbal communication books. It also sets the theoretical perspectives taken in the following sections. Section 1 introduces the student to the basics of research methodology. Our purpose here is to help the reader become a better consumer of not only this book but also other social science approaches to communication. The material on research methods has been expanded and helps establish a critical understanding both of what the researcher is doing and of what his or her advantages and limitations are, according to the method adopted.

The second section, "Subcodes and Studies," reviews the literature of nonverbal communication. This section presents the "meat" of what we know about nonverbal communication: material gleaned from a variety of sources, including scholarly journals, professional papers presented at conventions and conferences devoted strictly to the study of nonverbal communication, and where appropriate, material from more popularized sources. We believe that all sources of knowledge about nonverbal communication are important, but they must be balanced by the research questions asked and by the methods employed in drawing the conclusions they do about nonverbal communication. Hence, the second section builds on the first section. The second section's organization differs significantly from the previous editions. Although our presentation continues in its focus from the external environment to the internal environment, we have divided the chapters into more specific content areas.

We begin the studies on nonverbal communication with the space in which all people communicate from the space that is closest, touch (chapter 4), to that space which is farthest away, the environment (chapter 5). In chapter 6, we discuss physical appearance. After this, we examine how individuals communicate through their kinesic repertoire, and we identify and discuss a number of significant kinesic functions (chapter 7). Vocalic functions (chapter 8) such as conversational structure, deception, and messages of relationship are then examined. Chapter 9 examines the impact of nonverbal subcodes less obvious than those studied earlier. The impact of time (chronemics), smell (olfaction), and feedback systems on communication are examined as *biological* functions of communication, and their impact on the sociopsychological functioning of people in day-to-day activities is explored.

The first edition of *NVC* included a treatment of nonverbal communication that was unique at that time: the application of the studies to several significant contexts. Since the first edition, several texts have adopted this format, focusing mainly on nonverbal communication in specific contexts. Our treatment of this in Section 3, "Applications," continues to follow a more general approach to context. In this regard, we have actually generalized from the more specific treatments of the first edition. Our intent in these chapters is not to *prescribe* communication functioning, but to point out how nonverbal communication functions within three important contexts: in establishing and maintaining social contacts or relationships with others (chapter 10), in the nuclear and expanded family (chapter 11), and in occupational relationships (chapter 12). We have found that the discussion of these applications provides a point of departure from which students voice *real* concerns about their nonverbal communication and about its impact in contexts viewed by them as real and important. The final chapter (chapter 13) examines what we know and might want to know about nonverbal communication in the future.

Of the comments and commendations we received on the first edition, most focused on the degree of referencing and on the glossary. We have expanded the referencing even more, adding citations as up-to-date as possible, including some that will be unique to this treatment of nonverbal communication. As with the previous editions, we have included a glossary of all important terms and definitions.

At this point, we wish to thank several people who have made this book possible. Because much of the art work from the previous editions has been included in this edition, we express our appreciation to Debbie Allen and Teresa Brooks, for their able assistance in providing the photographs and many of the illustrations in the book. We would also like to thank all of the students who have taken nonverbal communication from us, for providing insight and enthusiasm for the original project and for the revisions. Many times these students walked into one of our offices with an article, newspaper clipping, or art object they thought would fit with this edition.

Finally, we would like to thank all those colleagues, teachers, and friends who have influenced our thoughts about and approaches to the study of nonverbal communication. I (Don Stacks) would like to express my thanks to several important people. First, to Judee Burgoon, under whose direction I really came to understand nonverbal communication, I owe a great deal. Second, to my coauthor, Mark Hickson, a friend, colleague, and sometimes still teacher, thank you for bringing me into this field and for teaching me that when looking at communication, "it depends." Finally, to my wife, Robin, and to my "sorority"—Stacy, Katie, and Meg—for putting up with all the days, nights, and weekends that this book has taken, I give my love and affection.

I (Mark Hickson) would like to thank Tom Pace and Russ Jennings for teaching me that there is such a phenomenon as interpersonal communication. Second, I thank my coauthors through the years, especially Don Stacks who has taught me more about nonverbal communication than I ever thought I would know. Third, I would like to thank some of the "competition" at West Virginia University, especially Virginia Richmond and Jim McCroskey for encouraging their competitors. Finally, a personal thanks to Nancy, who has to put up with a lot of chronemic problems anytime I work on a book, and to my faculty, colleagues past and present, who allow me to indulge myself in projects such as this.

Although someone's name must come first in a text, it is important the reader know that this book represents equal effort on the part of the two authors; they take total responsibility for the final product.

Much assistance, however, was rendered to us by our congenial and challenging editor, Stan Stoga and his staff. We also want to thank the reviewers: Jean Civikly, University of New Mexico; Virginia Cooper, Old Dominion University; Lynnette Eastland, University of Delaware; Ken Frandsen, University of New Mexico; Joan Gorham, West Virginia University; Lawrence B. Nadler, Miami University (Ohio); and Doris L. Werkman, Portland State University. Their suggestions, comments, and critiques were most helpful in preparing the third edition of *NVC*.

Don W. Stacks
University of Miami, Coral Gables

Mark Hickson III
University of Alabama, Birmingham

Section One

Introduction

□　　　　　□　　　　　□

As you begin reading this text, you should keep in mind that you may already know much of what you read. This should perplex you. But, if you consider that much of what we talk about as "nonverbal communication" is *normative,* is expressed in terms of expectations and unwritten rules, then you begin to gain a greater understanding of the complexities of what we choose to call nonverbal communication. From this beginning then, we move on to Section 2, "Studies," which examines each *subcode,* or area of nonverbal communication, in some depth. At this juncture most textbooks stop; the reader must take what he/she knows and try to apply it to the "real" world beyond the words and ideas in the book. We feel that there is a sufficient data base already available with which to move beyond this point, and we do so in Section 3, "Applications." Section 3 is based on what we have studied earlier and examines how each subcode operates, both alone and in conjunction with the other subcodes, in three contexts: in social situations, in the family, and on the job. This final section, then, rounds out the study of nonverbal communication by examining its impact on daily activities.

Before we begin our journey, however, several things must be done. We must first agree on what nonverbal communication is. After you have read this section, you should be able to define nonverbal communication and, by so doing, know how nonverbal and verbal communication differ with respect to several important dimensions. You should also derive an understanding of the depth of the material studied, including its historical foundations. One fact that is stressed is that nonverbal communication cannot operate in a vacuum; that is, nonverbal communication usually functions with the verbal aspects of communication to "create" what we commonly think of as a "message." Upon reading this section, you should be able to explain these functions and how they help clarify what we communicate verbally; you will acquire a basic understanding of the subcodes that constitute what we will study in some detail.

1

The chapters you will be reading are based on research conducted by social scientists. As you will find, various researchers use various methods in conducting their studies. Chapter 2 discusses perception and nonverbal communication. Here we discuss a few of the factors that assist us in filtering the nonverbal messages we receive. Chapter 3 serves to introduce you to research methods and techniques. We have included this chapter early in your study of nonverbal communication for two reasons. First, all research is only as good as the methods used to answer the questions, or to test the hypotheses, advanced. Learning about the conduct of research will help you better understand the strengths and weaknesses of the research reported. Second, you may wish to replicate or test some of the assertions and hypotheses advanced in this or other texts. An understanding of research methodology will help you find answers to *your* questions.

This first section, then, provides the foundations for what we later examine in some detail. We will attempt to identify several significant aspects of nonverbal communication for later study. As noted earlier, much of what we examine will seem rather obvious and may be something you already know. What might surprise you, however, are the anomalies, the effects of violating expectations based on the nonverbal subcodes, and how you are continually being manipulated—and manipulating others—by means of nonverbal communication. Throughout this text, then, we will look at how you use nonverbal communication to manipulate and how you are manipulated by it.

Chapter One

Foundations of Nonverbal Communication: Definitions and Historical Contexts

Key Concepts

Definitional Processes and Problems

Approaches to Nonverbal Communication

Considerations of What Nonverbal Communication Is

Verbal—Nonverbal Distinctions

Nonverbal Functions Related to Verbal Communication

Subcodes of the Nonverbal System

For Juan, a typical sophomore communication major at State University, it's a typical Monday morning. It's that day for an eight o'clock class once again. The electric alarm clock makes its familiar "buzz" at exactly 6:30. Juan, in the middle of a snore, turns over to the other side. His roommate, Bob, awakens slowly.

Bob gets out of bed and softly steps across the bedroom floor to take a shower. The soft, creeping sound awakens Juan again, and this time he gets out of bed. While Bob is in the shower, Juan goes to the dresser and begins to pick out his socks and underwear for the day. He can hardly distinguish the black socks from the blue socks, but he reasons that at this time of morning, if he can't tell, no one else will be able to either. Juan slowly picks up the electric shaver and begins to change his physical appearance.

Meanwhile, Bob is finishing his shower and washing his hair. He gets out of the shower, then blows his hair dry. Next, he brushes his teeth. He sprays on underarm deodorant, shaves, and splashes on after-shave. He puts on his underwear and walks back into the bedroom.

Now Juan proceeds into the bathroom, and Bob begins the process of choosing his "wardrobe of the day." He is particularly careful on this Monday because he wants to impress Gayle, the girl who sits next to him in his ten o'clock history class. In a matter of forty-five minutes or so, the young men are on their way to the University Union for a quick breakfast.

Upon arriving in the dining hall, the two can easily see that they will probably not have a place unless they reserve a table. Juan and Bob go to a table near where they usually sit. Each puts his books in a chair at the designated table, believing that leaving the books is, in effect, reserving a place. Then they queue up in line, each selecting his own breakfast.

For some of us, many of the events performed by Bob and Juan are typical. Others may be unusual. You will probably notice that much of the day so far has been spent in **nonverbal communication.** That is to say, they have been behaving without using many words. You may think this is typical of the beginning of the morning but that it does not continue during the rest of the day. In fact, we spend a considerable amount of time in nonverbal communication. One researcher, observing how feeling is transmitted in messages, found that as much as 93 percent of the emotional meaning is transmitted nonverbally.[1] This research further indicates that in face-to-face interaction, the total message may be sent as follows:

38 percent of the emotional meaning of the message is VOCAL

55 percent of the emotional meaning of the message is expressed via FACIAL EXPRESSION

7 percent of the emotional meaning of the message is expressed VERBALLY

Most researchers looking at the impact of nonverbal communication suggest that these figures may be a little high (93% of our communication being nonverbal), but at the same time, they accept the relatively high impact of the other-than-words dimension we will call nonverbal communication. In general, we accept Ray Birdwhistell's approximation that nonverbal communication accounts for at least 60–70 percent of what we communicate to one another.[2]

If this information is accurate, you should be asking the question, "Why haven't we studied this important phenomenon before?" Your question is obviously a good one, especially when you consider that we study verbal communication from the time we are infants through at least the sophomore level in college. Although we have had many courses in learning verbal "language," most of us have never had a course in nonverbal communication. What makes matters worse is that most people do not even know very much about it, even though we communicate nonverbally a vast majority of the time.

Because we do not study nonverbal communication much, we tend not to know much about it. The formal study of nonverbal communication, when compared with verbal communication, is still in its infancy. Nonverbal communication, as we will find, tends to be more elusive, is more difficult to define, and is more "natural," yet we do not think about it as much as we think about the more symbolic, verbal form of communication. As Paul Ekman and Wallace V. Friesen noted:

[Most people] do not know what they are doing with their bodies when they are talking, and no one tells them. People learn to disregard the internal cues which are informative about their stream of body movements and facial expressions. Most interactive nonverbal behavior seems to be enacted with little conscious choice or registration; efforts to inhibit what is shown fail because the information about what is occurring is not customarily within awareness.[3]

In summary, we are seldom aware of the nonverbal communication of others, and we are almost always unaware of our own nonverbal communication. This is not to say that *all* or even *most* of our nonverbal communication takes place unconsciously. Most of the time we simply act and react to the event, person, or object on a spontaneous basis; however, the reaction or action may take the form of an apparent unconscious yet planned or rehearsed act. Although we discuss this later in the chapter, one should realize that nonverbal communication is not totally symbolic; that is, what you communicate nonverbally cannot in most cases refer to something that is not present.

Verbal communication, as we shall see, is more symbolic (although not totally) and more conscious in terms of its presentation. The ''nature'' of nonverbal communication, then, is something we tend to take for granted (unless, of course, we have violated a nonverbal expectation or we find a need to manipulate that aspect of it).

Basic Definitions

To understand nonverbal communication, we need first to define what we mean by the term *communication*. We believe that **communication** is an interactive process whereby people seek to induce some form of change in attitude, belief, or behavior. We also agree with Judee K. Burgoon and Thomas J. Saine, who contend that communication may be defined as a ''dynamic process [of] . . . creating shared meaning from sending and receiving messages via commonly understood codes.''[4] Through communication we control ourselves, others, and our environment. Communication, then, involves a reciprocal process—one that is dynamic or on-going—whereby we intentionally alter the course of future communications. Although we believe that *most* communication is intentional, we also contend that the question of intent (which we address later) may be more a perceptual and motivational aspect of communication than a functional one.

What is nonverbal communication? To begin with, let us assume that the *nonverbal part of communication is that aspect of the communication process that deals with the transmission and reception of signs that are not part of natural language systems.* Whether they are spoken or written, words are considered part of verbal interactions. Any phase of communication that does *not* include words is considered *nonverbal*. However, we will be dealing only with those aspects of nonverbal communication that are perceived through one or a combination of the five known senses.[5] Although ESP and other versions of nonverbal communication (such as dreams and dream analysis) are generally excluded from our discussion, a short discussion of their impact is given later.[6]

We should remember that nonverbal communication may be a characteristic of the speaker (flattop hairdo, raspy voice, cutoff blue jeans, digital watch, raised eyebrow); it may be a characteristic of the receiver (looking bored, asleep, anxious); or it may be a feature of the situation (cold room, institutional green walls, light bulb burned out, the smell of medicine in a hospital). *Or* nonverbal may be the interaction of all three: **the speaker** (dress, voice, distance maintained from other), **the receiver** (posture, expression, maintenance of the distance adopted), and **the situation** as perceived by a receiver (the context, the environment, the time).

By now you should have some idea of what nonverbal communication is. It is something more than being merely ''beyond words,'' or as Edward Sapir once suggested, ''an elaborate code that is written nowhere, known to none, and understood by all.''[7] Nonverbal communication is complex, it is both behavior and communication, or at least has the potential for communication. It may be shared *between* people or *within* people. It may be either intentional or unintentional. Sometimes it may even be symbolic.

Considerations for Definitions

Before we state exactly what we believe nonverbal communication to be, we must address some of the considerations just mentioned: behavior versus communication; intentionality; sign versus symbol; and, finally, the process structure of the nonverbal ''code.''

Behavior versus Communication   First, and perhaps most importantly, we should distinguish between nonverbal **behavior** and nonverbal **communication.** Granted, some writers do not make this distinction; however, we attempt to do so here. As we have already stated, the perception of green walls is part of nonverbal communication. Only living things behave. Walls may ''communicate'' only because living things interpret them in certain ways and act accordingly. In a given context, the size of a room may communicate; you probably feel quite awkward when you have a class with five members meeting in a room designed for 200 students. At the same time that inanimate objects may communicate, we might find that humans may behave without communicating. It is true that we cannot *not* behave. We can, however, *not* communicate. In our discussion, we will be using the word *communicate* only when a receiver has interpreted a message as having some meaning. Thus, for communication, a receiver must be present and must interpret (decode in some way) the transmission of symbols (messages), whether they are verbal or nonverbal.

With the possibility of confusing the situation even more, we can also consider the sender as being his/her own receiver. That is, you can communicate nonverbally with yourself. In this case, however, there may be a fine distinction between behavior and communication. What is critical here is the control the sender exerts over the communication and the receiver's awareness of the communication. As A. T. Dittman points out, a message may be controlled and yet subliminal (below the level of consciousness) and not perceived.[8] For example, suppose you are driving down the highway. You are the only person in your car. You have this desperate urge to pick your nose. You look around and see that no cars are approaching. There are no other people around. So you pick your nose. Is this nonverbal communication or nonverbal behavior? It is nonverbal *communication* because you yourself have interpreted the message—you have perceived a need, considered others, and had a **social cognition** (e.g., you weighed the social consequences of the act). If you merely acted, the act becomes a behavior.[9]

Intentionality   Second, we need to understand the concept of **intentionality** as it relates to nonverbal communication. In verbal communication, we are most often deliberate in what we say. In the nonverbal system, however, there is often the unintentional transmission of messages. For example, if you have an itch, most often you will scratch it. In the event that you think it is socially inappropriate to scratch this particular part of your body in front of these particular people at this particular time, you may decide not to scratch it.

An example of intent is demonstrated by the head scratch. Usually you scratch your head in a general context and it means nothing. However, in the early 1980s the *Head and Shoulders* shampoo advertisers created a new meaning for scratching: dandruff and all the negative connotations, according to the commercial, of having flaky scalps. What had been a simple reaction (behavior) to a felt need now may be interpreted by others as an intentional (and negative) communication between you and them. The *perception* of some form of intent is enough to be considered nonverbal. Thus, communication did occur, although you may not have intended the message that was transmitted. Nonverbal communication takes place when a message is decoded (or interpreted) as having meaning, regardless of intent on the part of the sender. Most of our *verbal* communication carries with it a greater amount of intent, but *nonverbal* communication tends to be more primitive and less controllable than its verbal counterpart. Michael Burgoon and Michael Ruffner go so far as to assert that if verbal communication is not perceived by a receiver as intentional and if that same message was not intentionally sent by a source, then that message is *not* communication.[10] They imply that intentionality, as far as verbal communication goes, is a necessary prerequisite for communication. If, for example, the source does not intend the communication, the action is labeled as *ascribed communication,* communication that fails to provide an explicit meaning for what is said (like overhearing someone talking about you out of context). If the source intends a message and if the receiver fails to perceive intent, the action is labeled a *communication attempt.* In this case the source has failed to be understood.

In the nonverbal area, however, such distinctions are not as readily made. What you communicate nonverbally may be perceived as intentional even if you do not intend it (the *Head and Shoulders* advertisement, for example). L. Malandro, L. Barker, and D. Barker, have suggested that ''goal-direction'' helps to explain nonverbal communication and intentionality.[11] Their explanation closely follows that already presented: If you intend to send a nonverbal communication, and it is perceived as intentional, it is communication; if you do not intend a message, but that message is perceived as intentional, it is communication; if you intend a message, but that message is not perceived as intentional, it is communication. However, if you do not intend the message and no one perceived the message as intentional, then it falls under the category of behavior.

Sign versus Symbol   Next, we need to examine how verbal and nonverbal communication operate in guiding or directing ourselves and others through the use of signs and symbols. Verbal communication, almost by definition, is *mediated* by the type of code material it contains. By this we mean that because of its symbolic nature, this code is something we must agree on; we must create a socially shared system of agreement. The perceived intentionality of verbal communication creates a need to share with others just what we ''mean'' when we use the words that compose the elements of the verbal code of communication. Nonverbal communication, however, may be symbolic or nonsymbolic.

One of the more difficult areas in distinguishing between verbal and nonverbal communication deals with the distinction between a *sign* and a *symbol.* In the verbal code, we have the **symbol,** that is, something takes the place of something else—something *represents* an abstraction such as beauty, God, or wealth. That verbal communication is symbolic is inherent in the very abstractness of words. The phrase ''Sticks and stones will break my bones, but words can never hurt me'' is, as most of us know, wrong. Words, because of their symbolic nature, often hurt much more than an actual physical attack. To prove this point, one of your authors puts on the board in large letters prior to class: ''WARNING: STUDENT SEATED IN THE FOURTH ROW FROM THE DOOR, THIRD SEAT BACK, HAD SYPHILIS.'' Even though we know that we cannot get the disease from a student's chair, that chair remains empty for the class period. Obviously, one cannot get syphilis from a chair or toilet, but no one wants to be identified as the student with syphilis. Other professors we know ask students to erase the word *syphilis* with their hands. Many refuse. A **sign,** on the other hand, is a natural representation of the event or act. It is *it.* Fever is a sign of one's being ill. Much of what we call nonverbal communication falls under the rubric of a sign, but not all. Nonverbal communication can, and often does, yield a symbol. People expressing emotions do so nonverbally; once they have emitted the emotion—smiled, cried, frowned—we tag the behavior with a symbol—''happiness,'' ''sadness,'' and ''displeasure.'' Once some receiver has the potential (to include him/herself) for receiving the message, it becomes symbolic.[12] What we try to do in many cases is infer meaning from a sign. This process is unnecessary with the verbal code, which must depend upon a socially shared meaning assigned to the abstraction by the society that uses it.

Although verbal communication is quite *explicit* about what it represents, nonverbal communication is more *implicit*. Albert Mehrabian first distinguished between explicit and implicit communication by noting that "Verbal cues are definable by an explicit dictionary and by rules of syntax, but there are only vague and informal explanations of the significance of various nonverbal behaviors.[13] We take Mehrabian's explicit-implicit dichotomy one step further by noting that much of what we communicate nonverbally involves expectations. These expectations become normative and yield appropriate and inappropriate behavior. Distancing zones, appropriate dress, hair length, speech rate, amount of touch, and other nonverbal elements differ by culture and even by subculture. They take on different normative expectations that we can either maintain or violate. Violation of such a norm, as we shall see in later chapters, can yield both beneficial and hazardous effects.

Take our opening example of Bob and Juan. When they got up for school, they began something that is normative for most of us: they showered, cleaned up, dressed, went to eat, reserved their place with a book, and generally behaved as *expected.* Over a period of time such expectations become the norms that govern behavior and communication patterns. Although verbal communication is symbolic and must be analyzed each time it is used (e.g., we must "think" about what we are going to say—or at least we wish we had at times), the nonverbal code is less symbolic and more normative in nature.

Because of these expectations, we assume, often inappropriately, that nonverbal communication is less manipulative and more "true" to our feelings than is verbal communication. That is, nonverbal communication is considered more sincere and believable than is verbal communication. Exploring nonverbal communication in more detail shows us that this relationship really does not exist in the ways we imagine. In the case of Bob and Juan, unless there is a particular reason for changing their thinking about nonverbal communication, people usually just act and react in accordance with everyday normative expectations, which often mold their verbal communication.

We would define **nonverbal communication** as a process whereby people, through the intentional or unintentional manipulation of normative actions and expectations (other than words themselves) express experiences, feelings, and attitudes in order to relate to and control themselves, others, and their environments.

Nonverbal communication, then, operates in a manner similar to verbal communication; it seeks to provide us a means of control, although in a more subtle, spontaneous, and natural way. Aside from the differences in terms of expression (symbolic versus primarily nonsymbolic or spontaneous), the nonverbal code allows for interpretation of messages not intentionally sent if the receiver perceives the messages as intentional. As such, the nonverbal code, while containing much more information, loses specificity of content. The nonverbal message by itself may be ambiguous; in almost every instance, it needs the verbal message to complete the process of communication. Although there is seeming agreement about what constitutes nonverbal communication and what does not, there are considerable differences of opinion about how to approach the study of nonverbal communication. In the next section, we discuss some of these approaches.

Approaches to Nonverbal Communication

An **approach** is simply the way one sees things. Our approach to the study of nonverbal communication suggests several factors. First, it implies that we either include or exclude several elements in our study. Second, our approach "colors" how we see the event—and may even determine whether we can see it at all. Third, an approach involves some research methodology:

a method of classifying what we are observing, a way of understanding what we see based on that classification, and, finally, a basis for predicting future behaviors. As you might guess, there are many approaches to the study of nonverbal communication.

An approach is often identified either by a field of study or by one's research methods. Nonverbal communication evolves from the biological sciences—through the work of Charles Darwin. More recently, we find the works of Robert Ardrey, Desmond Morris, Ray Birdwhistell, Edward T. Hall, Ashley Montagu, Jurgen Ruesch, Albert Mehrabian, and Erving Goffman. D. Druckman, R. M. Rozelle, and J. C. Baxter have indicated that we might want to distinguish between nonverbal communication and nonverbal behavior.[14] They suggest that the study of nonverbal behavior may yield nonverbal communication, but this would identify researchers only from their own (psychological) approach as representative of their theoretical approach. What should be of interest to the communication student is the fact that almost no speech communication research is represented, even though its basic premise would seem to run throughout such research. This, then, is the problem with identifying an approach with any specific discipline. Even though researchers may cross disciplinary lines, they are identified primarily by *approach.*

Another way of examining approaches to the study of nonverbal communication is on the basis of what people assume to study and how they study it. In this regard, Judee K. Burgoon and Thomas J. Saine have laid out a theoretical analysis of how people approach the study of nonverbal communication.[15] Although their analysis is rather complex, they conclude that the approach one takes results in several effects. First, your approach focuses your attention on what you seek and sets your priorities as to what is important and not important. Second, your approach is governed by the assumptions you make about the behavior you are studying.

Third, the approach you take will indicate that one behavior may cause another behavior, or that certain past experiences or conditions will cause a behavior. We might interpret someone's shaking a fist as a vestige of our primitive past. By examining other primates who may engage in the same behavior when angered, we may draw a parallel conclusion. On the other hand, if you believe that socialization is the major cause of behavior, then the response to a wave of the hand should elicit a similar behavior. The communicative value of the act might be that of friendship. Finally, an approach may involve a method of studying nonverbal communication. It may set the perimeters of the study: when to begin and where to end. If, for instance, your approach is more psychoanalytic, then you are more interested in past experiences; if your approach is more behavioral, you may be interested in present experiences.

Although specific theoretical and disciplinary approaches *may* be associated with specific ways of carrying out research, this is not necessarily the case. Anthropologists may take an *ethological* approach, in which the nonverbal behavior of human beings is associated with the nonverbal behavior of other animals. Such is the case, for example, in Charles Darwin's analogy of human communication with the communication of lower animals. Some anthropologists, following such an analogy, use an ethological method. Other anthropologists, however, research human nonverbal communication as it relates to human verbal communication. This *linguistic* approach (sound makes words, words make sentences, sentences make paragraphs, etc.) has been used extensively by Birdwhistell. A *functional* approach looks at the purpose for which the nonverbal communication is used. Figure 1.1 illustrates the method of research employed. Contemporary nonverbal research and theory, however, draws upon *all* lines of study in order to understand how we communicate. Although specific researchers may adopt particular approaches, they are still aware of the contributions of other approaches to the study of nonverbal communication.

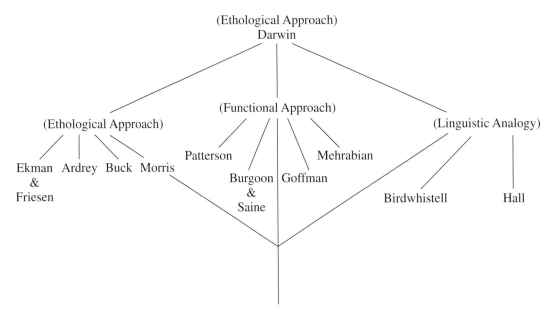

FIGURE 1.1   Approaches to Nonverbal Communication.

Functional Synthesis

Approaches filter what you see and channel your data (behaviors) into a system for interpretation. As Burgoon and Saine point out, there are many approaches to the study of nonverbal communication—some of them formulated by the same researchers.[16] We believe that no one approach is "right" or "correct." We believe that we often take something from one approach and add it to another to create our own approach. Certainly, most communication researchers have borrowed heavily from many diverse approaches to the study of nonverbal communication.

As we begin to examine the differing areas of nonverbal communication (subcodes), we draw from many approaches. How we put these together, then, may yield a "new" or hybrid approach to the study of nonverbal communication. We believe that several perspectives or approaches are more useful to us; these have had significant impact on our thinking about the study of nonverbal communication. Such approaches include material gained from anthropological roots, as advanced by Edward T. Hall and Ray Birdwhistell; from psychological roots, as put forth by Miles Patterson and Albert Mehrabian; and from a newer, neurophysiological approach as advanced by Richard Restak and Stuart Litvak. Evidently, too, we have been influenced by the work of people in the speech communication field, including Mark Knapp, Judee K. Burgoon, Dale Leathers, Randall Harrison, and Janis and Peter Andersen. This last group examines nonverbal behaviors for *communicative* value, as framed by the earlier works of A. T. Dittman,[17] Paul Ekman and Wallace Friesen,[18] and Albert Mehrabian,[19] and the neurophysiologial work of Andersen, Garrison, and Andersen,[20] which seems to be gaining acceptance.

Even the approaches to nonverbal communication by people in the speech communication field differ significantly. Mark Knapp, one of the earliest nonverbal communication researchers, stresses the developmental approach.[21] Dale Leathers takes a more general systems approach.[22] Judee Burgoon and Thomas Saine conclude that of several approaches, the functional is best suited to their research.[23] And L. Malandro, L. Barker, and D. Barker seem to take a more psychological approach.[24] Having been influenced by all these people, our approach will include some of each. It should be obvious by now that the approach you take to an object or problem will influence how you perceive it. In this regard, the approach you take will *define* what you see.

We believe it is desirable at this juncture to digress somewhat and examine the ''roots'' of the study of nonverbal communication. We do so for two reasons: first, because knowing where we began and knowing the differences that have evolved over a long period of time affords us an opportunity to understand more about what we are studying; second, it is essential to realize that the nonverbal code of communication has been studied and, at various times in the past, may have been as important as it is today, if not more so (in periods of cultures that were primarily oral/verbal rather than written/verbal, for example). We may also begin to understand why we have not been exposed to nonverbal communication. First, we discuss how the study of nonverbal communication began.

A Short History

Mark Knapp has traced interest in the study of nonverbal communication back to the early Hellenic period, about 400 to 600 years before Christ.[25] Although this starting point may be somewhat arbitrary, it falls within the purview of the study of discourse as a means of influence. The early Greeks, with primarily an oral culture, would have been interested in the delivery portions of any public communication. One might argue, however, that the study of nonverbal communication on a more basic survival level may have begun once *Homo sapiens* began to evolve into a social animal. Harry J. Jerison has suggested that the development of both nonverbal and verbal communication complemented each other.[26] He has argued that the spatiotemporal aspects of the nonverbal code began along with that of wolves and primates, for example. As humans began to interact as social predators, nonverbal communication became more refined and was associated with an awareness of time and place. As these images became further refined, they took on the shape of objects, which as evolution progressed, became symbolically linked to a ''language.'' Over time, this language became the major form of intentional communication with other people.

Probably the beginning of the study of nonverbal communication as we know it today is to be found in analyses of the writings of Charles Darwin. In 1872, Darwin published *The Expression of Emotions in Man and Animal.* One of the first to associate nonverbal behaviors of man with other species, Darwin's influence on the study of nonverbal communication has been great. What should be of interest to communication researchers is the movement from analyzing nonverbal communication as primarily a *mode of delivery*—association only with the verbal stream of thought and presentation—to seeing it as a function that may *indicate* a mood, an attitude, or a feeling. Darwin's investigations inaugurated the modern study of nonverbal communication, a study that may or may not be as closely associated with the verbal message as before. What Darwin did, however, was to establish a line of thought that is still prevalent. As we examine some of these trends, we will note different perspectives of what is nonverbal and of how we approach the study of nonverbal communication. Our concept or interpretation of communication influences (1) how we approach the study of nonverbal communication, and (2) how we decide what nonverbal communication, is and, conversely, what it is *not*.

This position—that of evolution—suggests a perspective from which to study nonverbal communication. Those of you who have taken a course that analyzed Darwin's theory of evolution should see some striking similarities between Jerison's position and Darwin's: language evolved to ensure survival. Nonverbal communication functioned as a beginning point for language and became the primary means for *input* to verbal communication. During the centuries between the early Greeks and Darwin, however, little was accomplished in the study of communication. Indeed, much of what was being studied consisted of simple analyses of speech delivery. Scholars in this period were interested in classifying systems of speech and proper delivery techniques.

In the late eighteenth century, however, some interest in other aspects of formal speech began to develop. In 1775, an Irishman, Joshua Steele, began to analyze the voice as an instrument of communication.[27] Later, in 1806, Gilbert Austin developed a system of gestures that is somewhat similar to the more modern systems applied today.[28] Austin's system, like many **elocutionary systems,** provided a speaker with ''appropriate'' gestures for delivery of speech. A more complex system, developed by Francois Delsarte in the mid-1800s, was based on movements or gestures aimed at expressing attitude.[29] As we note in later chapters, much of what Steele, Austin, and Delsarte began is still being investigated, especially in the area of kinesics, or bodily communication.

Thus, there are several approaches to the study of nonverbal communication. Some of these approaches were begun many years ago. Darwin studied nonverbal communication as an aspect of his theory of evolution. Steele wished to improve the vocal skills of actors, as did Delsarte. Austin was concerned with improving the gestures of speakers. Today we view the study of nonverbal communication as a method for observing normative behavior and for improving our skills for speaking, participating in interviews, avoiding embarrassment, and increasing our overall communication skills. To accomplish these goals, we must study each of the subcodes of the nonverbal communication process.

The Subcodes

To this point, we have talked about what nonverbal communication is, and we have used numerous examples. By now you understand that we can look at many actions or expressions and call them nonverbal communication. What we choose to study and how we group these subjects together reflect both our definition of nonverbal communication and our approach to its study. We believe it best to examine the **subcodes,** those component parts of the major nonverbal code, as dimensions related in four areas: spatial use, physical appearance, overt body and vocal communication, and covert body-temporal communication. We feel that these four areas, with their appropriate sub-areas, constitute nonverbal communication. We feel that such a categorizing system makes both theoretical and practical sense.

Spatial Use

We communicate in some environment or physical setting. Accordingly, we believe we should begin with an analysis of the environmental impact on our communication. This helps establish the context of the communication. Consistent with this premise, we examine in Section 2 the influences of feature dimensions, color and aesthetic appreciation, environmental size and shape, and temperature and humidity. Within this environment, we structure the space around us. We do so in two ways: we establish territories, and we expect certain amounts of personal space to be available to us. Thus we look at how we structure our territory and our personal space, what types of communications can be expected in each, and what the norms are regarding both aspects of proxemic (use of territory and personal space) behavior. We examine the total lack (absence) or violation of space as well as touching behavior. Commonly refered to as haptics, we may substitute *zero-proxemics* for the study of touch. Finally, we examine the impact of violating normative expectations with respect to distancing and touch.

Physical Appearance

We examine the impact of our body on communication. In this regard, we look at body shape, body image, physical attractiveness, clothing, and accessories. We consider how the body is used as a communicative tool and how we perceive the bodies of others. Such things as stereotypical judgments, relationships between body size and IQ, salary discrepancy, and expectations are examined for their day-to-day impact. Finally, we examine the impact of artifacts/accessories on people's perceptions of others.

Overt Body and Vocal Communication

Overt body communication deals with gross and minute bodily behavior that can be visually observed. We view overt body communication in two ways: the use of gesture and facial expression, and the use of voice. In the first section, Birdwhistell's kinesic system is explored in some detail. Based on this, we then examine a different system, Ekman and Friesen's more meaning-centered approach to bodily movement. We examine the relationship of blending behaviors, of creating differing emotive communications. We examine the relationship between eye behavior and communication, both between people and as an analysis of the brain's activity during communication.

The second section examines the unique contribution the voice makes to our communications, or our "vocal expressiveness." We explore some of the stereotypes we have of others based on their voices' masculinity, femininity, assuredness, and cooperativeness, to name a few. We look at sound and its attributes, such things as loudness, pitch, duration, articulation, and silence. We examine the paravocal aspects of voice qualities (what is a good voice and what is a bad voice, how they are used, and with what effect), characterizers, and qualifiers. Finally, we examine vocal segregates, including the effects of dialect, accent, rate, and nonfluencies, and we consider their correlation with such characteristics as body shape.

Covert Body-Temporal Communication

The final chapters in Section 2 examine phenomena we normally do not ''see.'' The chapters consider the impact of the olfactory system (language of smell and bodily odor), as well as the telepathic system or perceptual aspects of nonverbal communication and its potential for use. From this we look at the biofeedback aspects of nonverbal communication, including possible deception detection. We examine the impact of time (chronemics) on our communication, based on biofeedback rhythms, as well as the cultural and subcultural expectations of how we use and perceive time.

We continue our introduction to the first section by observing how studies of nonverbal communication are undertaken. Chapter 2 provides background information on perception as it relates to nonverbal communication.

□   **Summary**   □

From this discussion, you should have gained the following information: First, nonverbal communication is important. It accounts for between 65 and 93 percent of the communication we have with one another in face-to-face interactions. Second, there have been several theoretical and methodological lines of thought in the study of nonverbal communication. Third, although nonverbal communication differs from verbal communication in many ways, the two systems function together. In addition, you should be able to distinguish between nonverbal communication and nonverbal behavior. Finally, you should be able to identify and define nonverbal communication in terms of four basic dimensions: overt body (kinesic) and vocalic communication, spatial use (proxemic/haptic), physical appearance, and body-temporal communication (covert, olfactory, chronemic).

Chapter Two

Nonverbal Communication and Perception

Key Concepts

Nonverbal Communication Functions

Sex and Gender Differences

Brain-processing Structures

Age, Culture, Race, and Status Differences

Most researchers agree that the communication process begins with **perceptions.** Perceptions are the way that we look at things. As such, these ways of looking have two components: (1) sensation; and (2) interpretation. A sensation takes place with one of the five senses: sight, or the visual sense; sound, or the vocal sense; smell, or the olfactory sense; touch, or the tactile sense; and taste, or the gustatory sense. These sensory organs are illustrated in Figure 2.1.

After a stimulus has been sensed by one or more of these sensory organs, we interpret this stimulus in the brain. In a sense, we "place" the particular stimulus within what Don Stacks, Mark Hickson III, and Sidney R. Hill, Jr. call a "memory bank of perceptions."[1] Through this process of perceiving, stimuli from the external world become part of what we refer to as knowledge.

Knowledge, in nonverbal communication, is typically related to *how we intend to evaluate the message.* As such, nonverbal communication provides us with a message about the message (a metamessage). Here we are saying that nonverbal communication tells us, for example, whether the other person is being serious, joking, or sarcastic when she says, "I love you." This evaluation might be based on the other person's vocal tone and facial expression when the message was sent. Figure 2.2 illustrates this perceptual process.

FIGURE 2.1   Sensory Organs.

There are a number of factors which **filter** our interpretations of nonverbal messages. These **filters** include function or purpose, sex and gender, process structure, culture and race, age, and status. A number of the functional theorists claim that one of the most important is the **function** of the interaction as determined by the sender or the receiver. These include: (1) identification and self-presentation; (2) control of the interaction; (3) relationship of interactants; (4) display of cognitive information; (5) display of affective information; and (6) deception.[2] The following section indicates how each of these factors relate to the various subcodes.

Purposes of Interaction

Identification and Self-Presentation

Identification and self-presentation deal with who you are and who you are trying to make others think that you are. Thus, how you dress, the extent to which you wear makeup, the way your hair is cut are means through which you make a self-presentation through physical appearance. Your accent, your loudness of voice, whether you stutter, how fast you speak all involve how you present yourself to others through vocal mechanisms. How broad your gestures are, how uptight you appear, the extent to which you express yourself with your face are all elements of how you present yourself through kinesics. How close you stand or sit to another person provides elements of self-presentation through proxemics.

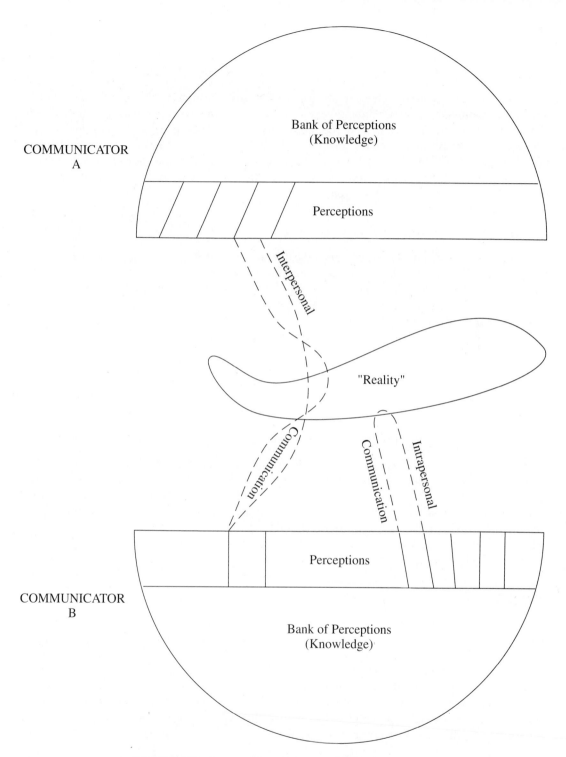

FIGURE 2.2 Interpretation of Sensed Perceptions.
Source: D. Stacks, M. Hickson III, and S. R. Hill, Jr., *Introduction to Communication Theory* (Ft. Worth, TX: Holt, Rinehart, and Winston, 1991).

Control of the Interaction

If you are wearing a suit and others are dressed less formally, you probably have the opportunity to control the situation more than the others in the group. In this way, you can control the interaction through physical appearance. If you talk loudly and leave few pauses for others to enter the conversation, you are controlling the interaction through vocalics. If you raise your hand or touch the other person to ''gain the floor,'' you are using kinesics to control the conversation. If you are standing in front of the room and others are seated some distance away from you, you are controlling the conversation through proxemics.

Relationship of Interactants

When you wear a matching outfit, you are indicating to others that you are ''together,'' a physical appearance mechanism for showing your relationship. When you talk softly to another person or whisper, you are showing that your relationship is closer than it might be otherwise. Thus, you are using vocalics to show your relationship. When you hold hands and sit close together, you are showing the nature of your relationship through proxemics. When you wink at another person and have a great deal of eye contact, you are indicating something about your relationship through kinesics.

You may also show *negative* aspects of a relationship through nonverbal cues. Standing farther away, wearing a three-piece suit among bikers dressed in leather, silence, and pointing one's finger at another might show such negative evaluations of the other.

Display of Cognitive Information

Cognitive information is simply knowledge that could be transmitted through words rather than how you *feel* about what you are saying. For example, wearing a uniform provides cognitive information to another person through the use of dress identification. Thus, you might be saying nonverbally, ''I am a police officer.'' Gestures such as ''1'' or ''OK'' can be used to supply cognitive information. Placing your briefcase in the seat next to you on a plane probably says to others, ''I don't want anyone to sit here,'' or ''This seat is reserved for a special person.'' Stating a sentence with sarcasm, says to the other person, ''I mean the opposite of what I am saying.''

Display of Affective Information

Affective information shows the other person how you feel about what you are saying. If you are usually loud and boisterous but today you are quiet, you might be saying, ''I don't feel well, so don't take much of what I am saying too seriously.'' If you usually are well-dressed but today you are not, you might be saying, ''I didn't feel like getting well-dressed today.'' If you start avoiding people you usually interact with, you might be saying through proxemics that you are not in the mood to talk today. If you close your office door when usually you do not, you are saying through proxemics, ''I don't feel like talking with anyone; I have other things to do. I need my privacy.'' All of these affective information cues relate to how the person *feels* when she or

TABLE 2.1   Sex Differences in Human Interaction

VARIABLE	FEMALES	MALES
Purpose	To negotiate	To control
Place	Private	Public
Orientation	Cooperation	Competition

he is communicating. In addition, affective information includes the **intensity** with which the person sends the message. "Look out" and "LOOK OUT!" show different intensity by virtue of vocalics and perhaps other elements of nonverbal communication.

Another filtering element in perceptions is sex and gender. This demographic and biological variable we take with us in many ways "programs" the purpose we see in an interaction.

Sex and Gender

Deborah Tannen has published a book about the nature of interaction between males, between females, and between males and females.[3] Table 2.1 summarizes some of her findings. The first of these findings has to do with the purpose of interaction. Tannen has found that males tend to use the communication process to *control,* while females use the communication process to *negotiate.* As an analogy, we will use a tennis match.

For males, the purpose of "playing a point" is to win the point. One of the ways to win a point is to "slam the ball down the opponent's throat." Another, perhaps more sophisticated means of winning the point, is a soft shot down the other side of the court or a drop shot just over the net while the opponent is in his or her backcourt. At any rate, the purpose is to win, to persuade.

For females, however, playing a point may be about trying to keep the volley going so that the result is a longer-lasting match with less competition and perhaps more fun. The female's purpose is to communicate, to negotiate, to be informative.

A third type of interaction, used by both sexes and genders, is **catharsis.** Here the server is simply trying to release tension—to feel better. As a tennis analogy, it's more like hitting the ball against a wall. In a sense, it doesn't matter whether there is another player (receiver) or not.

The second element of human interaction that varies by sex and/or gender is *where* people interact. According to Tannen, females tend to prefer interacting in private (one on one and small group) situations, while males tend to prefer public situations. Each of these factors, then, affect how we communicate nonverbally.

The third element is orientation. As we have explained, negotiation is based on cooperation, controlling is based on competition.

What else do we know about how males and females (or people with masculine orientations and people with feminine orientations) in terms of the communication process?

Ray L. Birdwhistell has divided the characteristics that differentiate the two sexes into three categories.[4] The first type, *primary,* is based on whether a human produces ova or spermatozoa. *Secondary* characteristics are anatomical in nature, and *tertiary* characteristics are essentially psychosocial. Whereas primary and secondary characteristics are biological, tertiary traits are learned. For our purposes, it is the *gender,* or learned, traits that are of greatest importance. An overview of the research on **gender** differences between males and females reveals the following:

Facial expression
    Women tend to be more prone to reveal their emotions in their facial expressions; males do not reveal as much overtly but have a faster heartbeat and more activity (internalize the nonverbal); women are better at remembering names and faces of classmates; women tend to smile and laugh more than do men.

Posture and bearing
    Women have legs together or crossed at the knees or upper legs; males have their legs apart at a ten- to fifteen-degree angle. Females keep their upper arms close to the trunk. Men assume a more relaxed posture than women. Communicators are more relaxed with females than with males.

Eye contact
    In most situations, women maintain more eye contact than do men; women look at other women more and hold eye contact longer with one another than men do.

Gesture
    In approval-seeking situations, women gesture more than men. In general social conversation, men use a greater variety of gestures than women.

Clothing, grooming, and physical appearance
    Females use physical appearance to get higher grades from male professors; physical appearance has a persuasive effect on both sexes; one's attractiveness is more important for female speakers than for male speakers.

Use of space
    Women are approached by both sexes more closely than are men. Men have more negative reactions to crowding.

Touch
    Although traditional studies found that males were more likely to initiate touch, more recent research has not supported that conclusion. Women do not necessarily interpret a man's touch as a sexual invitation, but men often interpret a woman's touch that way.[5]

Reports concerning kinesic, proxemic, and tactile differences are summary products of the preceding research. However, we can also present a general review of vocalic differences:

Sound development
    Girls begin talking at an earlier age; girls' speech is more comprehensible at an earlier age; they use shorter sentences earlier; and from 12 months on, they are more fluent than males. Female speech organs mature sooner than those of males. Mothers vocalize to female children more and receive more feedback from female children. Male children play outside more and have less experience with adult conversation. Girls' toys usually require more verbalization than boys'. Boys use more "sound effects" in playing with their toys.

Physiological differences
    The male larynx is usually larger than a female's. Males tend to have longer and thicker vocal cords than females; therefore, they usually have voices that are lower in pitch. More males than females tend to have speech defects.

Sex and speech patterns
    Pronunciation: Males more often leave the *g* off of *ing* words. Females speak more standard American dialect. Males think it's masculine to use nonstandard, blue-collar English.

Pitch: The stereotype is low pitch for males and high pitch for females.

Intonation: Women use ''excited'' speech pitch more than men do. Women use patterns of uncertainty and indefiniteness more than men do. Women have a distinct pattern that expresses confirmation at the same time as conveying hesitancy; for example, ''I live in the dorm?''

Volume: Males generally speak louder. Intensity is increased when speaking to a member of the opposite sex.

Vocal typecasting

Some men find it difficult to verbalize feelings of tenderness or strong emotion.[6]

Thus, it should be evident that sex can often be determined solely on the basis of voice. Although there are gender differences in how messages are transmitted, there are also gender-related differences in perceptions of others' nonverbal communication. Vocally, women are generally viewed in terms of sociability; men are perceived in terms of physical and emotional power. Vocal quality cues are more salient in judging women than in judging men. As a general conclusion, we can also state that *women are more accurate in their interpretations of nonverbal cues and are more responsive to nonverbal cues* than are men.[7]

Additional research has been undertaken on how males and females perceive one another. L. Powell, S. R. Hill, Jr., and M. Hickson III undertook a study to determine how males and females perceived a public speaker of the same sex and one of the opposite sex.[8] The subjects viewed a videotaped speech; afterward they were asked to evaluate the speaker. Three types of variables were observed: (1) attitudes of similarity; (2) inferences of credibility; and (3) interpersonal attraction. When confronted with a stranger on videotape, only females viewing a female speaker made an assessment of *social attraction.*

Another study of gender differences was undertaken by Erving Goffman.[9] He studied magazine, newspaper, and television advertisements and found that marketing and advertising specialists have taken advantage of the common stereotypes of gender differences. Six general types of ''genderisms'' were found. Males were found to be larger than women in *relative size;* women are portrayed as outlining and touching objects with their hands and fingers more often than males (the *feminine touch*). In terms of *functioning ranking,* males are portrayed as having the more executive, superior, or active role. The *family* is used in many advertisements; whereas sons are shown as inferior to their fathers, mother-daughter combinations generally note more equality.

The *ritualization of subordination* shows females physically ''lowering'' themselves to males or generally lowering themselves in the advertisements. The sixth genderism is referred to as *licensed withdrawal.* Here women are shown ''engaged in involvements which remove them psychologically from the social situation at large, leaving them unoriented in it and to it, and presumably, therefore, dependent on the protectiveness and goodwill of others who are (or might come to be present).''[10] An example is ''daydreaming'' during an interaction.

The mass media apparently reflect the gender nature of our society and also contribute to it. D. Archer, D. D. Kimes, and M. Barrios noted some factors not dissimilar to Goffman's findings.[11] Studying photographs in newspapers and magazines, they observed that more of the bodies of females were shown, whereas pictures of males usually contained only faces. Based on these differences, then, it should not come as a surprise that in almost any social situation, we have a certain set of expectations about how to communicate.

A third type of perceptual filtering that we do in nonverbal communication involves the process structure of the nonverbal code. Here we are discussing how the brain (or, as we will learn, brains) codes the stimuli that come into the brain.

TABLE 2.2   *Summary of the Characteristics of Spontaneous and Symbolic Communication*

CHARACTERISTICS	SPONTANEOUS COMMUNICATION	SYMBOLIC COMMUNICATION
Basis of Signal System	Biologically shared	Socially shared
Elements	Signs: Natural, externally visible aspects of referent	Symbols: Arbitrary relationships with referent
Intentionality	Spontaneous: Communicative behavior is an automatic or a reflex response	Voluntary: Sender intends to send a specific message
Content	Nonpropositional motivational/ emotional states	Propositions: Expressions capable of logical analysis (test of truth or falsity)
Cerebral Processing	Related to right hemisphere	Related to left hemisphere

Source: R. Buck, ''Spontaneous and Symbolic Nonverbal Behavior and the Ontogeny of Communication,'' in *Development of Nonverbal Behavior in Children,* ed. R. S. Feldman (New York: Springer-Verlag, 1982), p. 38. Reprinted with permission.

Process Structure

We begin with an examination of how we process verbal and nonverbal communication. Some texts use *hemispheric differences* to refer to processing differences; however, we prefer **hemispheric style.**[12] For most people, the left hemisphere of the brain is responsible for *most* of our verbal communication. This side of the brain is specialized in an abstract, logical, and analytical way that is best used in the analysis of language. The right hemisphere (sometimes called the ''minor'' hemisphere) is specialized for the spatiotemporal, gestalt, emotive forms of communication for which nonverbal is best suited. For many years, we thought that one side dominated the other. Lately, however, we have begun to realize that each hemisphere's specialization includes a small share of the other's specialty. There is some right hemispheric language, which is either automatic or tied to emotions, that becomes almost spontaneous and at times even unconscious.[13] The left hemisphere also processes some nonverbal communication.

It is essential to note, however, that each hemisphere of the brain is specialized to analyze either verbal or nonverbal communication. In terms of differences, we might look at a model that implies that nonverbal communication is spontaneous, whereas verbal communication is symbolic. According to Ross Buck, spontaneous communication is related to the right hemisphere, is an automatic or reflexive response, and is nonpropositional (lacks logical analysis).[14] His dichotomy is presented in Table 2.2.

One final approach to hemispheric processing has been proposed by Don Stacks.[15] Stacks postulates that the two brain hemispheres differ only in terms of style; that is, each is best suited for either verbal or nonverbal communication. He theorizes, however, that each hemisphere contains the processes necessary for language, but those in the right are unconscious or repressed by the left (which is the analytical, logical aspect of reality). His analysis also encompasses an evolutionary perspective, first set forth by Paul MacLean, postulating that the human brain is actually three evolutionary brains, each connected to the other and specialized for different purposes.[16] For example, the most recent brain (the **Neomammalian**) is responsible for language, symbols, signs, and the creation of rules, and it is representational. This "neocortical" level is found in higher mammals, but only the asymmetrical (right-left hemisphere) nature of the human being permits the manipulation of symbols. This brain controls the two lower brains. The next brain (**Paleomammalian**) is found in the limbic region. This brain is imaginative and primarily emotive in its analysis. Finally, the oldest brain (**R-Complex**) is found at the brain stem and is related to sensorimotor actions. This brain is best described in terms of instinctive behaviors. Stacks argues that when the Neomammalian brain loses control over the Paleomammalian brain, we observe more emotional reactions. If the right hemisphere's style is dominant, such communication may be reflexive, emotive to a degree of nonlogical expression, and usually not within the consciousness of the sender. When the R-Complex brain has free reign, such behaviors as encroachment, territorial defense, and aggression may be found.

The operating style of each brain hemisphere also helps determine what type of code material is used. Because the left hemisphere is more analytical and logical, most communication researchers find its material more discontinuous or arbitrary.[17] Based on the work of P. Watzlawick, J. Beavin, and D. Jackson, Burgoon and Saine conclude that verbal communication is more digital, much like that found in a computer: highly arbitrary, discrete, and in finite units. Nonverbal communication, however, is more continuous and natural. Burgoon and Saine label this as **analogical.** By this they mean the code material is composed of continuous, infinite, and natural representations of what we observe.[18] Going back to the color spectrum, which exists in infinite colors from white (combination of all colors) to black (the absence of all colors), our symbolic representations of such colors are arbitrary (ever try to figure out the difference between aquamarine and sea blue?), finite, and discrete. When we verbally communicate about them, we lose much of what occurs in nature. In the same way, a gesture is continuous, infinite, and a natural form of communication. Analysis of that gesture forces us into a finite analysis that looks at discrete and highly arbitrary elements.

Finally, we must examine the structure of the two codes. As might be expected, nonverbal communication is much less structured. Many researchers would indicate that nonverbal communication has no particular set of rules (although Ray Birdwhistell might question this statement), no grammar, no syntax. The verbal code can reflect on itself (be self-reflexive about that of which we are aware); can be indicative of past, present, and future; and can be expressed in a number of different languages. Nonverbal communication possesses no set of rules, grammar, or syntax; is bound to the present; and is its own natural language. For example, although speakers can talk about speeches they gave or will give (and how good or bad they were), they cannot do so nonverbally without first providing a **context** through verbalizing. Consider a smile. What does it reflect? Without some other information, we have no idea; although we may infer many things, we really need a verbal message to understand what the emotion is all about and when it may have been communicated.

Nonverbal communication, because of its rather singular need to be in the present, tends to be highly contextual. Different situations or environments produce different nonverbal messages. The way you act in class or with a friend would not be proper in a job interview or at work. The context tends to help us in some ways to decide what norms to follow.

Age

As we will see in future chapters, age is a primary factor in the communication process. For example, children stand closer to one another when they are younger. As we get much older, we need to stand closer to others because of hearing problems. For those in-between ages, we tend to stand farther away from people. Our voices change with age so that our vocalics are different. Depending on what age we are, we may become more or less concerned with our physical appearance.

Culture and Race

Nonverbal aspects of communication vary according to culture and race. In some cultures people stand very close to one another; others kiss one another's beards; women do not shave their legs and underarms in some cultures; and some cultures' pace of life is different from ours in the United States. Culture and race are important filters for us to understand nonverbal communication.

Status

How we interact nonverbally with a superior and how we interact with a subordinate may differ; in addition, our nonverbal communication sending and receiving processes differ when we are with peers.

Summary

It is important to understand that we receive and send the nonverbal code to others through a number of filters. Our filters assist us in interpreting the various stimuli that we sense. These filters include the purpose of the interaction (according to each of the interactants), the sex or gender of the interactants, the brain processing of the nonverbal code, age, culture and race, and status. As we go through the chapters in this book, you should remember that these filters help determine what you gain from a nonverbal encounter. To understand the studies in Section 2, we will next review how nonverbal studies are undertaken.

Chapter Three

Foundations of Nonverbal Communication: Methods of Research

Key Concepts

Steps in Nonverbal Research

Theoretical Perspectives

Methods of Conducting Research

Collecting Data

Limitations of Research

We believe that students should gain a basic understanding of how nonverbal research is carried out. This knowledge should (1) help the student better understand the limitations of the research reported in this and other books, (2) help make the student more critical of what he or she reads, and (3) enable the student to conduct nonverbal research projects. This review should correlate and combine the complex and often misunderstood components of research. By now you have a fairly well-grounded knowledge of nonverbal communication in general and of certain subcodes in particular, and also of how these areas function to influence our communication in a variety of contexts. This chapter examines how such research is undertaken and reported.

Nonverbal Research

The study of nonverbal communication is no less rigorous than any other branch of the social sciences. Research in nonverbal communication is difficult, however, because of the need to isolate the subcodes when studying their impact. How well we can isolate each subcode—how we *control* our research—often determines what type of research we undertake. Nonverbal investigation is represented in all types of research. We believe that research in nonverbal communication involves at least six steps: (1) review of the pertinent literature; (2) theoretical perspectives; (3) methodology; (4) collection of data; (5) analysis of data; and (6) application of the findings. Most research in nonverbal communication includes laboratory experiment, survey, field experiment, or field study methods. The literature review step seeks to combine and consolidate the many areas of study. We begin by analyzing how such a review is undertaken, with the understanding that all research really begins with a thorough review of the literature.

Review of the Literature

Like research of any type, nonverbal communication research requires that we first look at what has previously been researched. Although many would consider the literature review a historical method, it really is quite precise and may even include formal hypotheses (predictions of what the outcome of the research will be). According to Don W. Stacks and John E. Hocking, the literature review, as a component method of critical investigations, serves several functions, including the collection and verification of primary and secondary sources of information, as well as interpreting and making conclusions based on that information.[1] Review of the relevant literature may, therefore, collate existing knowledge and assign data into categories that are theoretically interesting and that provide the background for developing hypotheses to be tested.

   The general procedure in the review of literature is to examine journal articles, books, and published papers to determine what research has been undertaken. Don Stacks and Mark Hickson have provided a systematic way to undertake a library search (see Figure 3.1).[2] In addition, two indices specifically devoted to nonverbal research have been compiled.[3] The review of literature should be as exhaustive as possible. You should try to obtain all relevant material during this phase of your research, looking for data and studies that support your position as well as material that nullifies or invalidates your hypothesis. The best procedure is to prepare notecards on each article or section of a book. You may also cross-index each area of study (e.g., proxemics, personal space, violations). A list of journals that often publish articles on nonverbal communication is found in Table 3.1. When all the sources have been consulted, you should consider your theoretical perspective.

Theoretical Perspective

Normally we would begin a literature review with some theoretical perspective. A theoretical perspective, as noted in chapter 1, is a way of viewing the phenomena under study. From this position you will theorize that certain relationships exist between the variables of interest. In some cases, you may not have developed a theoretical perspective. In other cases, your position or outlook may be changing. In the course of time, most perspectives tend to change as researchers and disciplines mature.[4]

   For the novice researcher, there are several available sources in which to search for theoretical views. Among them are books by Frank E. X. Dance, Ernest G. Bormann, B. Aubrey Fisher, and Stephen W. Littlejohn.[5] Littlejohn, in particular, has noted two approaches to the study of nonverbal communication: the structural and the functional.[6] This distinction is especially important when we consider the perspective of Birdwhistell and Hall (structuralists) versus Ekman and

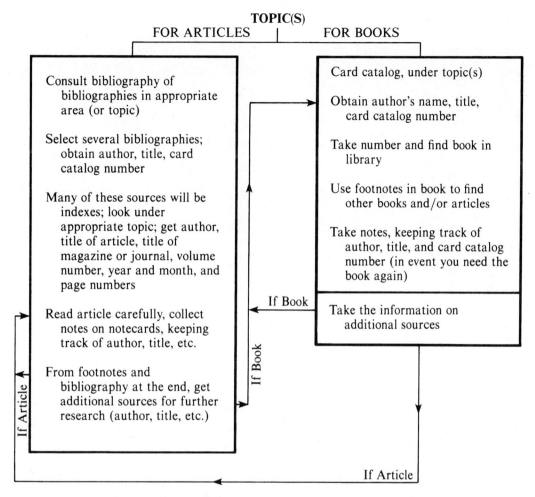

FIGURE 3.1   A Programmed Approach to the Literature Review.
Source: D. W. Stacks and M. Hickson III, ''Research: A
Programmed Approach,'' *Florida Speech
Communication Journal,* 2 (1974), 22.

Friesen (functionalists). In addition, Judee K. Burgoon and Thomas J. Saine present an excellent overview of many perspectives on the study of nonverbal communication.[7] By examining these sources, the researcher should be able to know in advance his or her position on processing differences, the origin of nonverbal communication, intentionality, and so forth.

One's theoretical perspective, then, provides guidance for interpreting the literature. How the researcher posits and tests research questions or hypotheses are influenced by this perspective. Understanding the theoretical background of a researcher may also help you interpret the results, and then, if such findings differ from yours, it may present a reason for such difference.

TABLE 3.1   Pertinent Journals with Articles on Nonverbal Communication Research

Acta Psychologica	Journal of Communication Therapy
American Anthropologist	Journal of Consulting and Clinical Psychology
American Journal of Psychiatry	Journal of Experimental Psychology
American Journal of Psychoanalysis	Journal of Nonverbal Behavior
American Journal of Psychology	Journal of Parapsychology
American Journal of Sociology	Journal of Personality
American Psychologist	Journal of Personality and Social Psychology
American Sociological Review	Journal of Social Psychology
Annual Review of Psychology	Merrill-Palmer Quarterly
Archives of General Psychiatry	Nature
Behavior Therapy	Perceptual and Motor Skills
Behavioral Science	Plastic and Reconstructive Surgery
British Journal of Psychiatry	Psychological Bulletin
British Journal of Social and Clinical Psychology	Psychological Reports
Current Anthropology	Psychological Review
Communication Education	Psychology
Communication Monographs	Psychology Today
Communication Quarterly	Psychiatry
Communication Research	Psychological Record
Communication Research Reports	Psychonomic Science
Communication Studies	Psychotherapy
Communication Theory	Quarterly Journal of Speech
Dissertation Abstracts International	Science
Environmental Perception and Behavior	Scientific American
Ethology and Sociobiology	Semiotica
Human Communication Research	Sex Roles
Human Ethology	Signs
Human Factors	Small Group Behavior
International Journal of Social Psychiatry	Social Forces

TABLE 3.1   Continued

Journal of Abnormal Psychology	Social Problems
Journal of Applied Communication Research	Southern Communication Journal
Journal of Clinical Psychology	Western Journal of Speech Communication
Journal of the American Institute of Planners	World Communication
Journal of Communication	

Methodology

Once the research literature has been reviewed and a theoretical approach has been formed, it is essential to consider methodological questions. To do this, it is necessary that the research question or hypothesis be carefully stated. When this has been done, the researcher should consider his or her methodology. Usually, our methodology will be consistent with what we were taught; that is, our training will, to a degree, influence the methods we select later in our research.

W. B. Pearce, V. E. Cronen, and L. M. Harris have outlined one view of seven methodological approaches to social science research.[8] They note that several questions must be asked about the method you use. These can be grouped into two major areas: (1) What counts as data? and (2) How do data count? How you answer these two questions will determine what method you follow. For example, when we consider what counts as data, we specify which (if any) units of analysis we will use, what type of observational unit we will approve, and what kind of data we will accept. In the study of proxemics, we may note that the unit of analysis is typically *discrete* (we might break continuous spatial use into four subareas: public space, social space, personal space, and intimate space). Our unit of observation may be defined as existing within "proxemes." Our type of data is *interval* if we consider the inches between the interactants and the responses to some questionnaire as data (assuming interval-level data). Answering the question of how we count our data, we examine how the data relate to causation and to our theory. Here we might look at statistical associations (probabilities) and how such data contribute to the interpretation of the event we have witnessed or manipulated.

The researcher should consider which approach is being used before attempting data collection. The approach will define what the unit of data is and how it is perceived. It will also indicate how we should analyze the data and interpret our findings within the general theoretical framework we have adopted.

Data Collection

Generally speaking, the data for study in nonverbal communication will be in one of four forms: (1) information from a laboratory investigation; (2) information from a survey questionnaire; (3) information from a field experiment; or (4) information from a field study. The first three methods of data collection will generate quantitative data; the fourth will generate qualitative data. All four are important and contribute to our body of knowledge concerning nonverbal communication; each has advantages and disadvantages; and, finally, each has researchers who advocate one approach over another. Table 3.2 illustrates the levels of research.

TABLE 3.2   Levels of Research

	PERSON	NATURE	METHOD
More ''Objective''	1st	Act Recording	Act VTR Audio Recording Paper Recording Participant-Observation • as participant • as participant-observer • as observer-participant • as observer
	2nd	Synthesis	Self-Report (and interpretation by subjects[s]) Historical Report and interpretation— from primary source
	3rd		Historical Report and interpretation— from secondary source • Self-Report • Historical Report Interpretation • Self-Report with stimulus (lab) • Historical Report with stimulus
More ''Subjective''	Omniscient narrator	Fiction	Contrived

Source: M. Hickson III, J. B. Roebuck and K. S. Murty, ''Creative
Triangulation: Toward a Methodology for Studying Social Types,'' in *Studies
in Symbolic Interaction,* ed. by N. K. Denzin, *11* (Greenwich, CT: JAI Press,
1990).

What really makes each different, however, is the amount of *control* the researcher has over the variables under study. Generally, control is most evident in the laboratory ''experiment'' and is reduced as we approach the field ''study.'' Whereas the laboratory experiment isolates the particular variables under study from others, thus deriving as ''pure'' a finding as possible, the field study places few or no constraints on the variables. One major problem with laboratory research is that it is seldom possible to generalize results from the laboratory to the field due to the effects of other variables artificially controlled in the lab. Similarly, the field study encounters difficulties when one tries to specify causes and effects. Each, however, contributes to our knowledge of nonverbal communication.

Laboratory Experiments   Most of the research reported in this book comes from studies conducted in the laboratory. In the laboratory experiment we attempt to control all of the variables in a situation except for those being tested. Even those being tested, however, are controlled in that they are carefully manipulated and their effects noted. The typical laboratory experiment begins with some question or hypothesis in mind, a proposition or supposition derived from a review of or a familiarization with the literature in a particular area of interest. Specific questions or hypotheses are then stated concerning the relationship(s) between the variables under study. Procedures are created and tested to maximize any potential sources of information by manipulation and, at the same time, to reduce other sources of information that might "contaminate" the manipulations.

In the laboratory experiment, there are two types of variables. First, there is the **independent variable.** This variable can be controlled or manipulated. Such manipulations may include dress, distance, time, or all three. Second, there is the **dependent variable,** a factor in comparison with which we judge the effects of the independent variables. Dependent variables may be such elements as source credibility, attitude change, attraction, decision to buy or get married, and so forth. We usually test the independent variables to determine how they produce different results among the dependent variables, either in isolation or in combination.

When the procedures and variables have been identified, the study is initiated. To carry out a research project, we need participants, people who have been chosen, either randomly or for a particular reason, to participate in the research. The participant will normally be assigned to a **condition,** a particular group that receives one or more manipulations. Usually we randomly assign a participant to a condition; this reduces the probability of error due to the participant's past or knowledge, enabling the researcher to exercise some form of control over the results. Once the participant has been manipulated, he or she is then exposed to the dependent measures, which become data to be analyzed (or, if the dependent measures tested how the participant reacted and were either filmed or coded by assistants, these become the data).

An example of the laboratory experiment is the study by Mark Hickson and others on smoking artifacts.[9] Figure 3.2 indicates the conditions created in this study, which randomly assigned college students to one of three treatment groups or a control group. One group viewed 16 slides of a man smoking a pipe; another (the control group) viewed 16 slides of the same man in the same poses except he was not smoking. Two other groups viewed a set of slides showing the same man smoking either a cigarette or a cigar. After viewing the slides, the groups filled out forms on the man's attractiveness, credibility (believability), and homophily (perceived similarity) to the participants. The independent variable was seeing the man either smoking one of the three types of artifacts or not smoking. The answers to the questionnaire comprised the dependent variables. One major criticism of this study is that the subjects were not asked whether they smoked; hence, some loss of control might be expected (especially for the homophily variable, which might be affected).

Survey Questionnaires   A second way to gather data is to administer surveys to randomly selected people. A survey is one way to collect data in the field while still exercising some control over the research. Typically, surveys are carefully devised questionnaires that ask specific questions, which have been pretested so that no bias results. Moreover, there are specific and rigorous ways of ensuring that the people selected come from the general population under study. These people compose the study's *sample.*[10] A study on body image reported in *Psychology Today,* for example, consisted of questionnaires cut out of the magazine and mailed back to the editors.[11] Because the survey was only filled out by readers of the magazine, the sample was biased in favor of college-educated, middle-class people.

FIGURE 3.2   Smoking Artifacts Study.

Survey questionnaires enable researchers to obtain as much data as possible while still exercising some control. Control is maintained by selecting the sample of respondents and by developing the questionnaire. A second form of surveying is the face-to-face interview. Much of what is reported on job interviews is obtained through such dialogues.[12] The type of data may differ from the laboratory experiment. Often the results of the interview must be analyzed by using a content analysis system.[13] Such systems may include the ways respondents reacted to open-ended questions (questions asked for a general response rather than for one response out of several given them by the questionnaire).

The survey is often the most economical and feasible way of collecting data. Consider, for example, a study that seeks to find out whether college students perceive a professor's dress any differently than noncollege persons. To conduct this study by means of the laboratory experiment would be both time-consuming and almost impractical. (You would be able to induce some students to participate, but nonstudents would be a real problem.) A survey questionnaire, with pictures of professors in various dress might work very well. You would randomly select the college sample and the noncollege sample, transmit the questionnaires to your respondents, and then compare the results. You still exercise a degree of control by randomly selecting your sample (being careful to include all possible respondents) and by formulating your questionnaire to avoid biased responses.

Field Experiments The field experiment attempts to combine the advantages of two procedures. First, it tries to control the variables under study as much as possible by manipulating degrees or levels of the variable under study. Second, the field experiment allows other variables that would normally be controlled in the laboratory to influence results. The major advantage of the field experiment, however, is that it allows the study to be carried out in a ''natural'' setting.

The research conducted by Leonard Bickman in his study of clothing is a good example of the field experiment in nonverbal communication.[14] Based on a confederate's type of dress, Bickman tried to determine whether a dime would be returned from a telephone booth. Rather than use college students, who might suspect that something was being tested on campus, he used whomever he could find at the telephone booth. The major problem here, of course, is the inability to randomize participants. By chance he could have selected an area that had ''high- or low-return'' people. In the field experiment the researcher simply has to use the participants who show up in the course of the experiment. A typical field experiment might be a scientific ''candid camera'' routine.

The field experiment can exercise some degree of control for randomization of participants. Although most field experiments do not control for participants, claiming that the value of data collected in the natural setting offsets any loss of rigor, you can still maintain some type of control. One study, conducted by Don Stacks, for example, tried to control for subjects while still conducting the research in a natural setting.[15] The two independent variables were physical attractiveness (high or moderate) and distance (close, far, or the normative distance that participants and confederates initially adopted). There are six conditions in this study. Furthermore, the study was conducted in the field: two high-density places were chosen as the locales for the research (Union or Lounge area). The number of participants (anyone who would participate at *either* locale) was counterbalanced by location. By this we mean that an equal number of participants were exposed to each condition at each locale.

Through statistical means, we can determine whether the location made any difference. If it did not (it did not in this study), then the analysis can be made as with the laboratory experiment, but now adding a control for location differences. These results can then be compared to experiments conducted in the laboratory to determine whether the participants reacted to the variables under different conditions. In some field experiment research, the results conform to laboratory findings; in many, however, they do not.[16]

Field Studies   Whereas the field experiment is controlled for the most part, except for the sampling of participants, field studies have little control except for the objectivity of the researcher.[17] In the field study, the researcher enters a natural setting in an attempt to answer general research questions. For example, Mark Hickson studied the nonverbal and verbal communication of people on a commuter bus in Washington, D.C.[18] Hickson's participants in this case were those people who regularly rode the bus. In this type of study, he could examine what he labeled "typical" and "atypical" situations as they occurred naturally.

One problem with the field study is that the researcher is both the participant and the observer. The researcher must find a way to unobtrusively record the variables of interest while still acting as a participant in the interaction. In the case of Hickson's study, he pretended to read while recording behaviors on the bus. A second problem with field data is the subjective nature of the data. A. Mazur's study of proxemic norms and personal spacing on benches in several cultures is biased, due to the differing size of benches in different locations.[19] (See Figure 3.3.) If Mazur had set up a field experiment, had controlled for the size of the bench, his results would have been more valid.

Although there are several disadvantages to the field study, the major advantage to this method of data collection is that you obtain truly natural results. The primary disadvantage, other than questionable objectivity of the researcher and loss of control over participant selection, is the fact that the field studies usually take much longer to conduct than do the other methods. Over time, many things can happen that might influence how the participants behave. The field study, however, has produced some significant nonverbal findings for most subcodes.

Data Analysis and Application

After the data have been collected, the researcher must analyze what has been observed or collected. At this stage, the researcher will make some kind of interpretation based on the analytical method appropriate for the theoretical position taken and for the type of data collected. Most researchers in the area of nonverbal communication will use some type of inferential or descriptive statistics (based on mean response per condition or percent responding). In the case of qualitative data, the researcher will examine where the data accumulate in his or her coding system and make some type of inference based on what is found. In most cases, the reporting will be predicated on the probability that only five percent of the results, or less, are based on chance (the outcome being the result of the manipulation ninety-five out of 100 times).

Once the data have been analyzed, the researcher must then demonstrate their usefulness. In this regard, you will usually find a discussion section in the report. Here the researcher summarizes what he or she set out to find, what was actually found, and what impact this might have on any number of things. The application section should point out: (1) where the study breaks new ground and how it can be used in dealing with other communication phenomena; and (2) what limitations there are on the findings. Sometimes the limitations on the research will reveal more about the study and its impact than will the discussion or the literature review.

FIGURE 3.3   Problems in the Field, as Might Have Occurred in the Mazur Study.

Limitations of Nonverbal Communication Research

We need to stop for a minute to caution you about a phenomenon we have observed when students are about to finish their nonverbal communication courses. It is at this stage (although it may happen earlier) that other people become interested in what you have been studying during the term, and they ask you to do analyses. At this point your knowledge is like a loaded gun: it can go off in any direction and possibly injure those around you.

You are acquainted with the basic concepts from which to study and analyze nonverbal communication. Like most people who possess the fundamentals, you may apply what you have learned where it is not applicable. When someone comes out of nowhere and asks "What does this mean?" you are at a disadvantage if you try to reply. You must rely on data; you must know how the participant has reacted in the past before you make judgments. Because you are not in control of the situation and have not carefully conditioned or controlled the other person, the reactions may be *idiosyncratic;* that is, your results might be from an unusual case.

At one time, a colleague called on the office intercom to ask what was going on in the parking lot below his window. He noted that a male and a female (ages uncertain) were kissing each other. What nonverbal message was this, he asked. The only response possible was, "I guess that they like each other." Although other responses could have been given, lack of knowledge about a number of factors prevented this. One must be careful, especially when inferring that something may be occurring because you once read about it. Some people, such as psychiatrists and psychologists as well as certain police personnel, can and do "read" other people's nonverbal communication with some degree of accuracy.[20] These individuals, however, have been trained over a period of years to make this type of analysis.

Your initial knowledge of what constitutes nonverbal communication and how it is used should provide you with the information needed to better understand the communication of others. In many cases you will conclude that people use nonverbal communication as a manipulative tool; by knowing how this is done, you will be better prepared to counter such influence. By now you have probably created your own manipulative strategies and tested a few of them. As noted in the chapters on application of nonverbal communication, we use our nonverbal communication in a number of contexts, and these may change the expected nonverbal message.

The context is not only important in everyday usage of nonverbal information, but it is also important in nonverbal communication research. Those studies in nonverbal communication that yield the most useful results are those that have been undertaken at different times, under differing conditions, using different methods, incorporating the most recent reviews of the literature, undertaken by a number of different researchers in differing locations—or what Norman K. Denzin refers to as "triangulation."[21] A good example of triangulation is a series of studies beginning with Sidney Jourard's 1966 study of touch and human body parts.[22] Jourard asked students to fill out a questionnaire that showed twenty-four human body areas. The students were asked whether they had seen others touch or whether they had been touched by four other persons (of differing relationships) on each of the twenty-four body areas. The four "types of relationships" were mother, father, same-sex friend, and opposite-sex friend. The results of Jourard's study are presented in Figure 3.4. In general, the results indicated that females allowed greater access to their bodies than did males; opposite-sex friends and mothers were found to do the most touching, whereas fathers usually touched no more than the hands of the other person.

In 1976 (ten years later), L. Rosenfeld, S. Kartus, and C. Ray replicated (reworked) Jourard's study, using only fourteen basic body areas (but including the front and back areas for a total of

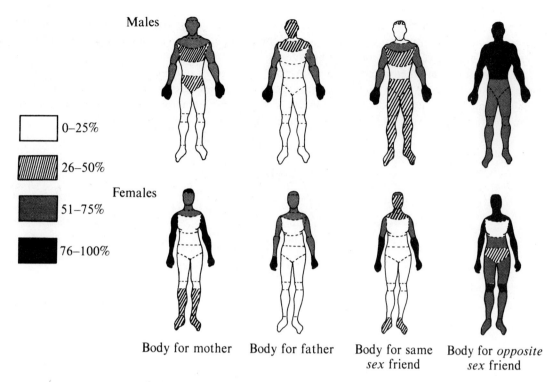

FIGURE 3.4 Comparison of Touch by Sex and Relationship.
Source: S. M. Jourard, "An Exploratory Study of Body-Accessibility," *British Journal of Social and Clinical Psychology,* 1966.

twenty-eight body areas). Rosenfeld and associates found that over the ten-year period, there had been some dramatic shifts in body accessibility (see Figures 3.5 and 3.6).[23] For instance, they found females were less accessible in the neck area but had increased accessibility from the chest to the knees (see Figure 3.6). Thus, the results of Rosenfeld's and Jourard's work illustrate that sex and relationship are important variables in understanding the norms of touch, norms that change over time.

Basing their study on a revised review of the literature, Stanley E. Jones and A. Elaine Yarbrough replicated the study in 1985.[24] In addition, Jones and Yarbrough asked their participants to write down information about *actual* touches. Their data were gathered over one and one-half years. The participants (five distinct groups) kept track of who initiated the touch, who the other person was, where the physical location of the touch was, the time of day, what was said, whether the touch was accepted or rejected, the type of touch, who else was present, the relationship with the other person, the nature of the social occasion, the status of the other person, the race of the other person, and whether the touch took place while sitting or standing. A copy of the "observation" form is reproduced as Figure 3.7.

More than 1,500 touches were recorded in the 18-month period. Using this combination of field study and survey methods, much more information was collected. Jones and Yarbrough found that most touches were *cross-sex*. They also found that both males and females initiated touch but that females initiated touch more often. And, as might be expected, they found a wider range of touch meanings and ambiguity than was suggested in the previous research. Finally, they found that context was a critical factor in touching behavior.

Thus, we find that when a particular nonverbal cue is analyzed, many times we accumulate more significant data. As you go through this text, take special care to note whether a study has been replicated, when it was conducted, how many researchers were involved, who the participants were, and so forth. In your use of the results found in this text, be extremely cautious.

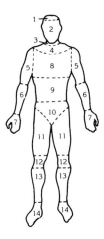

FIGURE 3.5   Potential Body Access Zones for Touch Studies.
Source: Lawrence B. Rosenfeld, Sallie Kartus, and Chett Ray, ''Body
Accessibility Revisited,'' *Journal of Communication,* Vol. 26, No. 3 (1976), 30.

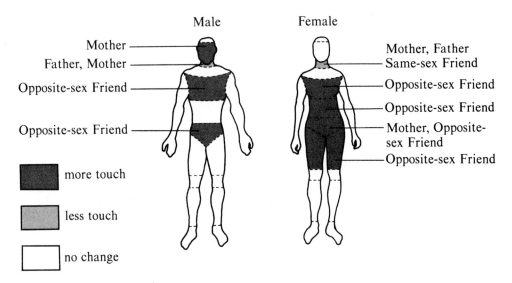

FIGURE 3.6   Summary of Where People Touch Other People.
Source: Lawrence B. Rosenfeld, Sallie Kartus, and Chett Ray, ''Body
Accessibility Revisited,'' *Journal of Communication,* Vol. 26, No. 3 (1976), 30.

You should remember that both the verbal and the nonverbal function together to create a "total" message, and that the information you possess is only basic, entry-level information. If you find this subject exciting and seek more, enroll in other courses on communication and nonverbal communication. We have found nonverbal communication to be a lifelong study, but one that is not isolated from our verbal messages. We hope that you will find the study of nonverbal communication both productive and continuing.

TOUCH OBSERVATION FORM

Name _____ Date _____
Use arrows to line entries which are part
of the same interaction. Ex.   1.
                                ↓
                               2.

Indicate where applicable: BM—Best Male Friend;
BF—Best Female Friend; MO—Mother; FA—Father

1. *Initiator of touch* A. Me B. Other C. Mutual D. Unclear (1 letter)	2a. *Parts of body when initiated* (1 or more letters @ blank: note 2-handed touches) Initiator touched with: / Receiver touched on:	2b. *Parts of body when mutual or unclear* (1 or more letters per blank) Me: Other:	3. *Place* A. Mine B. Other's C. Neutral (Specify bldg. and room)	4. *Time of day* (Include A.M. or P.M.)
1._____	_____ _____	_____ _____	_____	_____
2._____	_____ _____	_____ _____	_____	_____
3._____	_____ _____	_____ _____	_____	_____

5. *Accompanying verbal statement* (Paraphrase if necessary) *When:* A. Immediately prior to touch B. Immediately after touch C. During *By:* (M) Me; (O) Other	6. *Touch translated into verbal statement* (Make into short sentence if possible; note voice tone or facial expression if critical to meaning)	7. (Mark "Psych" for touches you reject internally only) *Acceptance/Rejection* A. Touch accepted by me B. Touch rejected by me C. Touch accepted by other D. Touch rejected by other (Spec. with letter; explain how & why t. is rejected)
1._____	_____	_____
2._____	_____	_____
3._____	_____	_____

FIGURE 3.7   Touch Observation Form.

TOUCH OBSERVATION FORM

Name _____ Date _____
Use arrows to line entries which are part
of the same interaction. Ex.   1.
                                ↓
                               2.

Indicate where applicable: BM—Best Male Friend;
BF—Best Female Friend; MO—Mother; FA—Father

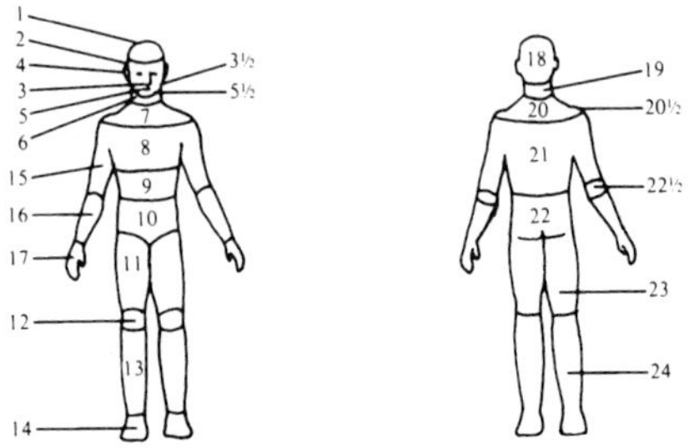

8.
Type of touch
A. Caressing/holding
B. Feeling/Caressing
C. Prolonged holding
D. Holding/pressing ag.
E. Spot touching
F. Accidental brushing
G. Handshake
H. Pat I. Squeeze J. Punch
K. Pinch L. Other
(1 or more letters)

1. _____
2. _____
3. _____

9.
Purpose of participants
A. Give/get into (spec.)
B. Ask/give favor
C. Persuading
D. Persuaded
E. Casual talk
F. Deeptalk
G. Greeting
H. Departing
 I. Any other (specify)
Me: *Other:*

___ ___
___ ___
___ ___

10.
Others present
(Male and/or female)
(Specify relation to you
using letters from Category
11)

_____
_____
_____

11.
Relationship to other
A.   Relative (spec.)
B1. Close Friend
B2. Not close friend
C.   Acquaintance
D.   Co-worker
E.   Superior
F.   Subordinate
G.   Stranger
H.   Other (spec.)
Spec. if intimate

_____
_____
_____

12.
Nature of social occasion
A. Work
B. Class
C. Party
D. Informal meeting
E. Other (spec.)
For public places, specify function (bar, etc.)

1. _____
2. _____
3. _____

13.
Status of other
A. Higher 1. Formal
B. Lower   2. Informal
C. Equal
(1 letter and 1 no.)

___ ___
___ ___
___ ___

14.
Age of other
(Approximate)

_____
_____
_____

15.
Sex of other
(M/F)

_____
_____
_____

16.
Race of other
A. Anglo
B. Black
C. Chicano
D. Asian
E. Other (spec.)

_____
_____
_____

17.
Standing or sitting
Me: Other:

1. ___ ___
2. ___ ___
3. ___ ___

18.
Any other contextual factors you think influenced your touches:

_____
_____
_____

FIGURE 3.7 *Continued*
Source: From S. E. Jones and A. E. Yarbrough, ''A Naturalistic Study of the
Meaning of Touch,'' *Communication Monographs,* 52 (1985), pp. 19–56.

☐   **Summary**   ☐

In this chapter we have examined some of the ways we study nonverbal communication. In particular, we considered in some detail how a research study is carried out. We have recommended a six-step process for the study of nonverbal communication: (1) review the literature; (2) develop a theoretical perspective; (3) develop a methodology; (4) collect the data; (5) analyze the data; and (6) apply the findings. Four general methods for research have been described: (1) laboratory experiments; (2) surveys; (3) field experiments; and (4) field studies. As you read through the remainder of this text, you should analyze how the studies were conducted. The next section of the text will provide ample opportunity for you to use your newly acquired skills in research criticism.

Section Two

Subcodes and Studies

☐   ☐   ☐

Now that we have a basic understanding of what constitutes the nonverbal code, we can examine in more detail the subcodes we manipulate. We begin at what we consider the most appropriate place: the use of touch (zero space). We establish this starting point on the fact that we communicate in some medium or environment, and based on this environment, we define or delineate a territory or personal spacing zone. Sometimes, however, people within the environment misread the cues we establish to ''tell'' them what we expect in terms of communication; sometimes they may even touch us. Messages such as these signal many things to others. Knowing what these messages are, what the **normative expectations** are for subcode use and spatial violations, provide us with the information we need to study nonverbal communication.

After we consider the impact of the environment and spacing behaviors, we turn our attention to the next subcode: physical appearance. It should not surprise you that how we perceive someone is greatly influenced by that person's physical appearance. Given the importance of physical appearance, we attempt to change such characteristics as our body image, attractiveness, and body type by the use of clothing, accessories, and body adaptors. What the physical appearance subcode conveys to us is a major determinant of whether or not we want to communicate with someone. It is greatly influenced by the environment and the distances we maintain (if you think someone is attractive, you try to get closer and may invade this individual's territory and personal space).

Chapter 7 examines what most people would consider *the* nonverbal subcode. What we call **kinesics,** or body language, has been popularized and considered by many to be typical of nonverbal communication. We will expand on this later, but you should note that the kinesic subcode deals with such subjects as the communication of emotion, both in terms of what that emotion is and how intensely it is held, and communication through gesture. Beyond that, however, we can observe such relationships as status, attitudinal disposition, warmth, and quasi-courtship behaviors. In many instances the gestural/kinesic subcode provides us with the information we need to understand better what people ''mean'' in their communications with us.

We then turn to the vocal aspects of nonverbal communication, a second feature of the body's communication. Based on *how* we say things, the meaning of what we say may be altered. Such communication outcomes are based on stereotypical judgments we make regarding such variables as pitch, breathiness, raspiness of voice, and so forth. Many times we use our voice to contradict, such as sarcastically telling someone how *much* you admire their hairdo. The verbal communication may indicate one thing while the vocal communication may be entirely different. In this section, we will also explore the effects of such vocal segregates as dialect, accent, and rate of speech. The vocal subcode, then, serves to stereotype or identify people, and it enables them to alter the impact of their verbal messages.

Finally, we round out this section by examining some of the less obvious, yet nevertheless important, aspects of nonverbal communication. Prime examples of this area are the use of time (chronemics) and the use of smell (olfaction) in everyday communication. Consideration is also given to less understood and less acceptable aspects of nonverbal communication such as telepathic systems (or perceptual systems) and biofeedback systems. This examination looks at the internal states and their possible impact on our communication.

By the time you have completed this section, you will have the necessary information to *begin* to understand how nonverbal communication operates. As noted in the first chapter, however, nonverbal communication does not operate in a vacuum but is considered to be multichannel/multimessage oriented. Nonverbal communication is also dependent upon the context in which it is studied and upon the norms prevailing in that context. By this we mean that the artificial division of nonverbal communication into subcodes, as we have done, makes the study of this complex subject seem simpler than it really is. Knowing where and how the various subcodes function, however, enables you to make predictions as to what the effects of each subcode are in a given context.

Chapter Four

Haptic (Touch) Studies

Key Concepts

Zero-Proxemics

Touch

Tactile Development

Touch Factors and Functions

Touch Substitutions and Violations

The study of touch and touching is known as **haptics.** For all practical purposes, we can refer to touching as **zero-proxemics.** Shirley Weitz has written, "the logical end of proxemics is touching. Once two people touch they have eliminated the space between them, and this act usually signifies that a special type of relationship exists between them."[1] As Ronald Adler and Ralph Towne point out, touching (or tactile communication) is very important:

> Besides being the earliest means we have of making contact with others, touching is essential to our healthy development. During the nineteenth and early twentieth centuries a large percentage of children born every year died from a disease called marasmus, which translated from the Greek means "washing away." In some orphanages the mortality rate was nearly one hundred percent, but even children from the most "progressive" homes, hospitals, and other institutions died regularly from the ailment. . . . They hadn't been touched enough, and as a result they died.[2]

Research investigations have proven that this dramatic statement has some validity. Anthropologist Ashley Montagu has discussed a pilot study involving 173 breast-fed and non-breast-fed children. That research indicates that children who had not been breast-fed had four times the respiratory infections, twenty times more diarrhea, eight times as much eczema, as well as more hay fever, asthma, and other diseases.[3] Tactile deprivation has also been associated with learning problems involving speech, symbolic recognition difficulty, and lack of trust and confidence.[4] Marc H. Hollender has described female psychiatric patients who resorted to ''sexual enticement'' because of their need to be held.[5] Nancy Henley concluded, ''. . . despite extremes of touch-avoidance, it is probably true that people fervently wish, even need, to be touched, and satisfy this desire in whatever way they can.''[6] This ''wish to be held'' has also been associated with depression, especially among females.[7]

Before we examine tactile communication among humans more fully, we need to review briefly some studies carried out on other animals. Specifically, we consider how touch deprivation affects growth and development. After discussing animal haptic behavior, we will discuss frequency of contact, types and functions of touch, factors influencing touch, and touch avoidance.

Animal Studies

Harry Harlow and R. R. Zimmerman undertook a study concerning the physical contact between a monkey mother and her infant.[8] They found that laboratory-raised baby monkeys attached themselves to cloth pads in their cages. When researchers attempted to replace the pads, the infant monkeys engaged in ''violent temper tantrums.'' Harlow then built a terry cloth ''surrogate'' mother with a light bulb behind her to radiate ''body'' heat. A second surrogate mother was made of wire mesh. Dual-mothers were placed in cubicles attached to the infant's cage. In half the cases the wire mother provided milk and the terry cloth mother did not; in the other half, the situations were reversed. The infants could spend as much time as they wanted with either of the mothers. Figure 4.1 demonstrates how the infants spent their time. In general, it was found that the infants spent time with the cloth mother for tactile ''affection,'' as opposed to the wire mother even when the wire mother provided food.

Touch is an important factor in the communication of lower animals. In newts, sex recognition and courtship involve tactile signals as well as other aspects (visual and chemical signals). W. H. Thorpe noted: ''In many species a sudden leap by the male sends a strong water current to the female, sometimes even pushing her aside.''[9] Thorpe has also reported that among certain parasitic water mites, sexual recognition can only be made through tactile communication.[10]

Aside from its sexual and courtship aspects, touch plays an important role in the development of animals. Two significant activities that adult animals, especially the female in most species, engage in at birth are *gentling* and *licking* behaviors. F. S. Hammett, in the early 1920s found that stroking or touching newborn rats, gentling them, yielded a gentler and less frightened rat than those not gentled, and the less frightened rats were more resistant to operations done on their thyroid and parathyroid glands.[11] According to L. Malandro, L. L. Barker and D. Barker, licking behaviors in animals immediately after birth serve to stimulate certain bodily functions, such as excretion.[12] Although this line of thought has been extended to humans, the ''maternal bonding'' between a human mother and her infant and its effects are still rather controversial, as are such actions as warm water immersion after birth.[13] Some hospitals now include a period during which the baby is slowly brought down to normal temperature of the room, rather than simply placing the infant on a cold bed (along the lines of Harlow's findings).

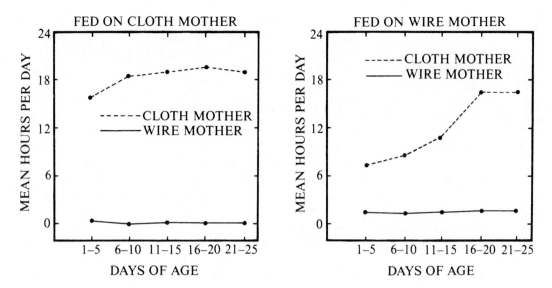

FIGURE 4.1 Comparison of Time Spent on Surrogate Mothers.
Source: H. H. Harlow and R. R. Zimmerman, "The Development of
Affectional Responses in Infant Monkeys," *Proceedings, American
Philosophical Society* 102 (1958), 501–509.

Tactile Development in Humans

In his study of tactile communication in American children, V. S. Clay found that children fourteen
months to two years old received more touching than infants younger than fourteen months. He
also found that female children received more tactile affection than baby boys.[14] Of the available
forms of communication, touching is the first form developed in infant children. Babies explore
their own bodies and their environment through touch. The child's first orientation toward the
world is discovered through tactile communication.[15] As children grow older, they become more
dependent on symbolic communication. Infants are given a feeling of vibration, touch, and rhythm
even before they are born. Desmond Morris writes: ". . . before birth the baby is undoubtedly
capable of hearing (and feeling) the steady thump of the maternal heartbeat, seventy-two times
every minute. It will become imprinted as the major sound-signal of life in the womb."[16] Morris
postulates that the heartbeat rhythm is so important that the ideal rocking speed for a cradle is
sixty to seventy beats per minute. Touching, according to Morris, continues to be a significant
aspect of communication throughout life. "If the baby's message was 'hold me tight,' and the
child's message was 'put me down,' that of the adolescent is 'leave me alone.' "[17] Then, with
young lovers the cycle moves back to the baby's "hold me tight."

   The development of healthy individuals seems related to the amount of touch they receive as
infants. If we examine Harlow's findings and suppose that they can be transferred to humans, then
the amount of touch a child receives in infancy may affect later development. Judee K. Burgoon
and Thomas J. Saine infer that touch needs in infancy result in four major values: biological,

communicative, psychological, and social.[18] The importance of biological value is found both in Harlow's studies and in modern delivery techniques. The communicative value comes from behavior much like Harlow's monkeys: when fed, when assured, when cuddled, the infant is touched by the mother. At this stage the only communication between infant and adult is either touch or crying; you may observe that the quickest way to quiet a crying baby is to touch it (the same may hold true for adults!). Psychologically, the infant, through self-exploration, begins the process of achieving self-identity, environmental identity, security, and well-being. Finally, the social value of touch can be found, again in the Harlow studies, and in the research that indicates not only such features as Montagu observed, but also speech difficulties and learning disabilities in later life.[19] James Prescott's studies of cross-cultural pleasure support the relationship between violence and pleasure, pleasure being associated with touch.[20] Such findings would support the notion that the more touch an infant received during development, the better adjusted that child, adolescent, and adult should be.

Most adult communication using touch is limited to greeting or symbolic gestures. Each culture has its own norms and expectations regarding touch behavior, and these vary greatly from culture to culture. There are, for instance, handshakes, kisses, embraces, rubbing of noses, back slapping, and the kissing of beards—all indicative of greeting behaviors. Not only do we expect different types of touch in different cultures, but we also differ between cultures regarding who touches whom, when, and where. Several researchers have examined the frequency of contact and the type and functions of touch. A brief review of their findings should provide the information needed to understand this most basic form of communication.

Frequency of Contact

Sidney Jourard counted the frequency of body contact between couples in various cafes in different cities and countries. He found differences in cultures with the following number of body contacts per hour.[21]

San Juan, Puerto Rico	180
Paris, France	110
Gainesville, Florida	2
London, England	0

Jourard was also interested in what parts of the body were touched the most often. For this reason, he asked students to fill out a questionnaire that listed twenty-four body parts. (See chapter 2.) Jourard's studies, as well as other, more recent research discussed in chapter 2, provide us with information about who is touched according to sex and relationship in the United States. Other variables related to touch include status, positive attitude toward the other, immediacy, and the perceived meaning of the touch.

In another study, L. T. K. Haung, M. H. Hollender, and R. Phares examined the influence of cultural attitudes on the wish to be held.[22] Subjects were five groups of women living in Malaysia and consisted of the following groups: Chinese-educated Chinese, English-educated Chinese, Malay-educated Malay, English-educated Malay, and English-educated Indians. Haung and colleagues found that Chinese-educated Chinese had the lowest body contact and most often regarded the wish to be held as ''something to be kept secret.'' Interestingly, this group preferred being

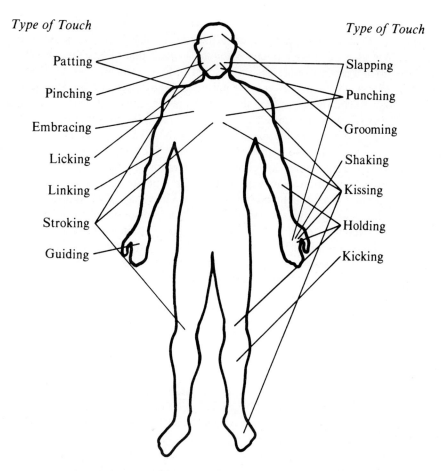

FIGURE 4.2   Type of Touch and Associated Body Areas.
Source: Adapted from M. Argyle, *Bodily Communication* (New York:
International Universities Press, 1975).

held over talking while angry. English-educated Chinese were the least likely to regard being held as something secretive and were least likely to prefer holding to talking. The other nationalities and educational backgrounds followed the Chinese-educated in this order: English-educated Indians, English-educated Malay, Malay-educated Malay.

Types and Functions of Touch

Just as the research has indicated that we have different frequencies of touch, we also have different types or kinds of touch. Two studies, in particular, point out the differences we perceive in type of touch. In 1975, Michael Argyle asserted that sixteen types of touch occurred commonly in western culture (see Figure 4.2) and that these touches communicate attitudes, regulate the interaction, or fall into a ''meaningless'' category (are incidental).[23] Richard Heslin states that we can classify touching behavior into five categories, based on the nature of the interpersonal relationship.[24] At one end of the relationship, we have the *Functional/Professional* level; this level includes such actions as a nurse's or doctor's touch, a touch that is both functional (it is doing something for you) and professional (it is impersonal). Moving toward an interpersonal level, we have *Social/Polite* touches, which are representative of handshakes and other socially prescribed touching behaviors. Heslin theorizes that such touch acts to neutralize the status differences between people. The next category is called *Friendship/Warmth.* Heslin states that this type of touch is most difficult for people to interpret because it is easily mistaken for love or sexual attraction and is often carried out when alone with the other person. The last two categories, *Love/Intimacy* and *Sexual Arousal* are quite interpersonal in nature. The former represents touches indicative of intimacy and requires appropriate interpersonal contexts. The latter is probably the most idiosyncratic and most variant type of touch and obviously the most intense. Heslin further states that as you move from the Functional/Professional level to other levels, you increase the individuality of the relationship and ''humanize'' the other person; he argues that the most appreciation of others is found in the middle category of Friendship/Warmth.[25] Morton Goldman and others found that touch added to the ''foot-in-the-door'' technique often used by salespersons. In their study, Goldman and his colleagues had a confederate touch participants while asking directions and the confederate touched participants in the process of recruiting volunteers for a telephone survey. In both instances, the confederate achieved greater compliance when touching the participant than when there was an absence of touch.[26]

Factors Influencing Touch

In addition to the work of Rosenfeld, Jourard, and Argyle (in chapter 3), others have found sex and relationship to be important variables in touching behavior. Anne Anastasi and Albert Mehrabian have concluded that the tendency to have more tactile contact with others is consistent with the idea that touching is one way to communicate liking.[27] Thus, the extent of intimacy, liking, and sex are related to touching behavior.

T. Nguyen and associates have examined the meaning of various types of touch as they are applied to different parts of the body.[28] Their subjects were opposite-sex, unmarried friends. They were concerned with four types of touch: the pat, squeeze, brush, and stroke. Examining how the different types of touch were related to eleven areas of the body (top of head, face, shoulders and top of back, chest, back, arms, stomach, genital area, thigh and buttocks, legs, and hands), they found that touch is generally considered a positive phenomenon. Strokes usually communicate warmth and sexual desire; pats communicate friendship and playfulness, whereas brushes and squeezes are ambiguous. Responses of males and females were also found to differ. Females discriminated among their body parts more than males. The touching of breasts, for example, was not seen as friendly or playful. Females perceived the squeezing of hands as loving and friendly. Males were less concerned about specific body parts; males felt that almost any meaning could be derived from touching almost any area of the body. However, touching of the thighs and buttocks tended to be better suited to communicate playfulness, the genital area sexual desire. Males were more concerned about the type of touch than the area of the body touched. Both sexes agreed as to which kinds of touching indicated sexual desire; however, males related sexual desire to pleasantness and love, while females considered sexual desire the opposite of playfulness, friendliness, pleasantness and love.

Mehrabian has formulated what he calls the immediacy principle: People "are drawn toward persons and things they like, evaluate highly, and prefer; and they avoid or move away from things they dislike, evaluate negatively, or do not prefer."[29] The immediacy principle and its relationship to touch is consistent with available research on interpersonal attraction; that is, we tend to touch the people we like and avoid those we do not like.[30] The concept of immediacy has also been found to be important in the context of classroom learning. V. P. Richmond, J. S. Gorham, and J. C. McCroskey found that factors such as "vocal expressiveness, smiling at the class, and having a relaxed body position had the highest positive association with learning"; however, touch also had a positive, albeit low, affect. Miles Patterson, Jack Powell, and Mary Lenihan found that such touching, through immediacy, increased getting help from subjects in their study.[31]

Karen Stolte and Paul Friedman examined the type of touch and the perceptions about that touch during labor.[32] What they found further supports the notion of immediacy and suggests a relationship with anxiety. Their subjects were full-term pregnancy patients who were interviewed as soon after childbirth as possible. Each was asked ten questions concerning how she felt about touch and her perceptions of touch during the labor period. In general, touch was thought to be positive during labor. Women ages twenty to thirty-four viewed touch more positively, however, than women aged fifteen to nineteen. Whites perceived touch more positively than nonwhites; single or divorced women perceived touch more negatively than married or separated women. The area most frequently touched during positive experience was the hand; the most negative touch was reported to be the physician's touch in the abdomen or pelvic area. The individuals reported as providing the most positive touch were husbands and family members, followed by the nursing staff. Hence, both physical and attitudinal immediacy, along with perceived meaning (professionalism) contributed to the women's perception of the touch behavior.

Thus, we can conclude that factors influencing touch include type of touch, degree of liking or disliking in the relationship, and the situation at hand. Additionally, David R. Maines has found that touch has been associated with "background" homophily. That is, we prefer to be touched by others of the same race and sex.[33] This finding, particularly regarding sex, is countered by others. Stanley E. Jones, for example, contends that females in general initiate touch more often than males and initiate control touches over males more often. Other researchers report that the idea that females touch more often is true in elderly nursing-home patients.[34] Jones is inconsistent with Nancy M. Henley's findings. It may well be that women do initiate control touches over males, but as indicated by Maines, males may not like it. Debbie Storrs and Chris L. Kleinke found that in interview situations, females were not influenced by the status or sex of the interviewer who touched them. Males, however, were less favorable toward equal status and female interviewers.[35]

The concept of whether we do or do not like to be touched is a significant one. As Peter Andersen and Kenneth Leibowitz note, there are many variables that affect perceptions of touch, of which age, race, and religion seem to be important.[36] We seem not to mind touch in most *professional* situations. In addition, we seem to like touch if that touch is consistent with the relationship and message(s) of the moment. At other times, however, we feel that we have been violated by touch. The most serious of these violations are in the form of assault and battery, but we also dislike being touched unexpectedly and out of the message context.

TABLE 4.1 *Comparison of Responses to Likelihood of Being Touched in Specific Situations*

	OTHERS MORE LIKELY TO TOUCH WHEN	OTHERS LESS LIKELY TO TOUCH WHEN
Information	Giving	Asking
Advice	Giving	Asking
Order	They're Giving	You're Giving
Favor	Asking	Agreeing to Do
Persuade	They're Trying	You're Trying
Worried	You're	They're
Excited	They're	You're
Conversation	Deep	Casual
Place	Party	Work

Source: N. M. Henley, *Body Politics: Power, Sex, and Nonverbal Communication* (Englewood Cliffs, NJ: Prentice-Hall, 1977), p. 105. Reprinted with permission.

Violations of Haptic Expectations

Little is known of what happens when we violate touch expectations. Much of what we do know would seem to imply that three variables are important in evaluating the touch we receive from others: the **location** of the touch, its **duration,** and the **intensity** of the touch. For instance, if we specify the location as the facial cheek, the duration as long, and the intensity as soft, we are defining a positive touch. On the other hand, if the location is the same but the duration extremely short and the intensity hard, we ascribe another meaning. When we examine the impact of touching behavior, we should keep location, duration, and intensity in mind.

What does the research indicate? Despite the prevalence of touch communication, not very much research has been carried out. What we do know, however, seems to indicate that touching another person "accidentally" leads to more positive evaluations, like those previously discussed. Although the implications should be obvious, at times people will either squeeze another person's hand during a handshake or be too "feminine," resulting in impressions that may not be intended. The "American handshake," for example, is supposedly one that is firm, but not too firm, and consists of two and one-half shakes.

Other research indicates that there are certain expectations about how we touch that are conditioned by situation or power. Table 4.1 shows what we should expect in terms of touch in nine situations. Table 4.2 implies that both power (or status) and sex interact but that usually it is the superior in a relationship who initiates touch. What we know indicates that there are expectations about touch behaviors, but how people react to these expectations or how they respond when they are actually touched are questions that require more research.

TABLE 4.2   *Touching by Status and Sex Relationships*

Superior touches Subordinate		25
Male:Female	1	
Female:Female	3	
Male:Male	16	
Female:Male	5	
Subordinate touches Superior		14
Male:Female	9	
Female:Female	1	
Male:Male	4	
Female:Male	0	
"Equal" touches "Equal"		13
Male:Female	11	
Female:Male	2	

Source: N. M. Henley, *Body Politics: Power, Sex, and Nonverbal Communication* (Englewood Cliffs, NJ: Prentice-Hall, 1977), p. 116. Reprinted with permission.

Researchers have attempted to study the impact of touch on both attitude and credibility. In a study conducted by J. D. Fisher, M. Rytting, and R. Heslin, librarians provided "incidental" touch to randomly selected students checking out books. They found that the librarians were evaluated more positively after incidental touch than after no touch.[37] Another study had male and female confederates "interview" students in randomly selected areas of a college campus, each interview beginning with one of the three types of handshakes: (1) a "normal" handshake (see above), (2) a "hard" handshake (the confederates practiced this handshake until an amount of excessive pressure was applied equally by both males and females), and (3) a "soft" handshake (only the thumb and index and middle finger touched the participant).[38] Findings indicated no differences for male interviewers across the three handshakes for either perceptions of credibility or change in attitude toward tuition (which was the focus of the interview and where participants were provided arguments concerning a needed tuition increase), although the mean responses were best for the normal handshake, followed by the hard and soft handshakes. For females, however, the hard handshake produced significantly higher perceptions of credibility, but no differences regarding attitude (normal handshakes produced slightly higher evaluations than did soft handshakes).

One study that merits discussion was undertaken by Beth Pressner.[39] She was interested in the effect of touch both on attitude toward clinical sessions in speech pathology and on learning. Her study was simple: She had clinicians use normal touch (operationalized from observations of the

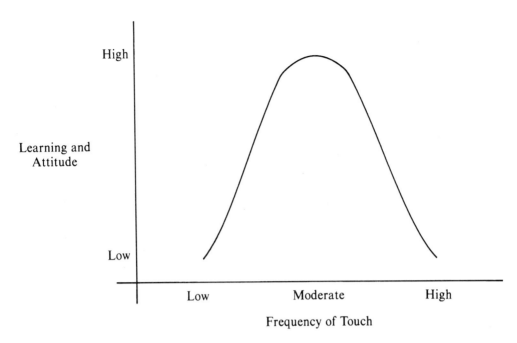

FIGURE 4.3   Frequency of Touch and Outcome.

number of touches clinicians used on a number of patients) at one of the three levels of touch: low, moderate, or high. Touch was defined as contact (usually manual) with the patient during the clinical session in a random form; the frequency of touch ran as follows: Zero to six touches per session was low, seven to sixteen touches per session was moderate, and sixteen to twenty-five touches per session was high. Her general findings were that touching in moderation seemed to produce the best results, although the number of patients studied may have been too small to detect any real differences. Figure 4.3 indicates the predicted relationships among touch, attitude, and learning. Low amounts of touch are expected; moderate amounts may indicate interest and an interpersonal awareness of the patient; high amounts of touch offer too much ''reward,'' and the frequency becomes expected rather than rewarding.

Despite the fact that we often avoid and even plan to avoid touch, we maintain a need for touch in our lives. For that reason we search out what are often considered ''substitutes.'' In the final section on touch, we discuss some of these substitutes.

Substitutes for "Real Touch"

As we grow up, various senses achieve a different sequence of precedence. As children our senses tend to follow the sequence: (1) touch, (2) visual, and (3) aural. As adults, and with the learning of language, the precedence changes to (1) visual, (2) aural, and (3) touch. Thus, as adults we tend to become ''touch-starved'' (at least in American society).

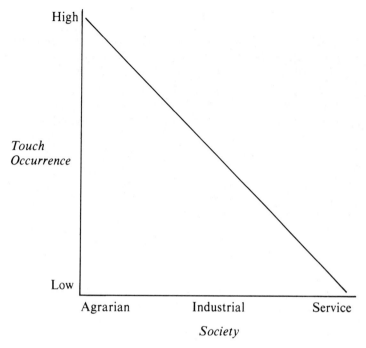

FIGURE 4.4   Relationship Between Touch and Type of Society.

Because we become starved for touch, we tend to buy ''touch-for-hire.''[40] Desmond Morris has stated that we hire ''licensed touchers'' such as beauticians and masseuses to take care of our need for bodily contact in a socially acceptable way. Such entities as encounter groups often satisfy the same needs. Other substitutes are used such as petting dogs or cats, sucking thumbs, or smoking cigarettes. This lack of intimacy that we ordinarily experience, and its substitutes, Morris calls a major social disease. Thus, as adults we need touch, as we did as infants, but the need is satisfied in unusual and unnatural ways. It appears that adults almost have an approach-avoidance complex about touch. We want to touch and be touched, yet there are social norms that pressure us to avoid touching. Perhaps one of the reasons for such a norm in American culture is the lack of working with the hands, the lack of touch. Most college students, if you ask them, feel that they are in college to avoid getting their hands ''dirty.'' As noted in Figure 4.4, there may be a relationship between the type of society (agrarian to service-oriented) and the amount of touch expected. Societies in which people engage in working with their hands seem to find touch natural; societies that have progressed beyond this point find touch less attractive.[41]

It is interesting to note that Manfred Clynes found that humans can transmit emotions to people who speak a different language through touch and gesture. However, investigating this notion in a laboratory, Steven J. Trussoni, Anthony O'Malley, and Anthony Barter found this could not be done because of idiosyncratic touch behaviors.[42]

☐   **Summary**   ☐

Touch is a prominent aspect of our development and occurs as a major form of communication. Although cultures differ in their expectations of what amount, type, and location of touch is appropriate, the need is still there. Touch is essential in the development of the person; it is needed in the development of intimate "relations." Touch, although so urgently required, is also approached with a puritanical avoidance. Learning about how touch operates and its significance should make us better communicators in one sense and, perhaps in another sense, wonder why we do not touch more.

Chapter Five

Studies on Personal Space, Territory, and the Environment

Key Concepts

Personal Space

Territories of the Self

Territorial Violations

Animals' Use of Space

Environmental Dimensions, Territory, and Personal Space Norms

In Chapter 4, we discussed touch as a basic nonverbal device that is part of the subcode we refer to as proxemics. In fact, we wrote that haptics may be referred to as zero-proxemics. Certainly most of us consider touch to be a significant factor in terms of our space; therefore, we touch relatively few people and we are touched by relatively few people. As we move outward from touch to personal space we will consider the nonverbal communication aspects of that space we carry around with us—an invisible bubble. As we move farther out from the body, we will find the concept of territory, which is usually a static—as opposed to dynamic—area for which we claim possession either in terms of social norms or laws. Finally, we will discuss the environment, those natural or artificial factors that affect how territories look, feel, and assist or inhibit us in communicating with one another.

Proxemics

Edward T. Hall has defined proxemics as ''the interrelated observations and theories of man's use of space as a specialized elaboration of culture.''[1] One can hardly dismiss the importance of space. In general, land values are going up every year, funeral plots are becoming more expensive, traffic congestion characterizes urban areas from 6:00–8:30 A.M. and from 4:00–7:00 P.M., and people are queuing up everywhere to see the latest smash movie, a rock group, or a selected politician.[2] Space is important to all of us, and, in western culture, there are many laws about space. At the same time, we need to remember that individuals have different spatial conceptualizations, as do different cultures, racial groups, sexes, and ages; still other perceptions are based on the situations in which we find ourselves. Proxemics is best defined, however, in terms of the two major subareas that constitute how we use the space around us: personal space and territory. We turn first to the study of personal space.

Personal Space

Edney has classified the use of space into three basic categories: (1) individual; (2) small group and interpersonal relations; and (3) communities.[3] Much of the research in this area has been strongly influenced by anthropologist Edward T. Hall, who first noted the communicative potential of personal spacing.

Classification Schemes   Hall has classified space according to the amount of distance between two individuals in the process of communication.[4] The first distance is referred to as **intimate.** This distance measures from zero-proxemics (touching) to eighteen inches in the United States. The next distance is **personal** and ranges from eighteen inches to about four feet. **Social** space ranges from four to ten feet, and, finally, **public** distances range from ten feet on up. Within each distance ''zone,'' we have units, or **proxemes.** These units are generally classified as ''inner'' or ''outer.'' The inner proxeme of the personal zone, for instance, might run from eighteen to twenty-five inches; the outer proxeme for that same zone might run thirty-two to forty-eight inches. The proxemes allow us to establish subranges within each distancing zone. How we view the zones may be examined in terms of topic of communication.

Much like the notion of territory, which is based on accessibility, personal spacing is based on the intimacy of the topic. As the topic of conversation becomes more intimate, we reduce the space between us. Also, you may observe that other people view the perceived intimacy of conversation on the basis of the amount of distance between you and the other person.

Hall, however, associates a number of factors with the various distances we adopt in daily interaction. As indicated in Figures 5.1 and 5.2, there are numerous features other than intimacy that contribute to our perception of personal space. Hall includes *postural-sex identifiers.* Sex refers to the sex (male-female) of the two people involved in the interaction; postural refers to whether the interactants are prone, seated, or standing. A second factor that is compared with distance is the *sociofugal-sociopetal axis.* As indicated in Figure 5.2, this factor refers to the ''angle formed by the axes of the interactants' shoulders.'' At level 0, the interactants are face-to-face (maximum sociopetality); at level 8, they are back-to-back (maximum sociofugality).

Amount of *touch,* ranging from none to mutual caressing (on a six-point scale), is the third factor. *Kinesthetic* features (parts of the body touching one another) is the fourth factor. The *visual code* (amount and kind of visual interaction) is based on areas of the eye, specifically of the retina. The *thermal code* has to do with the amount of heat detected by the people in the interaction, as given off by the body. The *olfactory code* has to do with the detection of body odor and breath. And, finally, *voice-loudness* refers to the volume of the oral aspect of verbal language. All of these factors are related to the distances people adopt, and they help to explain why we have certain distancing preferences or norms with different people at different times.

The interaction of these factors and the intimacy of topic allow us to examine why people adopt spatial distances. We should remember, however, that as distance increases or decreases, other nonverbal codes come more or less into play. The interaction of Hall's eight factors results in an

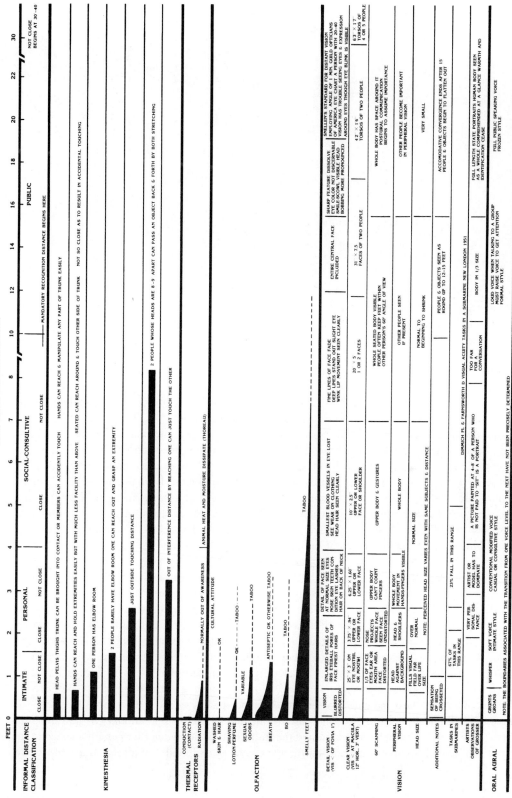

FIGURE 5.1 Chart Showing Interplay of the Distant and Immediate Receptors in Proxemic Perception (lines).
Source: E. T. Hall, "Proxemics," *American Anthropologist*, 65 (5), 1963. Reproduced by permission of the American Anthropological Association. Not for further reproduction.

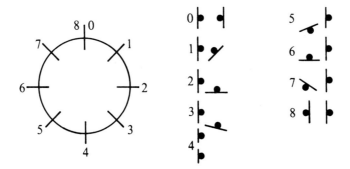

FIGURE 5.2   Sociofugial-Sociopetal Axes.
Source: E. T. Hall, ''A System for the Notation of Proxemic Behavior,''
American Anthropologist, 65 (5), 1963. Reproduced by permission of the
American Anthropological Association. Not for further reproduction.

equilibrium among the nonverbal behaviors.[5] But there are a number of other factors that influence distancing: age, sex, culture, race, task, degree of relationship, personality, and environmental structure help determine what distances we adopt with others.

Definitions and Need   Before we begin to examine these factors, we need to establish distancing zones with which we are really concerned. The emphasis of much of the rest of this section is on the personal spacing zone. Although we also consider the intimate and the social, much of our interpersonal communication is found in the personal spacing zone.

   Personal space is referred to either as an ''invisible, flexible bubble that surrounds us''[6] or as a ''body buffer zone.''[7] Both descriptions are correct. Personal space seems to be attributable to the need to protect our body territories. In that regard, personal space is a ''body buffer zone,'' a zone of space—unmarked, unlike territories—that serves to protect us from the intrusion of others. Personal space is also flexible; it surrounds the individual but is usually larger in the rear, with less distance needed in the front and to each side. Personal space is also influenced by vertical as well as horizontal factors.[8] What we have, then, is a sphere of space that surrounds us totally, from the floor to the ceiling, from front to back, and from side to side.

Need for Space   Research has indicated that, much like our need for territory, we have a need for personal space. **Body buffer zone** implies a definite psychological need. Other researchers have found (through the use of electrocardiogram, electroencephalogram, galvanic skin response, and other physiological indicators and from actual physical reactance) that people react to personal space physiologically[9] as well as psychologically.[10] Indicators of strong psychological and physiological needs are found in reactions to other people as compared to relations with inanimate objects, in verbal and nonverbal reports of anxiety, and in the placement of figures based on expected distances in given scenarios.

   Perhaps one of the best indicators of the need for personal space is the research first reported by Nancy Felipe and Robert Sommer and later replicated by Kristina Krail and Gloria Leventhal and S. M. S. Ahmed. This research examined the impact of violating another person's space in the library.[11] Felipe and Sommer first studied the expectations of females studying at a table alone.

In this research a confederate sat in one of several different seats at the same table as the studying females. When the confederate sat close to the subject, a series of behaviors were found to occur; the students would almost always (1) engage in eye contact with the confederate and give ''dirty looks''; (2) begin to build barriers (establish markers on the desk with such items as books, purses, paper, pencils); (3) begin to exhibit body shifts (moving the body around, as if uncomfortable); (4) use the body as a barrier by turning away from the confederate; (5) begin subvocal expressions or muttering; (6) engage in decreased eye contact (eye contact would go to the material in front of them); (7) assume a nonperson orientation (react as if the confederate was an extension of the chair or as an object); (8) exhibit anxiety movements, such as drumming of fingers, variant eye contact, and so forth; and (9) finally leave the table (give up their space and established territory, as based in the markers at step two) within 10 to 30 minutes.

Krail and Leventhal and Ahmed each replicated this study but added several variations. First, they had males and females invade students of both sexes studying alone in the library. Second, they introduced a verbal claim to the space. They found that the same behaviors occurred but that these were much faster if the confederate was of the *same* sex. They also reported that the females gave up their space more readily than did the males when verbally challenged (they suggested that females are taught socially to share more than are males, who are taught to defend things that they possess). During their menstrual period, females distance themselves farther from males, but not from other females.[12] In any case, these three studies indicate a strong need for space, with both psychological and physiological reaction when someone ''violates'' a spatial expectation or norm.

Factors Influencing Distancing Expectations   As might be concluded from the research already discussed, there are quite a few factors that influence our expectations as to how much space we maintain between ourselves and others. Judee Burgoon has classified these factors as arising out of three groups of variables: interactant, interactional, and environmental.[13] Within these groups are a number of related variables. In this section, we examine in isolation the more significant variables, although you should remember that they operate together in determining spatial norms.

Age Differences   In general, as the age of the person increases, so does the expected distancing. This holds true, however, only for interactions where there is a discrepancy in the ages of the interactants. With same-age people, distancing expectations are closer than with those who are older or younger. Several studies lend support for this generalization. One by Gay Tennis and James Dabbs found that older subjects (age being defined as students enrolled in the first, fifth, ninth, and twelfth grades, and college sophomores) preferred greater interpersonal distances than younger subjects.[14] In another study, researchers found that invasion of personal space, in a re-freshment line of a drive-in theatre, was influenced by age of the invader. With a five-year-old invader, adults were facilitative; with eight-year-olds there was no particular response; with ten-year-olds the adults displayed avoidance and excess motor activity.[15] J. R. Aiello and T. C. Aiello reported that students from ages six to sixteen maintained greater interaction distances as age increased, but this distancing trend leveled off at about the seventh grade, and distances did not increase significantly.[16]

It should be noted that age is significantly affected by both the sex and the race of the people involved. A number of studies have found that up to about age seven, sex is not an important factor in distancing norms; however, after that age the more commonly associated closer distances are found for female-female and male-female interactions, and farther distances are found with male-male interactions.[17] In terms of race, S. E. Jones and J. R. Aiello found that black and white elementary school children adopt different distancing norms. First-grade blacks adopted less personal space than whites, but by third grade, the difference between the races began to diminish and to reverse by grade five. Jones and Aiello also reported sex differences in distancing norms.[18]

Sex Differences   As noted, distancing preferences for either males or females are influenced to some degree by the age of the interactants. However, there are some generalizations that can be made based solely on the sex of the individual. As noted, Tennis and Dabbs found that males usually prefer greater distances when interacting with one another than do females.[19] F. N. Willis found that speakers usually stood closer to women than to men.[20] Terri Rosegrant and James C. McCroskey found that in an interview situation, male-male dyads established greater distances between them than any combination containing at least one female.[21] Not all research has confirmed these findings; Darhl Pedersen and Anne Heaston and Jeffrey Fisher and Don Byrne have reported contradictory findings.[22] It would seem that females prefer less distance when interacting than do males.[23]

In terms of approach behavior (an indicator of distancing preferences), several studies indicate that males tend to approach females closer than females approach males, but that this may be affected by the angle of the approach.[24] In this research Pedersen and Heaston reported that females allowed others to approach closer to their sides than to their front; males allowed others to approach closer to their front than to their sides; males were allowed to approach more closely off-center to the left than were females, although no difference was found for off-center to the right. Michael Hendricks and Richard Bootzin noted that males reported significantly more discomfort in approaching a female confederate than did females.[25] And, finally, R. M. Tipton, K. G. Bailey, and J. P. Obenchain found that traditional females maintain greater distances from males than do feminists, but do not differ in their approach distances with other females.[26]

George Banziger and Renee Simmons reported that interpersonal distance may be affected by the level of attractiveness of the confederate.[27] They measured the street-crossing times and reported the emotions of street crossers who were approached by—intruded upon—an attractive or unattractive female. Their research design was simple but effective. Another female confederate then approached each participant *after* they crossed the street and asked what two emotions the participant felt in response to the intruder. Positive emotions were more prevalent when the intruder was attractive, and negative emotions were more prevalent when the intruder was unattractive. The researchers theorized that spatial invasion increases arousal, but the nature of the arousal (i.e., positive or negative) is dependent upon the attractiveness of the invader. This particular finding, the role of physical attraction, has also been tested by Judee Burgoon and her associates, who defined *attraction* in several ways.[28]

Generally, it appears that sex differences play a major role in determining distancing norms. Males tend to expect and receive greater distances when interacting with other males. Males tend to approach females closer than females approach males, and although it is not possible to explain exactly why, approaches seem to differ by angle or side of approach.

Cultural Differences   The main thrust of cultural research has been advanced on the assumption that two types of cultures exist. Anthropologists have categorized cultures as either "contact" or "noncontact," the former maintaining closer distances than the latter.[29] Whether these differences really exist has been questioned. Several researchers have maintained that this distinction is not viable and may be a feature of faulty analysis.[30] Others have found that significant differences exist between contact and noncontact cultures.[31] Examination of this body of research indicates, however, that cultures differ in their *expectations* of what distances *should* be maintained when interacting. The differences, however, are more country specific and less culture specific. Citizens of Denmark, for example, maintain a high value for social interaction. As with Americans, the Danes spend most of their time in the workplace and in the home. To contribute to their feeling *hygge* (comfort, coziness, cheerfulness, and friendliness), they use furnishings, light, and limited body contact. Social gathering centers on the coffee table in a circle of light. Danes attempt to achieve expected distances differently. Hall has suggested that Americans generally do not like the Middle East because the Arabs get too close to them and breathe on them.[32] Whereas Americans go to great extents to avoid spatial violations, Hall states that the Arabs have no word for ''rape'' or ''trespass.''

An examination of different cultures implies doubt that all countries in a given culture operate on the same distancing norms. J. C. Baxter, for example, noted that Mexican-Americans maintained closer personal spacing than did Anglos, who in turn maintained closer personal spacing than did blacks in a natural setting.[33] J. Lorenz examined the cultural norms of three nationalities and found that the placement of figurines in relation to each other was largely contingent upon culture: South Americans had the largest personal spacing, Iraqi the smallest, with Russians being intermediate.[34]

D. B. Roger and E. E. Schalekamp investigated the body zones of South African black prisoners and found that South African blacks have larger body zones than reported for American black prisoners. They explained the difference in terms of contact versus noncontact cultures, with the American culture as more prone to contact. The differences between the two cultures were also viewed as possibly the result of cultural anomie, because South African blacks represent the opposite status pole of whites and reject African values forced upon them by the minority white population.[35] An alternative explanation is that the blacks may form a distinctly noncontact *subcultural* group and, as a result, may maintain a tendency toward greater personal space norms.[36]

Robert Shuter has noted that within a large culture, differences occur in personal spacing. From observations made in Costa Rica, Colombia, and Panama (all presumably contact cultures), he found that Costa Ricans interacted closest, Panamanians at the farthest distance, and Colombians were intermediate.[37] He also investigated the interaction patterns in Germany, Italy, and the United States. In this study, he observed dyads of males and females and found no significant differences between cultures with respect to male-female, male-male, or female-female dyads, although Germans interacted least directly in both sex pairs. In terms of male-female dyads, Italians interacted at a more direct angle than did Americans; however, American female dyads communicated more directly.[38] In an observational study of seating patterns on park benches in three different cultures, A. Mazur found no difference between the distances adopted by strangers.[39] His results, however, may have been an artifact of measurement due to differing bench lengths in different cultures. In several studies, methodological problems may also have contributed to such findings. For instance, Robert Forston and Charles Larson found no significant differences in interpersonal distancing between contact and noncontact cultures; however, the subjects were noncontact people who had been living in the United States for a period of time prior to the study.[40] Similarly, in his finding of no differences in subcultures, Jones may have been biased by the settings and the ways the data were collected.[41]

In general, it would appear that cultural differences, to include the possibility of subcultural differences, do exist in spacing expectations. That they do not necessarily exist for a dichotomy as large as "contact" or "noncontact" should not surprise us. We may have a stereotypical view of appropriate interpersonal distancing, but as Shuter found, that stereotype may or may not be accurate, depending on what nationality or subculture we are studying.

Racial Differences   No clear-cut generalizations can be made regarding racial differences and personal spacing expectations. Part of this problem follows from our discussion of cultural, sexual, and age factors. But in most cases, the results of research are mixed. In one study, for instance, Baxter found that in the United States, about one-third of the explanation for distancing expectations could be attributed to race.[42] Other researchers have found that the distance between interactants was greater for blacks than whites, although a number of factors (age, sex, culture) may also enter into the interpretation.[43] With college-age students, however, Ernest A. Bauer found that blacks stood closer to one another than did whites;[44] this was basically the same as Rosegrant and McCroskey reported, except that sex of the individual also affected the interaction distances. They found that in an interview situation, "Female-black interviewees established closer interpersonal distance to all interviewees than did any other sex-race interviewee combination."[45] Based on this, J. K. Burgoon, D. W. Stacks, and W. G. Woodall suggested that same-race interactions would be more rewarding (would result in closer interpersonal distances) than opposite-race interactions, but they failed to support such a hypothesis.[46] Thus, at this time no clear-cut conclusions can be made about race and personal space.

Personality, Liking, and Status   Several factors that influence our distancing expectations are brought to the interaction with us. These are features that change according to perception. In this regard, we can look at such manifestations as the individual's status or personality or the degree of liking one holds toward the other. In general, research has determined that people who are of higher status expect *and* receive more interpersonal distance than those of lower status.[47]

Personality differences function to create different personal spacing expectations. Although there is a rather large body of research in this area, the variables that affect the process of establishing spacing expectations are still not completely identified. What we know, however, would seem to indicate that introverts and extroverts differ in their spatial use, with extroverts using less space. Anxious and neurotic individuals tend to prefer more space but perceive less space to exist between them and others than do less anxious and neurotic individuals.[48] Aberrant or deviant personalities also affect the distancing patterns between people.[49] Violent people need more space than do nonviolent people. Schizophrenics use and expect others to use space differently than nonschizophrenics. Finally, emotionally disturbed people use space differently than do nonemotionally disturbed people; if that disturbance deals with violence, greater spatial preference is observed.[50]

Finally, the degree of liking in the interaction helps determine personal spacing expectations. Liking, however, can be viewed as more than simple "liking" and is related to such things as physical attraction, degree of acquaintance, and approval. In general, we approach others we see as being physically attractive more closely than we approach those we perceive as less attractive; people who wish to demonstrate liking also establish closer physical distances.[51] Moreover, people tend to establish closer distances from someone they are acquainted with than from someone who may be a stranger.[52]

An area that has received less attention is the finding that people maintain greater distances from others who have **stigmas.** Goffman noted that one ''possessing an attribute that makes him different from others in the category of persons available for him to be, and of a less desirable kind—in the extreme, a person who is quite thoroughly bad, or dangerous, or weak'' is one who possesses a stigma. Stigmas may be of two basic types: physical and social. *Physical stigmas* would include being in a wheelchair, being blind, being an amputee, having a burned face, and so forth. One group of researchers, for example, found that pedestrians allowed a legally blind person with a white cane 33.8 inches of personal space as opposed to 5.6 inches when there was no cane.[53] *Social stigmas* would include reputations based on such factors as being an ex-convict or having a social disease (one that cannot be seen, VD or herpes, for instance). In general, we maintain more space between ourselves and those with stigmas.[54]

Environmental Structuring   How we structure our environment obviously has a great impact on our personal spacing. In many instances personal space research would seem to be mislabeled, especially when we talk about seating preferences and furniture arrangement. However, if you think of such areas as a way of expressing ourselves by means of the distances we either choose or are made to choose, then we begin to acquire a better understanding of how personal spacing expectations and norms are structured.

In a classroom setting, J. Heston and P. Garner found that distances between students fell within Hall's intimate zone, with seating preference for a U-shaped arrangement.[55] This arrangement seems to direct attention away from immediate neighbors and may explain the closeness of the preferred distance. Research in task-oriented and social-oriented interactions indicates that the purpose of the interaction along with the environmental constraints may dictate distance and seating arrangements between interactants. Several studies report that the kind of interaction (i.e., casual or conversational, cooperative, competitive, or coactive) produces different preferences for seating arrangements that reflect different distances between individuals. Corner or adjacent seating preferences are found normally in cooperative task situations; opposite seating arrangement is usually found in competitive situations, where a greater distance keeps other people from surveying progress; and for coacting people, a greater distance is preferred.[56] Mark Cook notes that in bars, where the conversation is intimate or social, seating preference is for the side-by-side or adjacent cross-corner arrangement. When the purpose of dining is added, the preference is for larger distances and an opposite-seating arrangement.[57] M. Reiss and P. Rosenfeld found that when specific impressions were desired in a group interaction around a table, the position taken helped to indicate that impression. They had people choose one of several seats around a table to convey the impression of (1) leadership and dominance, (2) nonparticipation, (3) attraction, and (4) dislike. To show leadership, 80 percent of the people in the study took one of the two end chairs. To show nonparticipation, 64 percent chose one of the corner seats, farthest from the head. To present themselves as attracted to other group members, they chose chairs more in the middle. To show themselves as disliked (cold, unfriendly), they chose the farthest seating possible.[58] Other researchers on group processes have similar findings: leadership coming from the ends of the table; where there are fewer chairs on one side of the table and no chairs at the end, leadership comes from the side with fewer chairs.[59] One reason for this is that those positions control eye contact.

In other situations, such as being outside, the type of environment may affect personal spacing expectations and norms. J. J. Edney and N. L. Jordan-Edney found that situational determinants of size of groups and place may be significant factors in determining personal spacing. They observed spacing on a large, open beach.[60] Their concern was how naturally occurring groups divided their territory and the use of space within the territory. They found that (1) group territories did not necessarily grow with group size, instead individuals decreased their personal space; and (2) females claimed less territory than males.

The use of space, to include both territory and personal space, communicates many things. When we think of territory, we are examining something that is more fixed or marked than the more flexible personal space zone around us. These concepts are related, however, because personal space is an outgrowth of our need for some form of protection from others (e.g., we protect our bodies by erecting a psychological barrier). Many factors influence the amount of space we have around us, including the type of territory we are in. The best conclusion is that we form expectations based on norms associated with such characteristics as sex, race, culture, personality, status, location, and so forth. Like the environment, space helps communicate perceptions of relationships and indicate how we perceive others.

Violations of Personal Space

The final section deals with the violation of proxemic expectations. In general, we perceive a violation of expectations as either positive or negative and dependent upon several factors.[61] We will examine in some detail the dimension of space and how people react when we violate expectations based on personal space.

The research that has thus far been reported indicates that people, as well as other animals, have concepts of territory and personal space. Within cultures and subcultures, there is a recognition of this ''right to space.'' As in other societies, residents of the United States have proxemic norms.[62] Most of the research on proxemic norms has consisted of field experiments in which a confederate violates the space of subjects. Probably the most familiar of these studies includes the Felipe and Sommer and similar investigations of library invasion noted earlier.

When someone violates one of our territories, we tend to react, at least in our culture, with defensive devices. Again, the research of Felipe and Sommer is concerned with such invasion; however, if that territory is either the home or the body, then reactions become more violent. In most states the act of ''defending'' home or body is defined in such a way as to make homicide ''legal.'' For the most part, however, research has been interested in less intensely held territories and has found that we engage in the following behaviors: (1) we avoid conversation (we do *not* challenge unless challenged, and even then it will depend upon the sexual configuration of the interaction); (2) we avoid eye contact (in cases where a stranger sits down at a restaurant table with us, after the initial glare, we look almost exclusively at our plate); (3) we place objects between ourselves and the other person; and (4) we focus our attention, body orientation, and eye contact elsewhere.

Not all spatial violations are territorial. Just as unnerving are personal spacing violations. Indeed, because we have no real markers around us, we form an expectation of appropriate distancing and then expect that this distance will be maintained. It is precisely this type of thinking that led Judee Burgoon and her associates to propose a theory of personal space expectations and their violations.[63] This theory postulates that we can predict the outcome of a spatial violation based on three factors: (1) the ''reward'' power of the violator (what aspects he or she brings with him to the interaction: attraction, power, status, for instance), (2) the direction of the violation (closer or farther than expected), and (3) the degree of the deviation (how much closer or farther).

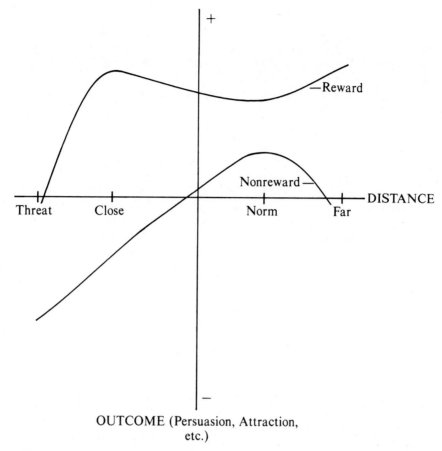

FIGURE 5.3   Predicted Outcomes for Violating or Maintaining a Spatial Expectation.

    In general, this theory posits that rewarding violators will produce better outcomes than will nonrewarding violators (see Figure 5.3). The outcomes, however, are conditioned by the amount of deviation and direction. If the violator deviates too closely, the impact of reward is not strong enough to reduce the tension, uneasiness, anxiety, and pressure associated with extremely close distances. If the violator is rewarding and deviates in moderation, then generally positive outcomes are observed. If the violator is nonrewarding, however, any deviation from the expected norm produces lower, even disastrous, outcomes. Partial support for this theory has been demonstrated for such outcomes as perceived attraction, credibility, and persuasiveness.

    The impact of such research points to strategies we may want to examine in a little more detail. For instance, suppose we know that others perceive us as being rewarding. This spatial theory infers that we will be perceived as more credible, attractive, and more persuasive if we deviate from the expected distance. On the other hand, if we know that we are nonrewarding, then we should maintain whatever distance is ''agreed'' upon. Research has indicated that these findings can be used in both dyadic and small-group contexts.

Recent research indicates that attractiveness of the person is a factor in spatial violations. Gender and status, however, have relatively limited effects on spatial expectations and violations. Attractive females are expected to be relaxed or erect, but not tense. Regarding cultural differences, one researcher found that spatial invasions among Turks are much less than have been reported in the research literature. Finally, David Buller found that apprehensive people are aroused when closely violated. LePoire, however, disputes the findings regarding persons' having such defensive reactions to spatial violations.[64]

Other Violations

Goffman has identified a number of modalities of violation of the territories of the self.[65] Goffman's first violation is spatial invasion: the infringement of actual body space. Second is the defilement of another's sheath; here Goffman is concerned with using the body, including the hands, to inappropriately touch the skin or clothing of another. Third, Goffman discusses the visual violation. This is the glance, the penetration of the eyes. Certainly staring is an example. At the same time, we should briefly consider the wink as a visual approach to decreasing personal space. No matter how close or how far apart two interactants are, a wink tends to bring them closer in a psychological sense. The wink, then, certainly is an element in proxemic relationships. The study of gazes is discussed in more detail later.[66]

Goffman has also indicated that there are violations of acoustic space. Perhaps an example would help us understand this phenomenon. Suppose that you go to a restaurant to have lunch with a business associate. In addition to having lunch, it is your intention to discuss business. You sit down, order from the menu, and begin your business talk. After about five minutes, a group of people comes into the restaurant. After ordering food, they put four quarters in a juke box; seconds later the music is blaring throughout the restaurant. Certainly, you would feel that the other people have infringed upon your acoustic space.

Kendrick and MacFarlane found that horn honking, as an acoustic spatial violation, was related to environmental temperature.[67] Their study was conducted in Phoenix, Arizona, on fifteen consecutive Saturdays between April and August. They found that at temperatures over 100 degrees Fahrenheit, thirty-four percent of the people observed honked their horns when a red light turned green. When the temperature was ninety degrees or less, there was no honking. Additionally, they observed that honking was usually done by young males accompanied by other young males. Several of the honkers integrated their horn honking with verbal and nonverbal signals of hostility.

A final category of violations, according to Goffman, is related to body excreta. This concept may go back to what your mother told you: ''Always wear clean underwear; you may have to go to the hospital.'' Certainly, no one wants to go to the hospital in dirty underwear. Goffman identifies four types of bodily excreta as personal violations. First, there are those that can be transmitted by direct touch: ''spittle, snot, perspiration, food particles, blood, semen, vomit, urine, and fecal matter.''[68] Second, there are various odors, including bad breath, body odor, and flatus. Third is body heat transmitted in a number of places mentioned by Goffman. The final element Goffman discusses is plate leavings on the table. Goffman mentions that knives perform an interesting function in this regard: if a child bites into a cake, it can easily be detected; whereas if he/she slices off another slice, it cannot. Many, if not most, of these violations are based more on societal norms than on logical reasoning, as are many proxemic expectations. Goffman provides us, then, with some of the norms that may affect our reputation with others and therefore our ability to communicate effectively.

Territory

When two or more human beings occupy the same established territory, they usually establish some social norms in terms of what territory belongs to whom. Archie Bunker had his chair in the living room, as many fathers do. Even some pets have their own space; animals also have territory relative to one another. Wolves, chimpanzees, bees, birds, dogs, and cats have established means for marking their areas. **Territoriality** is the concept that an animal "lays claim to an area and defends it against members of its own species."[69] In acting thus, the animals assure the propagation of the species by regulating density.

S. M. Lyman and M. B. Scott[70] have identified four types of territories on the basis of their accessibility. The first type is **public territory;** this is an area that individuals may freely enter. Government buildings, schools, hospitals, and commercial enterprises generally allow individuals free access. You should note, however, that this notion of "public" is legislated. The school you attend, the class you sit in, is designated "public" in many states but in reality is restricted only to those who have a *legitimate use for that space* (try to sit in on a class without permission and observe the reactions as you violate the "public" space). The second type of territory is **interactional,** a mobile area in which individuals congregate informally, the boundaries of which are likely to move. In terms of access, interactional territory is more restricted; generally, someone exercises control. Examples of such territories are a movie theatre, a restaurant, and your classroom. Interaction territory, however, is also viewed as a more mobile or indefinite territory, such as the space you have as you walk on a sidewalk or the small group's claim to a territory at a party. Note that the boundaries here are not explicit and that other people may invade or "defile" that territory by walking through it.[71]

The third type of territory is **home territory.** In the home, we find free interactions by individuals who claim the territory; others, however, may not have free access. In most places in the United States, homes are locked when all of the occupants are away; they are also locked at night. In most states, trespassing laws provide us with legal recourse should others intrude upon our home territory; in some states you can legally defend your home territory with the use of deadly force *if the intruder is breaking into the home.* We may even build fences to keep others out of our yards. But the concept of home territory not only includes legal and physical impediments, it also includes social barriers. Outsiders do not usually come into our homes and use areas or objects within the home without the express permission of someone who lives there. One of the major problems for people who live with others occurs when someone they do not like is invited into the home by a roommate; in this case, the person's perception is that the home has been defiled.

The last spatial area is **body territory;** the space immediately surrounding us. Body territory is usually marked by the skin or by the clothing with which we cover our bodies. Body territory can be seen as an imaginery area or radius around our bodies, one that may be small for some and larger for others. When one enters another person's body territory, there is a violation. Because we, in this culture, do not like our bodies violated, we tend to have larger body areas surrounding us; this implies personal spacing expectations.

Territory is important for all animals, but especially for human beings. Two studies of other species of animals lend support for the importance of territory. Although we hesitate to compare other species' behavior to ours, some parallels indicate remarkable similarity to the behaviors in humans.

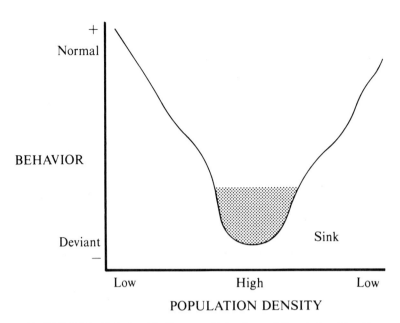

FIGURE 5.4   Relationship Between Behavior and Population Density.

Animal Correlates to Territoriality

Calhoun's Study of Rats   John Calhoun observed the conditions of overpopulation of Norway rats; his observations concerned three generations of rats over a period of twenty-eight months.[72] The rat population, in a quarter-acre pen, stabilized at 150. The rats "organized" themselves into twelve or thirteen colonies of about twelve rats each and were allowed to live normally, except that their lives were carefully controlled. Human intervention was minimal, except that the pens were constructed in such a way as to preclude other animals from entering. In other words, the rats were provided with plenty of food and water, but had no predators or enemies.

During the experiment, the rats developed what Calhoun has referred to as a "behavioral sink." The sink was an area in which gross distortions of behavior occurred. Such "deviant" behavior was observed disrupting normal nest building, courting behaviors, reproduction, and social organization. The occurrence of the sink was strongly related to the amount of territory (density of the territory) the rats had. As density increased, as Figure 5.4 indicates, behavior began to deviate from accepted norms until it reached the lowest common denominator: the sink. As territorial density decreased, the behavior became more "normative."

Most of the deviant behavior involved social actions. Most of the nest building, for instance, was undertaken by the female rats. In the normal area, the rats had no problems; however, females in the sink were unable to complete the nest building. Several types of distorted behavior occurred with male rats in the sink. Males mounted other males, young females, unreceptive females; others retreated from sexual intercourse entirely. Litters became mixed; some of the young were stepped on by others, and some were eaten by hyperactive males. The sink behavior was marked by extensive fights between males. Only one-fourth of 558 young rats survived to be weaned. Miscarriages increased, and various sexual disorders, including tumors, were found. There were other cases of unprovoked tail biting.

It is important to note that there was enough food to support all of the rats, but there was not enough space or privacy. A. S. Parkers and H. M. Bruce, for example, have indicated that the presence of a second male rat could block pregnancy.[73] Thus, in the case of Calhoun's Norway rats, the lack of territory caused social deviation and physiological problems.[74]

Sika Deer Study   A second study of the effects of lack of territoriality concerns deer found on James Island in the 1950s. James Island is about one mile off the Maryland coast in Chesapeake Bay. The uninhabited island is 280 acres (about a half a square mile). In 1916, four or five Sika deer were placed on the island. By 1955, the population had grown to 280 or 300, although support for such a population was no problem, given the adequate supply of food and water. About this time, however, a die-off occurred. John Christian, a biologist, had shot several deer for histological studies prior to the die-off. During the first three months of 1958, 161 carcasses were recovered. The population had stabilized at around eighty deer.

Histological studies of the carcasses indicated that the deer had not died of starvation. The researchers found, instead, that the deer had enlarged adrenal glands, which was attributed to a high level of stress. Christian concluded that the lack of relief from confinement caused stress, which accounted for the increased size of the adrenal gland, and the adrenal gland, in turn, increased the supply of adrenalin to the deer, resulting in death.[75] Thus, Christian's studies support the idea that for the Sika deer, it is possible that the lack of space produced stress which resulted in death.

Human Correlates of Territoriality

It is essential for us to note, however, that the conclusions of these studies of animals cannot be directly transferred to human beings. Humans in nonlaboratory situations can adapt by moving to other areas, but there are some situations in which this is not possible. We will examine a number of research projects that determine that humans can suffer from a lack of territory in a way similar to those results reported for lower species of animals.

Prison Studies   Gavin McCain and his colleagues observed crowding in prison environments.[76] They observed inmates at a prison and in a county jail in order to determine whether crowding/stress produced increases in illness complaints. Prior to visiting the prisoners, the researchers obtained detailed housing and medical histories of the preceding six-month period. Most of the illness complaints involved back pain, nausea, rash, sinus, constipation, chest pain, and asthma. In general, the researchers found more illness complaints from inmates living in dormitory housing than from those living in single or two-person prison cells. They concluded that it was probably the higher social density factor (total number of people in the unit), however, rather than the spatial (amount of space per person) factor, that accounted for the stress. In a similar study, D. A. D'Atri found that both systolic and diastolic blood pressure readings, as well as pulse rates, were higher for prisoners living in dormitories than for those in one- or two-person cells.[77]

James Bonta has severely criticized prison crowding studies, arguing that little effort has been made to show the overall relationship between population density and other factors in the prison environment. Bonta suggests that a prisoner's age and chronicity (length of exposure in the prison environment) might be important variables to be considered when interpreting territoriality in such environments. Other variables that Bonta suggests might affect territoriality findings include noise level, temperature, inmate turnover, and difficulty of surveillance.[78]

Cocooning Behaviors   In a series of studies done in the late 1960s and early 1970s by Irving Altman and his colleagues, human reaction to territory was vividly shown.[79] Altman's research was concerned with the problems associated with confinement to a particular territory for a long period of time. Such confinements might be equated with the behavior found in nuclear submarines on patrol for long periods of time, or in the case of a nuclear attack, the effect of long periods of confinement in bomb shelters. Altman's research indicated that when two people were confined to small rooms for periods of ten to twenty-one days (thus becoming ''home'' territories), a strict division of territory quickly occurred and in many cases, the individuals were not able to complete the confinement. Those who did, however, withdrew into their ''own areas'' after working hours. This behavior, a **cocooning** or withdrawing into oneself, is indicative of ''territorial behavior.''

Another study was undertaken using hospitalized children. The results indicated that changes in group density brought about changes in these categories of behaviors: aggressive/destructive, social, and boundary.[80] The researchers also found that autistic children withdrew to corners, whereas children who were normal or brain damaged reacted with increased aggressive and destructive behavior.

Territorial Claims

According to sociologist Erving Goffman, there are several types of territorial claims made by humans. In each case there is individual variation, cultural variation, sexual and ethnic variation, and variation by age. Finally, there is variation according to situation. Goffman notes, ''. . . to stand or sit next to a stranger when the setting is all but empty is more of an intrusion than the same act would be when the place is packed and all can see that only this niche remains.''[81] You can observe this if you are the only person in a movie theatre or large lecture room. A second person enters and sits right in front of you, although there are hundreds of remaining seats. This occurrence would probably upset you. On the other hand, if the only remaining seat in the room were directly in front of you, you would probably not have a second thought about the newcomer's sitting there. The situation changes with each new arrival and departure; an example familiar to us all is the elevator. Each time another person enters or leaves, the entire spatial configuration in the elevator changes.

Territories of the Self   Erving Goffman discusses eight **territories of the self.**[82] The first is **personal space,** which is essentially the same as Lyman and Scott's body territory. The extent to which someone violates this territory is dependent upon how large this personal space is from the perspective of the individual. Some individuals do not mind being touched by others, and some people do not like others within, say, eighteen inches of them.

The second type of territory is the **stall.** This is a well-bounded space, usually for use by one person at a time. The restroom stall, a single bed, a beach towel space, a telephone booth, and a parking space are examples. The desk you use at work also qualifies as a stall; usually only one person at a time works in this space.

The third type of territory mentioned by Goffman is **use space.** Such areas are claimed by individuals who are within one's line of vision, or areas that may be outside strict boundary lines but that are instrumental in performing a function. For example, areas around a tennis court, space around a golfer swinging a club, space between you and a magazine rack, and the space between you and a television set are all prime examples of use space.

Goffman's fourth category is more a temporal than a spatial dimension; it is called the **turn.** "Ladies first" and "children first" are basic examples, although our society has created more complex versions. Turn-taking requires not only an ordering rule but a claiming mechanism as well.[83] Thus, we must queue up, or we must hold a ticket number to assure ourselves of space at a certain time.

The **sheath** is the fifth type of territory. This territory includes the skin that covers the body and the clothing that covers the skin. The sixth classification is **possession territory**; this refers to objects we view as our own, our "personal effects." Jackets, hats, gloves, umbrellas, and cigarette packs are examples. The sheath and possessional territories are examined in more detail in the chapter on physical appearance. One researcher found that the most important possessions regarding a sense of self-identity were body parts, followed by objects, collections, memories, and, finally, people and pets.[84]

The final two types of territories deal with self and others. The seventh area is called the **information preserve.** It includes territories that contain facts about the self that we wish to control. Our thoughts, diaries, letters, and pockets are examples. Some preserves appear with sexual maturity, because they are associated with puberty. Females begin to control access to their purses, and males begin controlling access to their billfolds. The final area is the **conversation preserve,** which involves those who can summon us into an office or area to talk and those times when we can be called on or required to talk.[85] This type of territory may be associated with the person's status, power, or credibility.

Markers   To maintain a claim of these various territories, we need a visable sign of ownership. Goffman calls these signs **markers.**[86] There are three basic methods of identifying areas or possessions as our own. The most typical is probably the *central marker.* This is a sign used to indicate a claim radiating from the center. Thus, a drink on a bar means to others that we shall be returning to that seat to maintain ownership. Leaving a theatre program in a seat is another example. If you leave your sunglasses and suntan lotion on a space at the beach, you have left a marker. The second category of markers is the *boundary marker.* Instead of radiating from a center, they set forth boundary lines. For example, bars are often used in supermarkets to identify which groceries "belong" to whom. There are lines between seats or numbers indicating the seat on benches in a football stadium; fences are used between yards to indicate boundaries. The third category is the *ear marker.* This sign indicates a trademark, initials, or a name to show ownership. Name plates on doors and desks, and even inside automobiles; personalized license plates and monogrammed dress shirts are examples. Animals are branded with "ear markers." Robert Ardrey writes: "A territory is an area of space, whether of water or earth or air, that an animal or group of animals defends as exclusive preserve."[87] An invasion of a territory comes when one violates the boundary of a territory.

Purposes of Territory

We have looked at why territory is important in a general sense, but we should briefly discuss the purposes of territory among animals. Lawrence B. Rosenfeld and Jean Civikly suggest that territory is significant in that it does the following:

1. Defines an area for food gathering
2. Ensures an adequate food supply
3. Provides an area for mating and caring for the young; most animals tend to mate only with others within their area
4. Provides an edge in escape from enemies
5. Provides an advantage in fighting enemies
6. Helps in the regulation of population density
7. Helps regulate the spread of disease[88]

In *Human Territoriality,* Julian Edney reached several conclusions.[89] First, the human use of space is variable; we use space differently at different times. Second, the association between territory and aggression is not clear-cut; the human does not always increase aggression as density increases. However, we refer to territory and defend that territory if it takes on certain psychological identities; *Motherland, Fatherland,* and *Country* are three terms that we defend. Third, territory aids in providing food, shelter, recreation, and so on. Fourth, humans maintain several territories. Often we have territories at work, at home, and at play that differ; in some cases the three territories just mentioned may be the same, only the name changes (e.g., an office at home). In the same manner we "time-share" temporary territory and invade others' territory. (The notion of "time-share" has received attention in resort communities where you "buy" a week or two at a resort and others buy the remainder of the year. You actually "own" a week or two with all the associated privileges.) Finally, humans are the only animals that "visit" without antagonism.

Territory is important for people according to a number of dimensions. For example, the amount and location of territory one has may be an indication of status or power. Territory is important to animals and humans alike to show intimacy, to demonstrate power, or to illustrate ownership. However, some believe the importance of space has been overstressed. Several studies on crowding illustrate their point.

Crowding and Perception of Territory   Psychologist Jonathan Freedman believes that crowding has received unwarranted negative publicity through some of the studies carried out on animals. Freedman attempted to answer two questions: "(1) What effect does density have on performance on simple and complex tasks? (2) What role do temporal factors play?"[90] To answer these questions, subjects were placed in crowded and uncrowded rooms, with one to four persons in each room. Their behaviors were judged for a period of four hours; in some cases, subjects returned the next day for an additional four hours. The room sizes ranged from thirty-five to 180 square feet. In the high-density rooms (for example, four people in thirty-five square feet) each person had a chair. There was enough room for the people to be able to sit without touching, but there was no additional space. A less dense room allowed for as much as fifteen to twenty square feet per person.

Freedman found no significant differences in the ability to perform tasks as related to population density. He did find, however, that density influenced certain types of interpersonal behavior. Among high-school students, boys competed more than girls when in a crowded room. With different age groups, similar results were reported. In general, females liked the smaller room better, and males disliked the more limited territory. Freedman concluded that it is not the population density but the number of individuals with whom one must interact that produces substantial changes in human behavior. F. O'Brien found that people desired increased density in mission task situations that called for it. Thus, both the finite space (in this case, a submarine) and the nature of the task may cause people to accept undue density in most situations.[91]

Several researchers have postulated that crowding and density are related to more factors than the number of people present in the territory. Edwin Willems and David Campbell note that many variables lead to perceptions of crowding.[92] They infer that the interactive effect of such factors as number of people, spatial density, social density (perceived amount of space per person), environmental constraints, and physical variables (objects, placement of objects) affect perceptions of crowding. Even in the case of urban crowding, here too, perception plays a part. Bagley, for example, found that when murder rates in Bombay, India, and New York City increased with population growth, Bombay's murder rate increased ''only moderately'' while New York's increased ''dramatically.''[93] Perception of the environment or type of territory also seems to play a role in perceiving crowding. M. K. Fried and V. J. DeFazio, for instance, found that people expect smaller territories in public buses (where you cannot claim or own a territory unless you are physically present) than in an automobile (which is viewed by most as a form of home territory).[94] In general, the research on crowding is mixed, and the results may be dependent on how the individual researcher defined crowding.

Other research has found that crowding, or perceptions of crowding, can have an impact on family relations and even human sexual behavior. Alan Booth and John Edwards, for instance, found that the concept of ''love'' in the family was not affected by crowded conditions, but that crowding influenced the extent to which parents played with their children. Although neighborhood congestion does not affect sibling quarrels, mothers in crowded households reported more sibling quarrels than those in uncrowded households.[95] Booth and Edwards undertook a second study to investigate the effects of crowding on sexual behavior. Four types of crowding were considered in the study: objective (real) and subjective (perceived) household congestion, and objective and subjective neighborhood congestion. Booth and Edwards were concerned with how crowding related to marital relations, extramarital involvement, homosexuality, and incestuous relations. They interviewed people in all four types of crowding conditions to determine the effect of privacy on relations, the frequency of intercourse, and the extent to which intercourse was withheld.

The researchers found that privacy has an influence on marital intercourse, but it is the influence of perceived crowding, not the actual density. They found that only under stressful conditions was the frequency of intercourse affected by crowding. However, men and women reported greater sexual involvement outside of marriage when they were living in crowded conditions. With the interaction of stress and crowded conditions, more extramarital relations tended to occur. Finally, there were no significant relationships between crowding and homosexuality or incest.[96]

Although all of these studies on territory are significant, we should remember several facts. First, humans are not rats or deer; the differences between animal and human studies suggest that we can adapt to more stressful conditions, but lower animals may not. Second, laboratory studies cannot be undertaken on human beings for extended periods of time, as they can with animals. Third, as the research indicates, variables other than the simple size of the territory also affect how we behave and communicate. Territory, like the environment, affects our communication; as with the environment, we are not always aware of how territory operates or that it is operating. Knowing what types of territory we are in (e.g., Lyman and Scott's) and our claims to territory (e.g., Goffman's types) should help us better understand our communication and the communication of others.

Environment

Look around you. What you see right now is your immediate environment. Until now it has been unconsciously influencing your behavior. Most environments have been designed for some reason; they serve to tell you how you should communicate and behave. Environment also tells you something about the designer. If you stop and think about it, the environment really has quite an impact on you. As you read this section, you will note that all interactions between people take place in some environment—an area you attempt to structure, in which you attempt to create a mood or a response. If you are studying, for instance, your environmental preferences are different than they would be if you were looking for a good time. We expect a quiet, relaxing environment for study; we expect a little more noise, sensory input, and more tension when having a good time. Thus, we structure our environments for our preferences, and, in return, others structure environments according to what they consider appropriate for some expected outcome.

Mark Knapp has concluded that the environment is perceived in six ways.[97] His system examines the environment in terms of formality, warmth, privacy, familiarity, constraint, and distance. What we would look for in any environment are the degrees each "framework" possesses. For example, an office should be formal; somewhat cool (in terms of temperature); private (if meant for one person); familiar (we all know how to behave in familiar surroundings); fairly easy to leave, yet not "too easy" to leave; and put us in a position of power by distancing us from others. This may sound rather strange, but look at the environment you are in right now and see how it operates in terms of formality (informal to formal), warmth (comfortable to uncomfortable), privacy (private to open to others), familiarity (usual to unusual), constraint (temporal to permanent), and distance (how far away others are). Now, take another environment and do the same. If the two environments have been designed for the same purpose they should have similar "ratings." If not, they will differ along one or more of Knapp's "frameworks."

A second way of examining the environment is offered by Judee K. Burgoon and Thomas J. Saine.[98] They postulate that each environment is differentiated by nine dimensions: size or volume of space, arrangement of objects within the environment, materials used in the environment, amount of linear perspective, lighting and shading, color, temperature, noise, and sensory stimulation. If we juxtapose Knapp's frameworks with Burgoon and Saine's dimensions we find that the environment is structured to produce an aesthetic feeling. By taking the nine dimensions we create the frameworks identified by this juxtaposition (see Figure 5.5).

But these frameworks and dimensions occur in several ways. Edward T. Hall has suggested that the environment can be divided into three basic categories: fixed-feature, semifixed, and dynamic.[99] **Dynamic** is the type of space that is involved with people communicating; it changes as the people change. **Semifixed** features are those that enable people "to increase or decrease (their) interaction(s) with others, and to control the general character of (their) transactions, to

ENVIRONMENTAL ANALYSIS

I. Perceptual Features

```
              1    2    3    4    5    6    7
      Informal___:___:___:___:___:___:___Formal (FORMALITY)
 Uncomfortable___:___:___:___:___:___:___Comfortable (WARMTH)
         Open___:___:___:___:___:___:___Private (PRIVACY)
       Unusual___:___:___:___:___:___:___Usual (FAMILIARITY)
     Temporary___:___:___:___:___:___:___Permanent (CONSTRAINT)
  Others Close___:___:___:___:___:___:___Others Far (DISTANCE)
```

II. Environmental Features

```
      Low___:___:___:___:___:___:___High (VOLUME OF SPACE)
      Low___:___:___:___:___:___:___High (ARRANGEMENT/OBJECTS)
      Low___:___:___:___:___:___:___High (MATERIALS)
      Low___:___:___:___:___:___:___High (LIGHTING/SHADING)
      Low___:___:___:___:___:___:___High (LINEARITY)
      Low___:___:___:___:___:___:___High (COLOR)
      Low___:___:___:___:___:___:___High (TEMPERATURE)
      Low___:___:___:___:___:___:___High (NOISE)
      Low___:___:___:___:___:___:___High (SENSORY STIMULATION)
```

III. Environmental Patterns

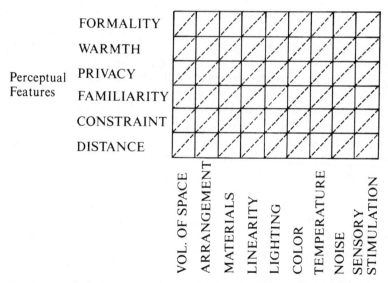

Example: Formality, as in office environment: volume = high (6–7), arrangement = high (6–7), materials = high (5–7), linearity = moderate (4–5), color = moderate (4–5), temperature = moderate (4–5), noise = low (1–2), sensory stimulation = moderate (4–5), would be an example of a middle/lower high-level manager's office.

FIGURE 5.5   Environmental Analysis.

some degree.''[100] People do this primarily by arranging furniture and other objects in the environment. **Fixed-feature** includes two phases: ''internal, culturally specific configuration, and external environmental arrangements such as architecture and space layout.''[101]

As we might imagine, depending upon the desired outcome, how we structure our environment includes all three of Hall's categories. For instance, suppose we wanted to design a room just for one purpose. How would this best be accomplished? First, ask yourself how you would like the person to respond to Knapp's six frameworks: is the environment to be formal/informal, warm/uncomfortable, and so forth. Then take Burgoon and Saine's dimensions and create that feeling.

There are several of these dimensions/frameworks that influence how we communicate or how we are expected to communicate in any particular environment. These include room color and aesthetic appreciation, room size and shape, temperature and humidity, and environmental structuring. As we examine each in greater detail, you should begin to understand how people use the environment to manipulate others or to create a first impression.

Room Color and Aesthetic Appreciation

Room color and the degree of attractiveness associated with the room are important environmental considerations. A. H. Maslow and N. L. Mintz examined the impact on human behavior of three rooms, each differing in the degree of ''beauty'' of the room.[102] The three rooms were engineered to be ''beautiful'' (with carpeting, drapes, etc.), ''average'' (a professor's office), and ''ugly'' (giving the impression of a janitor's storeroom). People were then placed in one of the three rooms and asked to rate the negative of a print photograph of faces. The photographs were rated higher in the ''beautiful'' room. Both the experimenters and the people responding reported more fatigue and a greater need to escape while in the ''ugly'' room.

James T. Kitchens and associates studied the interpersonal attraction of a confederate in a ''live'' situation.[103] To determine the influence of the aesthetics of the room upon ratings of interpersonal attraction, Kitchens asked people to rate live communicators rather than photographic negatives. The ''unattractive'' room had walls of dull green; light bulbs were unshaded, and the furniture was splattered with paint. A green couch with a broken leg and torn seat cushions was placed in the room. The ''attractive'' room was freshly painted and had been decorated by a professional interior designer. A regular classroom was used as a control to measure the impact of each room. The results of this study supported the conclusions of Maslow and Mintz; that is, the environmental aesthetics of a room influence both our behavior and our communications.

It is necessary to remember, however, that what is aesthetically pleasing to one may not be to another. Hence, we structure our environments partially to please ourselves and partially to please others. This difference may come from our geographic residence, our personality, our status, and so forth. Would you, for example, eat a meal in an environment that was formal, uncomfortable, nonprivate, somewhat familiar, nonconstraining, and cramped, allowing only a little distance (say six to twelve inches between people)? If you have ever eaten at a fast-food restaurant, you already have. Most fast-food restaurants seem to be rather large with seats arranged to maximize the number of people who can be seated at once; they also tend to use the hardest material possible to sit on. These features of the environment, when combined with a linear perspective—bright to harsh lighting, cooler than needed temperature, high noise level, and maximized sensory stimulation—all have one purpose: to serve as many people as fast as possible. To sit and have a ''chat''

TABLE 5.1   *Color in the Environment: Moods Created and Symbolic Messages*

COLOR	MOODS	SYMBOLIC MEANINGS
Red	Hot, affectionate, angry, defiant, contrary, hostile, full of vitality, calm, tender	Happiness, lust, intimacy, love, restlessness, agitation, royalty, rage, sin, blood
Blue	Cool, pleasant, leisurely, distant, infinite, secure, transcendent, calm, tender	Dignity, sadness, tenderness, truth
Yellow	Unpleasant, exciting, hostile, cheerful, joyful, jovial	Superficial glamor, sun, light, wisdom, masculinity, royalty (in China), age (in Greece), prostitution (in Italy), famine (in Egypt)
Orange	Unpleasant, exciting, disturbed, distressed, upset, defiant, contrary, hostile, stimulating	Sun, fruitfulness, harvest, thoughtfulness
Purple	Depressed, sad, dignified, stately	Wisdom, victory, pomp, wealth, humility, tragedy
Green	Cool, pleasant, leisurely, in control	Security, peace, jealousy, hate, aggressiveness, calm
Black	Sad, intense, anxiety, fear, despondent, dejected, melancholy, unhappy	Darkness, power, mastery, protection, decay, mystery, wisdom, death, atonement
Brown	Sad, not tender, despondent, dejected, melancholy, unhappy	Melancholy, protection, autumn, decay, humility, atonement
White	Joy, lightness, neutral, cold	Solemnity, purity, femininity, humility, joy, light, innocence, fidelity, cowardice

Source: J. K. Burgoon and T. J. Saine, *The Unspoken Dialogue: An Introduction to Nonverbal Communication* (Boston: Houghton Mifflin, 1978), p. 110. Reprinted with permission.

is simply not the purpose of this type of environment. (Try it, go to a fast-food place and sit with a friend for at least a half-hour *without* getting up; it's difficult.)

A second factor dealing with aesthetic appreciation is room color. As noted in the research of Maslow and Mintz and Kitchens and others, *room color* may play a determining part in how we perceive an environment. L. B. Wexner, for instance, found that certain colors were associated with certain moods. Thus, red was considered exciting and stimulating; blue was identified as secure-comfortable or as tender-soothing; and yellow was described as cheerful-jovial-youthful.[104] Burgoon and Saine (see Table 5.1) have identified various mood and symbolic meanings that we associate with different colors. Look around you to see whether such colors produce the identified mood. (If you are in a classroom, you might note that none of the colors are "exciting" or ''stimulating.'' Instead, the colors you see are pastels, shades meant to subdue rather than excite the student toward education. The halls, however, are usually more colorful and contrasting; consequently, talk and behavior is increased as compared to the classroom, where you are expected to sit and ''soak it in.'')

Room Size and Shape

A second feature of the environment is the size and shape of the room in which we interact. Robert Sommer has studied the effects of size and shape of classrooms on behavior.[105] He observed that various types of classrooms (seminar rooms, laboratories, windowless rooms, and rooms with an entire wall of windows) produce various reactions. Sommer found that students and professors alike had a distaste for windowless rooms and laboratories. He noted that in seminar rooms, fewer people participated, but they did so for longer periods of time. In seminar rooms, most of the participation came from those seated directly across from the instructor. In straight-row-seating classrooms, more participation came from students within range of eye contact with the instructor. He found that participation decreased as class size was increased; in addition, most of the participation came from those seated near the front or directly in front of the instructor.[106]

Other researchers have examined the impact of whether a room can be altered, and the resultant effects on communication. One study, based on dormitory students, found that people who could not alter their environment (beds, desks, and other major features were fixed) had fewer friends visit and did not stay in that environment as long as those who could change their environments. Generally, they found that the center of social life revolved around the more changeable room.[107] Imagine living in a room over which you have little control; many of us could not live in such a room.

Room shape does not appear to have a major influence on us. However, we should remember that nonverbal communication is also culture bound. We are used to an environment where our rooms are mostly linear; that is, we tend to prefer our environments square or rectangular. Living in a twelve-foot by twenty-four-foot block building would not bother most of us; however, people from cultures in which the rooms are circular—or the corners are rounded (as in some Spanish-style housing)—would find such a linear perspective odd. Generally, we perceive the size of a room more important than its shape. Other cultures may view this differently.

Temperature and Humidity

A third feature of the environment is the perceived temperature and humidity. We speak of ''perceived'' temperature and humidity because several factors can change how hot or cold we think a room is. For instance, the colors red and white produce different perceptions of temperature.[108] White rooms are almost always perceived as cooler (as much as five degrees cooler than red rooms). What effects do temperature and humidity have on us? How many violent union or protest strikes can you think of that occurred in November, December, January, or February? Now, compare your analysis with that of the summer months. It should not be surprising that the riots of the 1960s came during the hottest summer months on record.

What we do know about temperature and humidity makes good sense. For example, W. Griffitt found that as temperature and humidity increased, impressions of others' interpersonal attractiveness *decreased.* Another researcher noted that the outdoor temperature is more suitable for mental vigor if it ranges in the 50s or 60s rather than in the 70s. D. McClelland found that achievement motivation was higher when the mean annual temperature was between forty and sixty degrees Fahrenheit.[109] We must temper these findings, however, by noting that they were conducted in external environments cooler than some parts of the country. Anyone who has survived a south-eastern summer knows that eighty degrees can feel as cool as fifty degrees would to a northerner, considering the higher heat and humidity of the south.

Environmental Structuring

The last feature we examine is the structure of the environment. By this we mean how the environment and the objects within it are arranged and for what effect. We generally structure an environment purposefully, with an idea as to its effect. In this regard the environment may serve as a **metamessage,** or a message suggesting how to behave or communicate. The absence of an ashtray should tell a smoker not to smoke. The position of a chair should indicate how the conversation will go, how formal it may be, or the status differences between people. We probably have as much research in this area as in any area of the environment, and it all deals with either self-presentation or manipulation.

Consider, for example, an office arrangement; if the desk is in the center of the room and faces the door, we know that some type of power signal is being given. Michael Korda and Ken Cooper have discussed how to structure your environment to increase your perceived power and status.[110] Both of these investigators stress the need to understand how the environment is structured. In general, we find that the more permanent the environment, the more "plush" it is, and the larger it is, the more powerful is the occupant. Within the office we see emblems of power: diplomas, pictures, plants (again, the larger, the more power), size of desk, comfort of chairs, panelled rather than painted walls, access to windows, and so forth.

The structure of the environment also tells us how we are supposed to act. Anyone who has ever walked into a "bachelor's pad," or tried to put one together, knows that the subdued lighting, the shape of couch, texture of material, carpeting, and mood music are all tips as to what behavior is expected. But there are other environments that have been structured: a dentist's office, a professor's office, a church (especially one with great spaciousness that makes you feel insignificant), a bar. Each is structured to induce you to feel and act in a predetermined manner. The fast-food restaurant is another example of environmental structuring.

Have you examined other environments for their impact? Douglas Freeman and associates examined the environmental structuring in a supermarket.[111] They found, for example, that the most expensive items were placed at eye level. The attraction value of vegetables was important (notice that they are usually shining green, yellow, red, and so forth because they have been watered several times). One supermarket in Mobile, Alabama, found that by randomly placing Coca-Cola in the line of vision throughout the store, it sold more. Many stores place "sale" items in the front so that you see them as you walk in; did you ever notice that their price is the same, if not higher than those on the shelves? It is not an accident that they try to lead you to pass by the bakery as soon as possible (one store even gives cookie "credit" cards to children in order to attract them). In clothing stores, often the most expensive items are placed at the front of the store, and you must pass them to get to the "bargains."

All of these are examples of how you are manipulated by the environment. Consider that you, too, manipulate your environment for certain purposes. Other features that could be mentioned include music in the store or room (much has been made of this lately, with faster music getting you in and out faster, slower music inviting you to spend more time), lighting, temperature, and most of the other dimensions examined earlier. The critical intent, however, is that we communicate in and through our environments. These form the first line of communication, indicating how we should act and how we should view the inhabitants of the environment. This conditioning will determine how we create and perceive the space around us.

☐   **Summary**   ☐

The thrust of this chapter has been the study of space and how we use it to communicate. We looked at the environment and how, through its structuring and manipulation, we communicate to others information about ourselves; how we expect others to act; and how we should act. The environment, we noted, is the first line of communication, and its manipulation can alter other aspects of our communication. Space, we noted, consists of both territory and personal space. Territory consists of spaces or areas that are marked, have boundaries, and suggest ways to act and communicate. Personal space, on the other hand, has no markers, is flexible, and may be considered a zone around us. Both the territory we occupy and the personal space we expect and maintain are influenced by a number of factors, each operating in conjunction with the others to produce expectations of appropriate behavior and communication. Finally, we examined the effects of violating spatial expectations.

After reading this chapter you should have a better understanding of how we communicate in a medium: space. You should now understand better how and why we delineate and use space; you should appreciate better how people manipulate space, from environmental structuring to touch. The use of space is a powerful tool, one that deserves further research.

Chapter Six

Physical Appearance Studies

Key Concepts

Physical Attractiveness

Body Shape and Body Image

Purposes of Clothing

Body Adaptors

Effects of Accessories on Physical Appearance

Time after time we see an individual we have met before, and our immediate reaction is: "I don't remember the name, but I remember the face." Although some people often forget the name, they are less likely to forget what we look like. It is as if we remember people by their physical appearance, and we describe people, not by personality, but instead by their physical features.

Physical appearance may be said to include everything about us from "the tops of our heads to the soles of our feet." It is the first nonverbal factor to come into play during a relationship. Physical appearance is large in scope and includes such dimensions as body shape, body image, and physical attractiveness, clothing, cosmetics, hair, and accessories. We cannot prevent the formation of impressions based on these dimensions of physical appearance.

How important is your physical attractiveness? According to some people, physical attractiveness may account for the major reason two people communicate.[1] People, in this culture at least, prefer to talk to strangers they perceive as attractive. Because of this, we have a tendency to gravitate toward individuals perceived as attractive and away from others perceived as unattractive. We also tend to talk about people in terms of attraction— or lack of it. People are "beautiful" or "ugly." In some instances the degree of unattractiveness is more defined than attractiveness: people are "ugly," "uglier," and "ugliest." In sum, we tend to categorize people at one end of an attraction continuum or the other; either they are attractive or they are not, although most of us would probably be somewhere between these extremes.

In researching, evaluating, and studying the dimensions involved in physical appearance we are reminded of the numerous clichés that seem a bit trite but are nevertheless meaningful: "Beauty is in the eyes of the beholder," "Blondes have more fun," "It's the little things that count," "Clothes make the man," "Beauty is only skin deep," and "Black is beautiful."

Beautification of the body is a continuing project undertaken by individuals. Much money is spent yearly by individuals simply to alter their physical appearance. For what? As students of nonverbal communication, we believe that people are so concerned about physical appearance because they wish to communicate a better message about themselves to others. How we look, how we are shaped, and what we wear tell as much about us as anything else, and yet it is told without our uttering a word.

Physical appearance operates in several ways. Of primary concern to most of us is the visible aspect of our physical appearance: how we look naturally, including our body shape, height, weight, hair, teeth, complexion, and other natural endowments; and how we look in different types, styles, and colors of clothing. There is a haptic sense, too. That is, we wear what we feel comfortable in. Not too many of us would consider wearing burlap underwear. To some a starched shirt is necessary; to others that same shirt is considered a painful nuisance. The importance of such visual and haptic perceptions is discussed in this chapter when we consider such things as body shape, body image, clothing, and other accessories. However, we first discuss the importance of physical attractiveness.

Physical Attractiveness

Defining physical attractiveness in terms of absolutes is impossible. An old cliché, "Beauty is in the eyes of the beholder," seems to apply to a large extent. Although there are no absolutes in defining physical attractiveness, there is a high level of agreement as to what constitutes physical attractiveness. When asked to rate photographs of black women taken from *Ebony* and *Sepia* magazines, fifty black American males and fifty white American males reached a high consensus on which women were most and least attractive.[2] A similar study conducted in Great Britain questioned more than 4,000 subjects who varied in age, sex, occupation, and place of residence. Again, a high level of agreement was found as to which female faces were pretty. In both studies, however, it should be noted that what constitutes beauty is culture-related. In the case of black beauty, a separate Nigerian sample chose different women as being most attractive; those with predominately negroid features were preferred to those with caucasoid features.[3] Also, specific ideals of the beautiful woman or man undoubtedly vary over time. In addition, there is a variance in location. Wayne Henley, for example, found that well-dressed females received more money (for a telephone call) in airports, whereas poorly dressed confederates received more money at bus stations.[4] And look at old history books or turn-of-the-century European paintings of "beautiful" people. Most of us would no longer consider such people beautiful; instead, most would be classified as overweight!

Significance of Physical Attractiveness

Physical attractiveness has a major impact on how other people perceive us as similar to themselves (homophily). Attractiveness also affects evaluations of our credibility and general attractiveness (i.e., sociability, ability to work with others, stigma, etc.). The significance of physical attractiveness, then, merits considerable study.

Jerome Singer's studies considered the "use of physical attractiveness by females as a manipulative device to obtain higher grades from college professors."[5] He found a high positive correlation between firstborn, attractive females and grade point average. Upon further study, Singer
determined that firstborn females engaged in more "exhibiting" behavior such as sitting at the
front of the classroom more often, talking to the professor after class more frequently, and making
more appointments to see professors at their offices.

Singer also wanted to determine whether the better grades of these attractive females were a
result of intentional manipulation or due to luck. Consequently, he conducted a survey in which
he asked females to estimate their own body measurements and ideal measurements. A "manipulative intent" hypothesis was confirmed because findings indicated that (1) firstborn females more
accurately estimated their own body measurements, (2) firstborns were more accurate in estimating
the ideal female measurements, and (3) they were more likely to distort their own measurements
in the direction of the estimated ideal measurements than were later-born females.[6] It may be that
later-born females have their sisters to observe, to notice what is "covert" or not. The firstborn,
however, has to compare herself with idealized attraction standards. The Singer studies have not
been replicated using male subjects.

Judson Mills and Ellen Aronson conducted a study in which a woman delivered the same speech
to two audiences. For one audience, the woman dressed attractively (properly applied makeup,
neat and well-fitting dress); for the other audience, she dressed unattractively (no makeup, loose
fitting clothing, messy hair, oily complexion). The study showed that men were more persuaded
by the attractive female than the unattractive female.[7]

Social Interaction   Other research indicates that attractiveness has a significant influence on
perceptions of social interaction. A study by R. N. Widgery and B. Webster concluded that physically attractive people, regardless of sex, were rated higher on the character dimension of credibility than were unattractive persons. In a related study, Rebbeca Eiland and Don Richardson
found that differences in credibility and interpersonal attraction ratings of individuals are, in large
part, determined by race, age, and sex. Physical attractiveness does increase how likable one is;
however, it does not inherently increase one's status since it is an ascribed characteristic. Lonely
men were perceived as less attractive than men who were not lonely; however, women were
perceived no differently in physical attractiveness, whether lonely or not. People who provide
more spontaneous, uncensored nonverbal information were viewed as more physically attractive.[8]

H. T. Reis, J. Nezlek, and L. Wheeler were interested in the impact physical attractiveness had
on social interaction in general. They concentrated on the everyday activities of people of varying
degrees of attractiveness, rather than undertaking the usual experimental study of highly attractive
versus unattractive people. They had college students keep a journal of their daily activities and
related them to the students' physical attractiveness as rated independently. Their results indicated
five conclusions. First, physical attractiveness is strongly related to the quantity of social interaction for males, but not so for females. For males the interactions were rated more positively if
the other person was female; if the other person was male, the interaction was rated more negatively. Second, for both sexes (and in particular for cross-sex interactions) satisfaction increased
over time when the others were physically attractive. Third, females rated as moderately attractive
seemed to enjoy socialization more than others. Fourth, males who were rated as physically attractive reported more mutually initiated interactions with the opposite sex than self- or other-
initiated interactions. Finally, attractive males spent more of their time conversing and less in

activity, whereas attractive females spent less time in task interactions and more time on dates or at parties. In classroom interaction, researchers found that teachers associated personality characteristics with their judgments of their students' attractiveness. Turning the tables, S. T. Romano and J. E. Bordieri examined students' perceptions of the physical attractiveness of college professors. The attractive professors were seen as better teachers, as more likely to provide assistance, as less likely to be blamed for a student's failing a course, and as more likely to be recommended to other students. Female professors were rated higher than their male peers. Obviously, *physical attractiveness influences our perceptions of social interaction and how we structure that interaction.*[9]

Karen Dion and Ellen Berscheid conducted a study in which they sought to determine the relationship between attractiveness and liking among nursery-school children. The children were asked to name the classmates they liked best. The youngsters not only preferred the more attractive children but perceived the unattractive children as mean and aggressive.[10] The relationship of attractiveness to other traits has been explored. One study found significant differences in a subject's perceptions of physically attractive and unattractive individuals on fifteen of seventeen personality dimensions. People who were rated low in attractiveness were perceived in terms of negative and undesirable traits, whereas attractive individuals were judged significantly more positively with respect to these traits.[11]

The effects of attractiveness and intelligence have been studied by several researchers. M. M. Clifford and E. H. Walster, for example, asked fifth-grade teachers to evaluate a hypothetical student's academic record; the record included a photo of either an attractive or unattractive student, but the record was the same for both students. They found that the teachers perceived the attractive children as being more intelligent, as being more likely to attain advanced education, and as having parents who were more likely to be concerned with academic achievement.[12] Samuel Marwit noted that physical attractiveness also affected teachers' perceptions of transgressions made by students. He examined whether or not a student's physical attractiveness had any effect on teachers' ratings of transgressions and found that physically unattractive students were rated more severely than physically attractive students. Additionally, he found the effect to be more pronounced for black than for white students.[13] These findings, however, are not without their inconsistencies. R. Felson, in an examination of the role of physical attractiveness and deviance, found that physical attractiveness was not related to conduct grades given students, sociometric ratings of aggression by classmates, and student reports of teacher disciplinary actions.[14] Even with this finding, it appears that physically attractive people receive less harsh treatment, are more persuasive, and are perceived to be more intelligent.

Apparently, physical attractiveness not only affects people's perceptions of future success, but can also have a profound impact on immediate achievement. Jack May conducted a study involving attractive and unattractive waitresses. His results indicated that attractive waitresses received higher tips than did their unattractive counterparts.[15] The effect of physical attractiveness has also had a demonstrated effect on perceptions of journalists as to whether or not an individual was likable. Dominic Infante and associates had students read articles associated with either an attractive female's picture or an unattractive female's picture. Results indicated subjects felt the attractive writer would more likely succeed as a writer than would the unattractive writer, and they felt that the attractive writer's academic achievement was higher. Finally, they found that subjects perceived the attractive writer as having a better chance of obtaining a job with a major magazine.[16]

As introduced earlier in the book, a relationship has been established between proxemics and physical attractiveness. James Dabbs and Neil Stokes found that pedestrians walked closer to unattractive females than to attractive females.[17] As reported earlier, Judee Burgoon's proxemic violation theory is heavily dependent upon the reward "valence," or value, of the initiator of a deviation from an expected distancing norm. Interestingly, however, Judee Burgoon, D. W. Stacks, and S. A. Burch observed that high reward can have a "boomerang" effect.[18] For a southern sample, they found that enhanced physical attraction was viewed as less persuasive than "normal" attraction. Stacks hypothesized and supported this relationship in a field study.[19] He had two students dress either attractively or unattractively and ask students to sign a petition, after providing a number of arguments in favor of the petition. Preliminary tests indicated that the two female confederates were perceived as being significantly *more* attractive when in the physically attractive condition than in the normal condition. Attitude change was greater with the normal attraction condition than in the physically attractive condition.

Thus, we have discovered that physical attractiveness is an important asset. In receiving money for tips and telephone calls, attractive females were more successful. In other persuasive attempts, attractive persuaders were more successful and were rated higher on credibility scales. Academic achievement, too, appears to be higher among attractive people from elementary school through college. More recent research tends to support such findings relating physical attractiveness to many socially related outcomes; others, however, provide some evidence suggesting that physical attractiveness may be detrimental. In one study, researchers found that slides of attractive models (male and female) were more effective in persuasion attempts than were slides of "average-looking" models.[20] However, when Madeline E. Heilman and Melanie H. Stopeck investigated attractiveness as a factor in evaluating an employee, they found that attractiveness was only beneficial to those whose job type was *clerical*. In fact, they found that attractiveness was detrimental to favorable evaluations for female managerial employees.[21]

Norbert L. Kerr and associates found that the attractiveness of victims was an influential variable in moot court decisions. The defendant was more often found guilty when the victim was unattractive and had a crime-unrelated disfigurement than under any other combination of these two variables. The researchers contend that their findings are consistent with a "just world" hypothesis: faith in the world subsides if a careful, innocent victim is harmed. Consequently, jurors denigrate attractive victims to reconcile injustices.[22] On the other hand, Carol Austad and associates found that attractive, institutionalized psychiatric patients (male and female) were better able to adapt to discharge and successful recovery in their community than were those who were unattractive.[23]

It appears that attractiveness is becoming a more universal concept. Even though all the participants in Michael R. Cunningham's study were male Caucasians, they assigned similar attractiveness attributes to photographs of Caucasian, Oriental, and black female confederates.[24] The participants preferred large eyes, small noses and chins, and wide cheekbones. Although these results may be indicative of the participants in the study, it would have to be replicated with Oriental and black participants before any real sense of universality of attractiveness can be inferred.

Attractiveness, then, has an impact on communication. What exactly constitutes attractiveness, however, is another question. For many, the concept has been associated with sexual attraction. Sexual attraction, however, is associated with many variables other than physical attraction.

Sex Appeal   Just as there are no absolutes in defining physical attractiveness, there are no ab-solutes in identifying sex appeal. However, sex appeal is a result of an individual's experiences, attitudes, and preferences. It is affected by such factors as: (1) whether the person is known or is a stranger, (2) whether the perceived chances of ''success'' in a sexual encounter are high or low, and (3) early love experiences.[25]

In a 1978 survey, respondents were asked what they noticed first about the opposite sex. Results indicated that females noticed overall physique first. A close second was grooming and neatness of appearance, followed by eyes. Males noticed breasts first, followed by a general body shape and eyes.[26]

Studies indicate that women are not especially excited by large biceps or a bulging crotch. Women report being more interested in men with small buttocks and men who are slim and tall. ''The favorite male physique had thin legs, a medium-thin waist, and a medium-wide chest.''[27] This closely parallels the finding that females preferred a thin male.[28]

One way to determine what a man finds appealing in a woman is to study various beauty contest winners. Another method is to determine each man's personality from standard personality tests. The characteristics desired by men are correlated with their personalities. ''Men who like large-breasted women were . . . active in sports and dated frequently. The men who opted for small breasts drank little, held fundamentalist religious beliefs, were submissive, and mildly depressed. The results suggested that large women attract men with a strong need for achievement who drink a lot, while petite women are pursued by persevering introverts.''[29] Sex appeal is directly related to dating and marriage. Attractive college women tend to date more frequently, to have more male friends, to fall in love more often, and to have more sexual experiences than women of medium attractiveness. Elaine Walster and her colleagues conducted a study relating attractiveness and dating behavior. Many variables were considered (height, race, self-esteem, academic rank, reli-gious preferences, etc.), but physical attractiveness was by far the most important determinant of how much a date was liked by his or her partner and whether they would have a subsequent date. It was further concluded that physical attractiveness is just as important an asset for a man as for a woman.[30]

The how and what of perceived physical attractiveness seems to differ for males and females. A number of studies have supported a *similarity hypothesis;* that is, we tend to like those who do not distort our own view of ourselves (self-image) or who do not depreciate our own level of attractiveness. Roger Bailey and Tobian Schreiber, for instance, found that college-age people like and desire to date more partners who support or enhance their own self-view of physical attrac-tiveness. They also found that college students liked the opposite-sex person who matched their own level of physical attractiveness.[31] R. H. Stretch and C. R. Figby found that people like phys-ically attractive people better than the unattractive, and that males were more concerned with physical attractiveness than were females.[32] Both of these studies were concerned with more im-mediate aspects of physical attractiveness.

On a more long-term basis, two studies have established that physical attractiveness is also correlated with marital adjustment and success. James Peterson and Constance Miller studied middle-aged couples and found that couples could be matched for physical attractiveness.[33] Fur-ther, they found that attractiveness correlated with marriage adjustment; however, the correlation was stronger for husbands than for wives. Randy Jones and Gerald Adams found that males per-ceived attractiveness as being more strongly associated with success for females than for males.[34] They also found that for men and women, high self-assessed physical attractiveness was associated with the perceived importance of attractiveness to marriage selection and success for both sexes.

Finally, Elizabeth Tanke examined the male stereotype for female physical attractiveness. She asked 204 male undergraduates to give their impressions of females of varying physical attractiveness. The result of her analyses was a four-dimensional model of attractiveness. Of the four factors that she found, however, only ''sexual/social excitement'' was associated with physical attractiveness.[35]

From the above studies, it is fairly obvious that many factors influence sex appeal. Jonathan Finkelstein and Leslie Walker initiated a study in which they concluded that larger pupil size of the eyes was perceived as more attractive than smaller pupil size.[36] We must be careful, however, when we examine the pupil dilation research. Pupil dilation is regulated by the automatic nervous system, and we have very little control over it. Anything that we perceive as attractive will cause pupil dilation; this would include drawing an inside straight, seeing someone we view as attractive, or seeing a piece of steak if hungry.[37] The fact that we view dilated pupils as a sign of attractiveness goes back to the Middle Ages when women used the drug belladonna to enlarge their pupils. Advertisers seem to take advantage of this also. By touching up the amount of pupil dilation in female models' eyes, they can create two ''different'' moods: the one with pupils dilated will probably be seen as more attractive and could sell emotional or nonlogical materials, whereas the constricted pupils would be more businesslike.[38]

In a study by Chris Kleine and Richard Staneski, females with medium bust sizes were rated significantly higher in liking and personal attraction.[39] Finally, in a study by Sam Feiman and George Gill, results showed that white males indicated a preference for lighter female coloration, whereas white females preferred darker skin coloration in men.[40] In the study mentioned earlier, black and white North American males preferred lighter colored black females over darker colored females.[41]

Whether one is sexually appealing or physically attractive, then, is dependent on a number of factors. In the next sections, we focus on those factors as they relate to the body itself: body shape, body weight, and height. In addition, we discuss the importance of how we feel about our own bodies as well as the assessment of others' bodies.

The Body

Body Shape

We notice the bodies of others. Males notice females; females notice males; and whether we freely admit it or not, we observe the bodies of members of our same sex. Bodies are to be looked at. After all, body type is a most prominent natural feature. Unlike a person's hair, face, eyes, or legs, the overall body shape can be observed and judged from a distance. It is vitally important in the formation of impressions. We must ask whether the stereotypes concerning body shape are true. Is the fatter person a warmer person? Is the well-built person a more adventurous person? Is the thinner person more nervous?

Bodies can be classified according to their degree of muscularity, height, and weight. The three main body types are the endomorph, the mesomorph, and the ectomorph.[42] Diagrams of the three body types and brief descriptions of each are listed in Figure 6.1.[43]

The **endomorphic** type is considered to be soft, plump, short, and round. The **mesomorphic** type is properly proportioned and athletic, trim, muscular, and average in height. The **ectomorphic** individual has the tall, thin, frail body type. Because people can control their body weight and

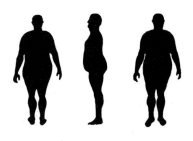

Personality Traits Associated:
Dependent, Calm, Relaxed, Complacent,
Contented, Sluggish, Placid,
Leisurely, Cooperative, Affable,
Tolerant, Affected, Warm, Forgiving

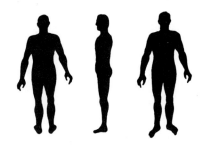

Personality Traits Associated:
Dominant, Cheerful, Confident,
Energetic, Impetuous, Efficient,
Enthusiastic, Competitive, Determined,
Outgoing, Argumentative, Talkative,
Active, Domineering

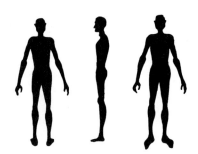

Personality Traits Associated:
Detached, Tense, Anxious, Reticent,
Self-Conscious, Meticulous, Reflective,
Precise, Thoughtful, Considerate,
Shy, Awkward, Cool, Suspicious

FIGURE 6.1   Personality Traits Associated with Endomorphic, Mesomorphic, and Ectomorphic Body Types.

physical fitness, it is a popular assumption that body type is viewed as a message about their personalities and their interests in the way they present themselves.[44]

It is thought that each body type encourages stereotyping by people in interpersonal situations. The endomorph is rated: fatter, older, shorter, more old-fashioned, lazier, physically weaker, less good-looking, more good-natured, more agreeable, more dependent on others, and more trusting in others. The ectomorph is rated: thinner, younger, more ambitious, taller, more suspicious of others, more tense and nervous, less masculine, more stubborn, more pessimistic, and quieter. The mesomorph is rated: stronger, more masculine, better-looking, more adventurous, younger, taller, more mature, and more self-reliant.[45]

Weight and Personality   Endomorphs and ectomorphs elicit negative reactions and teasing, whereas mesomorphs receive more positive reinforcement and are seen as more attractive. Along with the negative reactions that underweight or overweight children receive about their bodies, they also learn what behaviors are expected of them. Fat children are supposed to be fragile and awkward. However, *Family Weekly* recently reported that extremely overweight children rated eight to ten points higher on IQ tests than did thin children.

In a study of prejudices toward weight conducted by L. K. Karris, six male college students were divided into two groups. One male was obese, all the others were normal. Both groups visited eleven apartments available for rent. Five of the eleven landlords would not rent to the group with the obese male, three increased the rent, and two said the apartment was already rented to another college student. Women, however, feel weight is more important than do men. They also have more knowledge about obesity than do men. Female clothing sales personnel have less concern about eating behaviors than do college coeds. College students' radical changes in eating habits often results in the opposite problem from being overweight—anorexia nervosa.[46]

Height and Personality   Although weight is a factor influencing how others perceive us, height is also a determinant. In a study by D. Elman, college students were asked to assign trait ratings for a male college student, based on information in an application. When the informant indicated the applicant was tall, he was rated as more extroverted and attractive than when it was indicated that he was a shorter man.[47]

Eugene Lechelt sought to prove a correlation of physical height and personal esteem within occupations such as accounting, clergy, clerk, and so forth. The results showed that males and females tended to rate the physical height of members of occupational groups similarly. Males' ratings of physical height and personal esteem were highly positively correlated.[48]

There is a relationship between height and power, as Nancy Henley showed in her study of nursing students. The students were asked to estimate heights of known faculty and student members in their class. The heights of two staff members were overestimated, whereas the heights of two students were underestimated. Similarly, when other undergraduates were asked to estimate the height of a man introduced to them as any one of five academic ranks, the estimated height increased as the ascribed status increased. The conclusion was that people infer that persons in higher status are taller than they actually are.[49] As Mark Knapp has pointed out, except for Jimmy Carter in 1976, the taller of the two national presidential candidates has been the consistent winner since 1900. A survey at the University of Pittsburgh showed shorter men are discriminated against with respect to job opportunities and salaries. In American society, at least, there seems to be a preference for the taller man.[50]

Although we may examine the processes of stereotyping on the basis of possessing one of these three body types, in reality we all have a little of each. In extreme cases there may be medical or psychological reasons for the body type; glandular problems, hypertension, or anorexia nervosa may have caused the particular body type. In many instances, however, we possess a combination of body types that creates ''us'' at any given time.

W. H. Sheldon postulates that we can ''measure'' perceptions of our own body types.[51] He proposes that we use a 1 to 7 scale for each of the three body types. At the low end (1 or 2), you possess none or very little of these characteristics defining the body type. At the high end (6 or

7), you possess many of those characteristics. For instance, a mesomorph would be rated something like this: endomorphism—2; ectomorphism—2; mesomorphism—6 or 7 (depending upon whether or not the individual is tall or compact). For long-distance runners, the ratings might go endo—1; ecto—6; meso—4. For an NFL lineman: endo—6; ecto—2; meso—5 or 6. Note that the endomorphic and ectomorphic traits tend to be bipolar. All of these examples have dealt with men; how do women fit? The answer is, not very well. Most females would prefer a mesomorphic/ectomorphic body; this was brought out convincingly in the 1976 Olympics when a commentator asked the American female swimmers whether they would like to be more like the East Germans (who looked more masculine than some males—extremely mesomorphic)—their almost unanimous responses were "NO!" They would rather look like a female.

Finally, two studies indicate that perception of body type may correlate both positively and negatively. David Lester found a positive correlation between suicide rate and endomorphism in ten industrialized nations (as endomorphy increased so too did suicide). However, this held true only for males.[52] A second study found that mesomorphs were more often perceived as masculine.[53] Interestingly, of the females, fifty-six percent found the ectomorph to be feminine, and only twenty-five percent of the females found the mesomorph to be masculine.

Body Image

In day-to-day interactions, we do not typically describe ourselves as endomorphic, mesomorphic, or ectomorphic, or as any combination of the three. Rather, people tend to perceive their bodies in positive and negative terms, and they form attitudes toward their bodies that range from satisfied to dissatisfied. This is their **body image.** Body image is a concept that deals with the body as a "psychological experience."[54] Quite simply, it is the way a person views his or her body, including "attitudes and feelings." Accordingly, the body image helps to explain "personality characteristics" of those physically handicapped (e.g., after the loss of an arm, a person becomes "motivated toward high achievement or develops negative feelings toward himself").[55] A person's body image is both affected by and helps to influence others' perceptions of personality, attractiveness, sexual activity, and other features of that individual.

Negative Body Image   The concept of body image developed from research in neurology. In their book, *Body Image and Personality,* Symon Fisher and Sidney Cleveland described some fascinating distortions of the body.[56] They reported instances in which a patient thought "his paralyzed leg belonged to the man in the next bed," felt that the left side of his body was "lined with iron making it too heavy to move," and believed his head to be "filled with bricks." Eherenwald found that some of his patients thought their left arms (which were paralyzed) were "strange, ugly, disfigured, artificial, enlarged, shapeless, thickened, shortened, or snake-like." One patient even believed that the left side of his trunk and limbs had been replaced with a board.[57] Note that the negative body images became less and less paralyzed and more object oriented; almost as if the patient were saying, "It's not a part of me; it's something added, like a hook."

"Normal" Body Image   Not all of the studies on body image have been as extreme as those cited above. In 1972, E. Berscheid, E. Walster, and G. Bohrnstedt conducted a study on body image. Using a questionnaire, they surveyed some 62,000 readers of *Psychology Today.* The purpose of the study was to determine the relationship among body image and (1) attitudes, (2) self-esteem, and (3) experiences with the opposite sex.[58]

They used twenty-five body parts to measure "satisfaction" with the body. Attitudes of overall body appearance and facial appearance were measured, as well as attitudes on hair, eyes, mouth, voice, complexion, extremities, torso, sex organs, height and weight. Results indicated that only seven percent of the females and four percent of the males responding to the questionnaire felt "extremely dissatisfied" with their body appearance. Twenty-three percent of the females and fifteen percent of the males reported "slight dissatisfaction," whereas forty-five percent of the females and fifty-five percent of the males were "extremely satisfied" with their body appearance. The results indicated that fewer females than males were satisfied with their body appearance. Women also felt that "physical attractiveness" was more important for social interaction than did males, thirty-two percent and twenty-four percent respectively.

Considering the extent to which the American society emphasizes the importance of looking young and acting young, it could be assumed that older respondents would be more dissatisfied with their bodies than younger respondents. However, the results of the study by Berscheid, Walster, and Bohrnstedt indicate that, in general, there were no "satisfaction" differences among respondents of varying ages.

In the facial area, the most dissatisfaction for both sexes was with the teeth, followed by complexion and hair. The most frequently indicated area of dissatisfaction for both males and females was in the torso area. Males were more dissatisfied with the size of the abdomen (forty-seven percent) and buttocks (twenty-six percent); females were most dissatisfied with the size of hips (seventy-one percent), abdomen (sixty-nine percent), and buttocks (sixty percent).

Due to the emphasis placed on sex in our culture, it would be logical to assume that both sexes would be concerned with the size or appearance of their sex organs. However, according to the results, only one woman in four reported some dissatisfaction with breasts. Of that quarter, only nine percent were very dissatisfied. Fifteen percent of the males reported being worried about penis size, and six percent of those were very dissatisfied. An exception among male respondents was homosexuals. Male homosexuals reported a greater concern with size of their sex organs than did heterosexual males. No such distinction was found between female homosexuals and heterosexuals.

In another study concerning attractiveness of body parts, R. Lerner and B. Brackney asked males and females to judge the attractiveness of their own body parts.[59] Their findings showed that men gave their highest mean scores to eyes, teeth, general appearance, and face. The lowest scores among males were for ankles and hair. Females gave their highest scores for eyes, general appearance, and teeth, whereas their lowest scores were for hair color, ankles, and height. It was further determined that females consistently rated their body parts higher than males, demonstrating a higher overall satisfaction with body parts. This finding seems to contradict, to some extent, the conclusions of Berscheid, Walster, and Bohrnstedt.

A study by C. Kleine and R. Staneski related female bust size and first impressions.[60] Males and females rated color photographs of females exhibiting small, medium, or large bust sizes. Major findings were that females with large bust sizes were consistently evaluated as being relatively unintelligent, incompetent, immoral, and immodest.

The major emphasis in these studies indicates that there is something we can use as a norm to judge satisfaction or dissatisfaction with our bodies. Several studies have found that body image perceptions may be affected by other factors. W. Lucker, W. Beane, and R. L. Helmreich, for instance, note that sexiness, femininity, masculinity, and liking all have a strong correlation with physical attractiveness, especially for females.[61] These factors are all closely related to body image. John Higdon, examining paranoid schizophrenic, nonparanoid schizophrenic, and nonschizophrenic females found that ''in females the paranoid phenomena may result from some factor such as a feeling of deficiency'' in female attractiveness.[62] This female attractiveness may be attributable to perceived physical attraction, or it may also be a result of dissatisfaction with body image.

Body Image and Sexual Behavior   Although the size of sex organs may not be extremely important to body image, body image is important to sexual behavior. Berscheid, Walster, and Bohrnstedt report that positive body image results in (1) more sexual partners, (2) more sexual activity, and (3) greater enjoyment in sexual relationships.[63] Negative body image results in difficulty in relating to the opposite sex. According to Berscheid and associates, bachelors have more complaints about their body appearance than do married males. Apparently, unmarried males are more concerned with sexual performance; the lower their body image score, the more they feel that some body feature made them poor sexual partners and the more dissatisfied they were about penis size and shape. No such ''satisfaction'' distinction was found among married and unmarried females. It was further determined from the study that satisfaction with body appearance among males and females increased slightly for those reporting having had sexual relationships with ten or more partners.

The study by Berscheid and associates was replicated by T. F. Cash, B. A. Winstead, and L. H. Janda in 1985–1986. They found that women were still less satisfied with their bodies' overall appearance than were men. Their findings supported the idea that women are more critical of their bodies than men. The 1985 respondents were more dissatisfied with their bodies than were the 1972 respondents.[64] In a related study, T. F. Cash, S. W. Noles, and B. A. Winstead found that individuals with a poor body image reported greater depression than individuals with moderate or high levels of body image. They also found that others do not perceive depressed people as less attractive than nondepressed people. They did find, however, that depressed people distorted their body images in a negative direction, whereas nondepressed people distorted their body images in a positive direction.[65] Additional studies by Paul Rozin and April Fallon support the contention that women overestimate their body weight and believe men have a greater desire for thin women than they actually do, but Cash and Georgia K. Green found that overweight subjects did not differ significantly from others in estimating their body size. Underweight subjects, however, significantly *overestimated* their own body size.[66] This latter finding is consistent with research conducted by J. Kevin Thompson, in which he found that ninety-five percent of women overestimate their body size. Cheeks, waist, thighs, and hips were most often found overestimated.[67] This body image problem is especially important to persons with eating disorders such as *anorexia nervosa* and *bulimia.*[68] Not eating is just one way some people attempt to change the body to meet with the body image.

Effects of Plastic Surgery   People who are dissatisfied with their appearance have an option for change through a surgical procedure known as plastic surgery. There are two basic kinds of plastic surgery: (1) cosmetic or aesthetic surgery, which refers to improvements of the artistic and natural beauty of the face or body, such as face lifts and breast augmentation; and (2) reconstructive surgery, which refers to congenital or acquired defects such as harelip or scars.[69]

People who are dissatisfied with their appearance and consult plastic surgeons are remarkably consistent in their agreement as to what constitutes beauty. Many such dissatisfied people may seek advice from several surgeons and attempt drastic changes to ''improve'' their appearance. Often these individuals have a low self-esteem, grandiose ambitions too difficult to achieve, and vagueness concerning exactly what it is they are hoping to achieve. Frequently these patients are referred to psychiatrists.[70]

The motivation of the average patient seeking plastic surgery may be based on either internal or external pressures. External pressures include: (1) need to please others, (2) paranoid ideation (belief that he/she would please others), and (3) personal or social ambitions that seem obstructed because of personal appearance. The patient who is motivated primarily by external stimuli is apt to be disappointed after surgery, because the real cause of the patient's problem is not a defect in personal appearance. The patient who is motivated by internal pressures is more likely to feel satisfied with the subsequent change in appearance. The most common inner motivations are depression and a sense of inadequacy.[71]

Dale Leathers inferred that plastic surgery results in changes in communication behavior.[72] He reported a series of discussions and interviews with plastic surgeons, which reveal such changes in terms of self-image, body image, and communicative behavior. The following excerpt reflects the drastic changes that may occur after plastic surgery:

> Typically the change in communicative behavior after plastic surgery seems to manifest itself in a drastic reduction in inhibitions and in an openness, candor, and trusting type of behavior which is the ideal sought by so many authorities in interpersonal communication. For example, before plastic surgery some women with small breasts (those who later resort to plastic surgery) seem to ''have a behavioral disorder . . . they will never dress or undress in front of women . . . are very bashful in front of men. . . . After surgery for breast augmentation, however, a stunning change in behavior takes place.''

The same may be true of less dramatic changes such as having teeth capped, using ''elevators'' in shoes, or simply changing hair color. When these changes are made, modification of body parts leads to a new ''personality,'' or at least individuals begin to act the way they think that type of person would act. For instance, Leathers goes on to note that the women with the breast augmentation surgery, ''undress at the drop of a hat in front of everybody.''[73]

The overall conclusions concerning plastic surgery motivations are that a change in physical appearance alters the very foundation of personality function: the physical or body image. Plastic surgery results in a change in the reflexive image, the self-image, and in the communication behavior of the patient.[74] Plastic surgery is one means of voluntarily making changes in one's physical appearance that also tends to affect one's body image. Some other physical (and social) disabilities are more difficult to overcome. We often refer to these as stigmas.

Stigma

The concept of stigma was introduced in chapter 5. As stated earlier, one ''possessing an attribute that makes him different from others in the category of persons available for him to be, and of a less desirable kind—in the extreme, a person who is quite thoroughly bad, or dangerous, or weak'' is one who possesses a stigma.[75] People who exhibit stigmas include psychiatric patients, ex-convicts, divorced women, prostitutes, wheelchair victims, AIDS victims, and blind people.

Stigmatization can have rather dramatic negative affects on an individual and may interfere with the stigmatized person's attempts to achieve steady and essential interpersonal relationships with others. The stigma may be a source of embarrassment for the individual and may encourage the person to avoid interactions that might reveal the stigma. A second effect of stigmatization is that the individual may develop a sense of guilt regarding the affliction. Guilt may arise particularly if the source of the stigma is believed to be within the control of the individual. If a stigma lasts for a long time, the individual will be forced to alter his or her self-concept.

The central problem for the stigmatized person is how to attain "acceptance" from others. One method of seeking acceptance is to associate with "sympathetic others." These others are individuals who either share the stigma or accept it. A second method of coping involves the use of *disidentifiers,* methods of deemphasizing one's handicaps. Another technique for gaining acceptance from others is "passing." The individual who attempts to pass tries to pretend that he or she is not stigmatized. If the stigma is not severe, the individual may be able to pass as one who is not afflicted by a stigma, and therefore, may be perceived as "normal."[76]

Nonstigmatized individuals are cautious when interacting with those perceived of as having stigmas. M. E. Worthington's study, which was discussed in chapter 5, is an example of this phenomenon. Worthington found that individuals had a willingness to help stigmatized persons, but they did not wish to "catch" whatever the stigmatized experimenter had.[77]

In a related study, B. A. Barrios and colleagues found that individuals preferred to maintain an increased distance between themselves and a person with a social stigma (bisexuality). Stigmas, therefore, have a dramatic effect on the proxemic behavior of individuals as well as the stigmatized individual's overall acceptance by others. Michael Young, Melinda M. Henderson, and David Marx found that nursing students had more negative attitudes toward homosexual AIDS patients than toward heterosexual AIDS patients.[78]

We can expand upon Erving Goffman's notion of stigma by noting that people in this culture who are not physically attractive are generally stigmatized. Although this area has been only tangentially researched in terms of attractiveness, there is a body of research that suggests that stigmas associated with physical attractiveness may go much further than we think. Many people can remember the buxom female who developed before others in high school, or even in junior high. She was stigmatized for bust size in a rather negative way. Stigmatization can be looked at in other ways: rape, for instance. In Wisconsin a number of years ago, a judge was *recalled* by the electorate because he noted that a female was "looking for it" by the way she dressed. Obviously, the stigma in this instance was that of a prostitute.

A second area of stigmatization is described in research that examines compliance with a request. Much like Worthington's earlier research, this study indicated that people are more likely to help or comply with the request of an attractive person.[79] Several studies have examined the attribution process in trial situations. In almost every case, physical attraction was found to correlate with outcome. In a study presenting a hypothetical rape case in which the defendant was either physically attractive or unattractive, Shelia Deitz and Lynne Byrnes found a direct relationship between the amount of attractiveness and the defendant's ability to "manipulate" the jury.[80] As attractiveness increased, so too did the defendant's influence. S. Kanekar and M. B. Kilsawalla examined the relationship between retaliation and victim attractiveness and found that attractive victims were rated more positively than were unattractive victims.[81] Finally, J. E. Hocking, B. A. Walker, and E. L. Fink reported that attractive females were perceived by a jury to be *less* moral than unattractive females under the same immoral conditions.[82] As with Stacks' earlier findings, physical attractiveness does have its drawbacks.[83]

In general, the relationship between physical attractiveness and a variety of outcomes resembles an inverted **U.** As physical attractiveness increases, outcomes are generally more positive. However, at some point the person becomes "too attractive" and we no longer provide the same positive rewards. This person, then, may be stigmatized by being *too* beautiful. Perhaps moderation is best, with just a little enhancement of one's physical attributes and endowments.

Stigmas are often difficult to overcome through physical changes. Most people with stigmas compensate through their interactions with others. But we find that almost everyone wishes to make some changes in physical appearance from time to time. These changes are typically less drastic than undergoing plastic surgery but more involved than a change of clothing. Such changes can be made through **body alterations:** hairstyle, skin changes, and additions.

Body Alterations

Body alterations lead others to form perceptions about us as individuals. We convey messages, and offers hints and clues to our personalities through the decisions we make concerning the use of personal body alterations. As with other factors affecting our appearance, it is risky for a person to make use of body alterations without first understanding the implications. In a positive sense, body alterations can be indicators that a person's beauty is more than just skin deep.

There are numerous types and varieties of body alterations, including the style and cut of an individual's hair, the color and tone of the skin, and changes in the individual's perceived shape, weight, and height. Such changes can enhance one's popularity and increase attractiveness; that is, few people are attracted to those people who do not make proper use of the alteration and who fit the molds of "the plain Jane" or "the scum bum."

However, it is a point of interest that such religous groups as the Pentecostal Holiness oppose the use of such alterations, especially among female members of the sect. In this case, female members are not allowed to cut their hair or use lipstick, makeup, or other types of cosmetic treatments. Other extremes in their use and nonuse may be found among rock-and-roll performers. For instance, the rock group KISS found increased popularity with the idiosyncrasy of using painted faces on its male members. Another performer, Patty Smith, brought off a shock effect by not using body alterations, such as not shaving the hair under her arms.

Those changes made by an individual that affect his or her facial appearance seem of vital importance. For if clothes can be used to highlight the body, the body alterations must be used to emphasize and feature the face.

Hair and Hairstyles

Changes involving cranial, facial, and body hair have received the most attention among researchers in recent years. In 1976, Kelvin Peterson and James Curran found that short-haired men were rated as more intelligent, moral, masculine, mature, wise, and attractive than long-haired men.[84] However, beards appear to produce better effects than the clean-shaven look. Some studies have shown that college students attribute higher power and status to the male who wears a beard. But this may not hold true in business.

Historically, we seem to go through cycles in preference of hair. About 100 years ago, men had longer hair, beards, mustaches, and sideburns. In the 1920s there was a preference for a more clean-shaven look and shorter hair; in the 1940s and 1950s, one found the "butch" and "flattop"

FIGURE 6.2   Male Hair Styles.

haircuts popular, but facial hair was almost nonexistent. About this time, the ''Bohemian'' look began to invade our culture; the hair became shaggier, and goatees sprouted. In the middle 1960s, the ''Beatles,'' or ''moppet,'' look came in. During the unrest of the late 1960s and early 1970s, male hair became longer, beards flourished, and we returned to yesteryear. It is a little too early to say whether or not this cycle will repeat itself; however, the punk rock styles of hair might suggest a short period of a different cycle, with shorter hair once again the ''norm'' in recent years.

An issue of the University of Florida Placement Manual reported the results of a survey among 114 college recruiting officers and managers, determining which male hairstyles and beard styles have the most positive effect on hiring decisions. The short-haired, clean-shaven male received the most favorable ratings. Thus, it seems reasonable to conclude that hair and beard styles also influence the attribution of occupational status to the wearers.[85]

Figure 6.2 illustrates several hairstyles, hair lengths, and in the case of males, beard styles. Number 1 among the males is similar to the style that was rated the highest by recruiting officers, numbers 4 and 7 were rated the lowest.[86]

FIGURE 6.3   Female Hair Styles.

According to John T. Molloy, hairstyles for the businesswoman should be shoulder length, but no longer. It can be wavy, but not curly, and it can be short, but not masculine. He suggests that a businesswoman's hair must lay neatly in place without constant attention.[87] Thus, in Figure 6.3, numbers 1, 3, and 4 would be the more acceptable and successful style for females in business situations.

Daniel Freedman's 1969 studies concerning beardedness offer some interesting highlights into the issue, although the studies should not be considered conclusive. It should also be noted that the studies were conducted in the late '60s, a time when long hair and beards were seen as signs of rebellion. Freedman asked a group of undergraduate students how they felt about beardedness. None of the male subjects wore a beard. The majority of both men and women, fifty-six percent, used adjectives of youthfulness to describe the unbearded male. Of the men, twenty-two percent described the personalities of the bearded men as independent, and twenty percent described them as extroverted. Women who were envisioning an idealized husband in describing bearded men showed that *masculine, sophisticated,* and *mature* accounted for fifty-five percent of the adjectives they used. Freedman adds that people will stand closer to beardless men, whereas bearded men report they are less tense with unbearded male strangers than with other bearded men. Joseph Howard, identified as a graduate student at the University of Chicago, investigated women's thoughts on describing a man with a beard, and concluded that a beard heightens sexual magnetism. William E. Addison conducted a study at Eastern Illinois University in 1989. His 114 subjects (fifty-five men; fifty-nine women) rated bearded men higher on masculinity, aggressiveness, dominance, and strength.[88]

In a 1973 study concerning facial hair, Robert Pelligrini found a consistent pattern of description. The more hair on the face, the higher the ratings given to models on masculinity, maturity, self-confidence, dominance, courage, liberality, nonconformity, industriousness, and good looks.[89]

In summarizing the subject of cranial and facial hair, it appears that the length of a man's hair is a significant characteristic and a personal statement on how he views himself. To most people, long hair connotes an artistic, aesthetic, romantic, and casual mode of life. Discipline, seriousness, and business ethics are not suggested by long hair. Very short hair represents the energetic, precise, athletic, and youthful type, whereas the moderate length suggests pragmatic, executive, business-like, serious, and decisive qualities of an individual.

Beards, except for those persons in the areas of art, music, and education, are not recommended. Mustaches are not highly recommended, but when worn, should be kept trimmed and clean, and should not curve around the mouth or come below the upper lip.[90]

For facial and cranial hair, the amount, texture, length, style, and color can be varied to produce messages. Among females it has been noted by fashion experts and cosmetologists that the brunette is more of an authoritative figure, whereas the blonde is thought to be more of a popularity figure.

Another feature to be considered is that of body hair; in this case amount and location are the principal considerations. According to a recent survey, females currently prefer hairy-chested men to bare-chested ones.[91] However, the fact that body hair, in and of itself, elicits feelings of either appreciation or repugnance is the critical point. Body hair also seems to be important in judgments of attractiveness, illustrated by the often-heard comment, "I like him, but he's so hairy."[92]

A brief mention might be made of eyebrows as a part of facial hair. According to fashion trend magazines and other articles, eyebrows are best when little, if any, attention is called to them, for heavy, thick eyebrows tend to overshadow the rest of the face. They may be distracting. On the other hand, pale eyebrows tend to give an individual, especially a woman, a washed-out, weak look.

The Skin: Cosmetics and Colorings

Cosmetics are another body alteration. Makeup and other facial colorings such as lipstick cause people to form differing perceptions of others' personalities. However, research on this phase of body alterations is more limited. The applications of makeup, lipstick, and other skin colorings seem to be an extremely "trendy" issue. Thus, changes in cultural norms have occurred more frequently than the research on the effects of makeup and other colorings.

Interested in the effects of lipstick, W. J. McKeachie in 1952 had six male students interview six female students (three who wore lipstick and three who did not) and rate them according to personality perceptions. Women who wore lipstick were perceived as more frivolous and more overtly interested in males.[93] This study, however, would seem to possess little validity today. First, wearing lipstick is more generally accepted now than it was in the early '50s, and, second, there are more shades of lipsticks on the market today.

Knapp concluded that lipstick and other artifacts interact with clothing, facial, verbal, and body features, but under some yet unspecified conditions, they may be the primary source of information communicated about a particular person.[94]

A more recent study by Paul N. Hamid focused on the interaction between makeup cues and the presence or absence of glasses. Females wearing makeup were rated as wearing shorter skirts than those without makeup; the same held true for those without glasses as opposed to those with them. The woman with both glasses and makeup was perceived by males as artistic, intelligent, self-confident, and sophisticated, but low in shyness, seriousness, and sentimentality. Females also saw such a person as intelligent, but conceited and cold. The woman with glasses and no makeup was generally perceived as conservative and low in individuality. The woman with neither makeup nor glasses was perceived in a way similar to the woman with glasses and no makeup. The woman with makeup and without glasses was rated favorably on outward appearance, but unfavorably on personal traits.[95]

Today, one cosmetic change that may yield subtle results is eye color. In a study undertaken by M. Hickson, L. Powell, and M. L. Sandoz, eye color was found to be a significant factor in determining physical appearance.[96] They had participants view slides of a confederate. Half the participants viewed the confederate with brown eyes, the other half viewed the same confederate with blue eyes. In terms of physical attractiveness, participants preferred the blue-eyed confederate for social interaction, but preferred the brown-eyed confederate for working with on tasks. Eye color change is relatively easy using tinted contact lenses. One of the problems with this study, however, was that the confederate used blue eye shadow in both conditions.

Molloy undertook a study in which women aged eighteen to forty were judged wearing a minimum of makeup that they had applied and then wearing heavy makeup that had been applied by expensive professionals. The results showed that of 100 men under age twenty-five, ninety-two picked the minimum makeup picture as the most appealing. So did sixty-seven percent of the men aged twenty-five to thirty-five, and sixty-two percent of the men from ages thirty-five to forty-five.

Molloy suggests: If you are under thirty-five, wear lipstick and little else. But one should not wear lipstick that stands out. Also, eye shadow and eyeliner are out. Long fingernails and false eyelashes are for actresses, not the professional businesswoman. Colorless nail polish should be the only kind used. He states that mascara should be used with great discretion. As for skin coloring as a result of suntans, Molloy states that the sun can do three things: increase your sex appeal, increase your authority, and increase your chances of getting skin cancer.[97]

Additions

Although little research is available on them, other body alterations include such items that could be listed as: false skin, padded bras, false breasts, false buttocks, pantyhose, and artificial tanning creams or lotions. Eugine Mathes and Sherry B. Kempher found that the number of different sex partners for the female corresponded highly with the frequency with which she went braless.[98]

However, the other items mentioned in this section seem of less importance in altering an individual's personal appearance. First, they are worn beneath the clothing, and second, if the clothing projects the correct impression of the individual, then these other items, or the features they either accentuate or hide, will be less prominent and noticed.

Body alterations are relatively inexpensive compared to other factors that influence the overall body appearance. If used effectively, they can project a chosen personality type. If used haphazardly, they can cause an individual to pay a high price in lost appeal.

Our physical appearance can be changed by using cosmetics and changing coloring (including eyes and hair), by changing hairstyles, and by making additions to the body. However, the simplest and least expensive changes are made on at least a daily basis. These involve clothing and clothing accessories.

Clothing

Purposes of Clothing

Clothing is a phenomenon of the human species. Although other species use various appendages (feathers, fins, antennae, crests, bands, and the like) for ornamentation, only humans go to all the trouble of garbing themselves in textiles. It is generally accepted that humans wear clothes for protection and modesty. However, in his book *The Psychology of Clothes,* J. C. Flugel provides evidence to contradict these assumptions.[99] Charles Darwin observed that the natives of Tierra del Fuego did not wear clothes, despite the severe weather conditions, thereby disspelling the first theory. The theory that people wear clothing for modesty's sake may be true for more complex societies but does not hold true for all cultures. As a matter of fact, Americans distinguish between being naked and being nude. To be naked is to be deprived of clothes, which causes embarrassment. To be nude is to be confident about the body in an aesthetic sense.[100]

If man does not wear clothing for protection or modesty, then what is the purpose of clothing? As noted earlier, Ray Birdwhistell suggests that only a third of human communication is accomplished through words. Nonverbal communication accounts for the rest. Because what you wear is nonverbal communication, clothing is a means of communicating. You are constantly sending and receiving messages from other people based on dress alone.

Functions of Clothing

Although one purpose of clothing appears to be communication, the functions are varied. Clothing serves as a means of protection, sexual attraction, self-assertion, self-denial, concealment, group identification, and indicating status and role.[101] Many personal attributes can be communicated by clothes. These include such characteristics as sex, age, nationality, relation to opposite sex, socioeconomic status, group and occupational identification, mood, personality, attitudes, interests, and values.[102]

William Thourlby infers that there are ten decisions people make about each other based on clothing alone.[103]

1. economic level
2. educational level
3. trustworthiness
4. social position
5. level of sophistication

6. economic background
7. social background
8. educational background
9. level of success
10. moral character

Home economist Julia Ann Reed attempted to prove that the contents of a woman's wardrobe can indicate everything from her level of intelligence to her degree of sophistication. Results of her study showed that the "high-fashioned woman" considered herself religious, well-to-do, disagreed less with her parents, and spent more money on clothes. The "low-fashion female" perceived herself to be the all-American girl, possessing natural good looks, which she considered more important than money, clothes, or status. The "nonfashion female" thought of herself as conservative and usually came from a low socioeconomic background. The "counterfashion woman" viewed herself as more liberal, individualistic, and conscientious, but less status-minded and the least sophisticated. Results also indicated that the high-fashioned woman had the lowest grade point average, whereas the nonfashion woman had the highest.[104]

Clothing and Status   James H. Fortenberry and associates wanted to find out which mode of dress best served as a perceptual cue for status. They placed one male and one female confederate in a hallway at conversational distance. Anyone wishing to go by had to avoid them or pass between them. In one condition, the conversationalists wore "formal daytime dress"; in the second condition, they wore "casual attire." There was a significant difference between the behaviors toward the conversationalists when they were "formally dressed" as opposed to "casually dressed." Positive behaviors were observed toward the perceived high-status couple, whereas negative behaviors were exhibited toward the perceived low-status couple.[105] Wayne E. Henley has reported similar results in terms of assistance,[106] and M. Walker, S. Harriman, and S. Costello found that people are more likely to comply with a request from a well-dressed person.[107] Finally, both of your authors know of academic department chairpersons who suggest that graduate teaching assistants wear shirts and ties (if males) and dresses or skirts (if female) in order to create a "teacher-status" effect. Paralleling this, many professors forgo the coat and tie to reduce the status difference in the classroom.

Clothing and Wearer Characteristics   L. R. Aiken tested 160 women to determine wearer characteristics. Decoration in dress correlated with conformity, sociability, and nonintellectualism; comfort in dress correlated with self-control and extroversion; interest in dress correlated with social conformity, restraint, and submissiveness; and economy in dress correlated with responsibility, alertness, efficiency, and precision.[108] Another study on wearer characteristics was made by Mary Lou Rosencrantz, who found that working women with high clothing awareness were from the upper social class, belonged to many social and community organizations, had higher levels of education and verbal intelligence, had higher incomes, and were usually married to white-collar workers.[109]

Thomas Hoult conducted two experiments to determine whether "clothes make the man."[110] In the first study, male subjects were informally rated with no attention given to attire. They were then divided into three groups and judged again; this time special attention was directed to clothing. Results showed that clothing changes made no significant difference between the two ratings when the subjects were known.

In the second experiment, Hoult ranked photographs of the heads of ten college-age men according to attractiveness. He also ranked ten photographs of outfits as to their "appropriateness for college students." The photographs of the heads were then negatively correlated with the photographs of the outfits. There was a marked difference in the attractiveness ratings of the pictures between the first set of rankings and the final one; the attractiveness for heads initially rated low was improved when they were matched up with outfits originally rated high, and vice versa.

Clothing and Its Effects on Behavior   Leonard Bickman undertook two field experiments in which he observed the effects of clothes on behavior. In the first experiment, he wanted to test a person's "clothes-categorizing system" in regard to honesty. He enlisted three male and three female confederates who dressed in either high-status or low-status clothing. One of the confederates would put a dime on the shelf of a phone booth and leave. When a caller entered, the confederate watched to see whether the person took the dime or not. The confederate would then approach the booth and explain that he/she may have left a dime in the booth. Seventy-seven percent of the callers returned the coin to the confederate in high-status clothing whereas only thirty-eight percent returned the dime to the low-status person.[111]

In a similar study, Bickman wanted to find out whether or not uniformed individuals, acting outside their traditional roles, would still have greater influence than nonuniformed persons. His confederates varied in dress and level of authority. The lowest authority figure was dressed as a civilian, the average authority figure was dressed as a milkman, and the highest level of authority was represented by a guard. Bickman then set up three situations. In the first situation, the confederate stopped the subject and asked him/her to pick up a piece of litter. In the second situation, the confederate stopped the subject and asked him/her to put a dime in a nearby expired parking meter. In the last situation, the confederate approached the subject and asked him/her to stand on the other side of a "No Standing" sign (which means no parking in a bus stop zone).

Regardless of age or sex, the subjects were definitely more compliant with the requests made by the guard. As a matter of fact, eighty-three percent of the pedestrians obeyed the high-authority figure as compared to forty-six percent who obeyed the low-authority figure. There were no significant differences in the compliance shown toward the civilian and the milkman.

M. Lefkowitz, R. R. Blake, and J. S. Mouton were interested in people's conformity to violation. The chance of this happening seemed to increase if the original violator was perceived as someone of authority. The study took place at a traffic light at which a male confederate, wearing high-status or low-status clothing, violated the "wait" signal. Significantly more pedestrians followed the confederate when he was perceived to be a figure of authority. However, more pedestrians violated the traffic signal when the confederate, regardless of perceived status, initiated the violation than when the confederate conformed or was absent.[112]

Most of us, then, wear "uniforms" of some type. Some are not as obvious as others. However, some of these uniforms may be more important than we think. Bill M. Huddleston and Louise H.

Huddleston studied the legitimacy and competency attributed to male and female judges based on whether or not they wore robes in making their judicial decisions.[113] Although male judges were consistently rated higher, those males and females who wore robes were rated as being more competent. The highest ratings were given to male judges who wore robes.

Clothing and Success

Molloy has extensively researched wardrobe engineering. He has shown that what a person wears can determine ultimate success or failure in the business environment. His *New Dress for Success* describes the proper attire for the successful businessman. Suits represent authority, credibility, and likability. Darker colors transmit more authority. Although darker colors are preferred, black should be avoided as it is too powerful for most men and has funeral undertones. Dark blue and dark gray suits build credibility. Molloy recommends solid colors, but pinstripes and chalk pinstripes are acceptable.

Solid white shirts received better responses in terms of taste, class, credibility, and effectiveness. Pastel shades and simple, closely striped shirts are also acceptable. Molloy recommends that the shirt be lighter than the suit and that the tie be darker than the shirt. Solid ties have the best effect, but diagonal stripes are acceptable.[114]

In 1978 Molloy also wrote *The Woman's Dress for Success Book.*[115] His research shows that the best outfit for a woman is a skirted suit and blouse. A medium gray or medium blue suit with a white blouse expresses the most authority. Navy blue, charcoal gray and beige are acceptable for suit colors, and white on white, gray, and pink are acceptable colors for blouses. The "imitation man" look diminishes a woman's authority and should, therefore, be avoided entirely. What we wear may say much more than we realize. The more we understand about this component of nonverbal communication the more effectively we will be able to communicate.

Interestingly enough, what Molloy has described as "correct" has been bought by the business world. Consider, for example, what the average male bank executive wears: blue or gray pinstripes, white or off-white shirt—or pastel blue or brown—and a conservative tie (usually tied in a "false" Windsor knot). Consider, too, the female executive: not very many wear pantsuits anymore; that look went out in the late 1970s. Now we encounter people who are carbon copies of each other. Significantly, those who are in charge seem to set the "norm," even when no written dress code exists. Go into any business and observe what dress codes you find; most will be obvious.

Finally, as Kittie Watson and Larry Smeltzer found, in interview situations the dress "code" has become an expectation rather than a hit or miss procedure.[116] They noted that (1) top Fortune 500 interviewers listed clothing high on their lists of something to look for, and that (2) because of this and because of Molloy's influence, the actual impressions that were once made no longer prevail everywhere, that is, provided you do not violate the clothing "game." Further, they report that interviewers tend to hire in their own image. To succeed in an interview, dress much like the interviewer. (See Figures 6.4 and 6.5.)

Michael R. Solomon has indicated that despite the work of Molloy and others, we know little about appropriate dress in varying contexts.[117] He found, however, that (1) there is a connection between those who think they are actors on life's stage and their dress habits; (2) some therapists suggest buying new clothes as therapy for some of their depressed clients; (3) those who are "dressed up" in interview situations think more highly of themselves in the interview; (4) people

FIGURE 6.4   Proper Business Attire.   **FIGURE 6.5**   Improper Business Attire.

are more concerned about dress when they move into a new situation; and (5) according to business executives who interview women for managerial positions, ''feminine grooming and dress'' does not work.

Accessories

Like clothes, accessories can communicate many messages to an observer. Accessories can cast an individual into a specific role or group. Group identifiers include such items as wedding bands, fraternity/sorority pins, hearing aids, canes, crutches, walkers, and jewelry that reveals religious preference.[118]

One kind of group identifier is occupational identifiers, those accessories that signify a particular role or position. Police officers wear guns, badges, hats, and handcuffs. Doctors are distinguished by laboratory coats and a stethoscopes around their necks. Ministers wear collars and carry Bibles. Athletes suit up in gear designed for their specific sport. Those in the military are recognized not only by uniforms but also by colorful ribbons, stripes, insignia, and medals that distinguish the various branches of the service as well as rank. Workers may use hardhats, gloves, and goggles. The list is endless.

Jewelry alone can tell much about an individual. Besides classifying you as belonging to a certain group or occupation, jewelry can reveal your social status, economic background, self-image, religion, education, and availability. According to Molloy, businessmen should limit jewelry to a wedding ring and a thin, plain gold watch. Businesswomen might consider wearing a wedding ring even though they may not be married because the presence of a band projects an ''all business'' image.[119] A thin watch and gold post earrings are the only other pieces of jewelry a successful businesswoman should wear, according to Molloy.

Eyeglasses play a large role in one's appearance. P. Hamid in 1968 found that people who wear glasses were perceived as religious, conventional, and unimaginative.[120] In an earlier study, he used waitresses wearing makeup and/or glasses as subjects and found that if they wore glasses and makeup, they received the most favorable ratings. When the waitresses wore neither makeup nor glasses, they received the poorest ratings.[121] K. Beattie and associates, undertook another study, at Mississippi State University, and found no significant differences between students who wore glasses and those who did not.[122]

Alfred Poll, a prominent optician, concluded that how people handle their frames can make a statement about the wearer's mood and even the image one is trying to project. The person who compulsively folds and unfolds his spectacles, for instance, may be indicating boredom; the one who bends his temple bar may be revealing inner agitation. Someone who touches both temple tips together may be expressing intense concentration. Chewing on the temple tip is common among people who are tense, nervous, or under great stress. Poll goes on to say that the way you position your glasses on your nose is also significant. For example, if you prop your glasses on your brow to look at a visitor with the naked eye, you may be demonstrating honesty and openness. By contrast, sliding your glasses to the tip of your nose and peering over the frame may be a nonverbal gesture for ''You're putting me on.''[123]

Molloy recommended that a businessman should select heavy plastic or horn rims, which will make him look traditional, authoritative, and older. His glasses should enhance or offset the facial feature so that the upper and lower face become a ''compatible unit.''[124] In the case of the businesswoman, glasses will also make her appear more authoritative, but less appealing. Therefore, he suggested that contact lenses be worn for social affairs.[125]

Smoking artifacts may also be considered accessories. In one study comparing and contrasting pipe smokers, cigar smokers, cigarette smokers, and nonsmokers, the results indicated that the pipe smoker was perceived as high in credibility, high in similarity, and high in attractiveness. Cigarette and cigar smokers were perceived as low in credibility, low in similarity, and low in attractiveness. The nonsmoker tended to fall between the pipe smoker and the other two groups regarding most factors; however, there were no significant differences among pipe smokers and nonsmokers. One shortcoming of this study was that subjects were not asked whether they smoked and if so, what they smoked.[126]

Although they may be considered unimportant by themselves, accessories are vital to the overall effect. They are used as a means of identification, as an indication of status, and as a medium for nonverbal communication. The cliché ''It's the little things that count'' is particularly relevant where accessories are concerned.

Although these studies on accessories were generally carried out under scientific conditions, the studies on dress are more questionable. Much more scientific and controlled research needs to be undertaken on dress and the effects of dress. For example, will there be variations in the perceptions of dress among institutions and businesses such as banks, engineering firms, insurance companies, and book publishers? Is it possible that dress becomes more important in situations where the individual is coming up for promotion? When one gets a divorce? After one has been promoted to the top level? Most of the questions about ''dressing for success'' remain empirically unanswered.

☐   **Summary**   ☐

This chapter has been concerned with the social dimension of physical appearance, which includes overall body shape, body alterations, clothing, cosmetics, and artifacts. Because physical appearance is the first nonverbal cue to be noticed, it will have a profound influence on one's relationships with others. Physical appearance communicates meaning. Many stereotypes are based upon this first impression. Changes in physical appearance, either intentional or unintentional, alter an individual's perceptions and the perceptions others have of him or her. A person's appearance is a major factor in the development of one's self-image. Finally, a clear understanding of the importance of physical appearance is needed because its influence affects every aspect of one's life from an individual's self-image to one's interaction with others.

Chapter Seven

Kinesic Studies

Key Concepts

Principles

Kinesic Categories

Kinesic Functions

Influencing Variables

Decoding Accuracy

Kinesics may be defined as the study of human body movements, including such phenomena as gestures, posture, facial expression, eye behavior, and rate of walk. Kinesics has been a significant constituent of nonverbal communication for thousands of years, but the recent scientific interest has been rekindled by the works of Ray Birdwhistell.[1] Birdwhistell has outlined six general principles of kinesics, which are based on a scientific approach to the study of bodily movement. This approach is sometimes called the *linguistic analogy* to kinesics.[2] We look in some detail at Birdwhistell's contributions to the study of kinesics, but we also examine a second, more subjective method called the *functional approach* to kinesics. Each produces different interpretations based on how the researcher perceives the study of kinesics. (Remember, in chapters 2 and 3, we discussed what an approach signifies in both a researcher's method and interpretation; in this chapter we observe how such differences lead to different research styles and interpretations). We begin, however, with the work of Birdwhistell and his six general principles.

Principles

In one of his more important publications, *Kinesics and Context,* Birdwhistell outlined six general principles of kinesics.[3] Each deals with (1) how we study the area of body movement and (2) what the potential for such a study leads us to in terms of communicative value.

1. **There is a high degree of interdependence among the five body senses (visual, aural, gustatory, olfactory, and tactile), which together with the verbal, form the *infracommunicational system.***

Each of the five senses, then, is important in the determination of nonverbal meaning in face-to-face interaction. At various times or on various occasions, each of the senses may dominate an interaction. For example, if we perceive another person as being a ''cold'' person and that person hugs us in a greeting, the tactile sense may become dominant. In many instances, however, the senses *interact,* each adding a little to the perception of meaning in the interaction. What if that hug were given with a stiff body posture, around the shoulder area, with an extreme forward lean? Would that communicate the same as a ''warm'' hug? The kinesic variables (posture, lean, and gesture expressed by the location of the arm) offset what the haptic sense is telling us. The same is true when someone says he likes you but does not look you in the eyes.

2. **Kinesic communication varies according to culture and even among microcultures.**

Individual differences, then, persist in both the encoding and decoding of kinesic messages as a result of being in one culture as opposed to being in another. Kenneth Johnson, for example, has provided two ways in which black Americans' kinesic behavior differs from that of their white counterparts. Johnson attributes much of the difference to the African heritage of black Americans.[4] One of the differences is that blacks are more reluctant to look another person directly in the eye. The other is that blacks walk differently than whites. Johnson writes: ''Observing young black males walking down ghetto streets, one can't help noticing that they are, indeed, in Thoreau's words 'marching to the tune of a different drummer.' The 'different drummer' is a different culture; the non-verbal [sic] message of their walk is similar to the non-verbal [sic] message of young white males, but not quite the same.''[5]

In addition to these cultural variations, there are differences in kinesic behavior between subcultures. Desmond Morris and his colleagues have discussed some of the differences in western Europe.[6] Differences exist, too, even between microcultures, such as families.

3. **There is no universal body language symbol.**

As we have mentioned, the nature/nurture controversy persists. Birdwhistell's view is that nurture (learning) is the sole factor. This view, of course, has been disputed by Darwin and some contemporary researchers who are discussed later in this chapter.

Birdwhistell claims: ''We have been searching for 15 years and have found no gesture or body motion which has the same meaning in all societies.''[7] To exemplify this, an Arab may stroke his beard to convey the message, ''There goes a pretty girl.'' However, a south Italian will pull the lobe of his right ear with his right hand to mean the same thing. In attempting to convey the same message, an American male may move his hands in the air to form the shape of a pretty girl.[8] ''As far as we know,'' said Birdwhistell, ''there is no body motion or gesture that can be regarded as a universal symbol. That is, we have been unable to discover any single facial expression, stance, or body position which conveys an identical meaning in all societies.''[9]

4. **The principle of redundancy, as stated in information theory, is not applicable to kinesic behavior.**

According to information theory, some gestures may be reinforcing (and therefore, redundant) with verbal communication. An example would be when one says, ''A box is about twenty-four inches long," while simultaneously holding one's hands to indicate the twenty-four inches. Birdwhistell claims that kinesic behavior is *complementary to* rather than redundant with respect to the verbal behavior. As we will see in a later section, however, not all accept his notion of this complementary function. A prime example is the smile; we are not always complementing or reinforcing when we smile; indeed, we may even be masking a contradictory or negative message.

5.   Kinesic behavior is more primitive and less controllable than verbal communication.

Although both kinesic behavior and verbal communication are learned, it seems that we pay less attention to what we are "saying" nonverbally. There are numerous reasons for this, but one account is perhaps the most common. That is, we learn the use of verbal communication very early as a conscious process. However, we are not aware of our learning to "speak" nonverbally. Although we pay attention to the kinesic behavior of others, we rarely monitor our own nonverbal communication. This is probably most evident when a person takes a public speaking class. Although we "speak with our hands" naturally, when we get up in front of an audience, those gestures seem to disappear. Students must be "retaught" to use the gesture in such situations. In many instances, a speaker who is anxious about the speaking experience grabs the lectern and "hangs on for dear life."

6.   We must compare and contrast nonverbal codes time and time again in context before we can make accurate interpretations.

When we meet strangers, we tend to evaluate them. These evaluations are often based largely on nonverbal behavior. In many cases, we seem to agree with others as to what stereotypes we see based on kinesic behavior alone. R. G. Barker found, for example, that people can make similar (but not always accurate) judgments about others, based on just visual and proxemic information.[10] Birdwhistell indicates that we should attempt to evaluate kinesic behavior only after having significant information about that person. Even then we should consider the social context when making an interpretation. This means that we should have some base line behavior as a norm *before* making a judgment. What we have found, based on comments made by our students, is that other people will assume that because we are taking a course in nonverbal communication, you can "read body language." Although it is tempting to do so, you should remember that what you interpret from the other's kinesic behavior is only as valid as what you know about the person.

These underlying principles of kinesics provide a basis for studying the research undertaken by Birdwhistell. In this chapter, we view kinesic research by Birdwhistell and others. The principles of the science are examined, together with the different ways in which males and females send and receive messages, and how these messages can be interpreted in and out of context. Areas such as cultural variations and universal symbols are discussed. With each country and culture, a new set of meanings is linked to body language. Conversely, messages that have the same meanings may be transmitted in quite different ways. Aspects of status, facial expressions, and eye behavior are considered. Pupil size, conscious and unconscious facial expressions, and even our place in the chain of command help us to convey nonverbal messages. It should be noted before we begin this study of kinesics that a person's dominance in nature has come about as a result of his or her ability to communicate thoughts, to control both the environment and other people by means of communication. As the individual becomes better able to understand the complex communication processes observed in others, so that person can better understand those processes in himself/ herself.

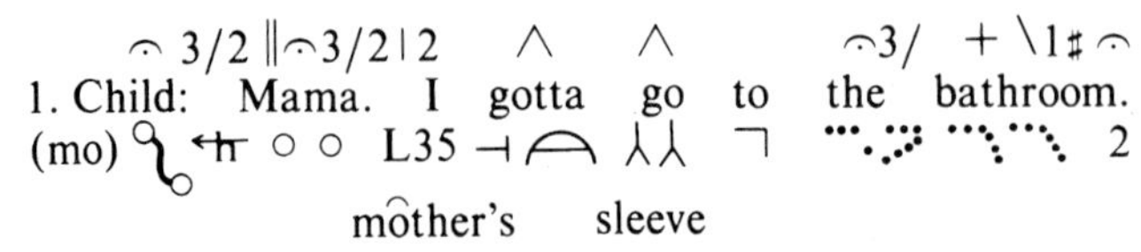

NOTE: The upper codes (ones above the descriptor) are paralinguistic cues. The kinegraphs are below the descriptor. See if you can match Birdwhistell's coding system to his description.

FIGURE 7.1 Kinesic Coding.
Source: R. L. Birdwhistell, *Kinesics and Context: Essays on Body Motion Communication* (New York: Ballantine, 1980), p. 358. Reprinted with permission.

Categories in Kinesics

Kinesics is a nonverbal area that is approached in a number of ways. Knowing these approaches and understanding how each differs in the interpretation of behavior makes possible better and more refined explanations of the communication of other people. This knowledge also enables us to understand better how others may interpret communicative behavior.

Birdwhistell's Linguistic Analogy

Birdwhistell observed kinesic behavior as an analogy between kinesics and linguistics in verbal communication. He has claimed that **parakinesic phenomena** are similar to factors that influence our verbal expression. He has further theorized that three factors are included in all parakinesic phenomena: (1) the degree of muscular tension (intensity), (2) the length of time involved in the movement (duration); and (3) the extent of the movement (range). These three phenomena yield a system of kinesic study that examines the structure of the movement and, based upon that structure, creates a ''meaningful'' statement, much like the building of a sentence.

For purposes of analysis, Birdwhistell devised what he refers to as an **allokine,** the smallest unit of kinesic behavior, generally too small to be meaningful. Birdwhistell has stated that allokines are rarely perceptible to the human eye, and there are 20,000 allokines in the facial area alone. When observing people, we must use **kines,** which are combinations of allokines. This level of analysis, however, is still beyond the meaningful and must be combined with other kines to create significant analysis. The next largest unit (the combination of kines) Birdwhistell calls **kinemes** (a group of kines that are not identical but that may be used interchangeably without affecting the social meaning). General American movement contains about fifty or sixty kinemes; most of these are in the head and face area. Kinemes combine to form **kinemorphemes,** which are sequential movements. Therefore, these categories may be considered analogous to categories in language from allophones to sentences.

The comparison to the linguistic system is simple. Allokines and kines are equivalent to the allophone and phone. Kinemes are equivalent to the morpheme; these combine to form words, or kinemorphic classes. Birdwhistell postulates that these can be analyzed by means of a coding system like that shown in Figure 7.1. (Notice how the ''shorthand'' almost duplicates the behavior.)

Morris' Derivation System

Desmond Morris has indicated that there are five categories of actions. These categories are: inborn, discovered, absorbed, trained, and mixed.[11] Morris states: ''Human behavior is not free-flowing; it is divided into a long series of separate events. Each event, such as eating a meal, visiting a theatre, taking a bath, or making love, has its own special rules and rhythms.[12] One category of actions is inborn actions; these actions are innate and exist at birth. One example is a newborn baby's ''reacting immediately to its mother's nipple by sucking.''[13] A second category is discovered actions, actions that we discover (such as folding one's arms) but that are limited because of the genetic structure of our bodies (in this case, our arms).[14] Absorbed actions are those ''we acquire unknowingly from our companions.''[15] Many of these actions are acquired in an unconscious attempt to synchronize our actions when we are together. Edward T. Hall has indicated that absorbed actions occur at an early age. Examples are the synchronized behavior of elementary students on a playground, such as skipping, dancing, and jumping.[16] Trained actions are those we have to learn from others; walking on our hands is an example. Finally, mixed actions are those we acquire in a number of ways. Infantile crying, for example, is changed as we become adults—in an attempt to ''cover up'' such behavior.[17] Thus, Morris's categories are based upon how we acquire the particular nonverbal behavior.

Mehrabian's Functional Approach

Albert Mehrabian categorized kinesic behavior into functional groups. These categories include: (1) a pleasure-displeasure dimension, (2) an arousal-nonarousal dimension, and (3) a dominance-submissiveness dimension.[18] In his research on body orientation, Mehrabian found differences between people who liked one another and those who did not. *Body orientation* may be defined as ''the degree to which a communicator's shoulders and legs are turned in the direction of, rather than away from, the addressee.''[19] Mehrabian found that a male interacting with another male has less direct body orientation with a well-liked person. Female communicators used a very indirect orientation with intensely disliked persons, relatively direct with persons they liked, and the most direct with neutrally liked persons. There was no difference in the openness of arms and legs, whether the two communicators liked each other or not. The *arms-akimbo* position (in keen bow) was used more frequently when interecting with disliked people. Mehrabian's general conclusion on his pleasure-displeasure (*liking*) dimensions is that relaxation is extremely low when one is talking to a disliked person; relaxation is moderate when we are talking with a friend.

Another dimension of Mehrabian's is dominance-submissiveness, or what we might refer to as *status* or *power difference*. Mehrabian found that people stand with a more direct body orientation when talking to a higher status person. People in inferior roles lower their heads more often. Individuals' legs and hands are more relaxed when talking with a lower-status person. A sideways

Physical violence / Verbal hostility / Neutrality / Immediacy / Intimacy

FIGURE 7.2   The Place of Avoidance-oriented to Approach-oriented Behaviors.

leaning posture is used more often by a higher-status person when talking to a subordinate. All are indicative of a relationship between the two interactants.

Mehrabian's research on status has induced others to view status as directly related to the sex of the individual. Nancy Henley has hypothesized that females nonverbally communicate from a lower status position, whereas males gain and maintain their higher status through the use of nonverbal symbols.[20] Erving Goffman found some support for Henley's hypothesis in his research on advertisements.[21] Finally, Michael Argyle and Marilyn Williams postulate that one reason for sex differences in regard to status may be derived from the perception of where the nonverbal behaviors are attributed.[22] They believe that females generally attribute nonverbal actions as feedback from themselves, whereas males tend to attribute nonverbal actions to others or to the environment. This line of reasoning could be further extended to infer that any minority (implying here that females may perceive themselves as a ''minority'' in terms of status, equated with, for example, blacks, Hispanics, or others) might classify the nonverbal actions as feedback from themselves as powerless, low-status people.

Mehrabian's third category is the arousal-nonarousal dimension, or *responsiveness*. High levels of arousal are shown both internally and externally. When we are interested in something or someone, we have higher blood pressure, higher pulse rates, and increased muscle tension; we respond to the stimulus through an aroused (or nonaroused) feeling. Also, our pupils enlarge (dilate) and we engage in more bodily movement. More recently, researchers have referred to responsiveness as **immediacy.** Immediacy involves not only kinesic cues, but, as Mehrabian has suggested, spatial cues, verbal cues, touching, loudness of voice, and the like. For immediacy, these verbal and nonverbal cues must be working together. Virginia P. Richmond, James C. McCroskey, and Steven K. Payne have indicated that immediacy can be found on a continuum, with physical violence at one end and intimacy on the other (see Figure 7.2).[23]

Obviously when two people get in a fist fight, they are close in space and they are ''touching'' one another, but they are not immediate. Robert G. Powell and Barbara Harville have defined immediacy as ''behaviors which reduce physical and psychological distance between interactants.'' They found differences in what constitutes immediacy across ethnic groups, as related to teacher clarity. Sanders and Wiseman, however, found that teacher immediacy enhanced students' cognitive, affective, and behavioral learning. Their subjects were white, Asian, Hispanic, and African-American. The relationship of immediacy to affective learning was more common in the Hispanic students.[24] Other researchers, looking at immediacy in the learning context, found that students reported a greater likelihood of resistance to the teacher if their techniques were *unexpected* according to perceived immediacy.[25] Judee K. Burgoon and Deborah A. Newton, in a study regarding relational messages, found that *high involvement* and the specific nonverbal cues associated with it conveyed greater intimacy, including immediacy and affection than did low-involvement nonverbal cues.[26] Thus, Mehrabian has presented three dimensions of nonverbal behavior: (1) liking, (2) power and status, and (3) responsiveness, or immediacy. Each of the three may function alone, or it may interact with another to communicate messages to another person.

Ruesch and Kees' Coding Method

Jurgen Ruesch and Weldon Kees provided one of the first category systems for nonverbal communication:

> In broad terms, nonverbal forms of codification fall into three distinct categories:
> *Sign Language* includes all those forms of codification in which words, numbers, and punctuation signs have been supplanted by gestures; these vary from the ''monosyllabic'' gestures of the hitchhiker to such complete systems as the language of the deaf.
> *Action Language* embraces all movements that are not used exclusively as signals. Such acts as walking and drinking, for example, have a dual function: on the one hand they serve personal needs, and on the other hand they constitute statements to those who may perceive them.
> *Object Language* comprises all intentional and nonintentional displays of material things, such as implements, machines, art objects, architectural structures, and—last but not least—the human body and whatever clothes or covers it. The embodiment of letters as they occur in books and on signs has a material substance, and this aspect of words also has to be considered as object language.[27]

A problem with this approach is the vagueness associated with what is and what is not nonverbal communication. Some of what Ruesch and Kees call nonverbal communication we have omitted in our definition of what constitutes the nonverbal code. It is useful to remember, however, that this is one of the earliest attempts at the scientific study of nonverbal communication.

Ekman and Friesen's Cumulative Structure

A more precise approach to kinesic behavior has been taken by Paul Ekman and Wallace Friesen.[28] This approach is sometimes called the *meaning-centered* approach to the study of kinesics because Ekman and Friesen are more interested in the meanings associated with bodily movement than the actual structure. They state that body movement can be analyzed in terms of five functions or categories of behaviors: (1) emblems, (2) illustrators, (3) regulators, (4) adaptors, and (5) affect displays. Because the approach is less ''structure'' oriented, it is easier to comprehend, but because of that same quality, it is more difficult to determine what specific behavior might be equated with what meaning.

Ekman has written that **emblems** have direct translations into verbal communication (usually a word or two or a phrase). Most people in the culture are familiar with the word or phrase and the emblem; emblems, then, are sent with conscious intent. The receiver knows that he or she is the recipient of the message, and the sender usually takes responsibility for the message. Some examples are the American emblem for ''OK,'' pointing one's finger like a pistol to indicate suicide, and crossing one's first fingers back and forth to mean ''shame on you.'' One of the most common messages in the United States is the emblem ''the finger.''[29] Its meaning is generally interpreted as ''screw you,'' but the intent may be seen as a joke when acccompanied by a smile and transmitted by a friend. In their European studies of gestures, Morris and others did not find the finger to be a dominant gesture. However, they found a number of substitutes, including the forearm jerk, the vertical horn-sign (index and pinky fingers up while the thumb holds down the middle and ring fingers), and the fig (the thumb between the index and middle fingers).[30] Figure 7.3 offers some American emblems that range from everyday to less common use.

The second category is **illustrators.** These gestures are used to support what is being said verbally. They are used particularly when giving directions. A. Cohen investigated the use of illustrators and found that (1) they were used more often in face-to-face interaction, and (2) they

FIGURE 7.3   Hand Gestures.

were used regardless of how familiar the communicator was with the directions.[31] In general, there are several classes of illustrators: those that emphasize words or sentences (such as shaking your fist and telling the other person *how* mad you are); and those that represent the thought processes (such as rolling the hand over as if trying to get a thought out or snapping a finger to create the impression of knowledge at a point in time). We also use illustrators to ''draw'' the shape of objects in space (such as drawing a circle with your fingers or calling someone a ''square'' while outlining the rebus in the air) and to represent some form of bodily action.

The third category developed by Ekman and Friesen is **regulators.** These gestures allow us to regulate when to talk and when to allow others to talk. Adam Kendon and Andrew Ferber have provided six stages of general interaction that serve to regulate or use the regulation function.[32]

1. *Sighting, Orientation, and Initiation of the Approach.*

2. *The Distant Salutation.* This is the ''official ratification'' (1) that a greeting sequence has been initiated and (2) of who the participants are. A wave, smile, or call may be used for recognition. Two types of head movements were noted at this point. One, the head toss,

is a fairly rapid back and forward tilting movement. Some people, however, tend to lower their head, hold it for a while, then slowly raise it.

3. *The Head Dip.* This movement has been noted by researchers in other contexts as a marker for transitions between activities or shifts in psychological orientation. This movement was not observed by Kendon and Ferber if the greeter did not continue to approach his or her partner.

4. *Approach.* As the greeting parties continued to move toward each other, several behaviors were observed. Gazing behavior probably helped signal that the participants were cleared for talking. An aversion of this gaze was seen just prior to the close salutation stage, however. Grooming behavior and one or both arms moved in front of the body were also observed at this point.

5. *Final Approach.* Now the participants are less than ten feet apart. Mutual gazing, smiling, and positioning of the head not seen in the sequence thus far can now be seen. The palms of the hands may also be turned toward the other person.

6. *Close Salutation.* As the participants negotiate a standing position, we hear the more stereotyped, ritualistic verbalizations so characteristic of the greeting ceremony, for example, ''Hi, Steve! How ya doin'?'' and so on. If the situation calls for body contact or ritualized gesture (handshakes, embraces, and the like), it will occur at this time.

Once the two parties have entered into conversation, decisions have to be made about who talks when *(turn-taking)*. Although a large portion of turn-taking behavior is paralinguistic (vocal), there are certain kinesic behaviors that control the flow of communication, and these differ from culture to culture. For the North American culture, as Starkey Duncan points out, the turn-taking sequence is typically me-you-me-you-me-you.[33] Within the interaction, we typically find such kinesic behaviors as gaze direction, head nods, forward leans, gesturing, and facing behavior used to control the flow of communication.[34] These kinesic behaviors have several functions: they may indicate a desire to continue with the conversation if you are speaking; they may signal a desire to turn the conversation over to you if you are listening; or you may use them to keep the other person talking.[35] Keeping the other person talking is usually the function of **backchanneling** behaviors, behaviors engaged in (1) to make the speaker feel he or she is being listened to and (2) to confirm interest in that person.[36] Here, however, you can also pace the speaker with head nods and smiles. (Try it sometime. As the speaker talks to you, slowly begin to backchannel with head nods; slowly increase the frequency of the head nod and note that the speaker's pace soon speeds up. Slow down the backchannel, and the rate of speech also will be slower.)

Judee K. Burgoon and Thomas J. Saine report a study in which the regulation of conversation took on a synchronous form.[37] People are synchronous in their behavior and communication when the ''flow'' of their actions takes on a continuous nature: one extends to the other and back in a rhythm. Although this research did not deal specifically with kinesics, the form of synchrony (swiveling chairs where the two interactants swiveled together during positive parts of the conversation and stopped swiveling during more negative parts) also brought them into a face-to-face, reciprocal gaze during the synchronous part of the conversation, which included smiling. The swivel and smile might be considered as backchanneling behavior. The lack of synchrony reflects a lack of backchanneling and is indicative of tension in the relationship.

The fourth category developed by Ekman and Friesen is **adaptors,** gestures that are learned in childhood. They are means of accounting for our behavior that may have been negative. Picking one's nose or scratching the body are two adaptors; they serve to satisfy a bodily function. When attention is focused on such behavior, we sometimes turn to objects instead. Hence, the fondling of rosary beads, the thumbing of a stone, or as Captain Queeg did in *The Caine Mutiny,* the rolling of steel balls in the hand, all function to reduce some felt stress or need. People who quit smoking turn to other object adaptors such as pens, pencils, their fingers, or candy. Adaptors, then, are used to adjust the body, to satisfy some bodily need, or, at times, to satisfy some emotional need.

The final category is that of **affect displays.** Ekman and Friesen have undertaken a number of research studies in this area.[38] Using subjects from a number of cultures, Ekman and Friesen have found six emotions that are universally expressed in facial expression: (1) fear; (2) anger; (3) surprise; (4) disgust; (5) sadness; and (6) happiness. (See Figure 7.4.)

Usually when we look at affect displays, we associate the specific emotion with the face and with the degree to which that emotion exists in the body. The body, by its tenseness, is indicative of what degree of emotion is being exhibited; as the body tenses, the emotion is usually greater. When identifying the specific emotion, however, we still rely on the face. According to Ekman and Friesen, we can examine the face for emotion by the area or region of the face from which the cue originates. This technique is called the *Facial Affect Scoring Technique,* or FAST.[39] A second technique, which has only recently been reported, is the *Facial Meaning Sensitivity Test,* or FMST, developed by Dale Leathers.[40] Although both tests are concerned with affect displays, FAST looks mainly for categorization of the specific emotion, whereas FMST looks for meaning within such a categorization. Both are useful. Within the FAST are three areas or regions: Region I contains the eyebrows and forehead; Region II is the area from the eyelids on down to the bridge of the nose; Region III comprises the nose, cheeks, mouth, and jaw.[41] (See Figure 7.5.) Within these regions, we can identify the six facial expressions Ekman and Friesen found. The best area in which to identify *fear* is from the eyes and eyelids,[42] the upper eyelid usually being raised and the lower eyelid tensed and drawn up. Fear may occur simultaneously with other emotions such as sadness, anger, or disgust. Varying from something minor to something life-endangering, the causes of fear can be physical, psychological, or both. The psychological harm of fear may be the result of loss of friendship, attacks on one's worth, or damage to one's self-esteem and sense of security.[43]

Anger is usually expressed through the cheeks (facial), mouth, brows, and forehead. Unless anger is registered in all three facial areas, there is ambiguity. Anger is usually aroused by frustration, physical threat, psychological hurt, and violation of moral values. Some of the usual signs of anger are an increase in blood pressure, a change in one's breathing, and a rising tension in the person's body. The direction to ''be still'' may be imposed because of the desire to strike.[44]

Surprise is the briefest of the six emotions that Ekman and Friesen consider to be universal. Surprise is triggered by the unexpected and by what might be called the ''mis-expected'' event. An unexpected surprise is an unusual event that is unanticipated, occurring when the surprised person is not expecting anything in particular to happen. In mis-expected surprise, the event need not be unusual to be surprising; it is the contrast with what is expected at the moment that is surprising. Surprise is not limited to the physical; it can also be in reaction to ideas and concepts. When it is not experienced as isolated emotion, surprise is usually followed by another emotion. It is the subsequent emotion that gives a positive or negative tone to the experience, fear being the most common sequel. Surprise may be used to mask or cover other emotions when you want to conceal how you are truly reacting or feeling.[45]

FIGURE 7.4 Facial Expressions: (1) Surprise (2) Anger (3) Fear (4) Disgust (5) Sadness (6) Happiness.

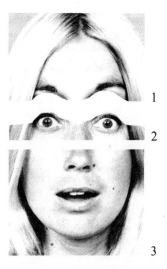

FIGURE 7.5 Three Parts of Facial Analysis.
Source: Paul Ekman and Wallace Friesen, *Unmasking the Face: A Guide to Recognizing Emotion for Facial Clues* (Englewood Cliffs, NJ: Prentice-Hall, Inc., 1975). Reprinted with permission.

The emotion of *disgust* often blends with surprise. Disgust is a feeling of repulsiveness, as a reaction to something or someone, and usually involves getting-rid-of and getting-away-from responses. The intensity of disgust may vary and can be closely related to contempt, a sentiment that is experienced only in relation to people or the actions of people. Disgust can appear in reaction to other people, ideas, actions, situations, or oneself, or in reaction to the sight, taste, smell, and touch of something.[46]

Sadness is expressed when the ''inner corners of the eyebrows are drawn up. The skin below the eyebrow is triangulated, with the inner corner up. The upper eyelid inner corner is raised. The corner of the lips are down or the lip is trembling.''[47] *Happiness* is shown when the ''[c]orners of the lips are drawn back and up. The mouth may or may not be parted, with the teeth exposed or not. A wrinkle (the naso-labial fold) runs down from the nose to the outer edge beyond the lip corners. The cheeks are raised. The lower eyelid shows wrinkles below it, and may be raised but not tense. Crows-feet wrinkles go outward from the outer corners of the eyes.''[48] One of the most prominent aspects of the emotion of happiness is the smile. Women, for example, use smiling to appease others but also to try to appeal to men. It appears that women smile more often than do men. Studies show that men are less likely than women to show teeth when they smile. Actually, males and females use smiling differently. In telling the truth or lying, males smiled more in telling lies than in telling the truth, but females' facial expression of smiling does not vary much in either case. Whereas Ekman and Friesen and Leathers use photographs to show facial expression, Randall Harrison has used a more simplified approach: drawings.[49]

Ekman and Friesen are continually undertaking research in an attempt to discover whether there are other facial expressions of emotion that are pancultural (exist across cultures). Most recently they have observed the expression of *contempt* and the startle reaction. Regarding contempt, the researchers found that, contrary to prediction, the contempt expression exists in Estonia, Germany, Greece, Hong Kong, Italy, Japan, Scotland, Turkey, the United States, and Sumatra.[50] Previously, Ekman and Friesen had thought that the emotion was simply a variation of disgust.

Unlike the other six, this emotion has not been found among other primates (it seems among the last to appear) and two of four such expressions of contempt involve unilateral facial actions. The other six involve bilateral facial actions. (See Figure 7.6.) In their study of the startle, Ekman and Friesen studied whether people reacted to the firing of a blank pistol. In addition, they fore-warned their subjects and asked them to suppress their startle reaction. They found the startle to be a *reflex, not an emotion.*[51] To this point, then, Ekman and Friesen have found *seven facial expressions of emotion:* happiness, sadness, disgust, anger, fear, surprise, *and* contempt.

Ekman and Friesen also state that an expression often shows two emotions at the same time; these they label **affect blends.** They also contend that there is a *neutral* expression. Predicated upon these various categories of nonverbal communication, we can apply some of the principles suggested by Birdwhistell, and others' interpretations or reinterpretations of them, to the variables involved. (For instance, Ekman and Friesen's notion of universality of emotions runs counter to Birdwhistell's principle of no universally held gesture.)

In opposition to Birdwhistell, Paul Ekman contends that Darwin's theory of universality of some emotions (and their innateness) is valid. He argues that there is evidence of universal facial expressions for such emotions as happiness, anger, disgust, sadness or distress, fear, surprise, and other sentiments. Ekman infers that we create the ''display rules,'' or norms; we learn regarding the appropriateness of facial expression. Such expression, however, has been measured on the basis of *surface appearance.* Ekman and Friesen have since developed a new facial expression

FIGURE 7.6   The Unilateral Pancultural Expression for Contempt.
Source: Paul Ekman and Wallace Friesen, *Unmasking the Face: A Guide to
Recognizing Emotion for Facial Clues* (Englewood Cliffs, NJ: Prentice-Hall,
Inc., 1975). Reprinted with permission.

measurement system based on *muscle movement*—the Facial Action Coding System (FACS). The
FACS distinguishes expression based on muscle (1) appearance change, (2) capability for independent action, and (3) feedback circuits that allow us to be aware of our own facial movement.
Other tests developed by Ekman and Friesen include the Requested Facial Action Test (REFACT),
which requires people to imitate facial expressions viewed on videotapes.[52] The importance of
such tests as the FAST, FMST, FACS, and REFACT depends on how well we recognize and
encode emotional expression and, just as useful, on the way we employ conversational signals
that emphasize such elements as linguistic comma, question, or exclamation point. The facial
expression is also used to signal agreement/disagreement or understanding/lack of understanding.

Ekman's research, especially regarding affect blends, has been one of the most heuristic areas
of study in nonverbal communication in the late 1980s and early 1990s. A number of questions
and critiques have arisen concerning the controversy over whether there are only seven basic
emotions expressed in the facial area. The controversy has brought about the following: (1) How
well are people able to encode and decode facial messages? (2) How do cultural differences relate
to the concept of universal expression of emotions? (3) Are there other emotions that should be
added to the seven developed by Ekman?

Skill in encoding and decoding certainly affects the results of studies on facial expression.
Coding abilities have been tested in regard to sex differences and personality. One researcher

found that males and females were equally capable of decoding anger. Others found females generally more accurate in encoding emotions of all types. Extroverts were more accurate in decoding facial expressions of emotion and were more confident in their assessments. Generally, however, *females are considered better encoders and decoders of emotion through facial expression.*[53]

Other researchers have found that knowledge of another's personality biases the decoding of that person's nonverbal messages. Also, children appear to learn to encode and decode more accurately as they get older.[54]

There appears to be a cultural bias in some of the research in this area. Makaremi found that Iranian students used crying as an angry reaction against their parents, peers, and teachers. These adolescents used verbal aggression more often with their peers. However, the overall aggressive behavior of Iranian adolescents was less than might have been anticipated by Western researchers. Matsumoto has expressed a more general concern with such cultural problems indicating that more research needs to be undertaken on the role of culture in formulating display rules. Sogon and Masutani observed some of these emotions as decoded by Americans and Japanese. They used as the seven emotions: joy, surprise, fear, sadness, disgust, anger, and contempt. Assuming joy is similar to happiness, these categories are similar to Ekman's. They also added what they called three "affective-cognitive structures": affection, anticipation, and acceptance. Sogon and Masutani found that Japanese and Americans expressed anger, fear, and sadness in a similar way. Joy and surprise were more culture-bound. Japanese subjects could not recognize disgust or contempt. [As has already been mentioned, Ekman had some difficulty in separating these two.] Affection, anticipation, and acceptance were culture-bound.[55]

Additional controversy has been brought as a result of two schools of thought. The first is the school that believes there are additional emotions. One general type of emotion that has received a great deal of attention is shame/embarassment/guilt. Margalit found that there are cultural differences and even subcultural differences in the display of shame by mothers of severely handicapped children in Israel. Sharkey and Stafford found that display of embarassment was situational and that, in large measure, such displays are related to the responses of the others who are present. Thus, the notion that embarrassment is a universal expression of emotion has been found not to be the case. From a more specific, physiological perspective Shields, Mallory, and Simon have investigated blushing. Blushing is more of an involuntary expression that some of these others; however, the researchers found that the amount of blushing decreases with age. Lang, Bradley, and Cuthbert refer to these affect blends as responses, but they claim there are also *reflexes.* Their example is the *startle reflex,* which occurs, for example, when one hears a gunshot. The startle reflex is prompted by pictures or memory images rather than overt, external stimuli at the time of the reflex.[56]

The second criticism of Ekman's research is undertaken by Orthony and Turner, who believe there is nothing basic about the emotions described by Ekman.[57]

A Practical Functional Approach

We have been discussing researchers who have developed a system for understanding human nonverbal behavior. Many of these researchers have taken a *functional approach* as we did in chapter 2. In the next few pages, we will describe how other research falls into the functional categories we have discussed previously.

1. **Identification and Self-Presentation**

We usually tell who a person is by physical appearance. However, we can also determine who a person is by how he or she walks, the expansiveness of gestures, and the like. Much of self-presentation and identification is related to the status of the person. Researchers have found that many of the kinesics cues of a higher-status person differ from those of a lower-status person.

C. L. Ridgeway, J. Berger, and L. Smith investigated the effects of power in accordance with expectations of status difference.[58] Eye gaze was used as the power indicator. As hypothesized, male subjects could perform tasks more easily when the confederate/observer (who maintained eye contact on the subject) was a female than when the confederate was a male. In both instances (male and female subjects), subjects performed better when they were under the impression that the confederate was a superior. Although the researchers ''linked'' male with superior, this should not necessarily be a condition for undertaking such a study. In fact, as a replication and extension of their findings, an interesting study might be to ''link'' higher status with the female confederate.

Status is not equal with power, but it is often difficult to differentiate between the two. Related to power, ''status refers to a person's social position and the judgments of that person by the social group.''[59] Our attitudes about characteristics such as physical attractiveness, age, and sex reflect the power of one's status. Mehrabian discovered, for instance, that posture is more tense in higher-status people, and the inferior tends to lower his or her head. The arms and legs of a higher-status person are more relaxed when talking to a lower-status person.[60]

An individual's place in the chain of command, or his or her status, may affect nonverbal communication. A study in Japan by Michael H. Bond and D. Shiraishi applied kinesic behavior measurements developed in the United States to interactions among the Japanese.[61] They were interested in how the variables of posture, status, the subject's sex would affect nonverbal behavior in certain situations. Actually, the status variable affected the subject's response. For the male and female subjects combined, higher-status interviewers elicited shorter pauses, more eye contact, more hand and head gestures, and greater total speech. Females were more responsive to the status manipulation than were males. The researchers interpreted these results as being generally consistent with the United States findings, except that greater tension was not seen in persons interacting with high-status interviewers; head and hand gestures are considered relaxation measures, but they increased when interacting with high-status persons. The higher-status figure initiates the distance or closeness of the relationship. This person also directs looks of greater duration toward those of lower status, and the lower-status person breaks eye contact first. The manner in which a person is addressed depends upon the degree of familiarity or equality of the acquaintance.

Closely related to status is dominance and persuasiveness. Kinesic variables influence perceptions of both. In terms of persuasibility and persuasion, we use more eye contact (especially if the person to be persuaded is a female), more head nods, more gesturing (especially if the person persuading is a female), more facial expression and activity, moderate relaxation (but if the person to be persuaded is a female, slightly more tense posture), smaller reclining angles, and differences in body orientation (male persuaders use indirect orientation; female persuaders use direct orientation; if the person to be persuaded is a male, more indirect orientation). Finally, try to use some ''open'' gestures (gestures that are outward rather than inward).[62]

Dominance, as expressed by kinesic cues, takes on several aspects. First is eye contact or gaze. Dominant people are those who can establish eye contact; however, whether that interaction is to be warm or cold will depend upon the eye contact (warm being more eye contact), smiles (warm being more smiles), and head nods (warm) versus head shakes (cold).[63] In another study, B. Schwartz, A. Tesser, and E. Powell found that elevation increased power and perceived dominance.[64] They had subjects look at pictures of people sitting or standing, and also sitting or standing but elevated. They found that elevated people were regarded as more powerful, regardless of whether or not the lower figure was standing. When both people in the illustration were sitting, the one elevated was perceived as more powerful. This would seem to confirm Ken Cooper's more anecdotal advice that to be perceived as powerful in a business setting you should arrive late and sit on something that will elevate you above the rest of the interactants.[65]

2. Control of the Interaction

The control of conversation is similar to Ekman and Friesen's notion of *regulators*. These are nonverbal attempts to enter or exit a verbal or nonverbal conversation. Greetings and farewells fall into this category.[66] One of the authors found an interesting concept while visiting Rio de Janeiro. People there often grab one another just above the elbow to get a chance to speak rather than interrupting verbally.

Students raise their hands to get a chance to speak when they are in a large class. In smaller classes, students may simply speak out or try to gain the teacher's attention through eye contact. Thus, we see that culture and context affect how we try to control the interaction.

3. Relationship of Interactants

The concept of relationship of interactants has to do with whether parties are trying to avoid one another, show others that they are with one another, or somewhere in between. One of the most positive affinity-seeking (showing liking) behaviors is what Albert Scheflen has referred to as **quasi-courtship behavior.**

Schlefen has provided a process model of what he refers to as quasi-courtship behavior, wherein both sexes note for one another a sexual interest. The model consists of four general steps or stages: (1) courtship readiness; (2) preening behavior: (3) postural cues; and (4) appeals to invitation.[67] Each of these steps involves specific kinds of behavior. For example, **courtship readiness** is expressed by increased muscle tone, reduced eye bagginess, less slouch, and a decreasing belly sag (note that some of these cues are functions of the automatic nervous system and others of the central nervous system). **Preening behavior** is accomplished through stroking the hair, rearranging makeup, glancing in a mirror, stretching one's clothes, leaving buttons unbuttoned (especially at the chest), adjusting suit coats, tugging at one's socks, and readjusting knots in ties. **Positional cues** are using the shoulders and legs to ''position others out'' of the invitation. **Appeals to invitation** include flirtatious glances, gaze holding, rolling of the pelvis, crossing legs to expose the thigh, exhibiting the wrist or palm, and protruding one's breasts. Both sexes, then, use nonverbal cues in an attempt to attract another of the opposite sex.

Quasi-courting occurs in nearly all situations when the participants know one another and are engaged in a common objective. It can also be observed in situations when there is a confusion over gender, that is, when some participant behaves in a way that is inappropriate to his or her gender. Moreover, it is present when a participant has been excluded or has withdrawn from the interaction.

Quasi-courtship behavior has a definite purpose in our interactions with others. It helps to provide a positive attitude and increased attentiveness or readiness to relate to the group or other person. It can make the participants feel more at ease with others. Scheflen writes that the result of quasi-courting is that "a group can become animated and cohesive enough to work together to complete a dull or tedious task."[68] The task may be simply to keep a conversation going, but quasi-courting helps bring forth activity and, therefore, new ideas. Quasi-courting also has an interpersonal dimension; by engaging in quasi-courtship behaviors, we make others feel attractive and needed, and we make ourselves feel needed. (See Figure 7.7.) Attraction is certainly a primary element as related to quasi-courtship behavior.

Dianne Berry and Leslie Z. McArthur found that adult facial structure that resembles that of a child carries particular characteristics. People with this facial structure are perceived as possessing qualities such as warmth, submission, less strength, more naïveté, less threat, and more honesty. Additionally, heightened eyebrows, dilated pupils, and wide smiles were perceived as attractive to females. The female face was generally perceived to be indicative of submission, warmth, naïveté, and weakness. There would appear to be a conflict between one's seeking affinity and one's attempt to control through status and power.[69]

Other researchers hypothesized that people who provided more spontaneous, uncensored nonverbal communication were perceived to be more attractive.[70] A positive correlation was found between physical attractiveness and nonverbal *encoding;* however, a negative correlation was found between physical attractiveness and nonverbal *decoding.*

4. **Display of Cognitive Information**

   Display of cognitive information is the presentation of information through Ekman and Friesen's *illustrators* and *emblems.* In the first case, gestures are used *to support* verbal information, and in the case of emblems, gestures are used to *substitute* nonverbal information for verbal information.

5. **Display of Affective Information**

   Display of affective information is Ekman and Friesen's *affect display.* It is used to show others how one feels at a particular time: happiness, sadness, surprise, fear, anger, disgust, and contempt.

The Blocking Function: Deception

Lying and acting provide a totally different set of functions in a sense. If the actor is intentionally deceiving the other person, all of the other factors are changed. In this section, we will discuss self-deception and the deception of others. Self-deception is similar to Ekman and Freisen's

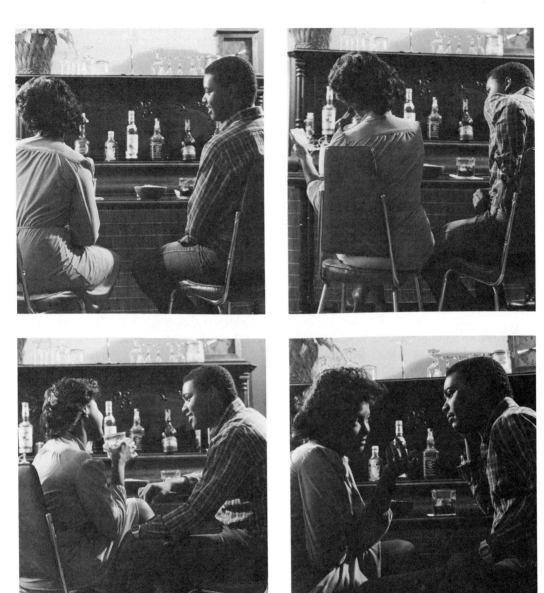

FIGURE 7.7   Stages in Quasi-courtship Behavior: Changes in Proxemics, Kinesics, Physical Appearance, and Paralanguage.

adaptors. This is a message to oneself that an error has been made or that one is tense in the situation. Although the intention is that these messages be limited to the transmitter, the receiver often interprets them.

Shelly Goldberg and Robert Rosenthal investigated self-touching behavior in the job interview.[71] They used four males and females to serve as interviewers in a variety of situations. They found that during a formal interview, self-touching seemed to be suppressed, and males tended to rate applicants higher when they showed a higher rate of self-touching than did females. Foot touching by the interviewees was a significant factor of favorable hiring.

Shari Friedman and Albert Mehrabian studied fidgeting behaviors.[72] Fidgeting was positively and significantly correlated with the tendency to engage in a variety of extraneous activities; fidgeting was also associated with unpleasant and arousable temperament. Other extraneous activities associated with fidgeting include binge eating, daydreaming, physical activities, consuming alcoholic beverages, and cigarette smoking.

The deception of others has received much attention of late. Deception here is defined as an attempt on the part of a sender to ''cover up the true information or affect that he or she feels at that moment.'' Paul Ekman has written that children begin to lie at around age four, usually to avoid punishment. As they get older, their views about lying change. They do not necessarily lie more, but they do improve at it. Ekman suggests that we look at the sound of the voice, the look on the face, and consistency between the movement of the hands and the words being said.[73]

Because deception is probably the most complex of all kinesic factors to determine and because of the importance of searching for consistencies, we will discuss both kinesic and vocal factors involved in deception.[74] J. O. Greene, H. D. O'Hair, M. J. Cody, and C. Yen found that an important variable regarding truth-telling and lying was the *type of lie.*[75] There are *prepared lies* and *spontaneous lies.* Prepared lies are those in which a liar knows that he or she is going to be asked about something. The spontaneous lie is one in which a surprise question is asked. The purpose of the study by Greene and associates was to determine deception by the latency and duration of response, eye contact, and body movement with immediate spontaneous lies and delayed spontaneous lies. Greene and associates asked that subjects respond to specific questions either truthfully or deceitfully to a confederate. Their responses were then surreptitiously videotaped for later analysis. The results indicated that liars exhibited shorter response latencies, less leg/foot movement, less hand movement, fewer illustrators, less affirmative head nodding, and less eye contact than truth tellers. Immediate spontaneous liars were similar to nonliars in response latency but exhibited significantly more head nodding, laughing, and smiling.

Other researchers found that, even without audio cues, subjects could distinguish deceptive messages from honest ones.[76] D. O'Hair, M. J. Cody, and R. R. Behnke studied deception as related to *communication apprehension* (unwillingness to communicate).[77] Highly apprehensive deceivers had higher levels of vocal stress when telling a lie than when telling the truth. Those with low apprehension did not seem to be affected in telling lies versus telling the truth. Mark A. deTurck and Gerald Miller found a number of differences between liars and people who were simply tense.[78] They found that liars spent more time adapting, gesturing with their hands, exhibited longer pauses and response latencies, and spent less time answering questions. Liars *increased* rates of gestures and response latencies; aroused truth tellers *decreased* behavioral rates for the same cues. Table 7.1 displays the results of these studies, which were similar to those of Ekman.[79]

TABLE 7.1   *A Comparison of Prepared Liars and Spontaneous Liars' Nonverbal Communication versus the Truth-Teller, Using Truth-Telling as the Norm*

VARIABLE	PREPARED LIARS	SPONTANEOUS LIARS
Time to answer	Shorter	No difference
Leg/foot movement	Less	More
Hand movement	Less	More
Illustrators	Fewer	
Adaptors	30% more	300% more
Head nods	Fewer	More
Laughing/smiling		More
Facial expressions	NOT A RELIABLE CUE	
Pauses		Longer/more
Speech errors		More

We may say, then, that there are discrepancies among the studies as to how we can detect deception. Generally, we can say that facial expressions are not valid clues to deception, that there is less eye contact and more averted gaze, that messages (particularly answers to questions) are shorter, that adaptors increase, and that there is more time between a question and a response. In addition to these kinesic cues, deception also varies from culture to culture. Deception is better detected when probing questions are asked (which shift a prepared liar to a spontaneous liar), when the liar is a friend or intimate rather than a stranger, when the decoder (receiver) is a male, and when there is more than one interview.[80] Finally, deception is also detected through vocal cues working with kinesic cues and verbal content.

In general, research suggests that we should look at speech rate, speech errors, pitch variation, response latencies, and pauses as major predictors of deception.[81] Tone of voice has been associated with deception, as B. M. DePaulo, M. Zuckerman, and R. Rosenthal, and L. A. Streeter and his colleagues found.[82]

Recent studies have explored the deception function in more detail. These studies indicate that the process of deception is a complex process influenced by several factors. Vocal cues, however, still seem to be relied on heavily by people attempting to detect deception. In a study examining the impact of deception in face-to-face interaction, James B. Stiff and Gerald R. Miller asked people to judge whether other undergraduates were lying or telling the truth.[83] They created the deception conditions by having a confederate ask to cheat on a test as part of the study; in the truthful conditions, no cheating was observed. They were then interviewed about the "strategies" the dyad had used to do so well on their task. Their findings indicated observers relied on several vocal cues. Specifically, they found that observers associated longer pauses and short responses with deceptive communications. Part of Stiff and Miller's study was concerned with how the subjects would react to positive and negative probing during the followup interview. They found that the type of probe produced different evaluations by the observers. Stiff and Miller found that negative probes caused truthful messages to be evaluated significantly more accurately and deceptive messages less accurately (i.e., a negative probe might be, "That's interesting. Come to think of it . . . that doesn't seem very plausible. Could you go into more detail on your strategy and how you thought of it?"; a positive probe might be, "That's interesting. Come to think of it . . . that seems quite plausible. Could you go into more detail on the strategy you used and how you thought of it?").

In another phase of the study, Stiff and Miller had people who were blind to the purpose of the study code the behaviors of the communicators as they were exposed to the probe manipulation. They found that interviewees receiving negative probes had shorter response latencies than did interviewees receiving positive probes. However, later analysis indicated that all the cues, although being relied on by raters judging the deceptive performance, had *no relationship to the actual deceptive performance*. That is, the observers relied on what they felt were deceptive cues, even though the cues were not related to deceptive performances. However, Stiff and Miller also found that *verbal content* was significantly associated with accurate detection of deception, indicating that what is said may be a better cue of deception than how it is said. It may be that we focus on the nonverbal cues to indicate that a deception is occurring; it may also be that once we think a deception is occurring, we fail to switch from the nonverbal message to the verbal.

Mark A. deTurck and Gerald R. Miller found that several nonverbal cues were associated with deception in both aroused (an environmental noise was added to the interaction) and nonaroused (no noise) conditions. Specifically, they found that deceivers encoded more speech errors and pauses, and engaged in increased response latencies and shorter messages; nondeceivers decreased rates on each cue and engaged in longer messages.[84] This finding is similar to that of J. O. Green and colleagues, who found that liars used significantly shorter response times when delivering a planned lie.[85]

What impact does a deceptive communication have on the encoder? D. O'Hair, M. J. Cody, and R. B. Behnke examined the vocal stress associated with deception in interview settings via a physiological measure of voice stress.[86] They also examined whether a person's apprehension toward communication differed from a nonapprehensive person's communication. As part of the study, researchers told subjects that they could earn $25 either by lying about their most recent employer (deceptive condition) or by telling the truth (honest condition). Questions asked by the interviewer (a confederate) were also manipulated so that deceivers would encode a prepared lie ("What was your most recent employment?"), a spontaneous lie ("What were your duties in this position?"), and a delayed deception asked later in the interview ("By the way, what was a typical day like at your most recent job?"). Their results indicated that only the highly apprehensive deceiver produced significantly greater vocal stress in the deception, and only in the prepared lie condition. Spontaneous and delayed deceptions failed to yield any differences in vocal stress. The vocal stress of people with low apprehension did not differ across the three conditions.

These studies demonstrate that deceptive communicators engage in vocal cues that may provide clues to the deceptive performance. However, they also indicate that many other factors are present in the deceptive performance. It is also apparent that being able to see the verbal portion of the message is still more effective in detecting deception than the vocal approach.[87] In daily interactions, we still may examine vocal cues (speech rate, speech errors, and tone of voice) as indicators of *possible* deception. If we find a possible deception occurring, then we can study other kinesic and verbal cues to determine whether we are being deceived.

Variables That Influence Kinesics

Kinesics, like personal space, is influenced by a number of variables. The following are variables that have been shown to affect kinesic communications.

Culture

Kenneth Johnson integrates the kinesic investigations with a detailed analysis of black nonverbal communication patterns. Johnson's hypothesis was that black-white kinesic differences resulted from different cultural backgrounds, the black's patterns having some distant relation to African body movement. Johnson's research deals mostly with walking behavior. Acccording to him, young blacks, particularly males, show defiance of authority by adopting a limp stance, which develops gradually during a conflict encounter: the head is lowered, the body extremely relaxed and motionless. In contrast, young white males assume the opposite stance in such a situation: body rigid, legs spread, arms still at their sides, and the hands forming fists. The young black's limp stance communicates that the authority is talking to thin air and might as well give up because the message is not being received.[88]

Geraldine Michael and Frank N. Willis examined cultural differences between classes and sexes in the United States with respect to the development of nonverbal interpretation and transmission skills in children. A dozen gestures were chosen for which there was an agreement as to meaning, and these were presented to children with no schooling or with one year of schooling. Decoding problems were presented by the interviewer's making a gesture and asking the child, ''What does this mean?'' Low and middle socioeconomic groups were compared, and all groups were racially mixed. Results indicated that middle-class children were ''superior'' to lower-class ones in both transmission and interpretation; boys were found to be superior to girls in interpreting gestures. Michael and Willis found in these experiments that for the interpretation of gestures, the first year of school is more important for lower-class children than for middle-class children.[89]

Other researchers have observed a number of differences in the way various cultures use gestures and what those gestures mean. Haig Bosmajian, for example, has identified 13 expressions that have different gestures in different cultures.[90] Other research indicates that the simple greeting can have many different gestures assigned to it.[91] In French Canada, for instance, typical ''American'' greetings are found (handshake for males; females may embrace if they are close friends). In Puerto Rico, women often greet by grasping the other's shoulders and kissing the cheek. In Italy, persons of the same sex can walk arm-in-arm and women often greet each other by kissing both cheeks. In Saudi Arabia, the most common greeting is a handshake with the right hand.

However males will frequently follow up the handshake by extending the *left* hand to the other's right shoulder and kissing the right and left cheeks. In China, where people do not like to be touched, a nod or slight bow usually serves as a greeting, but the handshake is also acceptable.

In terms of gestures used in other cultures, we find a number of differences. In Canada, for instance, most gestures are similar to those of the United States, with the exception of western Canada, where the smile seems more important, and touching of the other person as a gesture is more allowable.[92] In Puerto Rico, fingers waved downward generally mean "come here." A question of what is happening is sometimes associated with the wiggling of the nose, and people often point with the lips puckered rather than the finger. In Italian culture, gestures with two hands are not appropriate and one should use only one hand for emphasis. In Saudi Arabia it is impolite and offensive to point or to signal Saudis with your hand. Left-handed people must be careful not to eat, gesture, or send gifts or items with the left hand in Saudi Arabia. Pointing the soles of your shoes (such as the American way of putting the feet on the desk) at a Saudi or crossing your legs may be mistaken as signs of disrespect. Finally, in China, a smile is the gesture preferred over a pat on the back or handshake. Hand-holding with the same sex is common, and the Chinese use their open hand rather than a finger to point. They beckon others with their palm down.

Sex

Just as culture brings differences in kinesic behavior, so the sex of the person affects the way he or she acts and reacts. Facial expression is a result of training from childhood and is also a type of sex stereotyping. Boys watch adults and decide they cannot cry because it is not tough and manly. Girls are taught that frowning makes them less pretty. Both sexes learn that when they pout, get mad, cry, or seem sad, they do not look attractive. This is reinforced more for girls, and as a result, most girls smile or maintain a bland, expressionless face in an attempt to look pretty.[93]

In essence, children of both sexes are encouraged not to show *negative* emotions, and women are taught this to a greater extent than men. Males communicate authority, activity, and independence, but females communicate submissivensss, passivity, and dependence through their kinesic behavior.[94] In researching male and female posture, one observes that American women give off gender signals by bringing their legs together, keeping their upper arms close to the trunk, carrying their pelvis rolled forward, and presenting the entire body as a moving whole. The American male, on the other hand, tends to keep his legs apart, moves his arms away from his body, carries his pelvis rolled slightly back, and presents his trunk as moving independently from the arms and hips. In general, males tend to assume open, relaxed postures and expand into available space, whereas females tend to assume tense, deferent postures, taking up little space.[95]

It is generally thought that women have more body sway while walking than do males. Studies by Birdwhistell, however, indicate the opposite is true. The male may subtly wag his hips in a light-right-and-left presentation with a movement that produces a twist at the base of the thoracic cage and at the ankles. The female may present the length of the entire body as a moving whole; the male does not, but moves his arms independently of his trunk. "When around men, many women cross and uncross their legs incessantly, modify their voices, open their eyes dramatically, signifying animated interest in the male, and may also play with their hair."[96] Hence, some stereotypic kinesic behavior may hold true for one sex and not for the other.

As a final statement on the kinesic differences between men and women, it has been observed that during a conversation, women watch and look while listening to their partners.[97] This may be the primary reason women are more sensitive to kinesic messages and respond to them more readily. They may be taught this, and to take the position outlined earlier regarding attribution of behavior, they may be taught what to look for; the female is better able to send those messages also. Women, more than men, tend to smile, nod their heads, and produce a generally higher level of gestural activity; for example, when seeking approval, women tend to nod and smile, both of these being positive yet submissive signs.

Decoding

Our discussion of kinesic behavior has thus far focused on the encoding—or sending—of non-verbal messages. We now turn briefly to what we know about the decoding of nonverbal messages, especially in terms of facial expression and eye behavior. The primary conclusion we draw is that decoding ability is related mainly to the *sex of the decoder.*

Generally speaking, *women have been found to be more accurate than men in decoding honest nonverbal communication.* This conclusion is supported in almost all research associated with decoding differences;[98] however, one study found that men could better decode anger, women could better decode sadness. Additionally, depressed patients have been found to be less accurate in nonverbal decoding, except for the emotion sadness.[99]

Accuracy in kinesic decoding has been found to be related to Ekman and Friesen's emotions. Happiness is the most accurately decoded emotion, followed by surprise, disgust, anger, sadness, and fear. Research has also found that paralinguistic cues that might accompany emotion do not appear to enter into kinesic decoding. Deaf individuals and hearing individuals are no different when it comes to kinesic decoding, although it appears that the pleasantness of the emotion being displayed does differ in accuracy (the deaf are more accurate in unpleasant affective decoding, whereas hearing people are more accurate in pleasant affective decoding).[100] Additionally, people from low-expressive families have been found to be more accurate decoders than those from more expressive families.[101]

Decoding is especially prevalent in the area of the eyes. Studies on the decoding of eye behavior have yielded results in three general areas of investigation: eye contact/gaze, pupil size, and eye direction.

Decoding Eye Behavior

Eye Contact/Gaze Studies indicate that women engage in more eye contact than do men. In 1963, an experiment was conducted with groups of three women and groups of three men; these groups were asked to carry on discussions focusing on solving a problem. Group members were asked to find a name for a newly developed soap product. Each subject had privately selected a name prior to the group discussion. Visual interaction among group members was then observed through a one-way mirror as members tried to complete their task. Observers who were experienced in scoring visual behavior determined from this study that women engaged more in both mutual and nonmutual gaze and held the mutual gaze longer than did men. In later studies, using male and female partners instead of partners of the same sex, it was revealed that women did more looking than men. "Female subjects looked more than males while speaking, while silent, during the interviewers' speaking, and in informal discussions following the interview."[102]

In relationships encountered in daily life, eye contact can send important nonverbal information to others. "We look to the eyes for meaning, and find them so significant that our popular culture would have us believe that masking the eyes alone, while leaving all other personal characteristics—face, hair, clothing, body size, shape and gait—observable is enough to cloud the identity."[103] Eye contact has its positive and negative aspects. Experiments have shown that when people viewed videotapes of "engaged" couples, the couples that looked at one another the most received the highest positive ratings. On the negative side, our parents teach us that it is impolite to stare at others. "We don't like to be stared at, and believe it's impolite for us to stare at others."[104] Research shows that people dislike being stared at when the other person cannot be seen. An example of this is the resentment sometimes felt toward people with sunglasses. We need to be able to see the other person's eyes in order to receive the important visual information relayed through them. Further, the stereotype of "law enforcement" or "hell's angel" associated with chromed sunglasses prompted Don W. Stacks and Frederick W. Stacks to suggest that Auxiliary Coast Guard members remove their chromed sunglasses prior to conducting courtesy boat inspections.[105]

Eye contact is also useful in the regulation of interaction, most notably as a turn-taking signal for speech; eyeball watchers have established that a speaker, when nearing the end of an utterance, looks away from the other briefly, then, on ending, returns the gaze to the others, in effect conceding the floor.[106] This is the case for whites only. Blacks and interracial conversations use other nonverbal cues; in fact, they are almost the opposite. "A naturalistic observation of 63 black and 63 white dyads (same-sex and mixed-sex) corroborated the finding that black listeners gaze less at the speaker than do white listeners."[107]

Additionally, Steven A. Beebe found that "an increase in the amount of eye contact generated by a speaker in a live public speaking situation enhances the listener's perception of the speaker's credibility."[108] Somewhat ironically, in one-on-one situations, Phoebe C. Ellsworth and J. Merrill Carlsmith found that eye contact simply *emphasizes* the content of the message. With positive verbal content, frequent eye contact produced positive evaluations of the message, but with negative content, eye contact produced negative evaluations. Similarly, John Greene and Kenneth Frandsen found that a person's self-esteem is related to the amount of eye contact he or she maintains with others relative to the favorability of the message received: for people with high self-esteem, increased eye contact was found in the presence of a positive message, whereas decreased eye contact was found in the presence of a negative message; for people with moderate self-esteem, eye contact was found to be decreased for both types of messages; and people with low self-esteem used more eye contact when receiving negative messages than when receiving positive ones.[109] That is, eye contact becomes a gatekeeping mechanism whereby certain types of information yield more eye contact and others less. Andrew Abele found that gaze decreased as the other person's behavior became more *predictable;* in other words, averted eye contact by the listener might mean that he or she is bored.[110] Chris L. Kleinke reports that with high gaze, the person is evaluated as attentive, competent, and dominant; high gaze is also associated with perceptions of the person having good social skills, being mentally healthy, and having intense feelings.[111]

Judee K. Burgoon and associates found that there are at least two types of deviation from the expected conversational pattern in interview situations: (1) gaze aversion and (2) constant gaze.[112] Gaze aversion reduces the likelihood of hiring the offending interviewee. Interviewees exhibiting an aversive pattern were seen as incompetent, uncomposed, unsociable, and passive. With constant gaze the interviewee earned more favorable endorsements. The constant gaze interviewee was described in terms opposite to those used in describing averting gaze patterns. The aversion gaze effect was further supported in another study by J. K. Burgoon, D. A. Coker, and R. A. Coker, although constant gaze was *not* perceived as yielding significantly favorable results.[113] There were questions, however, regarding this conclusion, particularly regarding possible gender and confederate effects. Along this line of research, Anthony Mulac and associates investigated male and female gaze in same-sex and opposite-sex dyads.[114] They found no significant differences in gaze behavior of male/male and male/female dyads. However, they found that female/female dyads exhibited more mutual gaze/mutual talk, more mutual gaze/mutual silence, and less individual gaze/small talk than other dyad combinations.

Pupil Size   It has been said that nonverbal communication accounts for more than three-fourths of all human communication. This includes paralanguage, gestures, eye contact, use of space, and various other behavioral patterns. Even features as seemingly insignificant as the pupils have a bearing on what one communicates to those around him. Studies have shown that people who possess larger pupils are perceived as more attractive than those with smaller ones. Albert King, a researcher who studied pupil size and physical attraction, took identical photographs of a woman, and then enlarged the pupils in one photo. He then showed the two photos to a large sampling of people and asked them which picture they preferred. In almost every instance, those tested chose the photo with the larger pupils. When asked *why* they selected one photo over the other, they could not give a reason.[115]

Photographers today are preoccupied with the phenomenon of pupil size. Many fashion photographers for women's magazines actually attempt to enlarge the pupils in their photos. This is especially true for head shots in makeup and perfume ads. The photographer completely darkens the studio and uses a sudden bright flash to obtain this effect in the eyes of the models. The larger pupils tend to radiate an open warmth and can, in fact, be persuasive. "The fashion photographer makes his pictures more explicitly sexy because the climate of today's world is sexually liberated."[116]

The drug belladonna, derived from a poisonous Eurasian plant, also enlarges the pupils. The powder or tincture derived from the leaves and roots of this plant is also used to treat asthma, colic, and hyperacidity, as well as being used for various cosmetic purposes. Use of this drug enlarges the pupils and creates a more physically attractive person. On the other hand, people perceive those with small eyes to be untrustworthy, deceptive, and rather cold. Many people relate this to "criminal eyes."

One researcher has shown how the size of pupils can determine a person's perceived emotional state. He hypothesized that pupil size does not become a relevant variable in a person's perception until puberty. Because girls reach puberty before boys, more girls than boys of the same age should react to pupil size.[117] In an experiment, 121 students aged 11 to 16 years old judged which of two pictures of a teacher's face expressed a greater degree of positive attention and esteem toward students. The two pictures were identical except for pupil size. All age groups rated the pictures with larger pupils more positively. Sex differences occurred in the ratings made by 11- to 12-year-olds, exemplifying a greater degree of positive evaluation by females toward photographs with larger pupils.

An interesting aspect of eye behavior is the correlation between lying and pupil size. Though watching someone's eyes to tell whether or not he or she is lying may seem like an old wives' tale, this concept has been supported by a number of researchers in the field of nonverbal behavior. In 1964, a researcher experimented with four graduate and eight undergraduate students. Stimuli in the form of a series of two-digit numbers were presented to the subjects through headphones. The subjects were asked to listen and repeat the numbers in order when told to do so. It was noted that subjects' eyes constricted during the period between listening to the numbers and repeating them. When repeating the stimuli, the subjects' eyes were dilated as if to "let out" the information. The error rate and pupil dilation increased as information reduction decreased. Therefore, it can be assessed that pupil dilation corresponds positively with the number of internal transformations to be made.[118]

It was noted that lying, which definitely requires some internal transformation, was accompanied by smaller pupil diameters while the lie was being conjured up. Larger pupils were evident while the lie was being told. Ira Heilville observed that subjects' eyes are more dilated during deceptive answers than they were during truthful ones.[119] This and other evidence implies that pupillary dilation reflects the amount of mental effort required to perform a task. However, we do not train ourselves to observe the pupil dilation, relying instead on the frequency of gaze when looking for deception.

Eye Direction   We already know that the brain is divided into two spheres, left and right, and that each sphere controls the opposite side of the body. The amount of information one can derive from this is remarkable. As a general review, the right side, or hemisphere, of the brain controls the emotional and subjective actions; the left side controls the objective and rational functions.[120] The logical person uses the left side most, whereas the emotional person tends to use the right side. This may be called *dominance* or *preferred style,* as we noted in the second chapter. The engineer who calculates all day is probably left-hemisphere dominant, using the left hemisphere more often than the right.

The question arises as to how one may determine the dominant hemisphere. One of the ways is eye direction; a person will look in one direction relatively consistently when asked a numerical question. This indicates which side of the brain is dominant for that function. If a person looks to the left, the right hemisphere may be more dominant, and if to the right, the left hemisphere may be more dominant. There is also a tendency for a person to look in a different direction for a different type of question. In a study by Wayne Weiten and Claire Etaugh, four categories of questions were asked: verbal, numerical, spatial, and musical. The numerical and musical questions were the most obvious. The subjects most often looked right to answer numerical questions (they were consulting their left hemisphere) and left to answer the musical questions (consulting their right hemisphere).[121]

At least one stereotype can be related to these concepts. The origin of the idea that males are more adept at engineering and that females are more adept at liberal arts is possibly illustrated in this study. It was found that no matter what the question was, the males tended to look to the right. This indicates that they were consulting with the left, or numerical-objective, side of the brain. Females, on the other hand, seemed to be using the other, more abstract hemisphere.

As for the psychological aspects of eye movement, the right hemisphere has been associated with nonverbal and passive behavior. It follows, then, that the left hemisphere is more verbal and active. Racquel Gur and Ruben Gur conducted a study that tried to determine whether eye movement would indicate which defensive mechanisms one would be most likely to use. They tested for five defensive mechanisms: (1) turning against others; (2) projection; (3) principalization; (4) turning against the self; and (5) reversal, repression, and denial. Those with left dominance (looked right) tended to project and to turn against others as a defensive mechanism. Those who looked left (or right dominance) used reversal or repressed things and denied them. Principalization and turning against the self had no relation to eye movement.[122] Eye behavior is a real and visible aspect of kinesic communication; indeed, we can learn much about people just by watching their eyes.

☐   **Summary**   ☐

The kinesic subcode examines the impact of gestures on human communication. Gestures can be defined as any bodily movement, including gross corporeal motions and more subtle facial expressions. We examined several perspectives relative to the study of nonverbal communication, with major emphasis on Birdwhistell's and Ekman and Friesen's approaches. Eight functions associated with kinesics were identified, and the research substantiating their impact on human communication was reviewed. Kinesic variables such as culture and sex, which affect how we might interact with others, were then discussed. Finally, the decoding of kinesic behaviors was examined, with major emphasis on eye behaviors. The kinesic subcode helps us to understand better and to be better understood in our communication with others. We turn now to the study of voice.

Chapter Eight

Vocalic Studies

Key Concepts

Definitions

Sound and Its Attributes

Paravocal Communication

Vocalic Functions

Closely related to the study of bodily gestures (*kinesics*) is the study of the vocal "gesture." However, vocal gestures cannot be seen—they can only be heard. Indeed, in the early research, paralinguistic behavior included facial expression: what is said is modified also by the facial expressions that accompany the verbal/vocal message.[1] Over the years, the term *paralanguage* has been used to mean oral and vocal expression. Some researchers have labeled the study of the voice—and its impact on communication—*vocalics,* noting that paralanguage is sometimes confused with other kinesic (facial) expressions.[2] But it is important to realize that although we treat vocalics as a separate subcode, many people do not.

Definitions

Vocal refers to how we say words and includes accent, emphasis, vocal quality, pitch, rate, pause (including silence, a form of vocalic behavior), or anything that adds to the meaning we associate with the verbal. The voice in and of itself has major communicative value, and we are interested in the nonlinguistic aspects of communication.

Sound and Its Attributes

We are dealing primarily with the *sound produced* during speech or conversation. When dealing with sound, we can identify eight attributes, or areas of sound, that contribute to the paralinguistic meaning associated with the linguistic. Here we are talking about loudness, pitch, duration, quality, regularity, articulation, pronunciation, and silence as functions of the vocal cues we use. **Loudness** deals with the intensity of the voice; here loudness is more than simply volume. You can be loud without raising your voice: in many cases, lowering the voice produces the desired result. **Pitch** is the range your voice uses during conversation. Most of us have certain *pitch ranges* (extreme high pitch to extreme low pitch) in our voices. We do not think of pitch much, unless we "break" in the smoothness of transition from one level to another or use a different pitch for some effect.

Duration relates to how long the sound is made. It may also be considered as a *juncture,* or dividing point, between speech clauses.[3] **Quality** is a judgmental aspect of the voice that is associated with the speaker's timbre, tonality, and production of air flow through the glottis (opening in the throat where the sound is made). **Regularity** may be defined as the rate with which we speak and may include stress within the speech (increase or decrease of loudness within a speech clause). **Articulation,** which used to be a major concern of many, concerns the clearness and control of the sound being produced. **Pronunciation,** which is closely related to articulation, deals with both the clearness and control of the sound, the rhythm, and the rate of speech. Finally, **silence** refers to the lack of sound.

What our voices are, how they are interpreted, and how we use them for effect are related to these eight sound attributes. Based on these nonsemantic properties, the way we talk and the words we use convey different meanings.

Paravocal Communication

The conceptualization of paralanguage as content-free speech would seemingly produce an area that does not lend itself to study. After all, if the area is content-free, what can we examine? This problem still perplexes some researchers. However, in 1958 George Trager proposed a way to examine this content-free area and to bring the voice back into relationship with language:

> When language is used it takes place in the setting of an act of *speech.* Speech ("talking") results from activities which create a background *voice set.* This background involves the idiosyncratic, including the specific physiology of the speakers and the total physical setting; it is in the area of prelinguistics. . . . Against this background there take place three kinds of events employing the vocal apparatus: language; variegated other noises, not having the structure of language—*vocalizations;* and modifications of all the language and other noises. These modifications are the *voice qualities.* The vocalizations and the voice qualities together are being called paralanguage.[4]

The **voice set,** or prelinguistic area of vocalics, establishes the contextual features from which the voice is to be evaluated. The voice set provides the background against which we hear the voice. Just as you talk about things of differing intimacy in the differing personal-spacing zones, your voice will differ in the various contexts. Evaluating a voice without considering the context in which it is used results in faulty interpretation. Your voice is different in a quiet, indoor area than it is on a busy street. You use a different voice during a football game than during a speech. The context itself may create a different voice: your pitch levels may change after yelling and screaming at a game; your voice, after the game, is different than it was before the game; finally, you sound different at eight o'clock in the morning than you do at eight o'clock in the evening.

Voice qualities are modifications of the voice. These modifications are specific features of the voice itself and tend to be associated with particular people. Trager identified eight vocal qualities that accompany speech:

1. *Pitch Range:* the range in terms of frequency of pitch (highness or lowness) of the voice.
2. *Vocal Lip Control:* degree of raspness or hoarseness of the voice.
3. *Glottis Control:* the amount of air passing through the throat; ranges from breathy (too much air) to thin/tense (not enough air).
4. *Pitch Control:* degree to which the frequency of pitch is controlled during transitions (''broken'' voice is the image we conjure up when we think of someone with poor pitch control).
5. *Articulation Control:* degree to which the speaker is precise and clear in forming the sounds; yields an impression of pronunciation.
6. *Tempo Control:* rate of the voice (normal speaking rate is approximately 125 words per minute for the total U.S. culture; individuals from the South may speak slightly slower than this, and those from the Midwest or Northeast slightly faster).
7. *Resonance:* amount of reverberation in the head cavity, which helps to determine the timbre of the voice (try saying something while holding both hands on your cheekbones, you will feel a vibration [resonance]; now hold one hand on the cheekbone and use the other to pinch off the nostrils, you should feel less vibration).
8. *Rhythm Control:* the phraseology of the voice in degrees of smoothness; most of us have a particular rhythm to our speech, ranging from a jerky presentation to an almost sing-song phraseology (some stutterers can reduce their stuttering by adopting a sing-song phraseology when feeling a stutter coming on).

Each of these voice qualities tends to identify a particular speaker, and, as we shall see, may induce stereotypical judgments based on their vocal qualities.

Vocalizations are specific features of the voice that characterize a specific voice at very specific points in time. Trager states that we can examine three categories of vocalizations. (1) **Vocal characterizers** are nonlanguage sounds that can be placed on a continuum (usually from positive to negative or with those connotations). Vocal characterizers include laughing, crying, whimpering, yelling, sneezing, moaning, groaning, belching, and voice breaking. (2) **Voice qualifiers** are similar to the vocal qualities already discussed but fall into three categories: intensity (loudness), pitch height, and extent of held sound (duration). These qualifiers are features we sometimes perceive because they are relative to a given point in time. Here we must take into consideration the contextual features that have accompanied the sound production, such as echo, size of room, indoors or outdoors, temperature—all factors that affect sound production. (3) **Vocal segregates** are nonwords used to fill pauses. Formerly, speech teachers taught public speaking students never to fill a pause; in real life we use many vocal segregates, often to let the other person know that we are still speaking even though we may not know specifically what to say. Vocal segregates include such nonsense words as *uh-huh, um, ah, like, you know* (when used to fill a pause), *whatever,* and so forth.

Trager's system, then, allows us to understand the vocal contribution to meaning. Consider the voice qualities, for example, and how, through manipulation of these qualities, we can negate the meaning associated with a verbal statement. The following three phrases are indicative of how we use the voice to emphasize, deemphasize, or change the meaning of the verbal statement:

1. I love you.
2. I hate you.
3. Gee, you're nice.

Now, try to communicate each of the three statements in at least three ways (for example, ''I love you'' lovingly, sarcastically, and hatefully). It should not be too difficult; we use our voice for emphasis almost daily, and some of us are relatively skilled at the art of sarcasm, a paralanguage art form for certain persons.

Other ways of studying the vocalic contribution to communication have been proposed. These include the temporal characteristics of the vocalization—duration, interruption, reaction time latency—and such aspects as silences, pauses, hesitations, disturbances and dysfluencies, and other ways that we can examine the voice over units of time.[5]

Vocalic Functions

Much like the study of kinesics, paralanguage can be examined for the way it functions with the verbal message. These functions, however, are much less refined than those identified with kinesics. One possible reason for this lower level of refinement has been advanced by Hans-Peter Krueger, who suggests that vocalics exist as a small ''window of presence,'' without a past or a future. This window is limited further by having to rely totally on auditory cues that allow for no ''second look'' at the communication as found when studying a visual or spatial dimension.[6] Also, because the focus of study is on the *voice,* a content-free dimension of communication, judgments of meaning will necessarily be less refined.

In what way do vocalics function with the verbal message? The first function concerns identification and self-presentation of the speaker. This function deals specifically with the type of voice the speaker uses in the particular situation and with the speaker's perceptions of effect. The second function is controlling the interaction and concerns both encoder and decoder; it focuses on such vocal cues as hesitations, pauses, and interruptions. The third function concerns the relationship among interactants. The fourth and fifth functions deal with displaying cognitive and affective information.

Before turning to the first function, we need to examine briefly what the ''normal voice'' in ''normal conversation'' is like. Here, we look at the temporal dimensions of the voice and at how it is used in normal conversation over a period of time.

The ''Normal'' Conversation

The research of Hans-Peter Krueger examined normal vocalic communication *patterns* over time and with a variety of different people. His research is unique in that it uses a measuring instrument that is attached to the participant and that records data at preset intervals over a selected period of time. His instrument, LOGOPORT, measures three paralanguage parameters: duration of talk, pause between talks, and speech rate per talk (percentage of time a person speaks within a given talk). LOGOPORT, then, measures nonlanguage variables associated with day-to-day interaction; hence it does not rely on language but instead allows us to examine what a ''normal talk'' might be like. (A *talk* is defined as a conversation between the participant and others that lasts five seconds or longer.)

Krueger's data describe the talk patterns of sixty-six people (male and female students between twenty and thirty years of age) talking over a period of one day. He reports that people have between three and five talks per day. The normal talk lasted between twelve and thirty-eight minutes, and the speech rate varied between forty-eight and seventy-three percent of the talk, indicating, he notes, that about ten percent of the talk time is shared. Krueger also reported that talks have a typical form: a slow beginning period, an intensive speaking period, and a period he describes as ''fading out.'' He notes that this form was not deviated from in any of the interactions analyzed, suggesting ''a highly ritualized interaction behavior.''[7] In analyzing his data further, Krueger concluded not only that the talk patterns were of a particular form but that within talks, people exhibited highly stable speech behavior, regardless of the context in which the talk was conducted.

Now that we have an understanding of what is ''normal,'' we can turn to an examination of the five paralanguage functions identified thus far.

Identification and Self-Presentation

An important function of paralanguage is to help in the identification of others and to aid in interpreting their self-presentations through the type of voice chosen for effect. In this regard, we are talking about the voice type selected for a specific purpose. In general, **voice types** may be used for some sort of effect, or they may approach an ''idealized'' voice pattern. A second aspect of the voice type deals more with a socialization process than with the self-presentational effect. These are specialized vocal segregates that are associated with dialect and accent.

Voice Types   We noted earlier that people often use their voice for effect. Most of us possess certain voice qualities that tend to stereotype us one way or another. The fact that we sometimes use such stereotypes to characterize others or to play roles indicates that the voice type may be quite ingrained in this culture. How many of the following stereotypes have we heard? Males with a breathy voice are effeminate, whereas females with the same voice type are sexy; people who speak fast are brighter than those who speak slow; people who have no rhythm to their voice (are flat) are boring; people with high-pitched voices are weak, nervous, and argumentative; people with low-pitched voices are athletic or stoic. These voice types and the stereotypes we form of people who use such voice types are typical in this culture. Several researchers have examined the relationship between voice type and perceived personality; their results, however, have not always been consistent.

In 1964, Paul Heinberg theorized that there are eleven voice types based on the degree of pleasantness or unpleasantness associated with the voice.[8] Of the eleven voice types and their stereotypes, only one is perceived as ''good.'' The other ten are perceived as ''bad'' or ''unpleasant.'' The good voice type is associated with proper breathing, articulation, tongue position, control of pitch and resonance, and so forth. This is the voice we may ascribe to a professional announcer.

The bad, or unpleasant, voice types are generated from one's own specific vocal qualities. In most cases, these fall into one or more of the voice types, but use (and therefore recognition) identifies most by some type of effect. As you read the following, note which are recognizable.

1. *Breathy:* females perceived as sexy and spacy; males as younger, artistic, and effeminate.
2. *Tense:* older, anxious, nervous, uncooperative, less intelligent, and high-strung.
3. *Breathy-Tense:* four types, all of which are perceived as weak and nervous: husky, harsh, hard, and strident.
4. *Nasal:* whiny, argumentative, lazy.
5. *Denasal:* stuffy, as if the speaker had a cold.
6. *Oratund:* energetic, pompous, authoritative, proud, humorless.
7. *Flat:* bored, sluggish, withdrawn.
8. *Thin:* immature, emotional, sensitive (mainly for females).
9. *Throaty:* sophisticated, less intelligent, careless, older.
10. *Fronted:* artificial, aloof.

L. Malandro, L. Barker, and D. Barker believe that voice types and stereotypes are held by both males and females.[9] They infer that five major vocal areas influence stereotypes: nasality, screeching (shrillness of the voice), softness, monotone voice, and speed (rate). As we shall see, these areas do contribute to stereotypical judgments, but such judgments are made on additional vocal features also.

Ideal Speech   David W. Addington postulates that we type voices according to sex;[10] that is, females are typically perceived in terms of social features in their vocal presentations, whereas males are perceived in terms of physical and emotional power. Given the dated nature of such research (Addington's in 1968 and Heinberg's in 1964), and given the changes in perceptions of sexual stereotypes during the period following this research, one must wonder whether these personality types are still valid.

More recently, Cheris Kramer and H. Giles, J. Scholes, and L. Young have reported that vocal traits may yield an *idealized* voice.[11] Kramer's research utilized a questionnaire consisting of 51 language traits (both verbal and vocal) based on actual content derived from high school and college students. In one study, she asked 466 students from two high schools and a university to rate each of these speech traits as they compared to male and female use; hence she was able to tap the stereotypical "language" used.[12] Table 8.1 presents the fifty-one traits she found. Note that the majority are vocal in nature (marked with an *). She also found that males and females differed on many characteristics (see Table 8.2), with males differentiated on sixteen traits, females on twenty traits. Hence, there exist stereotypical paralinguistic (and language) traits we can associate with each sex. Much like the voice types discussed earlier, however, these traits are probably most identified with strangers; they also may be used for effect.

In a second study, Kramer sought to extend this finding to an idealized speech. This time she was interested in whether her subjects agreed on what an ideal speech type would be and in where males and females differed in their stereotypical perceptions. She found that males and females did not differ on fifty of the fifty-one characteristics identified.[13] The only difference between male and female perceptions of the idealized voice was that males thought it should be a *deep voice* whereas females did not. This finding strongly suggests that Kramer's subjects, both high school

TABLE 8.1   Speech Characteristics Identified by Kramer

*Demanding voice	*Militant speech
	Use slang
*Enunciate clearly	
	*Emotional speech
*Deep voice	
Boastful speech	*Authoritarian speech
	Use many details
*High pitch	
Use swear words	*Serious speech
Use hands and face to express ideas	
	*Forceful speech
*Dominating speech	Lounge, lean back while talking
Gossip	
	*Smooth speech
*Loud speech	Open, self-revealing speech
*Relaxed speech	*Enthusiastic speech
Concern for listener	Explain things thoroughly
Interesting speech	Smile a lot when talking
*Gentle speech	*Stutter
*Fast speech	*Patient speech
	Good grammar
*Persuasive manner while speaking	
	*Logical speech
*Show anger rather than concealing	
it	*Polite speech
Talk about trivial topics	
	*Nervous speech
*Wide range in rate and pitch	Opinionated speech
Look at listener directly when	
talking	*Casual speech
Straight to the point	
	*Aggressive speech
*Friendly speech	Gibberish
*Talk a lot	*Confident speech
Large vocabulary	Blunt speech
Assume listener knows what	Sense of humour in speech
speaker is talking about	

Source: Cheris Kramer, ''Perceptions of Male and Female Speech,''
Language and Speech, 20 (1977), pp. 156–157. Reprinted with permission.
*Vocal characteristic

and college students, perceived the *same* characteristics in their idealized voices. A second concern of her research was to see which characteristics males and females see as being different from the ideal. She found that males differed significantly from the idealized on forty-one traits, whereas females differed significantly on thirty-four of the characteristics. The paralanguage characteristics that did not differ between males and females included a wide range in pitch and rate, authoritarian speech, serious speech, and casual speech. Further, males did not differ from the ideal in high pitch, talk a lot, and emotional speech. Females did not differ from the ideal in dominating speech,

TABLE 8.2   *Speech Characteristics Differentiating Male and Female Speakers*
for Both Males and Females

TRAITS CHARACTERISTIC OF MALE SPEAKERS	TRAITS CHARACTERISTIC OF FEMALE SPEAKERS
*Demanding voice	*Enunciate clearly

*Deep voice
  Boastful speech
  Use swear words
	*High pitch
	  Use hands and face to express ideas
	  Gossip
	  Concern for listener

*Dominating speech	*Gentle speech
*Loud speech	*Fast speech Talk about trivial topics
*Show anger rather than concealing it Straight to the point	*Wide range in rate and pitch
*Militant speech Use slang	*Friendly speech
*Authoritarian speech	*Talk a lot

*Forceful speech
  Lounge, lean back while talking
	*Emotional speech
	  Use many details

*Aggressive speech
  Blunt speech
  Sense of humour in speech
	*Smooth speech
	  Open, self-revealing speech

	*Enthusiastic speech
	  Smile a lot when talking
	  Good grammar

	*Polite speech Gibberish

Source: Cheris Kramer, ''Perceptions of Male and Female Speech,''
Language and Speech, 20 (1977), p. 157. Reprinted with permission.
*Vocal characteristic

loud speech, gentle speech, show anger, militant speech, forceful speech, and aggressive speech. Finally, Kramer found that males and females differed on seven of the fifty-one characteristics, with females differing significantly from the ideal on the following characteristics (females were different from their ideal whereas males were not different from their ideal): females saw themselves as significantly less deep voiced, lower in terms of a sense of humor, higher on gossip, higher on trivial topics conversation, and higher on talk a lot. Males differed from the ideal on two of the characteristics that the females did not: males saw themselves as stuttering more and as being more boastful than the ideal speaker.

These findings clearly show that (1) stereotypical (idealized) voice characteristics exist, and that (2) males and females perceive themselves fairly stereotypically. How valid are these results?

In other words, would the presence of an actual *voice* have changed the results? Attempting to answer this question in part, Giles, Scholes, and Young replicated Kramer's studies with a British sample of eighty undergraduates. Their results were supportive of Kramer's findings in that they found thirty-nine differences between ideal, male, and female characteristics, with an overlap of thirty-two characteristics, and they found that males and females rated themselves as significantly different on forty-six and thirty-four characteristics, respectively.[14] But again, actual voices were not used; the method employed reaction to characteristics rather than to actual voices. However, both sets of research do indicate that fairly strong paralanguage stereotypes exist—and exist *across* cultures.

In 1990, Zuckerman, Hodgins, and Miyake found additional support for the ideal vocal stereotype, using human subjects. They found that vocal attractiveness is just as influential as physical attractiveness. Diane S. Berry found that vocal attractiveness increased strength, assertiveness, invulnerability, and dominance in the male voice; female attractive voices were rated as warm, honest, and kind. Naidoo and Pillay found that stutterers felt uncertain and uneasy in speaking situations.[15]

Vocal Recognition and Voice Prints   Based on the discussion thus far, it should be apparent that we can use our voices for a number of purposes. One purpose of the voice that has received some attention is the **voice print.** The idea behind the voice print is that the voice is unique, much like the finger print, and that we can identify people based on certain vocal qualities. Although we may be able to identify some people by their voices, the relative accuracy with which we do so is questionable.

When a voice print is taken, the voice is analyzed with a spectrometer, which displays a graph of the spoken language. What you actually obtain is a series of waves, some "thicker" than others, and blank spaces. This, then, becomes your identification. As you may surmise, however, the print is only as good as the voice that created it, and one must assume that it is as "true" as the person who created it; in other words, if we disguise our voice, the print will be distorted.

Shirley Weitz comments on the voice print in the following way:

> . . . it often happens [mistaking someone's voice for another] when I call my typist, Barbara Gombach, that I mistake the voice of another woman in her office for hers. Their actual voices are more distinctive than their telephone voices, however, probably because the telephone filters out many important voice characteristics and only carries sound in narrow frequency range.[16]

She goes on to note that the voice print has been used in some criminal investigations (notably recorded telephone conversations). Although some people claim that under proper conditions, "better than ninety-nine percent accuracy can be expected in matching voice samples,"[17] the methods used have been severely criticized. Typically, studies report that accuracy runs only a little better than fifty percent.[18] And although people may claim to be able to identify voices, in reality, accuracy drops off rather rapidly, and as McGehee noted, after about five months, accuracy is only about thirteen percent.[19]

To aggravate the situation, some companies have been selling pencils as "lie detectors." Actually, these are miniaturized stress evaluators. They claim to pick up the stress in a voice, which indicates lying. Can you imagine being told to report to your boss for no apparent reason, being informed that some money was missing, and then being asked whether you took it? Your voice might indicate some stress, which would be picked up by the detector, but this stress would be natural. Instead of recording the natural stress, the detector would indicate lying (a little light would go off, indicating the lie/stress).[20]

In view of what we know about the voice and our ability to "mask," or to use the voice for effect, the voice print should be approached with caution. Perhaps in the future, as we improve our techniques for identifying those features that make our voices "unique," the voice print will become an everyday tool. Until that time, however, we should remember that although our own voices are not particularly "good," we can alter them enough to confuse others. Often a simple thing such as a cold will create enough difference in the voice to deceive others.

How good are we at voice recognition without the help of mechanical aids? Some research indicates that we are not very good at recognizing voices—and that the blind are not any better than the sighted, which would seem to debunk the idea that with blindness, we become better at vocal cues.[21] E. Winograd, N. H. Kerr, and M. J. Spence had students listen to twenty masculine and feminine voices saying both the same message and a different message. In one part of their experiment, they found no differences in ability to recognize the various voices. In a second part of the study, they added a new message along with the old message; findings here indicated that subjects tended to recognize the old voice with the old message rather than the new message. Their subjects reported that the old messages sounded more familiar when they were said by speakers of the same sex as the subjects. The third part of the study examined sighted versus blind subjects' ability to recognize voices, but they found no differences.

It appears that we are fairly poor recognizers of voices, either personally or when aided by a voice print. It also appears, however, that as we become familiar with the voices and messages we hear, some increase in accuracy is obtained, but only when associated with previous messages.

Accents and Dialects   Trager defined a group of vocal characterizers as "nonwords." These vocal segregates can have a dramatic impact on the evaluation of another person's speech. We will take Trager's definition and expand it to include several other nonword classes: dialect, accent, nonfluency, speech rate, response latency, duration of utterance, and interaction rate. Each in its own way influences the positive or negative quality of the vocal message.

All of us speak with a special dialect or accent. This identifier tends to stereotype us according to some grouping. In the United States, for instance, we find three general dialects: Southern, Eastern, and general American (see Figure 8.1). Of the three, the general American is by far the most dominant. In reality, there are probably at least ten major regional dialect areas: Eastern New England, New York City, Middle Atlantic, Southern, Western Pennsylvania, Southern Mountain, Central Midland, Northwest, Southwest, and North Central (see Figure 8.2).[22]

We perceive differently those from dialect regions other than our own. Based on a number of studies, we can infer that people react to others' dialects or accents based on expectations. That is, we expect someone to possess a certain dialect, and if that dialect is present, we evaluate it more positively than if it is not.[23] Drawing on a number of research studies, Judee K. Burgoon and Thomas J. Saine present seven findings based on the credibility of a given speaker's dialect:

1. People don't have a preference for their own regional dialect; they don't consistently rate it highest.
2. General American speech (what Midwesterners speak) is generally viewed as more credible than Southern or New England speech.

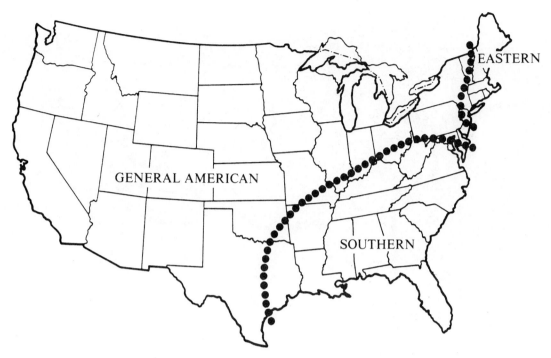

FIGURE 8.1   The Three Major Regional Dialects before 1940.
Source: C. K. Thomas, *An Introduction to the Phonetics of American English*,
2nd ed. (New York: The Ronald Press, 1958).

3. The speech of native-born speakers is rated as more dynamic, more aesthetically pleasing, and reflective of higher socio-intellectual status than that of speakers with foreign accents.

4. Both blacks and whites rate speakers of standard English higher than speakers using a nonstandard dialect (including black dialect). Black speakers who use standard English are assumed to be white.

5. People speaking with a New York accent are rated more dynamic but less sociable than those with a Southern drawl.

6. People speaking with a New York accent or Central U.S. pattern (which is equivalent to General American speech) are rated as more competent than speakers with a New England or Southern accent.

7. Finally, the effects of dialect on a receiver's judgment are short-term.[24]

Anthony Mulac indicates that we evaluate others' dialects along three primary dimensions. His research examined a number of dialects, both foreign and regional, and found that people evaluated others' dialects based on (1) sociointellectual status (status, occupation, income, literacy), (2) aesthetic quality (how pleasing or displeasing the accent or dialect is), and (3) dynamism (how aggressive, strong, loud, or active the voice is).[25]

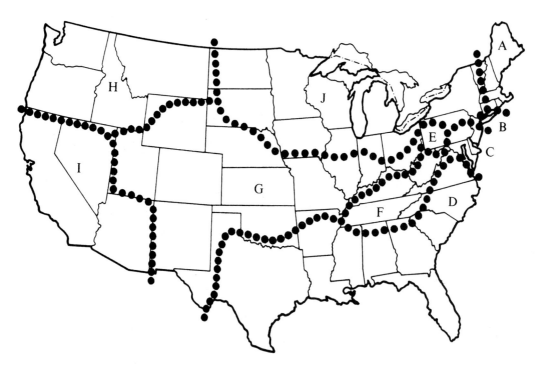

FIGURE 8.2   Dialect Areas: (A) Eastern New England; (B) New York City; (C) Middle Atlantic; (D) Southern; (E) Western Pennsylvania; (F) Southern Mountain; (G) Central Midland; (H) Northwest; (I) Southwest; (J) North Central.
Source: C. K. Thomas, *An Introduction to the Phonetics of American English*, 2nd ed. (New York: The Ronald Press, 1958).

Some researchers believe that accent or dialect has an impact on how people are perceived. Mary Jensen and Lawrence B. Rosenfeld reported that teachers rate children whose accents are different from the subcultural norm as culturally disadvantaged.[26] Other research also indicates that dialect and accent may serve as subtle influencers. Howard Giles, for instance, tested whether standard speech (that which is normal for the given area) would lead to higher perceptions of credibility and expertise for speakers attempting to influence others. He found that although the standard speech was more influential, it was influential only over the less prestigious accents found in the region.[27] This finding may suggest that we identify and prefer a normative level of accent; much like that discussed earlier in chapters 4 and 5 on violations of expectations,[28] it may be that certain accents—relative to our own subcultural accent—are more or less acceptable. Those accents closer to our own will be perceived as more rewarding (more credible, sociable, influential) than those at more extreme (noticeable?) dialects.

The impact of dialect, then, can have an effect on our perceptions of others. Although these perceptions may be short-term, they may influence our initial interactions or even create an impression that is totally wrong, resulting in not communicating with the other person. How specific the dialect and how good you are at identifying it depends upon how perceptive your ear is. It is not uncommon for people who deal with others from all over the United States to be able to place someone to within ten to fifty miles of his or her home town (assuming he or she has not moved recently). One of your authors, while serving in the Army, met someone who could place individuals within a fifty-mile radius of their homes; that person made quite a bit of money with this skill.

Vocal Expressiveness and Body Shape   Typically we expect that certain body shapes (somatotypes) produce certain vocal qualities. We expect the large male to sound like a large male; if he does not, we label him deviant. We expect the little, fragile, female to sound like that. Jim Nabors, in his role as Gomer Pyle, affected a voice that became associated with him, although it was not appropriate for his body type. When he began to sing, people flooded the network wanting to know who was singing for Gomer. Today some of us still have to think twice before associating Nabors' voice with his size.

Research indicates that such judgments should be accepted with caution. N. J. Lass and L. A. Harvey, for instance, found some relation between voice and body shape, but not as great as might be expected.[29] Most of the time, our expectations are based on physical rather than physiological factors. The large person may have a higher pitched voice than the smaller individual. We expect the opposite, however, and attach stigmas to those who do not meet our expectations. This attitude seems to be developing in regard to female athletes; we seem to expect them to sound more like a ''jock,'' with a deeper voice and a more gutteral vocal expression.

Controlling Interaction

A second vocal function concerns the flow and control of a conversation. This section explores the regulating and controlling function first, via the impact of disturbances within the flow of communication and, second, via the impact of interruption, speech rate, and talk duration.

Disturbances   Two areas of paralanguage that have received some attention are speech disturbances and temporal aspects of speech. Here we are referring to nonfluencies, speech rate, latency of response, duration of utterance, and interaction rate.

In the area of speech disturbance, George Mahl concluded in 1956 that speech disturbances can be classified into eight categories (see Table 8.3). His categories suggest anxiety can be measured by a *speech disturbance ratio* determined by the number of speech disturbances divided by the total number of words spoken.[30] As noted in Table 8.3, speech disturbances range from the use of the *ah* and *non-ah* (incoherent) sounds to the correction of sentences as an interruption. Some of his categories seem to be closer to an oral aspect of paralanguage than a vocal one, but a review of the research using his ratio indicates that the *ah* and *non-ah* speech ratio most frequently define speech disturbances associated with anxiety.[31] Interestingly, a study by S. J. Beckman found that males engage in more speech disruptions of the *ah* or *non-ah* variety than do females. Beckman speculated that the male role of assertion and dominance may be stressful and produce more speech disturbances.[32]

More recent research gives us a better idea of the vocal disturbance phenomenon. In a developmental study, Rosemary Dauterive and Donald Ragsdale found that hesitations such as *ahs* and unfilled pauses were used by both children and adults to cover hesitations.[33] They also found that

TABLE 8.3 Speech Disturbance Categories

CATEGORY	DEFINITION
Sentence Correction	Correction in form or content perceived by listener as interruption of word sequences
Sentence Incompletion	Interrupted expression with communication continuing without correction
Stutter	Stutter
Intruding Incoherent Sound	Unrecognizable sound that does not alter the form of expression
Tongue Slip	Neologisms, transposition of words from correct sequences, substitution of unintended for intended word
Omission	Words or parts of words omitted; generally terminal syllables of words
Filled Pauses; Repetition	Unnecessary serial repetition of one or more words
Ah	Definite occurrence of the ''ah'' sound

Source: R. G. Harper, A. N. Wiens, and J. D. Matarazzoo, *Nonverbal Communication: The State of the Art* (New York: John Wiley, Interscience, 1978), p. 41. Reprinted with permission.

the *ah* phenomenon increased with age, especially among females. Among the children studied, females decreased unfilled pauses, and males increased pauses as age increased, indicating a smoother emergent speech pattern for females. Dauterive and Ragsdale also reported that stuttering showed increased peaks at ages three, seven, and eight. The implication here, when combined with earlier research, is that females' speech patterns smooth out as they get older, whereas males' patterns tend to become more disruptive. Beckman assumed that as males begin to fulfill societal roles of assertion and dominance, they will indicate such change through their speech patterns. This study clearly supports such a view.

Verbal fluency has also been examined from both encoding and decoding perspectives. From an encoding approach, research indicates that speech patterns with the encoding of a message are less fluent (contain more pauses, filled pauses, hesitations) when involvement in the conversation is low and when the communication topic is novel or presented by people untrained in message preparation.[34] From a decoding perspective, more fluent verbal presentations have been identified with source authoritativeness, attractiveness, and professionalism.[35] Verbal fluency, however, also has a down side. Lawrence Hosman and John Wright found, for instance, that whereas perceptions of witnesses' authoritativeness and attractiveness increased with lower levels of hesitations, guilt-iness attributions *increased*.[36]

Temporal Dimensions   The temporal aspects of vocalics have been studied in some detail by Joseph Matarazzo and Arthur Wiens and their colleagues. This body of research has concentrated on the impact of the duration of utterance, the reaction-time latency (amount of time between two speech units), and the amount of interruptions in conversation.[37] Most of the research reported in this area has dealt with interviews in which the frequency of these three variables has been manipulated. What has been found is that by manipulating the duration of utterance, one person can influence how long another's utterance will be; the frequency of interruption by an interviewer produced similar interruption frequency by the interviewee. We can expect then, as we make our utterances longer or shorter, that we unconsciously influence others along a similar line. In terms of interruption behavior, the more or less we interrupt, the more or less will others. In a fascinating study, Michael Ray and Eugene Webb found that the frequency of President John F. Kennedy's response rate to a reporter's questions correlated highly with the length of questions posed.[38] Other research indicates that interruptive behavior is associated with less empathic listening behavior and lower interpersonal orientations toward others.[39]

Finally, there may be racial and gender differences in temporal speech. Melanie Booth-Butterfield and Felicia Jordan observed paralanguage behavior among black and white females in same-race and mixed-race groups. They found that black females in all-black groups were more nonverbally expressive than their white counterparts in all-white groups and that the black females interrupted other black females more than they interrupted white females. When the interaction was *mixed,* however, the black participants' level of interruption changed more than did the level of the white participants.[40]

Sexual differences in temporal behavior are less than conclusive. Although it has been reported that males have longer talk periods than do females[41] and interrupt more than do females,[42] such findings have been questioned.[43] In a study that reexamined these findings, Kathryn Dindia had 30 male and 30 female undergraduates engage in unstructured conversations (they were not told what to talk about) in same- or opposite-sex dyads.[44] Unlike earlier research, she found that (1) men did not interrupt more than women and that women did not get interrupted any more than did men; (2) interruptions were asymmetrically distributed in *both* same- and opposite-sex dyads, but it was *not* the male who interrupted more in opposite-sex dyads; and (3) women's less assertive behaviors were not interrupted—nor were their interruptions less assertive—and women's responses to interruptions were as assertive as males. Like the research reported by Kennedy and Camden in 1983,[45] she found more interruptions occurring in opposite-sex dyads than in same-sex dyads, but both males and females were more likely to interrupt and be interrupted by an opposite-sex partner than a same-sex partner. And, unlike West and associates' earlier findings,[46] interruption was not a function of sex.

Dindia did find that male and female interruption behavior did differ according to the type of conversation being carried out. In supportive conversations (where one partner seeks or gives agreement, acceptance, or approval), females were less likely to interrupt, but they were more likely than males to interrupt when the conversation was informational in nature (where one partner gives or seeks information, suggestion, or opinion), regardless of the sex of the person they were interrupting. Males in opposite-sex dyads were more likely than females to use disconfirming interruptions, and they were more likely to use disagreeing interruptions when interrupting another male than when interrupting a female (and were more likely to use disagreeing interruptions than was a female interrupting a male or female). Finally, Dindia found that males and females were *equally* likely to reinterrupt when interrupted; hence, interruption begets interruption, regardless of the sexual composition of the interaction.

One final area, that of interaction rate, implies that the stereotypical expectation that females interact more and talk longer than do males, is not true. *A significant body of research now indicates that men not only speak longer, use more words in the total interaction, and participate more in group discussions, but they also talk more than do females.*[47] The interaction rates for males and females differ, but not in the expected direction. This finding may be interpreted as stemming from a culture in which males are expected to be more domineering and assertive than females.[48]

Further support for rate of speech effects has been provided by R. Street, R. M. Brady, and R. Lee. Their research infers that perceptions of male and female sources' rate of speech are influenced by the context of the communication. They found that males were rated as significantly more competent and socially attractive when the rate of speech was fast to moderate. For females, however, only perceptions of competence were increased with faster rate. Moreover, the speakers were perceived as more competent on the basis of rates of speech when they were engaged in normal conversation than when they were in an interview setting.[49] In continuing this line of research, Street has also found that speech rate contributed to evaluations of interviewer competence and social attractiveness. His findings also indicated that male interviewer/male interviewee dyads converged on their vocal cues, whereas male interviewer/female interviewee dyads diverged on their vocal cues.[50]

Speech rate has also been correlated with personality. George Ray tested how the voice related to personality types and perceptions of competence and benevolence.[51] He found that rates of speech were related to judgments of competence, with rapid rates associated with more competence. The prototype competent speaker also exhibits a higher pitch range and is louder. The prototype benevolent speaker exhibits a low rate and a high-pitched speech.

Regulating the Conversation

Perhaps the major function of vocalics is the regulation of a conversation. These turn-taking cues—cues indicating that we want to maintain a synchronous interaction pattern, that we want to maintain our turn, that we want to get rid of our turn, or that we want someone else's turn—are examined in terms of Starkey Duncan's cultural turn-taking signals and through work on terminating interaction.[52]

According to Duncan, we structure our interactions according to a cultural rule that goes something like this: I have a turn, you have a turn, I have a turn, you have a turn. . . . This structuring of interaction is called **sequencing.** As long as the sequencing is synchronous, as long as the change from my turn to your turn is smooth, the structure of the interaction follows the cultural norm. However, there are times when that sequencing breaks down; although a number of things can disrupt the sequencing, usually two major reasons can be found. First, one of the participants does not want to take his or her turn in the conversation, thus yielding a long "switch pause." Second, one of the participants interrupts, crosses over into the other's turn. We examine instances of the first type.

Table 8.4 presents a graphic representation and a verbal sequencing of proper and improper turn-taking. Note that each turn represents the total speaking time each person has in the interaction (defined here as a simple interaction of four utterances). The space between the turns are pauses.

TABLE 8.4 Structuring the Interaction

A. Proper sequencing:

$Turn_{1.1}$ $Turn_{2.1}$ $Turn_{1.2}$ $Turn_{2.2}$ . . . $Turn_{1.n}$ $Turn_{2.n}$

        switch pause

B. Improper sequencing:
    $Turn_{1.1}$ $Turn_{2.1}$ $Turn_{1.2}$

C. Examples of sequencing:

    Jerry: Hi, how ya' doing?
     Bill: Fine, how's Nan and the kids?
    Jerry: Doing good. And Ashley?
     Bill: See you later.

D. Example of improper sequencing:

    Jerry: Hi, how ya doin?
     Bill: Fine, how[INTERRUPTION]
    Jerry: How's Ashley . . .

As long as the sequencing is moving synchronously, there are no problems; however, as the sequencing becomes more ragged or unsynchronized, problems may arise (remember that interruptions beget interruptions).

The impact of sequencing can be observed in the conversations of people who are of varying degrees of acquaintance. Thomas J. Saine maintains that the proper sequencing of an interaction may be in part a function of the similarity or level of agreement in the interaction.[53] This he calls synchronous behavior. Obviously, in times of stress or of initial interactions (where similarity is low), synchrony may be low. The degree of synchrony in a relationship may be indicative of the relational level of that relationship.

Turn Cues   Within a conversation you usually play one of two roles. You are either the speaker or the listener (sometimes called *auditor*). When you have your turn, there are certain cues you use to maintain that turn or to signal the listener that you are ready to let him or her talk. The other person may accept (and he or she is now the speaker), or that person may indicate that you are to keep the ''floor.'' Within each of these roles, certain cues may be used to signal a desire either to keep, to give up, or to refuse the turn. These cues fall into the categories of turn-maintaining cues, turn-yielding cues, turn-suppressing cues, and turn-taking cues.[54]

Turn-Maintaining Cues   When you are speaking and the listener seems to be signaling an attempt to take your turn (interrupting or engaging turn-taking behavior), you can suppress the other person by engaging in several paralinguistic cues. Taking an audible breath, using a sustained intonation pattern (falling or rising intonation patterns signal a willingness to stop talking), and using vocalized or filled pauses should inhibit the other's attempt.[55] Duncan suggests that the use of only a single turn-suppression cue will stop interruptions by the listener.[56]

Turn-Yielding Cues   When you want to stop speaking, there are several vocal cues available. First, create a rising intonation pattern, one that suggests a question has been asked. Second, use a falling intonation pattern or draw out the final syllable of the clause at the end of your statement. Third, stop speaking; silence usually induces the other to take the "floor."

Turn-Suppressing Cues   Suppose that you do not have anything to add to the conversation, or that you are afraid to speak. What cues can you use? When we discussed Paul Ekman and Wallace V. Friesen's approach to kinesics, you may recall, head nods and smiles were called *backchannelling* cues. You can do the same with paralanguage cues; the cues you use in this case to indicate agreement with the speaker would fall in the vocal segregate class. In this manner you would use such nonwords as *uh-huh, yep,* or *ahhh,* each confirming the speaker and indicating, "all right, I agree, keep on talking."

Turn-Taking Cues   Perhaps you want to say something, but the other person will not let you speak. Most of the turn-taking cues seem to be kinesic in nature (eye contact, facing behavior, leaning, raised hand, straightening of the back, etc.)[57] but there are at least two paralanguage cues available. One is called a stutter-start; you try to break in with a "b, b, b, but" or similar cue. The second is the interruption, in which you cross over into the speaker's turn and continue speaking. Remember, however, that interruptions seem to foster interruptions.

Pauses   One of the ways we can examine the structure of an interaction is by the use of pauses. Pauses also allow the speaker to maintain his or her turn, or they allow the listener a chance to gain a turn. In general, a **pause** is a silence in the turn or between turns. If it is within the turn it may be a *hesitation.* Hesitations are either filled or unfilled, and they yield the expected consequences. A second type of pause is the *switch pause,* the silence found between turns. The third type of pause is that imposed by others, *imposed pauses;* pauses of this nature are usually governed by some norm or rule. Tom Bruneau states that such imposed pauses are either a function of the environment (hospital zone, funeral) or in response to some role expectation.[58]

   Sometimes the type of pause yields the turn ending. The switch pause usually signals a synchronous exchange of turns. This type of pause results in closed turn endings; these turn endings are very short. Two other forms of endings are the *interruption,* which is an overlap of one turn over the other, and the *open turn.* Open turns are overlong spaces between turns and are indicative of nonsynchronous sequencing. These are usually found when relationships are just beginning or when stress is placed on one or more of the people interacting.

Impact of Turns   Recently, a number of researchers have been examining how turns operate in day-to-day interaction. As discussed earlier, turns are related to the synchrony of conversation between people. This synchrony is apparently learned early in life, even before formal education is begun.[59] Such a finding should not be surprising since conversational *coherence* is something that we pick up early in life; we learn at a very early age, "Don't interrupt," "Wait your turn," and "You can talk as soon as I'm finished." The impact of appropriate turn-taking and turn-yielding, however, has been found to be associated with such personality-related variables as interpersonal orienting, self-monitoring, and self-disclosing. Richard Street and Thomas Murphy report that people who are low in interpersonal orientation, especially males, are less vocally active and engage in *less consistent* communication (as measured by turn duration and backchannel responses). Their speech fails to converge with the other person's.[60] The implications of this study are twofold. First, a person's interpersonal orientation is expressed through paralanguage cues, which are directly related to the structure of the interaction. Second, highly interpersonal-oriented people "may be able to perform some behaviors, such as vocal and certain nonverbal behaviors, more consistently and to modify others behaviors, such as self-disclosures, to a greater extent than individuals less concerned with self-presentations [low interpersonal-oriented people or low self-monitors]."[61]

The implications of such a finding have been demonstrated in a study conducted by Deborah A. Coker and Judee K. Burgoon.[62] Coker and Burgoon were interested in finding what nonverbal cues were present when conversations become more involving. They hypothesized that increased involvement in a conversation would produce increased nonverbal cues on several dimensions, including paralanguage. They asked students to engage in dyadic conversations. After a few minutes, the dyads were separated, and one of the students was asked to act as a confederate in the next stage with the same partner by either increasing or decreasing the conversational involvement. They found not only that increased involvement yielded more vocal expressiveness and relaxed laughter, but that the interaction was better managed. Specifically, they found fewer silences and response latencies between turns and in general a more coordinated speech. This finding is similar to Street's finding of male-male convergence on turn duration and male-female divergence in an interview setting; Street's results may be due to perceptions of similarity and involvement on the part of male-male dyads.

Finally, there has been some research suggesting that turns around some types of silence follow a particular backchannelling pattern. In 1982 Margaret L. McLaughlin and Michael J. Cody found that conversations in which an "awkward silence" occurred due to a "minimal response" were sequentially repaired by a question/answer response.[63] This finding suggested that participants engaged in backchannelling behaviors (question/answer sequences) to repair the damage done to the conversation's coherence. Kathryn Dindia attempted to replicate these findings (in light of methodological and statistical advances unavailable to McLaughlin and Cody in 1982), but she failed to replicate the repair sequence.[64] Although she found that minimal responses did predict silence in an interaction, it did not predict much of the reason for that silence, nor was she able to find McLaughlin and Cody's question/answer repair sequence. It would appear that synchronous turn-taking behaviors are a function of many nonverbal behaviors; research on paralanguage cues and personality variables associated with turn-taking indicates that although paralanguage cues are important to conversational coherence, there are a multitude of other variables of equal or more importance.

Physiological Correlates of Regulation   The vast majority of research on turn-taking and regulation has used either an experimental or a field-experimental paradigm whereby conversations are conducted, and then the behaviors are coded for particular nonverbal behaviors such as silence, speech rate, vocal expressiveness, coordination of conversation, and so forth. Krueger has taken the observational study one step further with the use of LOGOPORT. His research suggests that turns occur in sequences over time and that vocal characteristics can help determine whatever lag may exist in such sequences. For example, he reports that flirtation is characterized by highly synchronous behavior, so synchronous that neither participant actually holds the floor because both parties enact both dominant and submissive roles in the communication. When engaged in a quarrel, however, when neither party is dominant *nor* submissive (or one would have ''won'' the argument), the synchrony is lessened.[65] LOGOPORT charts cued to the loudness of the interaction provide a convincing picture of the interactions. Interpretation of the charts is through the ''hills'' and ''valleys'' associated with the measured loudness. In the case of flirtation, oscillation periods are short, indicating that the turns are progressing quite synchronously; a quarrel, however, yields longer oscillation periods, indicating that synchrony is less and that sequencing is rougher. Also, the hills and valleys converge in a flirtation segment but diverge in a quarrel segment.

Class Variables in Turn-Taking It also appears that there may be a socioeconomic class difference in turn-taking behavior. O. Robins, S. Devoe, and M. Wiener have come to four conclusions regarding vocal behavior:[66]

1. *Working-class speakers* emit unfilled pauses, upward inflection, and open inflection behaviors significantly more often and in significantly greater absolute numbers than do middle-class speakers.

2. *Middle-class speakers* emit filled pauses and downward inflection behaviors significantly more often and in significantly greater absolute numbers than do working-class speakers.

3. *Working-class speakers* emit a greater variety of regulators that can be considered ambiguous in significantly greater numbers and significantly more often than do middle-class speakers.

4. *Middle-class speakers* initiate continuation regulators significantly more often and in significantly greater numbers than do working-class speakers.

Thus, the means of continuing or discontinuing conversations tend to vary according to socioeconomic class.

Relationship of Interactants

Vocalics also function to establish certain relationships between people. These relationships may be on several levels, but the ones of most interest to us can be split into two areas: (1) vocal cues of attraction, influence, and credibility and (2) vocal cues of *emotion*. In this section, we briefly examine the impact of the voice on such relational topics. The cues produced by the voice become greater than their sum total. Hence, we may get multiple messages from one or two cues, messages that may complement or contradict each other. We turn first to messages that indicate the relationship one person may have toward the other.

Attraction, Influence, and Credibility As should be evident by now, vocal cues function not only to establish how one person perceives the other, but also to establish whether one is trying to influence the other. As such, relational vocal cues may provide indicators of social attractiveness, composure, extroversion, competence, benevolence, warmth, and influence.[67]

Vocal cues associated with perceptions of personality variables were discussed earlier. A review of this research from a relational perspective suggests that a slightly faster rate, more pitch change, and low loudness is associated with credible speakers, at least as concerns speaker competence and benevolence, with pitch variation more important than loudness for benevolence. Perceptions of social attractiveness seem to be positively related to speech convergence, slightly faster speech, and shorter response latencies. Supportive conversations yield cues of expressiveness; interaction (fewer silences, latencies, and more coordinated speech); more vocal warmth, interest and pleasantness; and less anxiety (more vocal relaxation and attentiveness).

Research on apprehension, or reticence, suggests that the reticent speaker engages in more stressful vocal behavior. However, Judee K. Burgoon and associates demonstrated that the speaker who avoids communication engages in less vocal *potency* cues (loudness, tempo, intensity, and tempo).[68]

Vocal cues have a demonstrated effect on influence attempts. Research indicates that a faster rate of speech, more intonation, higher volume, and more fluent speech improves persuasiveness.[69] This pattern is similar to what might be labeled *pleasant* or *rewarding*. In 1980 Judith Hall found that people complied with a request more often when the voice was pleasant (warm, friendly) than when it was neutral (stiffer, colder, more businesslike).[70] In an extension of Hall's research, David B. Buller and Judee K. Burgoon added a neutral voice and also tested for receivers' sensitivity to nonverbal cues. Their results duplicated Hall's 1980 findings for the neutral (which approximated Hall's neutral voice) and pleasant voices, and found that hostile voices were perceived as nonintimate, tense, nonimmediate, and dominant. When looking at good versus poor decoders, they found that:

> poor decoders seem to discriminate the voices less on intimacy than good decoders and provide different arousal interpretations than good decoders to pleasant voices: the pleasant voices were seen as relatively tense by poor decoders and relatively relaxed by good decoders. . . . [Results indicated that] highly affiliative good decoders may employ positive, affiliative, composed, and sociable voices when attempting to gain compliance from them. . . . On the other hand, more socially anxious poor decoders may encode assertive, aloof, dynamic, and unsociable voices when attempting to gain compliance and prefer such voices when others attempt to gain compliance from them.[71]

Influence attempts, then, are a function of the relationship between the vocal cues and the decoding ability of the receiver.

Emotion   Much of what we communicate is abstract, and this abstraction is further muddied when we attempt to label our inner feelings. Nonverbal communication is especially relevant when attempting to identify emotions and emotional states. The role of the voice in this process is significant, yet not as well researched as kinesics has been. What we know of the vocal relationships with emotion are shown in Table 8.5, which was compiled from research conducted by Klaus R. Scherer[72] and by Judee K. Burgoon and Thomas J. Saine.[73] Scherer found that eight vocal characteristics were associated with vocal displays of emotion:

1. *Amplitude variation*—moderate (pleasantness, activity, happiness) and extreme (fear)
2. *Pitch variation*—moderate (anger, boredom, disgust, fear), extreme (pleasantness, activity, happiness, surprise), contour up (potency, anger, fear, surprise), and contour down (pleasantness, boredom, sadness)
3. *Pitch level*—high (activity, potency, anger, fear, surprise) and low (pleasantness, boredom, sadness)
4. *Tempo*—slow (boredom, disgust, sadness) and fast (pleasantness, activity, potency, anger, fear, happiness, surprise)

TABLE 8.5   *Vocal Cues of Emotion: Acoustic Parameters of Tone Sequences Significantly Contributing to the Variance in Attributions of Emotional States*

EMOTIONAL STATE	CUES[a]
Pleasantness	Fast tempo, few harmonics, large pitch variation, sharp envelope, low pitch level, pitch contour down, small amplitude variation (salient configuration: large pitch variation plus pitch contour up)
Activity	Fast tempo, high pitch level, many harmonics, large pitch variation, sharp envelope, small amplitude variation
Potency	Many harmonics, fast tempo, high pitch level, round envelope, pitch contour up (salient configurations: large amplitude variation plus high pitch level, high pitch level plus many harmonics)
Anger	Many harmonics, fast tempo, high pitch level, small pitch variation, pitch contours up (salient configuration: small pitch variation plus pitch contour up)
Boredom	Slow tempo, low pitch level, few harmonics, pitch contour down, round envelope, small pitch variation
Disgust	Many harmonics, small pitch variation, round envelope, slow tempo (salient configuration: small pitch variation plus pitch contour up)
Fear	Pitch contour up, fast tempo, many harmonics, high pitch level, round envelope, small pitch variation (salient configurations: small pitch variation plus pitch contour up, fast tempo plus many harmonics)
Happiness	Fast tempo, large pitch variation, sharp envelope, few harmonics, moderate amplitude variation (salient configurations: large pitch variation plus pitch contour up, fast tempo plus few harmonics)
Sadness	Slow tempo, low pitch level, few harmonics, round envelope, pitch contour down (salient configuration: low pitch level plus slow tempo)
Surprise	Fast tempo, high pitch level, pitch contour up, sharp envelope, many harmonics, large pitch variation (salient configuration: high pitch level plus fast tempo)

Source: From "Cue Utilization in Emotion Attribution from Auditory Stimuli" by Klaus R. Scherer and James S. Osinsky, *Motivation and Emotion,* 1, No. 4 (1977), p. 340. Reprinted with slight modifications, with permission of Plenum Corporation and the assistance of Dr. Scherer. Also from J. K. Burgoon and T. J. Saine, *The Unspoken Dialogue: An Introduction to Nonverbal Communication* (Boston: Houghton Mifflin, 1978), p. 205.

[a]Single acoustic parameters (main effects) and configurations (interaction effects) are listed in order of predictive strength.

5. *Duration*—round (potency, boredom, fear, disgust, sadness) and sharp (pleasantness, activity, happiness, surprise, sadness)
6. *Filtration*—low (sadness, pleasantness, boredom, happiness), moderate (pleasantness, boredom, happiness, potency, activity), and extreme (potency, activity, anger, disgust, fear, surprise)
7. *Tonality*—atonal (disgust), tonal-minor (disgust, anger), and tonal-major (pleasantness, happiness)
8. *Rhythm*—not rhythmic (boredom) and rhythmic (activity, fear, surprise)

As can be seen, vocal characteristics provide a lot of information relevant to emotional states, but note also that many of the emotional expressions overlap, making accurate judgments difficult with vocal cues alone.

Display of Cognitive Information

While the display of cognitive information is an important function of nonverbal communication in general, it is less important in vocalics than in some other areas such as kinesics. We must remember, however, that often when we try to instruct someone else, we do use the voice to gain their attention and to emphasize a point. Sometimes, when we feel the other is not understanding, we get louder, as if increasing our loudness will make us clearer.

Display of Affective Information

As has been indicated in other sections of this chapter, our vocal tone can tell others how we feel physically or psychologically. Certainly we can tell when one is intoxicated through vocal intonation, slurs, and the like. We can also usually tell when one is depressed, if we have a ''normal'' baseline to operate from. Screams of anger, fear, joy, and surprise all differ from one another. Parents often know whether to go to an infant's room based on the kind of cry.

•

□   **Summary**   □

Vocalics serve several functions. Of most importance, however, are the regulation of interaction and the stereotypic expectations we have of people based on their voices and vocal type. In many cases these expectations are either confirmed or disconfirmed. Thus, some of the more stereotypical judgments about sexual differences may not be true. Males may be the ones who talk the most, perhaps in compliance with a social norm that indicates they must be more assertive and dominant. This section has examined several diverse approaches to the study of vocalics. Trager's categorization system should provide us with a basic starting point, which some day may terminate in a true voice print. At this time, however, identification (through electronic or interpersonal means) should be approached with caution; we really are too good at masking our voices to concede complete effectiveness to such devices.

Chapter **Nine**

Studies on the Covert Subcodes of Nonverbal Communication

Key Concepts

Feedback Systems

Biofeedback

Olfaction

Chronemics

This chapter attempts to expand your knowledge of nonverbal communication through the study of a subcode that is less apparent than kinesics and vocalics. Unlike physical appearance, proxemics, and kinesics, it cannot be seen. Unlike vocalics, it cannot be heard. Despite touch being a sense that is used less often by adults, we find that the covert subcode is even less dominant. Here we are talking about low-conscious perceptions, especially the senses of taste, smell, and time.

Feedback Systems

There are systems that operate at or just below consciousness and that are important to nonverbal functioning. Here we are concerned with the psychological and physical systems that operate to establish our daily rhythms, moods, and emotions.

Gustatory Systems

Although there are many perspectives to the study of nonverbal communication, the one perspective that underlies most, if not all others, is that different nonverbal subcodes can be identified through the various sensory systems available to humans. To this point, we have discussed three of the five physical senses: the auditory sense (paralanguage), the visual sense (kinesics, proxemics, physical appearance), and the touch sense (haptics and possibly physical appearance). We have not introduced the gustatory sense, although some consider this sense to be a nonverbal subcode,[1] we believe it to exist within the ''invisible'' system. Gustatory (oral taste) tactile communication, we believe, is rightfully a part of the perceptual system, but more as a feedback system than as an actual nonverbal subcode. We believe that gustatory systems operate more as an information system.

In a series of studies that examined the perceptual system's accuracy as compared with other forms of assessment, Norman Lass and associates examined the feedback mechanisms that are associated with oral gustatory (tactile) perception.[2] According to Lass and others, there are at least three monitoring systems that provide information: auditory feedback, tactile feedback, and kinesthetic feedback. Lass was more interested in the impact of tactile feedback, especially in light of visual versus tactile (oral) recognition of shapes. In a series of studies, they found: (1) that the tactile system was as accurate as, if not more accurate than, the visual system, (2) that verbal feedback on shape (correct or incorrect) did not affect performance on a test of oral form discrimination; (3) that no specific learning appears to be operative (performance seems to be the same in the course of a number of trials); and (4) that location of the form in the mouth significantly affected performance. These findings, when added to those of the telepathic system, suggest two conclusions: (1) human beings can receive messages from other than ''normal'' systems (that is, for shape recognition at least, telepathic and tactile assessment are potential forms of communication); (2) there are other forms of communication, which may be unconscious (or at least found just below conscious awareness), that affect our behavior and our assessment of things, and that may influence our thoughts. Such forms may be examined as biofeedback systems.

In 1989, Murray Cox reported that the sense of taste is almost impossible to kill. He suggests that by the year 2000 we will shock our tongues with ''electric taste.'' Food will be electrically charged with positive or negative electrodes that will make our mouths erupt with flavor. Taste and smell are separate senses that work in concert with one another. He states that tastes change with the times and that they are also regional. People in the southwestern part of the United States prefer spicy foods while those in the Southeast prefer a smoked flavor. Cox has indicated that some 10 million Americans suffer from disorders of taste and smell senses—and often complain that food tastes like cardboard. Finally, as we get older our sense of smell decreases, but our sense of taste does not.[3]

Biofeedback Systems

Within the human being there are several types of biofeedback systems, each affecting the individual in a different way. In particular, we note that the skin, the musculature, heart rate, blood pressure, and brain waves serve as potential biofeedback systems.[4] We mention these because each operates most of the time at or below our consciousness. Of all major feedback systems, perhaps the skin is one of the most important. As Ashley Montagu has noted, the skin is a tremendous communication receptor. It serves as more than a protection device; it also serves to communicate back to the brain differences in the environment as well as the absence or presence of others.[5]

A second type of feedback is the muscle system. The muscle system, like the skin, serves an essential function, but one that is not completely understood. When we see someone we are attracted to, for instance, our muscle system changes, pulls or pushes, and alters our posture and even our pupils. Such changes are hardly noticed by the individual engaged in the communication;

they are usually subtle, yet effective. Such feedback systems may be the modern answer to the preening behaviors of lower animals or sexual display rituals.[6] We will examine more of this later in the chapter on social interaction.

Heart rate and blood pressure are related biofeedback systems. These subtle changes also have a communicative function; in many instances, however, they are interpreted as stress or other negative behavioral indicators.[7] Such findings as the Sika deer studies and Calhoun's rat studies are indicative of biofeedback systems functioning abnormally. The same may be true concerning some of the studies of crowding we examined earlier.

Finally, there are the brain waves. This system is gaining more attention as we learn how the brain operates. Several studies, some like those by the Soviets, indicate that different brain waves are associated with varying types of activity. As we have noted, perhaps there is a special "brain wave" receptor in the right hemisphere that receives such input, a receiving device that we may have been conditioned by the left hemisphere to ignore as illogical. A number of studies, however, suggest that alpha waves (those brain waves associated with a relaxed or rested state)[8] and lateralized alpha waves (those alpha waves that come from each hemisphere as a function of processing task)[9] can serve as significant biofeedback devices in a variety of communication modes.[10]

In general, the research on alpha waves and lateralized alpha waves indicates that we suppress this alpha activity when we are processing material or information that is associated with a particular hemispheric style. For instance, Monte Bushsbaum and Paul Fedio found alpha suppression in the left hemisphere when the activity called for the processing of linguistic information; right hemispheric alpha suppression was found for spatial tasks.[11] Other researchers have found similar results.[12] Further, at one time, the suppression of stuttering was examined for alpha wave activation, although the results of this type of research were not particularly positive.[13]

The supposition that brain waves refer to a biofeedback system also introduces chronemic variables to the feedback system under study. That is, we individually sync to a particular innate *rhythm.* Edward T. Hall suggests that "Rhythm is so much a part of everyone's life that *it occurs virtually without notice* [emphasis added]."[14] That is, rhythm is an unconscious perceptual state, one that may be associated with feedback. Hall goes on to note that the concept of the *self* "is deeply embedded in the rhythmic synchronic process. This is because rhythm is inherent in organization, and therefore has a basic design function in the organization of the personality."[15]

Research by William S. Condon has established the relationship between brain waves (rhythms) and self-synchrony.[16] The brain rhythms and frequencies associated with communication include the delta wave (1–3 per second), theta wave (4–7 per second), alpha wave (8–13 per second), beta I wave (14–24 per second), and beta II wave (25–40 per second). Condon has associated these waves with the following speech elements: delta—utterances; theta—words; alpha—short words and phones; beta I—short phones; and beta II—phones. Hall notes that the one-second delta wave is the basic rhythm of human behavior:

> The spoken (master) phrases fall into this one-second interval which bridges precisely three shorter phrases. These three phrases in turn encompass two to three words each (a total of nine words), which are made of twenty-five phones (sounds). *Each body movement is precisely synchronized with this four-level hierarchical series of rhythms* [emphasis added].
>
> This fragment of speech recorded on film . . . lasts for only one second. During this second the subject's arm is precisely coordinated with the theta wave pattern; her eye blinks are in sync with the beta wave pattern; the alpha rhythm is in sync with the words.[17]

Further, this biofeedback of language and gesture can be extended to interpersonal interactions. Condon has demonstrated that individual brain waves will synchronize with others to form a unified rhythm.[18]

Finally, there is the olfactory system and its influence on biofeedback systems. There is evidence to indicate that pleasant odors produce a state of relaxation because "when we savor a pleasant fragrance, we take deeper and slower breaths, relaxing our respiratory pattern much as we do in meditation."[19] Hence, olfaction—and perhaps olfactory memory—may be biofeedback systems that help control stress, hunger, and even pain. Research being conducted at Duke University and Yale University in "aroma therapy" may yield promising outcomes for olfaction and biofeedback systems.

Mood and Emotion

Feelings may be identified either as associated with a particular odor (e.g., fear, anger), or with a particular biofeedback device (including temporal rhythm). The mood state or emotive state we are in at any one particular time may be influenced by the biofeedback we receive from (1) ourselves and (2) others (including our environment).

We begin with the biofeedback we receive that enables us to judge our own perceptions. In 1964, Stanley Schachter proposed a two-factor theory of emotion that takes into account the physiological reactions we have toward things and the cognitive labels we apply to those reactions.[20] Schachter viewed emotion as

> a function of a state of physiological arousal and of a cognition appropriate to this state of arousal. The cognition, in a sense, exerts a steering function. Cognitions arising from the immediate situation as interpreted by past experiences provide the framework within which one understands and labels his feelings. It is the cognition which determines whether the state of physiological arousal will be labeled "anger," "joy," or whatever.[21]

In order for an emotion to be identified, both physiological arousal and past experience or other significant cues must be present if the label is to be correctly identified. When one component is missing, the individual will not be able to identify the emotion.

Extending Schachter's argument one step further, one may argue that the physiological arousal may be found in the form of some biofeedback system, one that is more perceptual than cognitive. Based on this line of reasoning, a perceptual cue (temporal, olfactory, rhythm) could be responsible for the arousal state. On the basis of the olfactory research of William S. Cain, for example, might not the odor given off by the individual arouse him or her to an emotional state? Harry Wiener reports people being hypersensitive to others' emotive and mood states.[22] Can we become more aware of our own internal states? odors? rhythms? Consider also the potential synchrony interpretation based on biofeedback as a rhythm: we feel relaxed at the alpha brain wave state (a wave about ten cycles per second); when disturbed, that wave rhythm changes to a different cycle, possibly alerting us that *something* has changed.[23]

The argument here is that the feeling of mood or emotion is a two-part sequence. First, the individual reacts to some perceptual change, a change probably based either (1) on an unconscious cue received exohormonally, or (2) on a form of synchronization between self and others. Second, based on this cue, the individual must then label the arousal. In an unpublished paper, Donald

Lombardi inferred that much the same thing may occur in the detection of deception.[24] That is, as we communicate with someone, we are receiving subconscious cues as to whether or not that person's nonverbal behavior is honest or deceptive. As the cues begin to add up, they take a more conscious form (notice that we are not identifying what cues may be available; in most instances they may occur in terms of microfacial expressions, exohormones, or nonsynchronous behavior). We are then forced to label them as either deceptive or not. If we label them as deceptive, we are then forced into a position of either keeping the deception going (and possibly cuing the other person by means of the same modes), or terminating the interaction.

Such a biofeedback model of emotion and deception would take into consideration a multi-channel form of communication. That is, we are constantly monitoring our system for change. This change may be perceptual, taking the form of unconscious events (of events that reside just below consciousness, or of sensed feeling [perception]), and whatever we can attribute it to in the near environment (to include past memory and experience) will produce a cognitive reaction to the event. If, for instance, we perceive the change as occurring olfactorily (as anger), we may interpret our biofeedback as fear, and react appropriately, or we may mask that feeling (deceive the other person).

Part of the feedback system deals with the recognition of deception. Paul Ekman evaluates the nonverbal behavior of people in two related situations: (1) when trying to withhold information, and (2) when trying to present false information in a credible fashion.[25] These instances are labeled as ''deceits,'' in which two basic mistakes are found. The first mistake is termed a ''deception clue,'' an expression or gesture that indicates a person is engaged in deception *but does not reveal the content of the deception.* The second mistake is termed ''leakage,'' and occurs when a person accidentally reveals information he or she wished to conceal.

An example might be the smile. A smile is a simple expression requiring only one muscle movement. Ekman and W. V. Friesen contend that smiles can be the most misunderstood of all facial expressions.[26] They not only conceal true feelings but can also convey false messages. Part of the interpretation of the smile, whether it is (1) *felt,* (2) *false,* or (3) *miserable,* is partially determined by the biofeedback and temporal aspects of the smile. For instance, felt smiles are those used with a positive emotion; they last from two-thirds of a second to four seconds. False smiles on the other hand, may be distinguished by the muscle used, laterality, location, and timing. False smiles may occur too early or too late, last too long, have short onset times, or not have a smooth offset. Miserable smiles do not mask emotion, as do the false smiles, but indicate accepted and contained misery. All three smiles are deliberate but are differentiated by both chronemic and biofeedback mechanisms.

In their work on muscle movements and facial expression, Ekman and Friesen infer that facial expression such as the smile may be distinguished by the muscles fired. Such analysis is based on (1) appearance change, (2) capability of independent action, and (3) biofeedback circuits that enable the person to be aware of his or her own facial movement.[27] In deceiving others, then, we have both biofeedback (muscles fired) and chronemic (onset and offset of the emotion) systems operating. Both systems would seem to be important when a deception, or a leakage, is attempted.

To complicate matters even more, there appears to be a general biological rhythm in all ''interpersonal'' communication. This rhythm, according to Paul Byers, consists of a ten-cycle-per-second synchrony between people engaged in nontask behavior.[28] Any change in this cycle would indicate a change in the relationship between people. As the behavior moved in and out of synchrony—or phase relationships—some perceptual feeling of the relationship is then observed, codified, and reacted to. As Byers notes:

> Although one organism may not directly perceive his phase relationship to another, I believe that, in the case of humans, the phase relationship is systematically related to the biochemical (endocrinological) [to include olfactory] states which are reflected in or perceived as feelings. It is particularly interesting to observe that the information carried by interpersonal rhythms does not move directionally from one person to another. This information cannot easily be conceptualized as "messages," since the information is always simultaneously shared and always about the state of the relationship.[29]

Byers' perspective clearly parallels those of Hall and Condon, suggesting an interpersonal synchrony that begins with self-rhythms meshing with another's self-rhythms. The degree to which we sync, then, may be related to the communication of affect and deceptive communications.

We have come full circle. Emotion, mood, and deception begin with the individual and move to encompass others. Once we begin an interaction, we perceive information from others and ourselves, based on perceptual systems, then act and react to it. What we may be able to do, however, is to use such features as subconscious memory (e.g., olfactory) to provide the cue to the emotion; that is, we may be able to self-cue as to the intended label for the arousal. If that self-cue was a particular odor in memory dealing with sex, the label might be identified as "love." If the cue was associated with fear, the label would then be "fear." Based on the perception, a mood state may be entered into, and possible interactions with others may be found to be either honest (mood shown) or deceptive (mood hidden).

Olfaction

Dale Leathers has suggested that "olfaction is truly the forgotten sense."[30] Although we use our olfactory sense daily, we actually do not think about what we smell unless it is especially positive or negative. We associate certain odors with some visual aspect in the environment: a person, a place, a thing. Each has its own particular scent, its own particular smell. In many ways, however, what we are smelling is a perceptual process, an action associated with the cognitive processes by which we label the odor.[31] Consider, for example, the odor of a field freshly fertilized with manure. What cognition comes to mind? Is it positive or negative? Before answering, consider a second example, the odor of a beach along the ocean or a lake just before sunset. What cognition comes to mind? Is it positive or negative? If the cognition is positive, then you probably designate such experiences with positive mental labels (perhaps you grew up on a farm or vacationed on a beach). Not only that, but the reaction to the smell will influence your behavior—as many advertisers have both found and demonstrated.

This section examines the olfactory process as it relates to communication. The "forgotten sense" will be shown to have great communication potential, but the process is even more perceptual than that of chronemics. We will see that the way we label the odor we perceive influences both memory and behavior. In some ways, we may postulate that the notion of **olfactory memory** is equated with the concept of deja vu. Before we consider that condition, however, we need to examine the olfactory process and how it relates to human behavior and communication.

What Is Olfaction?

The olfactory process is a complex chemical exchange that is only now beginning to be understood. The role of odor or smell in human behavior, however, has been present for a long time. We may note that what we normally perceive as olfaction may or may not coincide with the more scientific notion of olfactory communication. The scientific view is more concerned with how odor serves to communicate at a level just below the conscious; it concentrates more on how the particular chemical ''signatures'' we produce affect both our own behavior and that of others. We are also interested in this process, but we are more concerned with the social influence olfaction has on us in our daily routine.

Olfactory Processes

Olfaction is a process whereby we recognize certain odors around us. Those smells may come from the environment, from others around us, or from ourselves. We perceive the odor or smell through a pair of grooves high in our nasal passages. The cells there are closely linked to the lower, forward portion of the brain (the olfactory bulb). These cells are protected from the air passing through them by a thin film of flowing mucus, the area concerned with olfaction. This area that is sensitive to odors has a total surface smaller than the surface area of a dime. It consists, however, of about 600,000 specialized cells connected to the olfactory bulb. To be detected, an odor must first dissolve in the film or mucus. Then, as it passes close to the sensory cells, it is captured and held just long enough to be analyzed.

Unlike our other senses, the olfactory sense is connected directly to the same hemisphere or side of the brain as that on which it is found. By this we mean that whereas the right ear is *contralaterally* connected to the left brain hemisphere and the left ear to the right, the right nasal passage is *ipsilaterally*—directly—connected to the right hemisphere. This allows for an extremely fast exchange of information between sensory cell and brain area. This exchange, however, tends to occur so fast that much of what we perceive through the olfactory input senses may not be consciously received; it may not be labeled within our memory traces as adequately as are the more consciously received sensory messages.

It has been demonstrated, however, that odor remains in our memory much longer than what we see or hear.[32] Trygg Engen theorizes that the difference in terms of memory may be traced to survival as a species and to a linkage with the brain. He postulates that we possess an *odor memory* that lasts longer than other forms of memory: (1) because of the nearness of sensory input to the brain area receptive to the information, (2) because a more direct, quicker, and less edited type of message comes from olfactory information, yielding (3) a memory that is stronger due to associations between the odor and the situation.[33] The odor is received directly in the limbic (emotive) centers of the brain; such associations of smell and emotion, then, follow naturally. As we see later, advertisers are taking full advantage of this linkage. For the moment, however, we can expand upon the survival value of such a message.

For lower species, the olfactory message is received by a limbic system that has only one function: processing the sense of smell. This function enables highly specialized odors to communicate specific meanings. Thus, for example, we have the **pheromone,** a substance secreted by insects that serves as a sexual attractant. Although humans produce such a secretion, its effect may or may not produce the expected results.[34] There are some persons in the world of popular literature, television, and advertising who would have us believe that by wearing pheromones, we activate the sexual instinct in others.[35] Although this is entirely possible, the question of such an **exohormone** (a hormone secreted by one organism that, through olfactory reception, alters the behavior of another organism) functioning in the human being is highly speculative.[36]

What research we have concerning subconscious exohormone effects indicates that males and females react differently to a sexual scent. Such research, however, is both mixed and contradictory. These are certain odors associated with menstrual cycles that differ in terms of both pleasantness and intensity as the cycle operates.[37] Further, analysis of vaginal secretions both before and after coitus produce different chemical analyses. Studies also infer that exposure to at least two exohormones (androstenol and copulins, both found in sexually excited women) affects how people perceive each other; but this effect is more marked in females' perceptions of males than in males' perceptions of females. As the researchers concluded,

> We have apparently demonstrated, possibly for the first time in a controlled experimental situation, that a *complex human behaviour can be influenced by the odour of substances known to have pheromonal properties in animals* [italics added]. The effects obtained evidently interacted with cognitive and affective responses elicited by the reading of descriptions of individual persons in a way that resulted in a rather specific overall response that depended not only on the substance under test, but also the sex and other characteristics of the person described.[38]

It is interesting to note also that males and females differ in how they perceive the sexual odor. Females describe the exohormone as "musky," whereas males can only offer a vague response to its odor. Further, sensitivity to the odor seems to be highest at ovulation, when the odor is brought into consciousness. In a study examining the impact of the pheromonal effects of the musky exohormone (androstenone and androstenol), E. Filsinger, J. Braun, and W. Monte found that males and females differed in the perceived sexual attractiveness of a target picture. (These pheromones are found in the sweat of human armpits.) Specifically, males reported increased sexual attractiveness associated with androstenol, and females reported decreased sexual attractiveness associated with androstenone.[39] When compared with a no-odor condition, the musk odors decreased the self-rated sexiness of male participants. They also compared pheromones against synthetic odors and found little difference in sexual perception.

In the early 1970s researchers in both America and England found a social-grouping effect based in part on olfaction. This research reported that women who lived or worked together tended to synchronize their menstrual cycles.[40] Such synchronization is limited to a very close circle of acquaintances and may be due to the smelling of exohormones and suppression of certain hormones, based on some not-too-well-understood process. It is interesting to note, however, that "exposure to males" tends to counteract the synchronizing effect.[41]

Aside from the sexual aspects of olfaction there is also a social effect. There are some who suggest that emotions can be "smelled." That is, there are definite odors given off to communicate anger.[42] Other moods such as fear are also closely associated with differences in odor. Harry Weiner theorizes that these odors of emotion may be associated with steroids.[43] There is also evidence that psychotic behavior such as schizophrenia can be diagnosed through odor.[44] Kathleen Smith and Jacob O. Sines, for example, found that when sweat was compared, researchers could significantly differentiate schizophrenic from nonschizophrenic subjects.[45] Weiner reports that some psychotic patients are also hypersensitive to others' emotional states, and the psychotic patient may become more sensitive to the chemical changes going through an individual as emotions change.[46] As A. Hoffer and H. Osmond note,

> . . . olfactory percepts are very closely linked with affect, and in many persons they are extremely evocative of feeling. This suggests a possible explanation for the increasing apathy found in many schizophrenic patients. They are, in fact, being satiated with affect evoking stimuli, so that eventually indifference supervenes.[47]

Olfactory Identification

From what has been stated up to this point, it would appear that the only people who engage in olfaction are either sexually aroused or psychotic. This perception is not accurate. Each of us is influenced by the odors around us—more influenced than we might think. Besides the sexual attractant, there are hundreds of odors surrounding us at any given moment. How good we are at identifying them, however, may determine in part our inability to perceive them.

How good are we at identifying odors? According to some, we are "microsmatic"; we are poor sensers of smell. There is some evidence, however, that our sense of smell is much more developed than was thought earlier. This is especially true with **olfactory signatures.** Research, for example, has demonstrated that parents can tell which children are their own based on the child's own "smellprint."[48] This same research confirmed earlier research implying that siblings could also identify with high accuracy which shirts were worn by their brothers or sisters.[49] How early this ability is learned may be indirectly found in other research indicating that six-week-old infants seem to be able to "tell" the nursing pad of their mother (react more favorably to the mother's breast pad than to others' pads).[50]

According to research conducted by William S. Cain and associates, the linkage between odor and label may be the significant feature of remembering and perceiving an odor. They infer that the cognitive process is inherently important in perceiving an odor. Cain further notes that "names define odors, locate them in relation to other odors, and even give them an internal 'address' for retrieval from memory storage."[51] His research indicates that people, when presented an odor, may fail to identify exactly what they smell but will decide upon some type of label (usually responding that the label is "on the tip of the tongue"). This label, right or wrong, is then associated with the odor at a later time.

Interestingly, Cain has found that several features help increase our odor inventory. First, we must have an accurate label. The more accurate the label is, the better we can remember it; the more specific the label, the better we remember it. Second, females are much better at identifying odors than are males, although with training males can approach the female's ability in odor identification. And finally, there are age differences; older people have more problems with odor identification than do younger people. This may be due in part to decreased cognitive ability associated with age.

The importance of such a labeling process is not new. In the 1700s, Linnaeus suggested that odors could be best classified in a sevenfold-category system:

1. aromatic
2. fragrant
3. musky
4. garlicky

5. goaty
6. repulsive
7. nauseous

This listing of odor also falls within our modern range of preferences. You need not smell numbers 5 through 7 to know they are less positive than 1 or 2. (Musky is the smell most often associated with sexual appeal or pheromone, still a positive odor.) R. W. Moncrieff went so far as to have 16 subjects compare 132 types of odor and rank each in order of preference.[52] The rankings fell in the same general order as Linnaeus's.

Use of such labels helps us both to remember and to identify the odor. For example, below is a list of ten products now on the market. What odor do you associate with each? How positive or negative is it? How easy would it be to identify that odor?

1. Johnson's baby powder
2. Chocolate
3. Coconut
4. Crayola crayons
5. Mothballs
6. Ivory soap (bar)
7. Vicks VapoRub
8. Bazooka bubble gum
9. Coffee
10. Caramel

In a 1981 study reported by Cain, these are the top ten odor-identified products.[53] They were identified over the perceived top ten odors as listed by a group of 103 women (listed in order of expected identifiableness: ammonia, coffee, mothballs, perfume, orange, lemon, bleach, vinegar, nail-polish remover, and peanut butter). Hence, what we think we can recognize is not always what we recognize. Also, as might be expected, the label is very important.

A 1987 survey conducted by the National Geographic Society tells us more about our olfactory abilities. Avery N. Gilbert and Charles J. Wysocki reported the analysis of data collected in a huge research project titled, "The Smell Survey: Its Results."[54] National Geographic collected 1.5 *million* reader responses to a survey of six scents, asking their readership (1) to determine whether they could smell the odor and (2) to determine what that odor was. Gilbert and Wysocki then randomly selected 26,500 respondents from the United States and 100,000 respondents from the rest of the world for their initial analysis. They found that most people correctly identified most of the odors (which included sweat, banana, musk, cloves, gas, and rose). Table 9.1 presents the U.S. results for ability to smell the odor and to correctly identify it. A quick perusal of the results indicates that most respondents could smell the odors, although there were differences in their abilities to correctly identify the odor. Major findings suggested that:

> Women not only think they can smell more accurately than men, they generally can; reactions to odors vary widely around the world; and pregnant women, commonly thought to be smell-sensitive, may actually experience a diminished sense of smell . . . nearly two persons in three have suffered a temporary loss of smell and that 1.2 percent cannot smell at all.[55]

The importance of olfactory identification is probably more closely identified with species other than humans. Daily it seems, we read of dogs tracking down a lost child, an escaped convict, or a cache of hidden drugs. But human identification can be just as important—maybe more so. Boyd Gibbons, in an overview of the "Intimate Sense of SMELL," notes:

> During the World Wars, German soldiers claimed they knew the whiff of the English, and the English said likewise. More recently, North Vietnamese soldiers reported that they often smelled Americans before seeing them. Jack Holly, a Marine Corps officer who led reconnaissance patrols deep into the triple-canopy jungles of Vietnam, told me, "I am alive today because of my nose. You

TABLE 9.1   *Results of the National Geographic Society Smell Survey (United States Sample)*

ODOR	PERCENTAGE THAT COULD SMELL	PERCENTAGE CORRECTLY IDENTIFIED
Androstenone *(Sweat)*		
Total	66.6	25.1
Females	70.5	26.0
Males	62.8	24.2
Isoamyl Acetate *(Banana)*		
Total	99.1	51.3
Females	99.3	52.8
Males	99.0	49.2
Galaxolide *(Musk)*		
Total	70.6	28.8
Females	74.6	34.8
Males	66.7	22.9
Eugenol *(Clover)*		
Total	99.2	86.4
Females	99.5	89.6
Males	98.9	83.2
Mercaptans *(Gas)*		
Total	97.4	58.7
Females	97.8	59.3
Males	97.0	58.1
Rose		
Total	99.2	83.0
Females	99.5	84.5
Males	99.0	81.6

Source: A. N. Gilbert and C. J. Wysocki, "The Smell Survey: Its Results,"
National Geographic, 174 (October 1987), pp. 516–517.

couldn't see a como bunker if it was right in front of you. But you can't camouflage smell. I could smell the North Vietnamese before hearing or seeing them. Their smell was not like yours or mine, not Filipino, not South Vietnamese either. If I smelled that smell again, I would know it.''

Some years ago my mother, a former nurse, suspected that a neighbor might have stomach cancer when she detected the familiar odor of fermentation on his breath. In the days before high-tech medicine, physicians depended on all their senses, including their noses, to diagnose illness. An eminent diagnostician might arrive on a hospital ward, sniff, and announce that a case of typhoid fever must be in it. Typhoid smelled like baked bread. German measles smelled like plucked feathers, scrofula like stale beer, yellow fever like a butcher shop.

Patients with smallpox were said to smell like perspiring geese (whatever that is, since geese can't sweat). A surgeon on rounds will ordinarily smell the patient's bandage for infection by *Pseudomonas* bacteria. It has the musty odor of a wine cellar.[56]

Identification, then, provides significant cues to behavior, including survival behaviors. But some people now use these same findings to their advantage.

Olfactory Influence

As might be expected from the reported studies of the olfactory process, a certain amount of manipulation of others' behavior is possible through smell. Such manipulation indicates that olfaction can be used effectively to sell products, to make things more positive (or negative) than they are, and to help regulate other forms of communication. In this section, we examine in more detail the influence of smell on everyday activity.

Consider the following examples of olfactory manipulation. Bakers deliberately place fans over freshly baked loaves of bread, venting the scent out across the street to tempt others into their shops. Car dealers find that by using a ''new car'' scent, they can sell used cars faster. A musty odor can be created to make objects smell ''old'' or antique. A bakery vents its ovens during morning rush hour, sending the smell of fresh doughnuts to people caught in traffic (and has youngsters selling doughnuts as people wait for the lights to change).[57]

These are but a few examples of how we are manipulated by our sense of smell. Consider, too, a study carried out at Colgate University, which demonstrated how extensively a person can be subconsciously influenced by odor. Researchers used four batches of identical nylons, scenting one with a floral fragrance (narcissus), one with a fruity fragrance, one with a sachet fragrance, and one with its own synthetic odor. Women shoppers were then observed touching and inspecting the stockings. When asked which of the four batches they would prefer, fifty percent of them chose the floral-scented stockings as being ''softer and more durable,'' twenty-four percent chose the fruity-scented stockings, and eighteen percent chose the sacheted stockings. Only 8.5 percent of the shoppers chose the unscented pairs as being most desirable.[58]

Not only are hosiery perfumed without our conscious knowledge, but even such items as paper, fabrics, underwear, socks, cosmetics, and prophylactics are deliberately fragranced. In their initial stages, rugs are so strong smelling (''malodorous'') that they would not sell unless they were *reodorized* (changed to smell different). Aromatic woods such as cedar, apple, sandlewood, and hickory sell for more than do stronger smelling wood (pine, oak, birch); therefore, imitation aromatics are added to inferior-grade lumber to raise its price. How many people would buy a Christmas tree if they knew that the trees were actually cut and sprayed with a clear plastic spray odorized with "evergreen" scent in early September and kept in cold storage until just before Christmas? How would a Christmas tree lot be perceived if it did *not* smell like evergreen? Yet we can create almost any odor that can be described (such as "evergreen," for trees, "Johnson's baby powder," for bathrooms, and most types of incense).

One of the more pervasive aspects of our culture is the "clean Gene" feeling we have. We are constantly bombarded by the media to believe that if we smell bad, we will be socially rejected. Because of this expectation, people who do smell are stereotyped into a media role and generally *are* rejected until the situation is corrected.[59] This conditioning starts when a baby is born into a conditioned culture that has been sterilized, deodorized, and reodorized: the hospital room. Even the mother of the baby has been carefully shorn, washed, and deodorized with a variety of chemicals. Hence, we begin with a sterilized olfactory memory of the world.[60]

Children between the ages of two and six are exposed to at least 55 hours of television per week, the programming saturated with commercials promoting cleanliness and advertising hygienic products. By the time they are five, children have succumbed to a cultural conditioning that implies a negative reaction to body odors previously associated positively. (A child under age five usually perceives the bodily odors of adults—laced with pheromones or exohormones—as quite pleasant and natural.)[61] After age five, children begin to take seriously the ad, "Brand X takes the worry out of being close."

If we could take away our fears of being close, of being unclean, of being unattractive, we would almost eliminate an entire industry. Consider that body odors can be controlled or hidden (reodorized) through the use of toothpaste, mouthwash, colognes and perfumes, deodorant, hairspray, shampoos, razors to shave off hair that retains odor, scented pillows and sachets, washing powders, fabric softeners ("Will they notice I didn't use _____ ?"), preshave and aftershave, lotions, bath oil, body powders, and of course, soap.

If advertising did not manipulate us into thinking that our body odors were unclean and less than natural, would we need all these products? It is interesting to note that some deodorant commercials imply that men and women smell different mainly because they perspire differently. In fact, perspiration does not even have an odor. It is the action of bacteria outside of the gland opening that produces the stale, musty unpleasantness of an odor we associate with sweat. How we smell is most likely affected by our diets, medication, and health. People who eat red meat smell different from those who eat fish or vegetables. People on drugs such as penicillin have a distinctive odor. Many diseases can be diagnosed by smell alone.[62] Oral health problems are also closely associated with certain odors. The amount of body hair we have also influences our odors; those with more bodily hair smell more than those with less hair (a reason Orientals, whites, and blacks differ in their smells).[63]

Olfaction also serves as an identifier of socioeconomic class. We can, by use of reodorant, deodorant, diet, and other odors, establish some form of socioeconomic class or status. In our culture, the better off the person is, the better he or she usually smells. There is a major difference between *Chanel No. 5* and *Charlie,* between *Chaps* and *British Sterling:* cost. Walk into a house, and you can establish region of country or possibly even ethnic background by the smells of the cooking (a major difference between South and North is the frying of fats, for instance). According to Ruth Winter, prostitutes, aware of their unclean status in society, try to cover themselves up by lavishing on perfumes, hence the derivation of the phrase, "smell like a whore."[64]

Olfactory Memory

Olfaction serves as a major influence on both our thinking and our behavior. But advertisers have also found that *olfactory memory* is a way to sell products. By means of such devices as "scratch and smell" advertisements and vivid emotional labels, advertisers are able to influence or awaken our olfactory memory, a form of remembrance that, as noted earlier, has the highest memory capacity of all five senses. Its sensation, according to Wilson B. Key, is to awaken "vague and half-understood perceptions which are accompanied by very strong emotions."[65]

This invisible stimulus, emotion, supplies the motivation to buy. Different places, times, and things have distinct odors (for example a coffee shop, a dentist's office, a pipe, Christmas). Advertisers have found that vacations can be sold by memory. A picture of the seashore evokes memories of the smell of the sea, and a picture of the mountains evokes a memory trace of pine and fresh air.[66] Florists now advertise to "send springtime." The message is, of course, that the scent of flowers is to be associated with the smells of spring, a new love, a new start in life. Because odors produce memories tied to emotion, these emotions and odors are reproduced more strongly, and the emotions associated with them are perceived even more powerfully.

How lasting are these memories? Gilbert and Wysocki suggest that the memories associated with smell tend to be recalled with odor, but these memories tend to fade with age. They report that stronger odors produced more vivid memories; women not only found all odors to be stronger than did men, but except for the odor associated with flatulence, they reported more memories than did men; both pleasant and unpleasant odors are more likely to produce memories than middle-ranged odors; and odors correctly identified are more likely to evoke a specific memory.[67]

A closely related aspect of olfactory memory is that of smell adaptation.[68] Smell adaptation occurs when the odor you smell becomes a part of your environment or general background. For instance, if you are wearing a perfume or cologne you *like,* you will notice that it tends to wear off as times goes on; it is adapted, and you feel a need to replenish. If, on the other hand, you are wearing something you do not like, its adaption seems to take forever. One of your authors has his class wear a perfume or cologne they cannot stand for a class period. After about twenty minutes, the odor is so bad that doors and windows must be opened. On the next day, however, when the class members wear cologne they like, adaptation occurs.

One final aspect of olfactory memory needs to be addressed, **olfactory deja vu.** When we have the feeling that we have experienced something for the first time but have not in reality experienced it, we explain it away as deja vu. In some ways this phenomenon may be related to the olfactory memory traces we have of people, places, and objects. Remember, the olfactory process is one that occurs very rapidly and one that may not have conscious labels attached to it. Remember also that odors can be identified by association; if the association is generalized enough, the odor will trigger a similar memory that does *not* match the new stimulus. Consider, for example, an incident one of our colleagues tells us about. He was walking down the hall when he noticed a particular odor—a perfume—emanating from a female just ahead of him. He approached her, touched her, and mentioned her name. You can imagine his chagrin when the female turned out to be someone else. Actually, the female was wearing the same perfume he associated with another person, and she was of the right size, build, and hair color he associated with that person.

Although this incident may not classify as real deja vu, it implies the powerful suggestive ability of olfaction. The same type of occurrence may be true when you are certain you have been in a particular environment before but you know you have never before set foot in that environment.

There may be some unconscious odor lingering that is associated with something from your past. Although research has not addressed the question, it remains a possible way of explaining such behavior. Interpersonal versions of olfactory deja vu like that described earlier may occur on a more regular basis.

A recent study supports this interpretation. D. C. Rubin, E. G. Groth, and D. J. Goldsmith examined the impact olfactory cuing has on memory. They had undergraduate students describe the memory evoked by one of three cues: odors, photographs, or the names associated with 16 common objects. They were told to date the memory (when the focus of the memory occurred), rate its vividness, pleasantness, and how many times they had thought of the memory before the experiment. The results indicated that odor cues evoked memories that were rarely evoked by photographs or words, that there were no distinct age differences in the memories, and that inaccessible memories can be evoked by the olfactory cue. They also suggested that odors might produce more pleasant memories than the other cues.[69]

Time (Chronemics)

Chronemics is concerned with how we use and structure time. It is a significant area of nonverbal communication because we generally perceive our actions and reactions as a time sequence. We talk about what we will do tomorrow, what we should have done yesterday, how we have wasted time. Each of these statements reflects a general western view of how time should be used, of how it is abused; and this view sets forth expectations we use to identify others. Consider, for example, how you view a Latin American or a Mexican through his or her use of time. Is this person as energetic as we are (assuming North American expectations)? Does this person value time as much as we do? How does this individual use time? If you decide that Latin Americans differ from us with respect to any of these criteria (or more), then you view their chronemic orientation as different.

Time is generally perceived in three ways. First, we can examine time in an individual or psychological orientation. At this level, we are thinking about how we personally use and perceive time. We can also examine time on a more basic level, considering the biological "clocks" within us. This again is more personal and may differ from one individual to another. Finally, we can examine time on cultural (and subcultural) levels. It is at this level that we find major differences between people. Consider, for instance, Hall's description of the Tiv of Nigeria's use of time and contrast it with your expectations:

> The Tiv equivalent of the week lasts five to seven days. It is not tied into periodic natural events, such as the phases of the moon. The day of the week is named after the things which are being sold in the nearest "market." If we had the equivalent, Monday would be "automobiles" in Washington, D.C., "furniture" in Baltimore, and "yard goods" in New York. Each of these might be followed by the days for appliances, liquor and diamonds in the respective cities. This would mean that as you travel about, the day of the week would keep changing, depending upon where you were.[70]

You may note that this type of division of time is not so different from what *we* might have used a hundred years ago. Look at the *Farmer's Almanac* from that period, and you will find time divided by planting seasons in the several regions, a concept close to the Tiv's use of time. Many Americans learned of two major Southeast Asian time distinctions in the middle '60s to early '70s: monsoon and dry seasons.

The Structure of Time

Many of us have asked the question, "What is time?" In answering this question, we provide others with a glimpse of how we view life itself, almost like answering the question of the glass that is filled to the halfway mark—is it half full or half empty? How we structure time offers us the same type of insight: Are our days numbered? Does time for the person ever end? Or does it, as one student suggested, continue on as long as the person is remembered? Edward T. Hall suggests that it may better serve the student of time not to examine the specific "microstructure" of time, but instead to examine the *kinds* of time we hold:

> As people do quite different things (write books, play, schedule activities, travel, get hungry, sleep, dream, mediate, and perform ceremonies), they unconsciously and sometimes consciously express and participate in different categories of time.[71]

Hall suggests that western culture does not hold one specific view of time, which may differ from others, but that we perceive time as consisting of between six and eight *categories*.[72] Further, these categories are functionally interrelated into four major time pairs (see Figure 9.1) in a *mandala* of time (a mandala is a classification device that shows relationship) between ideas or variables in a nonlinear fashion; it allows for multiple influence among the ideas or variables. The eight individual categories combine to create what Hall has labeled the ninth and ultimate category, *meta time.* Meta time refers to the study of time from philosophical to scientific orientations based on some theory of how time operates. As such, Hall's *theory* of time is general and grounded in cultural derivations. We believe it provides an excellent base from which to examine the more specific theories of time as put forth by Tom Bruneau, Joost Meerloo, and Thomas Cottle.

Hall describes how the mandala characterizes time in both general and specific relationships between categories by noting:

> When one looks at the time mandala, several things become apparent. First, there are four pairs in which the categories appear to be functionally interrelated: (1) sacred and profane, (2) physical and metaphysical, (3) biological and personal, and (4) sync time and micro time. Second, the time positions on the opposite sides of the mandala also seem to bear a special relationship to each other. Sacred time and personal time are personal, and from what little is known of the metaphysical, it would seem that rhythm is shared with sync time in both. . . . These common elements, such as rhythm, are links connecting the different kinds of time. Third, the two axes going from lower left to upper right and upper left to lower right set things apart in other ways: group, individual, cultural, and physical. Fourth, the left side is explicit and technical (low-context) while the right-hand side is situational (high-context). All of this suggests that there are clusters of ordered relationships between the different kinds of time.[73]

To understand time, then, we must understand the different categories that function to make time "real." Later in this chapter, we see how Hall's meta time perspective helps us better understand how chronemic theorists perceive time from the different categories.

Time Categories   Hall's eight time categories range from the "imaginary" to the "real." At one extreme, we find *sacred time,* or a time rooted in mythology; it is magical and helps to define consciousness by determining where we are in relation to something not of this world. Sacred time for hard-driving workers, for instance, may be found in the ability to lose themselves in their work, leaving the problems of relationships, family, and so forth, elsewhere. Closely related to this time is *profane time,* or a time that is deeply rooted in the explicit time system found in cultures.

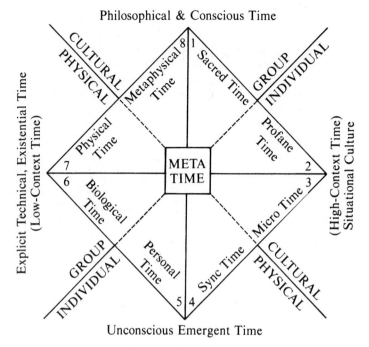

Note: To discuss complementary systems it is necessary to invoke Meta Time, which is where the integrative concepts are located.

FIGURE 9.1   A Map of Time.
Source: Edward T. Hall. *The Dance of Life: The Other Dimensions of Time* (New York: Doubleday, 1984). Reprinted with permission.

Profane time is formulated; it consists of centuries, decades, years, months, weeks, days, hours, and minutes. Tied closely to the sacred, profane time takes the magic and binds permanence to it—in western culture, for instance, Christmas is celebrated on December 25, not so in other cultures.

Micro time evolves out of the sacred and the profane. Micro time is culture-specific and a product of the differences in how time units are perceived by the culture. Micro time includes perceptions of informal time perspectives such as the meanings we place on waiting, punctuality, and other uses of time. *Sync time* links the profane with the micro. According to Hall, sync time is a relatively new western notion, yet one that has been around for centuries in other cultures. Sync time refers to the ability of people to move at various paces or beats. There are days, for instance, when we feel ''out of sync'' with others, when we and they operate on different time orientations. Sync time will differ both within a given culture and within a particular individual.

Because people differ in the way they sync with each other and with themselves, Hall suggests that a *personal time* exists. Personal time is the experience of time by the individual. For the individual, time may fly or crawl. In dream analysis, for instance, a nightmare may seem to last forever, yet it is typically over in less than a minute. Some students report that some classes go "too fast," and others report the same classes "drag." All are personal experiences of time within a given culture, closely linked perhaps to sync and profane time. From the personal we arrive at the metaphysical. *Metaphysical time* concerns the ability of the individual to escape from time and space—to go into a time warp for which contemporary science has no explanation. The concept of deja vu, Hall suggests, is represented by this time category, as are the feelings associated with transcendental meditation. Metaphysical time is neither sacred nor profane; it is highly personal and mostly unexplainable, at least according to western thought.

At the other end of this time continuum are physical and biological time. *Biological time* is cyclic, perhaps part of the sync between individual and environment. Biologically we live a cycle; doomed from the beginning to die, we live through other time categories. Biological time—*phasing expressed in terms of individual biological clocks*—concerns the ability of the individual to recognize and alter behavior due to some cycle they are in. Hence, the biological interfaces with the social to produce a perception of time that differs from the more personal, psychological time orientations discussed earlier. Finally, there is *physical time,* which represents the scientific observation of time and its effect on life. From primitive cultures that determine time on the cycles of the sun or moon to the most advanced cultures, time represents a physical reality, something to be measured precisely and that has a demonstrated impact. Albert Einstein, for instance, argued that as a human approaches the speed of light, 186,000 miles per hour, his or her life would slow down. Modern physical science now tells us that time may indeed go both forward *and* backward. The physical may, in some ways, help promote the sacred by altering the way we view time.

What Hall has tried to communicate through his mandala, however, is that time is not a simple continuum, as discussed above. Instead, time is *nonlinear;* it does not follow a strictly logical path—hence the use of the mandala as his model. Attempting to follow Hall's eight categories, as his mandala presents them, is something neither he nor we could do *logically.* Instead, he suggests we look at the time categories in groupings.

Functional Time   Although most time researchers prefer to examine time as a particular category or kind, the meta time perspective suggests that time categories function to establish usable groupings of categories. For example, at the cultural level, metaphysical, sacred, profane, and micro time function to define the particular culture's perception of time at a primary, or barely conscious, level. Time as a physical function is defined in terms of sync, personal, biological, and physical time categories, in which the emphasis is less on the sociological and more on the biological impact of time and time cycles. At the individual level, personal, sync, micro, and profane time become the focus of life. Here, we are more concerned with experiencing time and ourselves. Finally, at the group level, biological, physical, metaphysical, and sacred time interact to create a time perception suggesting permanence (physical and biological), which yields a subcultural life of its own.

The focus on meta time and its component categories suggests that all eight time categories interrelate to create our total perception of time. Theoretically, this is both interesting and educational; it helps explain how cultures and individuals differ in their structure and use of time. It does not, however, tell us much about the specifics of time. To establish a more formal structure of time we must turn to the work of Tom Bruneau.

Bruneau's Chronemic Structures

Just how is time structured? This question, as addressed by Tom Bruneau, seeks to go a step further than Hall's category structure. Bruneau's theorizing suggests that, much like kinesics and Ray Birdwhistell's kinesic coding system, time can be studied as a *microstructure* that yields units from which time messages can be analyzed.[74] Bruneau, opting for the term *chronemics* as the underlying construct of time, begins his analysis of time by noting that time is best equated with change and that change is variation of *process* and *duration*. Further, chronemics is the study of the dynamic interrelationships of both process and duration with "durations being a spatializing tendency and process providing motion or phoria and, with which, durations become more tensive and obtain[ed]."[75] In attempting to structure chronemics, Bruneau operationalizes time at three levels: macrostructural, metastructural, and microstructural. The first two levels, much like Hall's mandala of time, establish the philosophical nature of time and place chronemics as a place of study. At the microstructure level, however, the variables that create a notation system become operant.

Bruneau, then, goes one step further in his analysis of chronemics. He attempts to impose a structure on time, one that we hope will provide a handle on a vague and yet extremely personal concept. Bruneau's perception of time includes the sociocultural structures put forth by Hall and extends this analysis to the interdependence among macrostructure, metastructure, and micro-structure. In so doing, the analysis begins with process and duration, moves to the individual—personal—view of time, and finally provides a way of *scientifically* working with time.

As noted, Bruneau's philosophy of chronemic structure is found in the relationship between time as a process and time as a duration. Philosophically, he differentiates between the events we process and the way we perceive them (duration). In formulating this macrostructure of time, he suggests that cultures operate on a past-present-future trichotomy. But cultures, he notes, differ in their perceptions of each leg of macrochronemics. It may be better to examine the chronemic macrostructure from a *personal time perspective;* that is, how we—as individuals—relate process to duration. Bruneau argues that the interplay between personal time processes and durations alter how we perceive our world:

> We are basically and essentially temporal animals. Further, when we understand that our personal spatial realities expand and contract as our personal time varies [through perceptions of the event and the event's duration], we can begin to see change and to dissolve temporal categories, as well as begin to think about the relativity of human experience.[76]

What are the temporal categories that change? Bruneau suggests that time is inherently personal, that we view it as consisting of many things, most of which revolve around *becoming* and *being*. Becoming is related to the process of time and being is related to the duration of the category of time we become. Hence, he goes on to note, people view time as transitory and subjective and related to *now*. Where becoming and being are subjective, the now is measurable, it is the present moment; we may evaluate becoming and being as related to the now.

Those with a past orientation view change as a minimal element in their lives; they focus not on potential change nor on the immediate impact of the now, but on the stable and constant past. The future-oriented person views life in terms of novelty, seeking new perspectives on now and on old perceptions. The present-oriented person focuses on the now, living without analysis of the event, living for the immediate duration of the event, rather than for the event as a process (with a past or future), and experiencing time in the NOW.

Note that this macrostructure, beginning with process and duration, eventually works itself down to the individual. At the metastructural level of chronemics, then, we deal not so much with society or culture but with what concerns the now. And, as we may guess, the now is tied to the individual who experiences through one of the three chronemic orientations—or through a combination of chronemic orientations—*time*. The metastructures of time, then, are found at the individual level and consist of "personal and social rhythmicities, cyclicities, periodicities, actualities . . . eventualities, sequences, and a number of other processual and durational patternings such as personal and social timing, pacing, transition, pausing, etc."[77] Chronemic metastructure, then, becomes a biological-social relationship. How we view time may vary with changes in body rhythm and hormonal flux associated with our body clocks. These biological clocks then interrelate with social and psychological clocks—clocks that alter the biological rhythm we are born with and that create the unique orientation to time each of us has. Table 9.2 presents Bruneau's taxonomy of biological, social, and psychological clocks and their impact on our time-lives. The interaction of these clocks create a *temporal environment,* yielding drives, cues, signals, estimates, beliefs, motives, judgments, and values from which we test "nowness." The impact of these temporal codifications on behavior, as Bruneau notes, is such that they are unique to both individuals and groups, thus "When my time is not yours, or their time is not ours, dysrhythmia seems to occur."[78]

The making of moments is what constitutes chronemic *microstructure.* A moment is the now; a moment contrasts with the future and the past, what will or did happen. Moments can be viewed as nows, instances, or even points in time. Moments are potentially measurable and exist dynamically as units of the now. Bruneau suggests that we can define four levels of nowness. First is the *minimal unit,* the biological/physical/technical level of time. This level defines time as an objective, real concept that rarely changes. Minimal units include the speed of light, brain rhythms or waves, and perception. Minimal units have acquired labels such as *chrons, ergs,* and *oligons* and are measured in portions of seconds or milliseconds. The minimal unit, then, exists at a level below consciousness.

When that minimal unit enters consciousness, it becomes a *standard interval unit.* The standard interval unit is found in the pacing, regularity, and synchronized use of multiple minimal units. It is the "formulation of nowness" in such a manner as to be objectively measured and studied. From the objective, time moves toward a subjective, personal level. Here time becomes a *variable unit,* a conceptual "thing" that extends into the past and future. At this level, we speak of the psychological impact of time as a process/event first and as a duration second. That is, at this level, the event may be initially labeled as a standard interval unit—objectively stating the event— and then psychologically adding duration as a measure of how the process/event is felt or perceived. Finally, Bruneau suggests that time is also something that transcends consciousness. At this *point-instant* level "flashes of awareness or insight (which appear to be acausal) arrive in consciousness as sudden awakenings, revelations, images, visions, and the like."[79]

These four levels of time occur simultaneously. We are constantly guided by the physical into a perception of the present, which we may or may not use to enter the past or future. At times we are aware of sudden flashes of insight, intuition, or fear. These point-instances may be a function of one or all of the other chronemic levels. How to study such rhythms has been problematic. Bruneau suggests that a notation system similar to that developed by Birdwhistell might be employed. At this time, Bruneau has identified four elements in his chronemic notation system: a *chron* (a now or moment at the level of primary momenting), which is similar to the kinesic kine;

TABLE 9.2   *Chronemic Taxonomy of Temporal Variables*

LEVEL	CODIFICATION	DESCRIPTION
Biological	Temporal drive	Biorhythms; hormone periodicity; deals with primary momenting in terms of stimuli detection
	Temporal cues	Sensing and recognition of temporal drives of self and others; involves the products of primary momenting
Physiological	Temporal signals	Sensing and recognition of duration from the perceptual moment; involves the recognition of nonverbal action
	Temporal estimates	The beginning of duration; a sense of time and timing, habit and tempo, pace and pacing
Physio-psychological	Temporal signals	The beginning of process; a sensing of succession, duration, change, permanence, and perspective (past, present, future); the beginning of symbolization and the I-Time interrelationship
Psychological	Temporal beliefs	The beginning of a process-duration relationship; of establishing assumptions about the role and value of time
	Temporal motives	Establishing intention-time relationship; establishment of influence on a conscious level of drives, cues, signals, etc.
Social	Temporal judgments	Creation and testing of temporal beliefs and motives as exercised by many individuals and groups
Cultural	Temporal values	Creation of a metaperspective on time as a commodity (interplay of process/event and duration) and its impact on behavior

Source: Tom Bruneau, ''The Structure of Chronemics,'' paper presented at the conference on Current Trends in Nonverbal Communication: A Multidisciplinary Approach, Arkansas State University, April 1986. Used with permission.

a *chroneme* (chrons that occur regularly or habitually within the person, group, or culture), which is similar to the kinesic kineme; a *chronemorph* (the sequencing of chrons and/or chronemes into meaningful and symbolic patterns), which is similar to the kinesic kinemorph; and a *chrontax* (''the systematic utilization of chrons, chronemes, and chronemorphs in the conduct of individual and group communication behavior''[80]), which is similar to the kinesic kinemorphic class.

Culture and Time

Culture begins to educate each of us at an early age as to the value of and the means by which we distinguish time. Each culture has its own particular time norms, which are unconsciously followed until violated. When such violations occur, however, they are perceived as intentional messages associated with that particular culture. In this regard, each culture teaches its people what is appropriate or inappropriate with regard to time.

Hall has indicated that with respect to their use of time, cultures tend to fall into two general categories.[81] The first is *monochronic,* which is arbitrary, self-imposed, and learned. This is the way we tend to operate in American society. We are controlled by an arbitrary time device (clock, watch). We eat meals, not when we are hungry, but when the clock says it's time to eat. In *polychronic* cultures, several things may happen at once. Examples are found in Latin America and the Middle East where emphasis is placed on interactions and people, rather than on an arbitrary time device. This may also be seen in the Tiv example noted earlier.

Informal Time

Hall notes that each culture actually operates on three time systems, with each system operating simultaneously to create chronemic norms. Probably the most difficult to understand and adapt to is **informal time.** This is based on practice and takes on a more personalized or psychological orientation. At least six factors influence our perception of informal time: duration, punctuality, urgency, activity, variety, and monochronic/polychronic orientation. Notice that each of these factors seems to be definable on the basis of a personal time orientation; that is, they tend to run as we "see" them. Notice also that these six factors lend themselves to stereotypical types of perceptions.

North American culture is quite readily definable in terms of how we perceive these six time factors. Consider, for instance, **duration:** How long does something last? In the North American culture things last a short time, perhaps a vestige of our short history (compared to other older cultures). However, problems occur, even within the culture, in regard to such terms as *immediately, in a second,* (as contrasted with *in a minute*), and *forever.*

Activity deals with what we perceive should be done in a given period. In North American culture, we perceive a great deal of activity as necessary, but not too much. In the same way, we are more *monochronic,* we like to see things as *varied* within a given period. We create variety within a given period in a strange way, however, in that we treat each activity as a separate entity. In this sense we are monochronic, but within that self-imposed period, we establish other monochronic periods that imply both activity and variety of content. Look at any *TV Guide* summary of a daily TV schedule, and you will find examples of this. Other cultures, being more polychronic, do not place the same emphasis on activity and variety, leading to a "things will get done when they get done" perspective, which we perceive as lazy, nonambitious, and a waste of precious time. In some cultures, the polychronic norm may end with several people meeting to discuss business, whereas in our society, we would do so individually. The thought of meeting more than one person at a time upsets our monochronic norm.

Probably the most important, culturally defined, informal time system is that of **punctuality.** In our culture, we expect people to be punctual. By this we mean that we expect people to arrive at the appointed time or just before (five minutes). People however, tend to *sync* (or synchronize) differently. Hall has identified at least two major types of synchronizing that pertain to punctuality patterns that differ in their perceptions of where the time ends. For those of us who are *displaced,* who see a point in time as being the end, we operate as if a 4:45 meeting means just that: be there at 4:45 (actually, a couple of minutes early, just to be safe). For those of us who are more *diffused,* who see time as only an approximation, we would consider that same 4:45 meeting as an approximation and arrive about that time. For those who are displaced, there seems to be a need to be on time. For those who are diffused, the compulsion for punctuality is lessened. The diffused person, however, seems to operate more on a late basis than an early basis. Some people, for instance, are always X-minutes late, in fact, consistently late to such a degree that you can begin to depend on their "lateness."

Subcultural Informal Time   Within each culture there are subcultures that view time a little differently. In the North American culture, for instance, a southerner definitely views time differently than does a northeasterner. These differences occur in all cultures and may be defined as **time frames.** Frames, as originally defined by Erving Goffman, are attitudes and perspectives for viewing performances.[82] Within each culture there are subcultural "frames," or expectations based on appropriate time "performances." These time frames are unexpressed, or undefined, and are learned the hard way: we violate them in order to learn them. In this sense, we encounter such time orientations as CPT (Colored People's Time), or street time;[83] hauley time, or white person's time (hauley is a derogative Hawaiian term that referred to the early missionary's palid complexion), is contrasted to Hawaiian time, which is more lax.[84] In each case, the subcultural time orientation (Hawaiian and street time) refers to a more lax and unconscious perception of time.

Even at the conscious level, we note subcultural time differences. Judee K. Burgoon and Thomas J. Saine observed, for example, that if you are invited to a Mormon's home for dinner, you should arrive *early* because punctuality is extremely important.[85] In our culture, the meaning of *on time* differs significantly, depending upon the subcultural time frame within which we operate:

> . . . Arriving even five minutes late requires an apology. Yet for a cocktail party or picnic, it may be perfectly acceptable to show up an hour after the party is supposed to begin. In New York City, an invitation to a party from 5:00 to 7:00 may mean that you are expected to arrive about 6:30 and stay until the party is over; in Salt Lake City, an invitation to a dinner at 6:00 generally means that you had better arrive at 5:45.[86]

Formal Time   Formal time refers to the way that a culture views and teaches time as a conscious entity. It is this formalness that creates what we may view as the time system according to which we operate: seconds, minutes, hours, days, weeks, months, years, decades, centuries. We attribute great importance to time systems in our culture, allocating salaries, wages, and time spent with someone on a continuum of positive to negative effect. Such a perspective concerning time is consciously taught to us as a function of five discrete time variables: order, cycle, value, duration, and tangibility.[87] When we learn time, the first thing we learn is that time is *ordered*. That is, Monday comes after Sunday and before Tuesday. This time ordering indicates the beginning and the ending of a period (a week). We further order our time in terms of the number of days per week, weeks per month, months per year, years per century, and so on. Leap year, for example, is discomforting to many because they have an "extra day" to deal with.

A second feature of the formal time structure we learn is the *cycle*. We live in a cyclic society, one that expects things to occur in a particular order over a given number of units (days, weeks, months, years). We feel good when we can talk about something happening in a year or two, implying cycle, or when good or bad "seasons" occur (e.g., hurricane, monsoon, summer, winter, fall, spring). We view time as having a *duration,* temporal continuum, or depth. Our perception of depth, however, is not as long or broad as some other cultures. We viewed the ten years we spent in Vietnam as a terribly long period; the North Vietnamese, however, viewed this period as but a ''drop in the bucket of time'' (counting from the early Chinese invasions of their land to the French and American invasions). For us duration is short-lived. Finally, we view time as *tangible*. We spend time, we buy time (time-sharing, for instance), and we view how valuable we are based on our hourly pay. One of the first things people do when they obtain a job is figure out what they are worth per hour. This can be ego defeating for those on salary. By breaking down the hours people work (at home and office) in terms of the total weekly salary, they find themselves actually working for less than the minimum wage.

Formal time, then, differs from informal time in that it is more conscious and is taught. Like informal time perception, formal time may differ in various situations, but this difference is more evident on the cultural than on the subcultural level. We tend to stereotype people as being more different than they actually are, based on formal time (which may lead to informal time systems).

Technical Time   The last time system we can discuss is technical time. Technical time is a precise way of measuring the relationship between a variable and time. We speak of ergs per square centimeter, of the atomic year (365 days, 5 hours, 48 minutes, and 45.51 seconds, give or take a millisecond), and of $E = mc^2$ (where c equals time). Each of these times is precise and technical but not too useful in everyday communication. Listen to an engineer or physicist (or chemist), however, and you will hear him or her speak about different types of time. Hence, technical time becomes standard and useful.

In sum, cultural time orientations offer us different frames from which to view time. We can begin with those taught and see how informal orientations create differences. Or conversely, we can begin with the informal and note the differences. We need to remember that how we perceive time is based not only on cultural differences but also on subcultural differences.

Psychological Time Orientations

There are at least two major approaches to the study of psychological time orientations. Perhaps the best known is that advocated by Joost Meerloo.[88] A second time orientation has been proposed by Thomas Cottle, which differs sufficiently from Meerloo's to warrant investigation.[89] Both are similar in that they view the time orientation of an individual as the way a person views his or her own ''personal life span between birth and death.''[90] This Meerloo calls, **clinical time,** a conscious and unconscious use of time during the life span.

Meerloo considers psychological time as operating on one of four mutually exclusive levels. We may be in one of the four time orientations at any one particular point in our lives, but we generally only hold one orientation or level at any given point. Meerloo theorizes that our personal time orientations indicate how we relate to self and others. The first state is that of a **past orientation** to self or others. At this stage, we view time as a cycle; we relive the past in a sentimental way, and we learn from the past. Anyone who has had a blind date and is offered another one (the person has a ''good personality'') may react from the lessons of the past. If the past indicated that blind dates were good, then he or she might accept; if, however, the past indicated problems, then we would expect that the person would reject the idea of a blind date.

The **time-line orientation** differs from the past in that we take a more analytic view of what has happened. In this orientation, we tend to examine the past for its impact on the present then project this into the future; time becomes a systematic progression from past to present to future.

With a time-line orientation, the person's blind-date history would be considered with reference to present needs, then these needs would be projected into the future (the probability of a ''bad'' date, the need for the date, and the possible future consequences are all analyzed).

Meerloo's **present orientation** is conditioned by a view of time that speaks for the here and now. Present orientation does not take into account anything beyond the immediate past or anything very far into the future. Those operating on the present time orientation may be considered the ''me first'' type, requiring only immediate gratification and worrying very little about future consequences. In some ways the American culture is perceived as possessing only a present orientation in relations with other cultures. Consider, for instance, how we treat other countries every four years (as presidents change).

The final orientation is a **future orientation.** The futurist spends much time thinking about what will happen, projecting events and acts of the present into the future, and then considering the consequences beyond the present.

In some ways, we are almost forced to adopt different time orientations. Consider, for example, your education. Somewhere around the seventh grade, you were asked to project your thinking into the future to make a career choice. Based on that choice, you were assigned either to a college-bound or to a career-bound curriculum. That placement was, in part, based on a time-line perspective that examined your performance on certain tests (past), your current career choice (present), and your needs to meet your career choice (future). Based on this simple interaction, you began to be programmed for an occupational area (college versus noncollege in this case; the difference between shop and typing courses). Your problem, however, is that school (including college) places you in a very present orientation; you have too many assignments due too soon. Hence, you ''live for today,'' that is, you put off until tomorrow what you do not want to do today. It is only when you fail a course that you assume a past orientation. (The same sequence may be followed when someone decides to major in a field based on one good professor, one who is well thought of; it is all fine until you meet the one who is not so good.)

Cottle maintains that the psychological time orientations we hold are not quite as fixed as Meerloo's. He asserts that we view time either as continuous or discontinuous and that this orientation creates an ''attention to life.'' Cottle infers that the view of time should be more spatial/ mental rather than linear. This is especially true, he argues, if one considers John Dewey's idea that the future remains continually empty.[91] By this Cottle means that the future is only a fantasy, whereas the past includes real experiences retrievable through memory.

Cottle's orientations to time are similar to Meerloo: past, present, and future. Past orientation, he indicates, is an orientation in which the individual deals with things that are over, our experiences. Present time is that which is instantaneous, and is associated with segments of time that prepare for the future. But there are two types of present: past-present and present. In the past-present orientation, Cottle perceives the human being as an *observer* of action (one whose perception is tied in the past as it acts in the present). The present orientation, on the other hand, yields a perception of man as an *agent* of action, a person who makes events happen. The future orientation is also seen as existing as a dichotomy. In the future, we classify those who, with a genuine attraction to the future, view events from that standpoint, and those who view the future as a place in which to avoid the past and present events. Each will assume a distinct communication orientation and exhibit distinct behaviors.

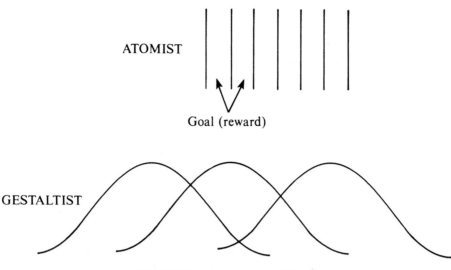

FIGURE 9.2   Perceptions of Time.

How these three orientations are perceived or pursued tends to separate Cottle from Meerloo. Cottle postulates that people perceive the three time orientations in gestaltist or atomist terms. The **atomist** confronts each time orientation as distinctly different and separate. The **gestaltist** sees not only a relationship between time zones but a temporal horizon where each zone affects the other. (See Figure 9.2.) The atomist is discontinuous and egocentric (holding a view that the present is but an intermediary period to be used to prepare for the future). The gestaltist views time as continuous and historiocentric (a view in which the time one has is shared with others collectively rather than through individual achievement). Cottle argues that the egocentric/atomist is faced with dissatisfaction in work and relationships when rewards and gratification are postponed and life becomes more incomplete.

The difference between Meerloo and Cottle is that Meerloo looks at ''levels'' of time, and Cottle looks at zones of time. Both deal with a psychological perspective suggesting that we work out our own conceptions of time flow and our own relationship between past, present, and future. The degree to which these relationships are continuous or discontinuous will predict satisfaction with life and hence influence or determine their communicative ''styles.''

Sex Differences   Cottle's major premise is that time perception also differs according to both sex and sex role. He believes that males tend to view their world in a more continuous way, one that is continually taking away from him; females seem more able to accept each moment as it comes along and not worry about how many moments are left.

> One's sexual and sex-role development bear heavily on one's perception of time. Women, for example, know that their childbearing period begins with the onset of menstruation; men experience no clearcut commencement of a period of childbearing years. They learn that at some point in time sexual potency increases, that at another point it diminishes, and that at still a later point it may cease altogether. Men, therefore, develop a sense of a fearful eventuality awaiting some time in the future.[92]

Social roles, then, require that men learn how to deal with the future, to plan for future courses of action; women are more concerned with the present. Whereas a man, based on his social role, is expected to maintain a steady course in life (more like the gestaltist orientation), a woman is prepared to change her perceptions about past, present, and future. Cottle argues that (1) the ''market orientation to perceiving time'' causes males to view time over a longer period, with a more temporal horizon; and that (2) females are better prepared to deal with time in a more atomistic way. He argues that because ''women still change their names in marriage and usually their place of residence,'' these factors may contribute to their predisposition to a more discontinuous view of time.[93] Whether this will hold true with changing sex roles is yet to be seen.

Time Talks

By now you should understand how time differs on three levels: cultural (and subcultural), psychological, and biological. Some researchers and writers in the area of nonverbal communication do not include time as a subcode. We believe that time is significant for two reasons. Time communicates a variety of messages, as Burgoon and Saine point out in an anecdote about Harry S. Truman:

> The story is told about Harry Truman, who shortly after assuming the presidency, was visited by a newspaper editor. After the editor had waited forty-five minutes in Truman's outer office, an aide went in to tell the President that the man was becoming very irritated about his long wait. Truman replied, ''When I was a junior senator from Missouri that same man kept me cooling my heels for an hour and a half. As far as I'm concerned, the son of a bitch has forty-five minutes to go.''[94]

In other ways, time talks. Be five minutes late for an interview, and you lose the job. On the other hand, be ten minutes early, and the secretary who sends you in will let the boss know through tone of voice alone that you are insecure.[95]

Time can be used as a relational message. Punctuality may produce two rather strange results. A female can make her date perceive her as more attractive (worth more) by having him wait a short time (''cooling his heels''). Much like Burgoon and Saine's example, we establish a message by how long we wait. Would you want to go to a doctor who did not make you wait? (What kind of doctor would see you as soon as you get into the *waiting* room?)

Second, time is very manipulatable. We manipulate others based on the amount of time we spend with them, by the amount of time we do not spend with them, and by the way we spend time with them. Sometimes we communicate punishment by the way we use time, as in silences. Silence can be the cutting edge in an argument. When people are in authority or power, silence is considered a sign of respect.[96] Silence is also necessary for interpersonal relationships. When we are comfortable in silence, there seems to be a positiveness associated with the relationship.

In what many Americans consider a hectic pace as a result of our culture, physiological problems occur that affect social behavior. Several studies have been conducted on what some refer to as Type A behavior (extreme impatience, aggressiveness, and hostility, competitive achievement striving, and time urgency). Perry, Kane, Bernesser, and Spicker found that college students who were identified as having Type A personalities were more likely to cheat on an examination than those who where described as Type B personalities.[97] College students who were Type A also reported having more daily hassles than those who were Type B.[98] Other researchers found that people had an inability to sleep when encountering a time zone change. They noted changes in

TABLE 9.3   *Fast Cities, Slow Cities: How They Rank*

	OVERALL PACE	WALKING SPEED	BANK SPEED	TALKING SPEED	WATCHES WORN	CHD*
Boston, MA	1	2	6	6	2	10
Buffalo, NY	2	5	7	15	4	2
New York, NY	3	11	11	28	1	1
Salt Lake City, UT	4	4	16	12	11	31
Columbus, OH	5	22	17	1	19	26
Worcester, MA	6	9	22	6	6	4
Providence, RI	7	7	9	9	19	3
Springfield, MA	8	1	15	20	22	7
Rochester, NY	9	20	2	26	7	14
Kansas City, MO	10	6	3	15	32	21
St. Louis, MO	11	15	20	9	15	8
Houston, TX	12	10	8	21	19	36
Paterson, NJ	13	17	4	11	31	4
Bakersfield, CA	14	28	13	5	17	20
Atlanta, GA	15	3	27	2	36	33
Detroit, MI	16	21	12	34	2	11
Youngstown, OH	17	13	18	3	30	6
Indianapolis, IN	18	18	23	8	24	22
Chicago, IL	19	12	31	3	27	13
Philadelphia, PA	20	30	5	22	11	16
Louisville, KY	21	16	21	29	15	18
Canton, OH	22	23	14	26	15	9
Knoxville, TN	23	25	24	30	11	17
San Francisco, CA	24	19	35	26	5	27
Chattanooga, TN	25	35	1	32	24	12
Dallas, TX	26	26	28	15	28	32
Oxnard, CA	27	30	30	23	7	34
Nashville, TN	28	8	26	24	33	14
San Diego, CA	29	27	34	18	9	24
East Lansing, MI	30	14	33	12	34	29
Fresno, CA	31	36	25	17	19	25
Memphis, TN	32	34	10	19	34	30
San Jose, CA	33	29	29	30	22	35
Shreveport, LA	34	32	19	33	28	19
Sacramento, CA	35	33	32	36	26	23
Los Angeles, CA	36	24	36	35	13	28

Lower numbers indicate faster speeds, more watches worn, higher CHD rates.

*Rates of coronary heart disease, adjusted for the median age in each city.

From Robert Levine, ''Pace of Life'' in *Psychology Today*, October 1989.

Reprinted with permission from *Psychology Today* magazine. Copyright
© 1989 (Sussex Publishers, Inc.).

sleeping patterns when there was an altitude change as well.[99] Finally, Robert Levine reported that cities with the fastest paces also reported the highest rates of heart disease. Table 9.3 lists the cities with the fastest paces in the United States of those studied. Levine defined pace based on the walking speed of pedestrians; how long it took bank tellers to give change; how long it took postal clerks to explain the differences among regular mail, certified mail, and insured mail; and whether people wore watches.[100]

☐ **Summary** ☐

This chapter has expanded the notion of nonverbal communication into areas of perception. A perceptual state, it was argued, exists when the information received exists around the level of consciousness. We examined biofeedback as a perceptual system that may be used to explain emotion, mood state, and possible deceptive communication.

We looked at olfaction as a nonverbal subcode. Not only are we subconsciously influenced by the odors around us, but we are much better at identifying such odors than was previously thought. Olfaction serves several purposes. On one level, it deals with the basic survival needs: the scent of emotion and sexual attraction. On another level, it is associated with the labels we ascribe to the odors we perceive. Such perception can make us fair prey to those who would manipulate both our perceptions and our memory. The perfume *Charlie* is associated with a strong and progressive young female. Not too many traditional females would wear such a fragrance. Olfactory memory is used to sell us on products that have some form of emotive connotation. Olfactory memory may, in this regard, act as a form of deja vu; we sense we've been there before, smell we have been there before, and associate that perception with the present experience. In any event, our ability to manipulate and influence by means of smell has great potential; it is an area that needs further research.

Finally, we discussed time. We usually act and react to time as though we take it for granted, with little thought as to the messages we send and receive. On the cultural level, time sets forth expectations and unfortunately leads to stereotyped differences between and within cultures. At the psychological level, time serves to establish a way in which to see the events around us and to describe a posture from which we perceive time (continuous or discontinuous). At the biological level, we observe how individual rhythms operate to synchronize us with those around us and with the environment, including our physical, intellectual, and emotional readiness to respond to others. Finally, time as a variable in the communication process serves as a message in a variety of ways.

Section Three

Applications

□   □   □

This section completes our study of nonverbal communication. To review quickly, we began our study of the nonverbal system by defining what we were studying, how it differs from the verbal system, how it functions with the verbal system, and finally, what its subcodes are. We are now ready to *apply* this knowledge in several contexts. At this stage in most textbooks, you are on our own. We believe, however, that sufficient information is now available to indicate how the various subcodes operate in social situations, in the family, and on the job.

We start with an examination of an area that has received some attention. Our discussion of how nonverbal communication is used in social situations begins by looking at the courtship and quasi-courtship behaviors in which we all engage. It considers why we do so and what to look for. We then move to power plays, or how we use nonverbal communication to increase our perceived power, status, credibility, and attraction. We also examine the process of identifying first impressions and how we manipulate them.

Next we move to the family and observe how we use nonverbal communication in day-to-day activities there. We look specifically at the spatio-temporal subcodes such as environment, time, and space; we also note how the physical appearance, zero-proxemic, vocalic, and kinesic areas impact home life. We look at the developmental aspects of nonverbal communication in childhood, in marriage, in adult life, and finally, with the aged. This chapter examines the processes by which we relate to people we care a great deal about, how that concern and that affection are communicated, and their impact on the growth of a ''nuclear'' unit.

Chapter 12 examines nonverbal communication on the job. We are interested in how the environment, the use and alteration of space, and the use of time interact to create impressions of how we work and who we are on the job. We consider the importance of building a nonverbal image through kinesics, physical appearance, and other subcodes. Finally, we examine in detail the process of getting a job—the nonverbal factors of the job interview—and how you can create an impression of power and credibility.

The last chapter sums up what we have been studying. It describes the problems associated with definition and functions. This chapter might be considered the ''quick review'' or ''guide'' chapter. It may be useful as a reference later in your academic or professional career.

By now you have the necessary information with which to begin to apply nonverbal communication. These final chapters expand upon the information found in Section 2 to provide application of nonverbal communication as each subcode operates to change the impact of your own, personal communication. Perhaps some strategy or theory will emerge from this material that enables you to increase your awareness of how you are manipulated and, in turn, how to deal more effectively with your environment and those in it. At the very least, you now possess the necessary information to understand others' nonverbal communication; based on this, you may be able to predict both intent and outcome.

Chapter Ten

Nonverbal Communication in Social Situations

Key Concepts

Intimate Behavior

Male-Male Friendships

Female-Female Friendships

Matching Hypothesis

The previous chapters have provided us with the results and conclusions of contemporary research on nonverbal communication, as obtained through laboratory investigations, survey questionnaires, and field experiments. In this chapter, we describe some of the nonverbal factors that operate in social situations (female-male; male-male; female-female).

The underlying assumption of this chapter is that social interactions are composed of the exchange of messages, which are often combined to form conversations. Ultimately, a number of these conversations are combined into what we call a relationship. From a communication standpoint, then, a relationship is composed of a number of message exchanges between individuals. The focus of these messages certainly varies from person to person, from situation to situation, and from culture to culture. The types of nonverbal norms discussed in this chapter are especially pertinent to white, middle-class American society. The situations in this chapter are concerned primarily with non-job-related and non-family-related, heterosexual relationships as well as general friendships, both cross-sex and same-sex. The focus is *liking,* the primary ingredient in such relationships, as opposed to family and job relationships, both of which contain a number of complex power and status differentials.

Meeting the Opposite Sex

As an example, we will look at the old-fashioned "blind date." In this type of stranger-to-stranger interaction, both parties know the general type of situation in advance. For a number of reasons, the parties involved (Jim and Jane) attempt to collect as much information as possible about one another before the face-to-face meeting. One of the primary reasons for doing this is to increase the predictability about the other person.[1] Thus, Jim and Jane acquire as much data as possible through an intermediary, Mary. Mary knows both Jim and Jane, and she believes they would enjoy being with one another.

As a "match-maker," Mary would probably use the **matching hypothesis;** that is, people tend to choose partners considered to be in the same category of physical attractiveness.[2] Unfortunately, Mary's perception may not be the same as Jim's or Jane's. Thus, when Mary says, "Jane has a nice personality," and "All the girls like her," Jim knows that Jane probably is not very attractive. Jim, like most males, is quite interested in physical attractiveness. As mentioned previously, physical attractiveness is the single most important quality in initial cross-sex interactions.

If Jim were to see three females sitting at a table in the local campus pub, he might or might not choose Jane as the one to dance with. Generally, if there were three females seated at the table, Jim would probably choose the one in the middle in terms of physical attractiveness. If Jane were with a more attractive friend and a less attractive friend, then Jane would probably be selected. Thus, for Jim, the matching hypothesis is a combination of physical attractiveness and "chance of success," in this case the chances of Jane's agreeing to dance with Jim. If Jim is unsuccessful with Jane, then as the night goes on, as the lights go down, and as he has a few more drinks, he may ask Jane's less attractive friend to dance. Generally, both very unattractive and very attractive partners are less preferred than those in the medium range.

While on the "blind date," Jim is going to be concerned primarily with physical appearance. His evaluation will be based on Jane's bosom, general body shape, and eyes. Jane's evaluation of Jim will be based on overall physique, grooming and neatness, and eyes.[3] Although personality and intelligence will have some effect on the probability of a second date, *the single most important factor is physical appearance.*[4]

A number of factors go into what one considers physically attractive. For example, when people who are in love rate the physical attractiveness of other, third persons, they rate them as more attractive than do people who are not in love.[5] Females are more in agreement about what constitutes physical attractiveness than are males.[6] Rainville and Gallagher found that a perception of dominance increases one's physical attractiveness, but less so for females than for males.[7] In television commercials, baby-faced experts were considered less expert but more trustworthy than their mature-faced counterparts.[8] Thinner figures are associated with more positive characteristics.[9] And, while unattractive female faces were associated with higher homosexuality ratings, the same was not found to be true of males.[10]

As the night goes on, Jim and Jane begin to talk. At first this conversation may be awkward. The awkwardness of the conversation is noticeable to both parties because of certain verbal and nonverbal exchanges. Jim and Jane frequently switch topics; they ask seemingly meaningless questions; they repeat statements and questions. In terms of vocalics, there are many stutters and stammers, but of most importance, there are many meaningless pauses. Laughter is sometimes quelled because each is unfamiliar with the humor of the other. Neither wants to appear "too serious" or "too flighty."

General Characteristics

These vocal cues are significant for another reason. Voice quality, assertiveness, response level, and intensity become meaningful aspects of physical attractiveness when two opposite-sex people interact in an intimate environment. Simply by being alone together in Jim's or Jane's car, the two find themselves in such an environment.

Both feel the need to increase the space initially, to allow more freedom for each one. The initial interaction is *strained* because neither knows what to expect from the other.

When Jim and Jane arrive at the basketball arena (the scene of their date), they find that some of the strain is gone and that they are actually physically closer to one another. Like their home team, State U., they are both somehow aware of "home territory."

Jim and Jane are now seated together as close as they have ever been. The advantage of being in the arena is that there are thousands of distractions to keep each one from paying too much attention to the other. Each of them has friends at the game who come by to speak. Each of them introduces friends to the other. At this point, physical appearance enters the situation once again. Now Jim is not only concerned about how Jane looks *to him* but is also concerned about how she looks *to his friends*. Jane has the same feelings about Jim.

Overall physical appearance becomes a factor. But what are the specific physical traits the two are seeking in one another? Essentially, each wants the other to "fit in" with his or her "crowd." Jim would be quite disappointed if Jane were excessively overweight. Perhaps he would have decided to forgo the basketball game. He may not have been pleased had Jane been exceedingly underweight, appearing to have *anorexia nervosa*. Thus, Jim prefers Jane to be the medium weight person she is.

When Jim first talked to Mary about Jane, he also asked Mary about Jane's hair color. As L. Malandro, L. Barker, and D. Barker have noted: "Blond hair has been the mark of both the princess and whore."[11] Blondes are known "to have more fun," to be the ones "gentlemen prefer," and are stereotyped as "dumb." Redheads are known for their tempestuousness and their tempers. Brunettes are probably found most often in American society. Jim had a preference to go out with a brunette, which is perhaps one reason why Mary selected Jane. Though Jim preferred a brunette, there is no evidence to show that males generally prefer females with any particular hair color. Some males have preferences for blondes; others have preferences for brunettes; still others prefer redheads. Also Jim probably does not know whether Jane dyes her hair or not, although more brunettes dye their hair blond than vice versa. Some also "streak" their hair. If Jim is very conservative, he probably does not like streaking (of the hair).

The conservative male also prefers hairstyles and lengths that are "typical" for the time. These variables may change from year to year, and they differ according to subculture. For Jim, very curly and long hair are "out."

Because he perceives himself as conservative, Jim also prefers little makeup for his date (or at least he thinks he does). Although he likes for a woman to wear some lipstick or lip gloss, he does not want it to be the first thing his male friends notice about Jane. He wants Jane to look "natural"; he really wants her to wear the *appropriate* makeup to look natural, rather than looking made-up or not wearing any makeup. Eye shadow may be the primary factor that distinguishes the well made-up versus the poorly made-up female. Both the color and the quantity of shadow influence how eye shadow may look. Some college coeds also have a tendency to overdo the use of blush, so much so that the term has lost its original meaning. Blushing is more often undertaken by females than by males anyway.[12]

Assuming Jane's hair, cosmetics, body shape, and neatness of appearance "meet with Jim's approval," the next concern is dress. John T. Molloy writes: ". . . dressing to succeed in business and dressing to be sexually attractive are almost mutually exclusive."[13] Molloy has looked at women's dressing for sexual attractiveness in terms of whom they are trying to attract (men with old money; men with new money; doctors, scientists, accountants, engineers; corporate businessmen; professional army officers; salesmen; blue-collar workers; lawyers; dentists; professors; men in high-risk professions; artists, musicians, writers; and men in high-fashion industries).[14] Unfortunately for Jane, Jim does not fall into any of Molloy's categories. As a college student, Jim can find at least five male dress stereotypes: the preppy, the greaser, the jock, the freak, and the nerd.[15]

In the college environment, Jane has much more flexibility than she would in other places. Designer clothes almost always appear appropriate. Traditional, but not "country," clothes are generally acceptable. Jane should appear in attractive, but not overly sexually appealing clothes.

On the other hand, Jane is concerned about the appearance that Jim presents to her friends. She does not want Jim to be overweight, nor does she wish him to be shorter than she is. Again, she may have a preference for a particular hair color, but this will be Jane's opinion. She probably would not like Jim to have a flat-top or to appear like a "hippie" of the 1960s. As you may note, there are more stereotypes for Jane to live up to than for Jim; there are stronger stereotypes for female attractiveness.

While they are still at the basketball game, the thoughts of intimacy or possible intimacy (**fantasy**) may run through their minds. We take note of what the research has to tell us.

Intimate Behavior

Desmond Morris has suggested 12 steps in animal courtship that appear to apply generally to human beings.[16] These steps vary from person to person, but they provide us with a hypothetical sequence of events. Jim and Jane may or may not *physically* go through each step, but remember, they are *fantasizing*. The first step is *eye-to-body*. Here the two parties seek out the general physical appearance of the other. The second step is *eye-to-eye*.[17] This is when the evaluation of the attractiveness of the eyes is made. Usually there is an initial gaze, looking away, and finally mutual gaze. A gaze held and reciprocated for more than three seconds usually indicates a desire to interact. At this stage individuals are attempting to gain information about character (especially trustworthiness). Staring is considered to be an act of aggression. As has been mentioned, the third stage, *voice-to-voice*, is an important variable in determining physical attractiveness. As a British friend of ours has stated, however: "I don't want to be just an accent object."

The fourth stage is *hand-to-hand*. While hand holding may occur briefly early in the first interaction, this hand holding will be limited in time and restricted to semiprivate situations (such as in a movie theatre or in an automobile while driving). *Arm-to-shoulder* is the fifth stage. This is the first stage toward intimacy. It can be used as an extension of the same method used with friends. However, it can be first trunk-to-trunk interaction. *Arm-to-waist* is the next stage. This stage separates the "friendly" arm-to-shoulder interaction from a more intimate interaction. The hand is now closer to the genital region. The seventh stage is *mouth-to-mouth*. There is a likelihood that physiological arousal may first appear in this stage. "The female may experience genital secretions, and the male's penis may start to become erect."[18]

Lenore Tieffer has undertaken an extensive study of kissing behavior. She writes: "Nothing seems more natural than a kiss. Consider the French kiss, also known as the soul kiss, or tongue kiss (to the French, it was the Italian kiss, but only during the Renaissance). Western societies regard this passionate exploration of mouths and tongues as an instinctive way to express love and to arouse desire."[19] According to Tieffer, the kiss may be used as (1) a sexual act, (2) a sign of friendship, (3) a gesture of respect, (4) a health threat, (5) a ceremonial celebration, or (6) a disgusting behavior. As some have said, kissing is simply the mutual exchange of saliva.

Clellan Ford and Frank Beach studied sexual customs in 190 tribal societies. They found that only 21 mentioned kissing. Four of these kissed by sucking the lips and tongues of their partners. They also found that Lapps kissed the nose and the mouth at the same time.[20] Even in the United States, Tieffer reports a study undertaken by Martha Stein, which showed little kissing among call girls. In that study, the researcher was in rooms, hidden from view, where she observed 1,230 sexual encounters among 64 call girls. In only 36 percent of these encounters did the partners engage in deep kissing. Thirteen percent of the encounters included sweet talk, seduction, adoration, and tongue kissing.[21] In Japan, kissing is acceptable only between mother and child. For the Japanese, "Intercourse is 'natural'; a kiss, pornographic."[22]

In Western culture, there are also nonsexual uses of the kiss, including greetings and farewells, affection, religion, deference to higher authority, making the hurt go away, sealing a bargain, blessing sacred vestments, making up, and showing betrayal (Judas kiss). The Hindus maintain four types of kissing that are not prevalent in western society: tongue-sucking, tongue-tilting, tongue scraping, and lip biting.

In summing up the importance of the mouth in human interaction, Tieffer states:

> Deep kissing causes other physiological changes. The presence of a lover's tongue in one's mouth induces the secretion of saliva, which is under neural control (seventh and ninth cranial nerves) and thus appears in response to any stimulus in the mouth. Most societies find juicy kisses more desirable than dry ones, but they seek a balance. Excessively wet kisses are unpopular (as the Danes say, "He's nice to kiss—when one is thirsty."), but a dry, tight kiss is usually regarded as either immature or inhibited.[23]

It is important to note that kissing is not a *naturally* sexually stimulating act. "Sex researchers generally agree that the only way infants and young children can be sexually aroused is by direct stimulation of the genitals." The arousal of kissing is largely caused by the attachment of sexual symbols with the act itself. "The frequency and intensity of kissing [in the United States] varies according to gender, social class, sexual orientation, and the degree of emotional intimacy that the relationship calls for."[24]

Alfred C. Kinsey and associates found that 90 percent of the married women in the United States reported deep kissing during marital sex. However, only 41 percent of men with an eighth-grade education reported tongue kissing their wives, whereas 77 percent of college-educated males reported doing so. Kinsey also found less tongue kissing among male than among female homosexuals.[25]

Kissing, then, may or may not be sexually arousing. Kissing varies by culture, gender, social class, sexual orientation, and degree of intimacy. Even in sexual encounters, kissing may be absent as a stimulating factor.

Morris's eighth step is *hand-to-head.* As has been noted in Sidney Jourard's and Lawrence B. Rosenfeld's studies, the head is an intimate part of the body. In this stage: "Fingers stroke the face, neck, and hair. Hands clasp the nape and the side of the head."[26] The final three steps increase intimacy drastically. Step nine is *hand-to-body.* Step ten is *mouth-to-breast.* Step eleven is *hand-to-genitals.*

The Diagram Group states that more than 45 percent of the men reported receiving fellatio in heterosexual relations, but only about 16 percent of them reported giving cunnilingus. Objections to *mouth-to-genitals* encounters have ranged from unnatural to sinful to unhygienic to unpleasant.[27]

Whether or not the two parties engage in all of the above steps, the last step will be *genitals-to-genitals.* Two irreversible acts can take place here. First, if the female is a virgin, the hymen is ruptured. Second, fertilization is often a possibility.[28]

Since the first edition of this book only a few years ago, the degree to which sexual promiscuity has occurred has decreased tremendously. The always present threat of venereal disease has had an upsurge. More significant, however, has been the media deluge of information about AIDS, a disease of startling proportions in which sexual histories are recorded in each sexual act. Certainly, sexual behaviors today are much more reserved than they were eight years ago.

Environment, Proxemics, Chronemics

By now the basketball game has been completed. The next thought for Jane is the uncertainty of where they are going now, how much intimacy Jim will attempt, and when he will take his next step. [We must remember that Jim and Jane are no longer strangers in the strictest sense; they have completed step three and may have completed step four if they held hands walking to the coliseum.] The environment in which the next interaction takes place will have a significant impact on the answers to the other questions. Albert Mehrabian has provided us with some information about numerous types of environments, including movie theatres, museums and galleries, stores, and bars.[29]

Because the ballgame ended after 10:00 P.M., it is unlikely that some of these places will be the next stop for Jim and Jane, but let's examine what Mehrabian has to say about them. "Movie theatres can be enormous, quasibaroque, reserved-seating palaces; chi-chi, medium-sized, first-run houses with lines going around the block twice; comfortable old nabes showing double spaghetti westerns of *Les Regles der Jeu* and *Les Enfants der paradis* for $1.50; or porn houses in which more is going on in the balcony and the johns than on the screen."[30] The first-run house is more typical for a college community. Often the theatre has two, three, four, or more films going on at the same time. The movie theater involves less control (or dominance) than a person would have at home watching television. However, if the movie theater is not too crowded, some intimacy among two partners and the film can be achieved if the film is of the appropriate genre.

"As physical environments, theatres [in general] are usually loaded and pleasant (exciting)."[31] These are usually high-status environments. The state of arousal a member of the audience may achieve at a concert or play is much greater than one would achieve in a movie theatre. The "live" performance generates excitement. In addition, the crowd itself may induce arousal. It is desirable, however, not to go to these events alone; someone should be with you to share the excitement. However, it is now too late for a play (at a theatre), and Jim has no desire for a museum environment either, although individual art may precipitate arousal also. Because they are in a small college town, the stores are now closed, too. For this reason, Jim decides to take Jane to the local bar. Naturally, as Robert Sommer has described them, bars are "designed for drinking."[32]

"In the pub there is a general freedom from anxiety—any man with the money can be certain of a welcome."[33] In the bar, a person may have some privacy, but the general rule is to be open to interaction with others in the bar. The nature of the particular environment ranges from place to place, based upon legal restrictions and social customs. The duration of one's stay in a bar will depend upon lighting, noise level, others present, other stimuli, types of alcohol, and the amount of funds available.

College towns usually have bars that cater to various types of audiences. Mehrabian writes: "At the high-load extreme, there should be a large dancing bar featuring 120-decibel acid rock, strobe lights, and a laughing, pushing, shouting, sweating mob."[34] Going to a bar allows the two to eliminate some anxiety and inhibitions. If dancing is allowed, the amount of touching is increased. At this point, the two begin to know one another rather well. When Jim takes Jane home, she asks him to come in for one last drink. The nonverbal, interpersonal processes that occur after this are pretty much left up to the interactants.

Cross-Sex Friendships

Male-female friendships almost always carry with them the undercurrent possibility of there being more to the relationship. Particularly if the two individuals have known each other for an extended length of time, both are aware of this undercurrent. Although the two may touch one another, and even kiss, they must be careful about the context, frequency, and nature of these tactile behaviors. Most people, however, report having few of these relationships because of the potential problems involved. Alan Booth and Elaine Hess, for example, found in one study that only 35 percent of the men and 24 percent of the women reported having cross-sex friendships.[35]

Same-Sex Relationships

Usually the sex variable becomes less important in same-sex relationships, but the power variable increases in importance. The variable of power in relationships has been studied extensively by Jay Haley and his associates.[36]

> If one took all the possible kinds of communicative behavior which two people might interchange, it could be roughly classified into behavior which defines a relationship as *symmetrical* and behavior which defines a relationship as *complementary*. A symmetrical relationship is one where two people exchange the same type of behavior. Each person will initiate action, criticize the other, offer advice, and so on. This type of relationship tends to be competitive; if one person mentions that he has succeeded in some endeavor, the other person points out that he has succeeded in some equally important endeavor. The people in such a relationship emphasize their symmetry with each other.
>
> A complementary relationship is one where the two people are exchanging different types of behaviors. One gives and the other receives, one teaches and the other learns. The two people exchange behavior which complements, or fits together. One is in a "superior" position and the other in a "secondary" in that one offers criticism and the other accepts it, one offers advice and the other follows it, and so on.

This simple division of relationships into two types is useful for classifying different relationships or different sequences within a particular relationship. No two people will consistently have one of the types in all circumstances; usually there are areas of a relationship worked out as one type or another. Relationships shift in nature either rapidly, as when people take turns teaching each other, or more slowly over time. When a child grows up he progressively shifts from a complementary relationship with his parents toward more symmetry as he becomes an adult.

Thus, we might say that some relationships are about "equal," that is, no one person is always "in charge." Others carry status differences and are unequal. An equal relationship may be defined as a "liking" relationship, and an unequal one may be considered a "power" relationship. We next investigate male-male friendships and female-female friendships and the nonverbal communication that accompanies each.

Male-Male Nonverbal Communication

The preoccupations that males share with one another appear to be sports (as participant, spectator, and Monday-morning quarterback), power (at work and at home), masculinity, and time. The fourth preoccupation finds males in a chronemic dead-heat run with themselves and with society in general. In the United States, males find that there is a rush to do more than their contemporaries; they must be better and quicker than other males. The interactions that take place between males involve power plays at work, quasi-leisure at the basketball and racquetball courts, and externally induced leisure at bars. In all of these cases there is an underlying tension, as if there is more to do in life; thus the chronemic focus is on the future. Although the competition with time and other men is a significant factor in the life of American men, most also attempt various interpersonal, complementary relationships.

Meeting the Same Sex There are various contexts in which males meet one another: on the job, through mutual friends, or at mutual recreation facilities. Unlike females, males generally disregard physical appearance in establishing relationships with one another. At the first meeting, there is a mutual attempt to determine the major interests of the other man. The conversation often leads to sports, when men define one another as baseball, football, or golf fans. One primary separation is the sports fan versus the nonsports fan. Once such a separation is found, the likelihood of a longterm relationship is lessened. A second separation is between team sports and individual sports. Males are taught the concept of being a "team player" early in life, and they are expected to maintain an interest in the team phenomenon throughout life. Examples of nonteam play may be "hogging" the ball when playing basketball, asking a best friend's girlfriend out on a date, and using "sneaky" means for beating out a competitor at work.

Males expect one another to be team players. They expect one another to accept differences (a fisherman versus a hunter versus a nonhunter) when working together on a common task. In addition, they expect one another to reward "good ol' boy" behavior and penalize those who do not engage in it. Upon first meeting, if there is tacit agreement as to conversation topics, and if the other is perceived as a team player, the chances are good that the two will maintain at least a short-term relationship. Lionel Tiger has indicated that the male relationship is likely to turn out better than a same-sex female relationship.[37]

In man's effort to be accepted into a group, it is necessary that he act as a team player, even at the cost of losing self-respect to the point of humiliation as a result of harassment and discomfort. This procedure is seen in high school and fraternity initiation rites, as well as in the types of behavior needed to be promoted to colonel in the army or to full professor in academia. To be accepted, one must learn to work with men to the complete exclusion of women. Athletic teams and military units cannot allow the influence of females to destroy the team effort. The advantages of female ''bonding'' are found along the lines of spontaneity and confidences.[38] The male role is based on **machismo.** According to this ''real man'' notion, males are viewed as independent, females as dependent. The independence carries with it a notion of control. Therefore, for males, nonverbal communication is controlled. Emotions are generally covered up, whether the actual *felt* emotions are positive or negative.

Males must also be in control of their roles, for they do not generally look at one another as complete human beings but rather as complementary role players: a tennis partner, a co-worker, or a drinking buddy. We now investigate how some of these roles are demonstrated in nonverbal communication.

The Environment   Males prefer same-sex environments that exclude feminine content. This is found in the bachelor apartment, the male bar, the poker game, the tennis court, and the office. The bachelor's apartment contains art objects, but not of the same type as would be found in a woman's apartment. Flowery objects and flowery-patterned coverings on furniture and drapes are omitted. Furniture fabrics are either solid or abstract, usually in earth tones. The music played on the stereo, while only males are present, is of the hard-rock, soul, or country variety. Generally, males do not prefer tender movies on television *in the presence of one another.* Instead, they opt for sports (even Australian football).

Bars where only men are present do not usually have flowers or candles on the tables. Tables do not usually have tablecloths. Beer is drunk from cans or bottles. Slot machines, pool tables, and game machines are likely to be present. In many ways, the dirtier the bar, the more *macho* it is.

The poker game allows males to get down to their undershirts and smoke cigars. Here the place can be ''messed up'' as much as desired, without any female influence. Conversations may be continuous, but males do not feel the obligation to carry on a continuous conversation, as women do. Much of the conversation takes the form of sports talk, the poker game, kidding one another, racist and sexist jokes, and storytelling. At the tennis court, the game is all business. Multicolored tennis balls, outfits, or racquets are less acceptable. Even in these games, activity is important. ''A major value in the American masculine world is to do—to be active and get things done.''[39]

The office is masculine also. Technical (mechanical and electronic) ''things'' are present; feminine ''things'' are absent. Diplomas, trophies, awards, and abstract art are present. Wood and bronze occupy the office. Plastic and too many plants are absent.

Friendly Interaction   When male friends talk with one another, there is little touching after the initial greeting—the handshake (except for team sports, where they ''pat'' one another on the behind or back to signify, ''well done''). There is little eye contact. In terms of proxemics, males sit close enough to talk with one another, but no closer. In movie theatres, male friends will often "skip" a seat between them if only two of them are there. At bars and in restaurants, they will generally sit across from one another or at corners but not next to one another (if only two are present). Although some males have at least one good friend, they reveal little to one another except in times of crisis or after a number of drinks. The following case serves as an example.[40]

> I have three close friends I have known since we were boys and they live here in the city. There are some things I wouldn't tell them. For example, I wouldn't tell them much about my work because we have always been highly competitive. I certainly wouldn't tell them about my feelings of any uncertainties with life or various things I do. And I wouldn't talk about any problems I have with my wife or in fact anything about my marriage and sex life. But other than that I would tell them anything. [After a brief pause he laughed and said;] That doesn't leave a hell of a lot, does it?

Although many males operate under a cloak of insecurity, this insecurity is rarely revealed to same-sex friends. However, the women's liberation movement has allowed some freedom for the new male.

The New Male Herb Goldberg has described eight factors he feels are descriptive of the "old male."[41] These factors Goldberg defines as self-destructive:

1. Emotional expression is feminine.
2. Giving in to pain is feminine.
3. Asking for help is feminine.
4. Paying too much attention to diet, especially when you're not sick, is feminine.
5. Alcohol abstinence is feminine.
6. Self-care is feminine.
7. Dependency is feminine.
8. Touching is feminine.

From this list, we see that factors 1 and 8 are particularly related to nonverbal communication. In the 1990s, the new male has discovered that emotional expression is human, not feminine. This change in encoding behavior also gives the new male a greater sensitivity to the nonverbal communication of others. In addition, the new sensitivity allows the male to touch others (male and female). Like the European male, some American males have learned that hugging male relatives and friends is a positive phenomenon.

Chronemics, however, remains the basic problem for the American male. Role-playing, as has been mentioned, plays an important part. Both sexes go through a similar process of socialization and development. Males, however, appear to feel a greater impact from aging, particularly in the middle years. Michael McGill writes: "Mid-life crisis refers to a rapid and substantial change in personality and behavior during the age period forty to sixty."[42]

The mid-age crisis may involve one or a combination of subcrises: (1) the goal gap, (2) vanity and virility, (3) the empty nest, (4) meeting mortality. The goal gap occurs when the individual finds that, in comparison with his peers, he is *falling behind* professionally. This "falling behind" is an example of the chronemic consciousness of the male. Some men accept their failure. Others go on to a new career and find new challenges; however, they often encounter failure in other areas of their lives. The wife of one of these men said: "Art got what he wanted, and the kids and I lost what we wanted. We are separated now—legally, that is. The divorce will be final soon. We have been separated ever since he took the other job because he changed when he married the other job.''[43] Other men have a crisis even when they have been successful in their work. They begin to lack goals.

A second type of crisis in the middle-aged man is concerned with vanity and virility. Several physiological changes occur during this ''male menopause.'' There is a slight change in gonadal functioning; there begins to be an inability to achieve erection or ejaculation. Other changes are also occurring: ''urinary irregularities; fluid retention and resultant swelling; hot flashes; heart symptoms such as pseudo angina; peptic ulcers; itching; headaches; and dizziness.'' Changes most apparent to others include ''liver spots, baldness, gradual weight gain, fatigue, insomnia, irritability, moodiness, and depression.''[44]

With these physiological changes, there are corresponding changes in behavior and personality. Males often turn to alcohol and other drugs. They may avoid sexual activity altogether, or they may seek new pleasures, often with a younger partner, the so-called ''Jennifer Syndrome.'' The daughter of one middle-aged man commented: ''. . . my father got old and he got horny. He began attacking every girl he got near—employees, patients, *my friends!* He cut Mom off physically and financially. He drove her to drink and worse. He's taken up with Marcia, who is my age, and their behavior together is disgusting. He's embarrassed and humiliated me and Mom just so he can stay young. This whole thing just makes me sick.''[45] To account for the problem of ''looking young'' men buy new clothes, jog, get hair transplants, dye their hair, buy sports cars, and so on.

The third type of subcrisis is the empty nest. The father is concerned about his age because his last child has left home. The fourth subcrisis, mortality, is probably the core of all of the problems. Thus, both physical and psychological problems occur for many males in the middle years. Females go through a similar crisis during menopause.[46]

Female-Female Nonverbal Communication

Studies indicate that women are better encoders and decoders of nonverbal cues than men are. However, men seem to be better encoders of positive emotion, whereas women are better at expressing negative emotions. But this statement may not pertain as much to encoding ability as it does to the perceptions of men and women. Because women typically smile more than men, negative emotions are detected more easily in women. On the other hand, smiles and positive expressions are rare in men; therefore, such positive expressions are more noticeable in men.

Women not only look at others more, but they also find conversation more difficult when they cannot see the person to whom they are speaking. Women, regardless of status, also tend to have less personal space than men. Moreover, women are approached more closely by both men and women. One study found that women dyads in waiting rooms sat closer than men pairs. Also, in crowded situations, women seem to become less irritated than men. Frank N. Willis found that ''women stood closer to close friends than did males.''[47]

Mehrabian's immediacy principle states that people are drawn to and touch those they like, withdrawing from and touching less those whom they dislike. In general, women and men both stand closer to people they like. However, women differ from men in that they use indirect body orientation with liked and disliked persons, using closer body orientation in neutral relationships. Body orientation also relates to status for both men and women. More direct body orientation is used with people of higher status.

Female-Female Relationships   Generalizations can be made about female-female relationships; however, these general statements seem to differ according to the intensity of the relationships. In other words, women behave differently with other women who are considered mere acquaintances than with other women who are considered to be close friends. Moreover, women seem to make the distinction between friend and "close" friend more often than men do.

In trying to distinguish among the various nonverbal cues that women exhibit in same-sex relationships, consider a hypothetical situation. Cindy is an office clerk who has been employed by the company for several years. Lisa is a new employee of the company and is working in the same office as Cindy. Although their jobs are independent of each other, Cindy has more power in the relationship because she is more familiar with the procedures of the company and Lisa is just the "new kid on the block." Cindy and Lisa are acquaintances with the potential of becoming friends because of the amount of time that they must spend with each other at work. However, for a friendship to develop (beyond the level of acquaintance), Cindy's power within the relationship must be diminished. Reduction of power in a relationship, in turn, increases the level of liking.

Assuming that Cindy and Lisa are still at the acquaintance level, what are the general nonverbal norms that each one observes while playing the role of acquaintance? At this point, the perception of power in the relationship is very keen by both women. Thus Cindy's nonverbal cues tend to indicate her power. She may have more direct eye contact for longer durations with Lisa than Lisa has with her. Lisa, however, might maintain a greater distance when approaching Cindy. This may be Lisa's subconscious recognition of Cindy's power. Also, some paralanguage cues might indicate more authority in Cindy's conversational voice and more friendliness (a subordinate role) in Lisa's.

At this point, although Cindy has the power in the relationship, there may be a third party whom both women would like to have as a friend. This creates an atmosphere of competition, especially if the third party is male. In this case, both Cindy and Lisa become very sensitive to the nonverbal cues that each directs to the man. Each woman will monitor these cues, especially personal appearance, trying to evaluate herself as a competitor.

How Female-Female Pairs Reduce Power and Increase Liking   One of the most common ways that women use to remove a power barrier with another woman is to find a common enemy or antagonist. This enemy may be in the form of a person (perhaps a boss or a co-worker), a situation (such as working conditions that neither Cindy nor Lisa likes), or a common goal. In the case of a common goal, the enemy the women have in common is their perception of any barriers that may interfere with the accomplishment of the goal or project.

As Cindy and Lisa move from acquaintance to friendship, there is a consequent reduction in the amount of power that Cindy has in the relationship. In other words, as Cindy begins to consider Lisa a friend and not just a co-worker, she must consequently relinquish some of the power she has over Lisa. This surrender of power is not usually a conscious act, but rather, by definition, it is necessary. As these changes within the relationship take place, there are several nonverbal cues that may be noticed.

As the two women become friends, the nonverbal signals they exchange with each other become more equally balanced. As the relationship becomes more friendly and Cindy loses power, both women become more equal partners in the relationship. Because of this equality, Cindy's nonverbal cues are no longer indicative of power and, in turn, Lisa's are less indicative of subordination in the relationship. This will increase the interpersonal interaction between Cindy and Lisa because, when a superior or a subordinate takes on the body language level of the other, the level of interpersonal communication consequently increases.

Female-Female Pairs Losing Friendship   Not only are there significant nonverbal cues that are indicative of people who are in the process of becoming friends, but there are also a few cues that may indicate that the ''closeness'' in a relationship is being lost. This closeness is the immeasureable aspect of a relationship that distinguishes friends from acquaintances. Because we seldom choose to discuss changes in our relationships, as they occur, most of these signals are nonverbal.

Often, women have very close relationships with other women. This is not to say that men are incapable or never experience this in same-sex relationships, but society allows women to express emotion more openly than it allows men to express their feelings. Because women feel more free to express their emotions, they tend to do so more openly. This freedom of emotional expression causes the relationships of women to be more readily defined in emotional terms, rather than in terms of function or comradeship, as in male relationships.

The more open emotional aspect of female relationships is one factor that causes the nonverbal cues of women to differ from those of men in same-sex relationships. Because nonverbal signals are more indicative of emotion than of cognitive thought, situations involving more emotional expression should draw different nonverbal responses than would those situations with less emotion.

□   **Summary**   □

In social situations, nonverbal communication differs according to the sex and the relative power of the interactants. As has been noted, increasing power decreases liking, and vice versa. As we begin to enter into social relationships, certain nonverbal communications are expected. These expectations, however, differ according to both the sexual composition of the relationship and the outcome expected (simple friendship or an increasing bond towards intimacy) by one or both parties.

Chapter **Eleven**

Nonverbal Communication in the Family

Key Concepts

The Home

Marital Nonverbal Communication

Children and the Family Relationship

Nonverbal Communication and Children

Nonverbal Communication and the Elderly

This chapter extends the study of nonverbal communication to a rather familiar context: the family. When we think of the family, we usually associate it with such terms as *development, relationships,* and even *training.* These perceptions or labels reflect a continuing relationship between self and others, or "significant others," in terms of parent and peer or husband and wife. We use nonverbal communication in our family relationships in the home. In spite of this, and partly due to problems associated with studying long-term relationships where they occur (in the home), the impact of the nonverbal aspects of the *home* has not been examined in any detail, although interest is beginning to mount in a number of disciplines. In a great many books on family communication, nonverbal communication is treated separately, as if it were only a simple unit rather than a condition that is found at *all* levels of the family.

As has been indicated in other sections of this book, the contextual aspects of our nonverbal communication seem to operate in both a predictable and understandable way; they even progress according to a "common sense" dictum: we meet someone socially (regardless of where we meet that person, it is still considered "social" in communication context); we progress through various stages of interaction, perhaps getting married and starting a home; and finally, we find that our home environment may affect our jobs (even create pressure to find a job). Much of our communication in the home, however, is expressed nonverbally. As we become more intimate, more relaxed with one another in relational terms, we speak less, feel the need to speak less, and communicate more nonverbally (whether this is good or bad will be the judgment of the individual reader).

The impact of nonverbal communication in the family can be found at a number of levels, fulfilling a number of functions. As we pointed out earlier, things change when two people move from the notion of the individual to that of the family. Many, if not most, of the problems associated with family communication are nonverbal in nature; they seem to be the root of many conflicts and often seem to follow from inaccurate readings of the others' honest and deceptive communication. Hence, nonverbal communication may be an important feature in the conflict found in many families. Control over others' communication is also a nonverbal function found in families. Finally, and probably more importantly, we find that families identify and self-present through their nonverbal communication.

Nonverbal communication associated with the home—where most family communication occurs—appears to function as a means of establishing a family self-presentation and the beginnings of relational development. We begin our study of the family here because most of us associate a *home* with a physical place, a sanctuary or refuge where we can hide from the world, an environment we sometimes use to express ourselves both publicly and privately. We do so, however, with the knowledge that little research has examined the impact of the home on communication per se. As we examine the home, keep in mind the identification and self-presentation functions associated with the nonverbal message.

The Home

Most of us, when we think of home, whether it be the place we grew up or the place we now call home, think of a geographical location. Home, therefore, may be more than a simple place of residence; the word may also have a psychological interpretation that adds to the impact of our communication. How many times have you heard someone say, ''Would you act like that in your home?'' even when that action takes place in your apartment, dormitory room, or a house you just bought? Home, then, means first of all some physical locale in which we place ourselves. It is environmental in that we express ourselves within it; it is spatial because we seek to use it as both territory and an extension of our personal space. We seem to think that time is different between home and other locations. Finally, we leave certain olfactory ''signatures'' in the home. Our behaviors, especially those relating to touch, change greatly in the home and even moreso in certain parts of the home.

Spatiotemporal Dimensions

Within the home, we generally perceive the spatiotemporal factors first. In the following section, we consider how the environment, space (territory and personal space), touch, and temporal and olfactory elements influence communication in the home.

Environmental Factors   Anyone who has thought of buying a house knows that there are many considerations that must be taken into account before the actual selection takes place. Consider, for instance, the appearance of the house; we usually live in a house that reflects our personality as well as satisfying our needs.[1] There seems to be a relationship between the type of house we purchase and such factors as social status, degree of liberalism/conservatism, occupation, perceptions of self, and other variables. Our house becomes, to a degree, an extension of self.

One of the major decisions we make when we decide on the house that will become our home is the physical layout of the rooms. Aside from cost and prestige (in terms of number of bedrooms and bathrooms), we want a layout that is pleasant, that is comfortable, and that best reflects on ourselves. Consider the three layouts in Figure 11.1. Which do you feel best fits your needs? Why? Would *any* be acceptable to you? Which seems more homey? These criteria may seem rather simple, but remember we noted that major determinants of liking an environment are the feeling of comfort and the ability to change objects within it.[2]

Consider, for instance, a typical dormitory room. This may be square or slightly rectangular. It is usually ''fixed'' in some way; by this we mean that the objects are either too large to move or are bolted into position in such a way that change is minimal. Would you consider such a place as your home? Many students do for the greater part of a year. They act as owners (part-owners or co-owners in the case of sharing a room), and as such they have many of the same needs and desires as others who live in apartments or homes. They place objects in and around the environment that reflect their own features or traits: their sex, things they like, and certain personality clues (such as posters, guitars, books, etc.), that serve as self-presentational devices. In some instances, they even have ''areas'' of the room set off for study, sleep, relaxation, and social interaction.

This use of space is not much different than what we create at home. What is the use of a living room, for instance, if there is also a den or family room in the house? Which would you use for self-presentational aspects, and which would you use for relaxed communication? Usually, we use the living room for more formal interactions and the den/family room for more relaxed activities.

How we use the space within the home also tells us something about the owners. Some families spend a great amount of time in the kitchen. Most of us know people who always meet in the kitchen and talk (gossip) over a cup of always-present coffee. We also know of people who would never sit in the kitchen and talk, feeling that this location is improper and that the den is much better.

The environment, then, lets us know much about the people living in the house. Whether it is a *home* may be better explained through the use of space: territorial demands and effects of personal spacing needs.

Space   An extension of the environmental factors in the home is the creation and use of space. Here we begin to look at *how* the home is used. As with the earlier treatment of space, we consider this area in terms of two subcomponents: territory and personal space.

Territory   Almost by definition, the home is a territory. According to S. M. Lyman and M. B. Scott's four types of territory, **home territory** is one of our most inviolate areas.[3] Nash suggests that this defense of home territory extends from the physical home and its component parts to any territory the family defines as ''the home.''[4] In a field study of family transformation of public territory (camp sites) to home territory, Nash noted that a wide variety of territorial markers were used to establish home territory and that once these markers were established, typical home territory defenses occurred. This finding only reinforces the impact of restricted access to home territory. When we are in our homes, we restrict access to those who are allowed to enter. As noted earlier, sometimes, when one member of the household allows someone not liked by another

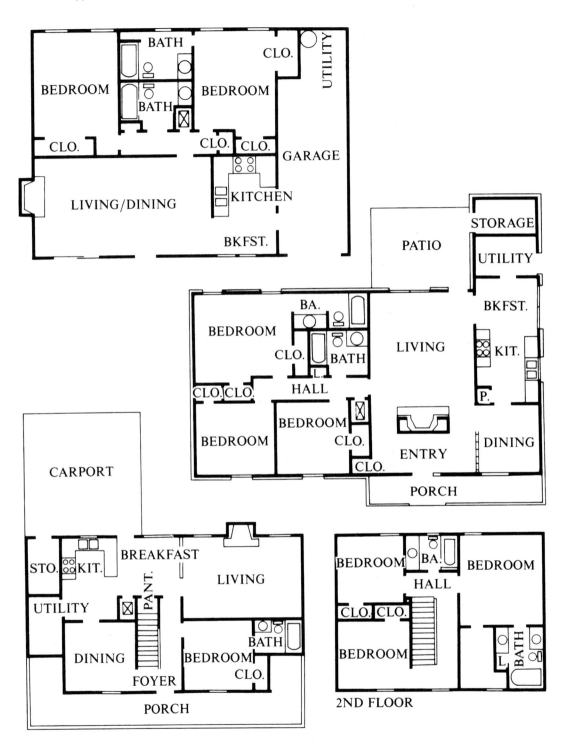

FIGURE 11.1   Which House Plan Best Reflects Your Needs and Desires?

member to enter, conflict can occur over even the largest and most open territories in the house. The impact of territory, however, is even greater when it is combined with privacy.

Judee K. Burgoon has formulated a theoretical overview of privacy.[5] Although it does not deal directly with the home (it is more general in nature), the notion that we seek, need, or demand some form of privacy seems natural. We need privacy for a number of reasons, including a need to get away, to reduce stress in a relationship, to engage in behaviors that cannot be carried out in public (e.g., bathroom behaviors), and other reasons. In terms of the home, it seems that privacy is perceived in the following ranking:[6]

Most private: bathrooms
             bedrooms
             kitchens
             dining rooms
             den/family rooms
Least private: living rooms (formal)

Other factors affecting how we perceive the home and various locations within it are defined by the uses we have for that space. For instance, if we examine the studies on territory by Irving Altman that were cited earlier, we may find some significant parallels in the home.[7] We usually use the bedroom as a place to **cocoon,** to withdraw from the pressures of day-to-day interactions. The bathroom, although most private, is in some ways treated both seriously and almost comically. On the serious side, we do our most private things in the bathroom; we also do other things: treat it as a ''reading room'' or library, as a place to address problems with children, as somewhere to hide. On the comical side, we use our bathrooms to present ourselves through color (what does a lavender bathroom tell you about the user?) and through placement of objects such as magazines and pictures, and, as caricatured in the media, it is a place that we fight over.

Sometimes our personality helps to establish territoriality in the home. Several examples include the office at home (which the IRS continually tries to establish as a single-use territory), the kitchen for the cook, and the workshop/garage for the handyperson. In addition, we sometimes have our own ''places.'' These are perceived differently within the territory. Archie Bunker has his own chair; heaven-help those who violate this territory. But there is more to this notion of territory than just the Archie Bunker type. As Julian Roebuck and Mark Hickson note about the American redneck:[8]

> In the home the ''man of the house'' has his space reserved—like ''Archie Bunker.'' Other space in the house is not reserved for anyone, except space for the redneck's few significant possessions (such as his truck, his tools, or his shotgun). Generally speaking, the woman in the house has no rights to social space and the children have few.

This description, although aimed at a specific subsection of the public, could really be extended to many other people. For the most part, we establish a territory we deem ''ours.'' Siblings, for instance, when possessing a room of their own, sometimes go to the extreme of locking the door so that others cannot get in. From this type of behavior—the notion of private property within the home—comes the feeling that a certain room is his or hers.

Personal Space An extension of the home is also perceived in the way we use personal space. Most notably, we design our homes to create the best of all worlds. We try to establish enough space to ''feel at home,'' yet we want our space close enough to feel as a family unit. Most dens or family rooms are laid out to accomplish two tasks: to view the television set throughout the room and to make conversation convenient and easy. Most of the time, however, we only accomplish one or the other. Hamid and Newport, in a recent study, found that children four to nine years old could perform a variety of tasks better, had a more positive mood, and showed greater physical strength in a pink room than they did in a blue room.[9]

Probably the most important aspect of personal space, other than arrangement, is the perception of space we have—**density.** As noted earlier, density can cause interpersonal problems.[10] As space decreases within the home, members are forced to be with each other more. This may seem to be a positive feature, but as noted earlier, as density increases, so also do family problems. The need to have some space, especially for males who react more negatively to crowding, explains the need for privacy even within the home.[11] The circle is now completed: we plan our house as a comfortable yet personalized environment; within this environment we create special territories that may or may not be set aside for the use of one or more family members; we then seek to limit our contact by arranging the furniture in such a way as to increase distances for normal interactions. (This may sound strange, but the next time a friend comes over, sit on a couch and observe whether he or she sits next to you or in a chair close by. As might be expected, however, this type of behavior may change if the person is engaged in a relationship with you.)

Touch   In the home, we may expect our touch norms to change. Inside the walls of the home our touch behavior becomes more idiosyncratic as it relates to the level of intimacy within the family. In public there are the usual norms; touch is usually withheld unless a ''proper'' occasion allows for it. On the other hand, we assume that within the home, the frequency of touching increases. Not much research has really focused on this point; within the home, it would seem, touch is still a rather strong message.

Touch is used to demonstrate both intimacy and to serve as punishment. In this regard, the research demonstrating a context to touch (i.e., location allows for touch or no touch), would seem to demonstrate that the home is one location where opposite sex touch is allowed.[12] The type of touch we may expect to observe would probably cover the entire range as noted by T. Nguyen, R. Heslin, and M. L. Nguyen.[13] We may expect, however, to experience more intimate types of touch, such as the last five stages suggested by Desmond Morris.[14] The more private the room, the more arousing the touch, thus implying that a ''love/intimacy'' and ''sexual arousal'' type of touch would change greatly even within the home, at least for most of the American public.

One area that the home and touch certainly affect is the degree of co-orientation found among family members. In general, the more touch found in the home, the greater the liking and the less the stress. As demonstrated in research concluding that people who are comfortable with each other will engage in more other-than self-oriented touch, the more touch one observes in a family, the better the relations between members.[15] Further, within the home some of the more stringent norms for adult-adult and adult-child touch can be relaxed. Even with this relaxation, however, the frequency of male parent-to-child touch is probably still quite low.

If we accept James L. Prescott's findings on socialization, then we should expect that as touch increases in the family, interpersonal relatedness should increase.[16] Research, however, has not examined this question thoroughly. In view of the prevailing conservative nature of the American public, it may not be too unrealistic to infer that touch norms, both in public and at home, are becoming more private. Thus, like our need for privacy and personal territory in the home, touching others may be decreasing as a way of increasing privacy. The more we set ourselves off even from family members, the less touch we should expect.

Temporal and Olfactory Elements   Not much is known about how time and olfaction are differentiated in the home. One may assume, however, that a different chronemic norm may be developing. Because we live in a time-conscious society, which views time as a function of almost everything valued positively, one might infer that the perception of time is more relaxed in the home. In other words, we observe time almost compulsively while on the job, but during our leisure hours we would prefer not to think about it.

   In terms of olfaction, however, there are several aspects we have been trained to observe about smells in the home. There is the **olfactory signature.**[17] When we enter a house, we initally smell several things. Such smells tell us something about: (1) the ethnic background of the inhabitants, (2) the hygienic habits of the inhabitants, and (3) how long they have lived here. Moreover, certain smells seem to linger: cigarette, pipe, or cigar odors; perfumes and other deodorizers; musty smells and other age indicators. In a culture that thrives on the notion of cleanliness, certain odors in the home may reflect negatively on the family. Finally, there is a certain, perhaps unconscious, odor that we associate with *home*. Most of us have positive emotional attachments to such smells, bringing back memories of days gone by. Such an odor seems to relax us, makes us feel more protected and perhaps young again.

Kinesic Factors

Within the home, our kinesic behaviors acquire a different meaning. In public we typically mask our facial expressions and reduce the degree to which we emphasize other expressions. In the home, however, we engage in both facial and body displays that are more "open" yet idiosyncratic. We explore kinesic variables in more detail in the next section on nonverbal communication and marriage, but for now, note that several features of kinesics in the home seem to be associated with this location. First, considering the relative intimacy of the home, we may be more open with our gestures in conversation. Second, because we are more at ease in the home, our body posture is more relaxed, and our gestures become more expressive. Finally, we may tend to create more emblems or emblematic illustrators in the home, using certain gestures with particular meanings. The "come here" gesture of the finger to the child, and the maintenance of eye contact with the spouse are two examples.

Vocalic Factors

Closely associated with the kinesic behaviors are the vocalic cues found in the home. It seems that silences tend to increase in the home. This may only be true for adults, however, because children view the home as the primary "work" and living place. As intimacy increases, the need for verbal communication appears to decrease. Long periods of silence are accepted and may become the norm. Whether this is good depends on the stage of relationship development; whether it is a function of the increased use of mediated (television, radio) communication forms is still open to debate and interpretation.[18]

Physical Appearance

The final subcode to be examined within the home is physical appearance. Within the home, physical appearance is often "let down." By this we mean that behind the barriers of the home, we can relax the constant pressure to "look good." In the home our choice of clothing changes; we seldom spend much time in the home dressed as John T. Molloy indicates we should dress on the job.[19] We tend to place less emphasis on such normal activities as showering and shaving (both sexes), and we dress in a more relaxed manner. In many ways, however, we change such behavior when we open the door. When the doorbell rings we normally re-dress, smooth our clothing, and sometimes have the "most respectable" person answer the door. Within the home, we also place less stress on accessories.

Review

Our nonverbal communication continues in the home and may be perceived as a function of the way we present ourselves to family members and to others. Although not much research into this phase has been undertaken, probably due to the way we perceive the home and the privacy it accords, there are certain behaviors that change. Future research will have to examine what we have discussed. Because the home is thought of as a physical or territorial entity, it influences our nonverbal communications. Indeed, it (the home) may even establish "new" norms, such as silence and touch. But the home is more than just a physical entity; it also seems to engender the notion of *family*. The next section examines the nonverbal aspect of the family in terms of control and relational development. The section after that considers the impact of nonverbal communication on children and the elderly.

Nonverbal Communication in the Marriage

Although families reside in homes, homes may consist of groups that are not families. The concept of family as associated with the home implies that within the physical home, there are differing degrees of family. We discuss these degrees in the next several sections. As you may recall from chapter 10, social interaction progresses in stages. We may consider the final stage of that interaction to be marriage. Once we have married, our communications with each other (partners) change. Sometimes a marriage will result in the bearing and raising of children. In the end, most of us want to grow old with someone (preferably the marriage partner). Thus the psychological home may be viewed as consisting of three stages beyond social interaction; the marriage, the children, and the elderly. Each of these has received some attention from social science researchers; the most research on nonverbal effects, however, seems to relate to the marriage and children stages and much of what we know of marriage comes from the *problems* associated with it. Of particular interest here is the nonverbal communication associated with relationship control, including aggression and development. Of obvious concern are those nonverbal messages that function as indicators of affinity (likableness or dislikableness), control of the other, and accuracy of nonverbal message encoding and decoding. Most of the nonverbal research on children comes from studies of development and training. In both cases, the research dealing with families, specifically the effects the family has on the nonverbal behavior of spouses and children, is limited.

There seems to be a widely held belief that once two people marry, things are different. Part of this perception may be based on the ''piece of paper'' that makes cohabitation ''legal.'' But this perception may be derived from the differing verbal and nonverbal communications that take place between the two people. Most of us assume that a successful marriage is one between two people of approximately equal attraction and of similar interests who are satisfied with each other's company. Within the marriage, and before the birth of children, comes a time of adjustment. This adjustment deals, partly, with sharing an environment and partly with changing nonverbal behaviors.

As noted earlier, much of the research concerning nonverbal behavior in the marriage comes from couples who are at a low ebb in their marriages. As Alan Sillars has noted, most of the previous marital research has been concerned with affective and dominance problems in the marriage.[20] Such problems often end up in a conflict *pattern* composed of verbal and nonverbal cues.[21] Although the majority of research in marital communication has been on the verbal aspects of conflict, the nonverbal elements associated with conflict patterns are beginning to be recognized. As Lynn Turner notes, ''conflicts are expressed in verbal *and* nonverbal behaviors [emphasis added].''[22] The emphasis on conflict, however, tends to isolate some nonverbal behaviors from others and to ignore other behaviors that (a) may predate the distressed behavior and/or (b) may not recognize it. In this section, we review the available research dealing with marital satisfaction and conflict, and we touch on some areas of potential interest.

Environmental Factors

Not much research has examined the impact of environment on marital nonverbal communication. We note, however, that some research extends the family to the social interactions in the community and infers a relationship between social and family relationships.[23] This analysis implies that family relations and social relations operate together: if the social aspect is altered, then the marital relationship may also change.

A second feature of the environment deals with who creates the home. Who is responsible for which room? The total decor? The exterior? These questions need to be answered. How many marriages, for instance, divide the environmental aspects and the placement of objects, according to marriage partner? As noted earlier, who ''owns'' which room? Informal analysis by students in our classes indicates that the female may have more of a voice than the male, but this is highly variable.

Space

Probably one of the best indicators of potential distress in a marriage is the increasing need for territory. Usually, satisfied married couples tend to spend a good amount of time in each other's company. However, as one female noted in an analysis of her forthcoming divorce (the husband was still living in the home):[24]

> My husband and I became informally maritally separated but with his continuing to live in the house while we continued with our marital counseling. He lived in another part of the house, and our interpersonal contacts continued to decrease . . . I beat a retreat to my bedroom, closing the door against the intrusion of the others . . . I began a lengthy siege there . . . emerging only when necessary.

During a positive marital experience, we expect that such behavior would not occur. However, there are times when we all need to get away from the presence of others, to cocoon for a while. Over time we would also expect our personal space to change. At the beginning of the marriage, personal space needs in the home are probably less than those at later stages. If the relationship continues and intensifies, we would assume that the expected personal space would change from closer to farther and then back to closer as the years continued. One reason for this may be found in the level of relationship as the couple moves from ''love'' to ''liking.'' As the transition from an extreme emotional bond to one of less intensity occurs, there may be a perceived need for more space (yet still less than that found in initial interaction and more than during courtship and newlywed stages). As the marital partners become comfortable with each other over time, the space need may decrease.

Touch

As with the physical home, the amount of touch exhibited by both partners will tend to be idiosyncratic. But we should note that as long as marital satisfaction is high, the *relative* amount of touch, the frequency of touch, should remain high. As dissatisfaction with the marriage increases, as the relationship becomes distressed, touch between partners should decrease and self-touch increase.[25]

Kinesics and Vocalics

A number of researchers have examined the impact of kinesics and paralanguage on marital communication. In general, it has been found that (1) the nonverbal codes are better discriminators (indicators) of distress in a marriage than are the verbal messages we send; and that (2) when asked to act *happy,* the nonverbal behaviors provided the only discriminating basis for distinguishing between distressed and nondistressed couples.[26]

A study by John Gottman and Albert Porterfield theorizes that the ability to read the other's nonverbal cues may be related to the degree of satisfaction in the marriage.[27] The results of this study indicate that when husbands receive their wives' cues, the relationship between marital satisfaction and nonverbal communication is positive. Comparing the ability to read the wives' nonverbal cues to strangers, Gottman and Porterfield found that satisfied husbands were better able to read their wives' nonverbal cues, whereas the husbands of dissatisfied wives were less able to read their wives' cues. Further research infers that marital adjustment and satisfaction are also influenced by the ability to send and receive ambiguous messages.[28] Patricia Noller and Cynthia Gallois examined the relationship between the type of message sent (positive, negative, neutral affect), the nonverbal cues used, and the degree of adjustment in the marriage. They found that wives were more accurate encoders and used more positive nonverbal behaviors (e.g., smiles) with positive messages; husbands, however, tended to use *similar* nonverbal cues (eyebrow raises and flashes) for both positive *and* negative messages. When Noller and Gallois examined the degree of marital adjustment, no differences in nonverbal accuracy were found for wives, but highly adjusted husbands were more accurate when exposed to positive messages than to neutral or negative messages.[29] Other research indicates that there is no general tendency for good nonverbal communicators to be married to good nonverbal communicators. R. Buck, D. Kenny, and R. Sabatelli, for instance, analyzed 48 recently married couples; their research supports this contention and the contention that marital complaints were negatively associated with the wife's nonverbal sending ability, but no relationship was found for the husband's sending ability and the wife's complaints in the marriage.[30]

The type of nonverbal messages reported in these studies included both kinesic and vocalic messages. The nonverbal cues included messages transmitted by means of facial expression, vocal inflection and quality, body positions, and general movement cues.[31] In most of these studies the nonverbal channel conveyed the more accurate message. J. Swain, G. Stephenson, and M. Dewey examined the function of eye contact and the relational intimacy of couples, strangers, and friends in conversation. They found that married couples engaged in *less* eye contact than did strangers or friends, thus casting doubt on the belief that the intensity of a relationship is manifested by the amount of eye contact during conversation.[32] One possible interpretation of this finding may be that eye contact diminishes after courtship as the partners become more comfortable with each other.

Within the marriage, we can also obtain an idea of the degree of satisfaction or adjustment by examining mirroring and synchrony behaviors.[33] When two people are attracted to each other and are positively associating the other with self, we tend to find mirroring and synchrony behaviors. In many instances the partners do not even know they are mirroring the other's behaviors. Husbands and wives seem to synchronize their nonverbal behaviors, which helps increase the accuracy of the communication. It may also reinforce the other's behavior and lead to a greater prediction of what the intended message is. As distress increases in the relationship, we would expect that the degree of synchrony would decrease and the amount of mirroring would be reduced.

Finally, the paralanguage cue of silence is found in the marriage. In most instances the amount of silence between the two partners should indicate a degree of comfort in the relationship. Silence, however, can communicate just the opposite.[34] The idea that ''silence is golden'' is only as true as the degree of satisfaction in the marriage. Much like the use of territory and increased personal space, we can hide behind our silences, using them as effective barriers against others.

Chronemics

The study of how time is perceived in the marriage has not received much attention. If we review Thomas Cottle's research, we do obtain a general notion that the husband and wife may perceive time differently.[35] Some research now indicates that the way we use time in the marriage may be related to marital satisfaction. Michael Lewis examined the impact of how married couples used time (in this case how task-related [work] communication affected relations in the home) and found that as the amount of time spent in task-oriented communication increased, marital satisfaction decreased.[36] This suggests that bringing the office home, infringing on marital and relational time, has a negative effect on marital satisfaction. Lewis' research included both the housewife and the working wife; hence the impact of any differences due to the sex of the working spouse should be negligible. What happens when both working spouses bring home their work, thus reducing the time to spend with each other, has yet to be reported.

Physical Appearance

The role of physical appearance and attractiveness has been examined in many interpersonal studies. As noted in the chapter on social interaction, our physical appearance and attractiveness have a major effect on whether or not we will interact with someone. The relationship between physical appearance and marriage, however, has not been studied in any great detail. What we know is generally divided into two viewpoints. One point of view maintains that attractiveness is more important during the dating stage; the other approach infers that dating is less of a commitment than is marriage and that we might, therefore, date someone less attractive during dating. Marriage, on the other hand, is of greater duration and importance and, hence, we would try to marry at or above our attractiveness.[37]

Marital satisfaction seems to be more influenced on the basis of whether the husband feels his wife is more attractive than he is.[38] Nevertheless, as Judy Pearson points out, the physically attractive are neither ''loved more by their partners nor do they love their partners more, than do unattractive persons.''[39] She further notes that the major factor in the relationship is found in the *differences* between attraction levels rather than overall attractiveness of one of the partners.

Amplifying the results of the attractiveness research, it appears that as the comfort level of the relationship progresses, there will be a different perception of what is ''good'' physical appearance. Here we can consider the type of clothing worn and the amount of time spent in preparing oneself for the other. At the initial interaction stage, it is extremely important for both male and female to make themselves as attractive as possible. (This would include the olfactory component also.) As time progresses, the amount of effort put into looking ''good'' may change. We may expect that the other person will be clean, but that they will dress and put the same effort into dressing as they did earlier in the relationship is not expected. This would seem to hold more true for males than females, perhaps because the stereotype for the attractive male is not as firm as that for the female.

We must also recognize that for a large number of women, the home is the primary place of work. Males typically dress for their jobs, changing into something different at home. Females in the home, on the other hand, may wear the same dress throughout the day. For females working outside the home, however, the same dress pattern as that of males should apply.

The Expanding Family—Children and the Family Relationship

We discuss the effect of the home on child development in the next section. First, we feel that it is essential to note that the birth of the first child seems to change the married couple's nonverbal communication. (The second and later children have less impact, with the exception of the time variable.)

The addition of a child to the home changes almost all the nonverbal norms. Before the child, couples have a certain amount of privacy and perhaps an extra room, office, or sewing room; all this changes. Extra space is given to the child, even though many parents initially have the child sleep in the same room as they do. For a while, the child's room becomes the center of attention.

In terms of space, privacy now becomes a secondary matter. Along with certain environmental sounds (noise, either external or internal), the general relationship between parents and home changes somewhat. As the child grows, the parents will probably find that they share everything with the child, including the bathroom. They will also find that the child requires touch—reassurance—and sometimes the parents will need to touch each other at times simply for reassurance about dealing with the child. Perhaps the variable that changes the most is time: a child knows no time. Time becomes precious for the parent who works outside the home. At the same time, the mother (or housefather) begins to need some time to her(him)self because the child will monopolize that time if allowed to do so.

In some instances special clothing may be worn. This may be for protection. In addition, there will be a different odor around the house. Depending upon what type of diaper or baby powder used, the house will smell different. The brand of powder or diaper will have a distinctive smell, often like the one parents had as babies.

Interestingly, these changes occur rapidly and are apparently accepted rather quickly. Many new parents have trouble remembering what it was like without a child. Although such changes are not always positive and may lead to marital dissatisfaction, the changes are perceived to be in the best interest of the child.

Some research has investigated the question of how the child-adult interaction affects the adult's own nonverbal cues. John Bates found that through facial observation, positive expressions, negative expressions, and forward leans, children are able to exert a subtle influence on adults.[40] Bates found that when a child played a high-positive role, adults nonverbally reacted more positively to the child than when the child played a low-positive role. The adults also allowed the child's nonverbal positivity to influence their written evaluations of intellectual and social abilities. Hence, we are more positive about children who indicate a more positive attitude toward us and react positively. Perhaps the idea that we train the child rather than the child training us should be reexamined.

Finally, there is some evidence indicating that the number of children in the family and the spacing of these births affects perceptions of marital satisfaction, as well as the parents' attitude toward the child and the care given. Philip Mohan notes that although families with four or more children account for only about 20 percent of the U.S. population, they contribute about 40 percent of the cases of child abuse.[41] Mohan implies that the number of children and their spacing are potential sources of stress. Parents who have a large number of children over a relatively short period of time are subject to more stress and may express more rejection and less protection toward their children, compared to parents who have fewer children over the same period of time.

Nonverbal Communication in Children

We now turn to the nonverbal communication we have with our children. For the most part, the research on child nonverbal communication deals with developmental stages of emotional and social learning. At this time the interplay between family members begins to shape the child's outlook on life, his or her relational development, an understanding of social norms, and the encoding and decoding of affect.

Infants   The process of communication, of learning to communicate, begins at birth. Once a child is born, it begins to receive a number of stimuli from its environment: sounds, feeling of temperature, light, and touch, to name but a few. These are *stimuli* because the child probably has no way of analyzing such information as communicative, although there are some who theorize that some precommunicative function exists to account for rudimentary processing of such "communication."[42] What we know of infant nonverbal communication has come from research that examines how the infant relates to its parents, other infants, and strangers.

The nonverbal code is the infant's major way of communicating. The infant will communicate bodily and emotional needs through eye contact, touch, and smiling behavior. Because the infant has not yet progressed to the stage of verbal language, the immediate messages communicated are nonverbal in nature. At a later stage (between two and six, for example, when the child is learning the language), the nonverbal code takes on a less important conscious role. As we shall see, however, the nonverbal code continues to provide information in several areas.

At birth, infants have some instinctive nonverbal communication potential. For example, some research indicates that an infant immediately after birth both recognizes and prefers human faces to abstraction.[43] After birth, facial display plays an important role in adjusting the child to the parent. Kenneth Kaye and Alan Fogel studied the interaction of mother and infant over a twenty-six-week period.[44] They found that when a mother was "on"—engaged in smiling, exaggerated facial expressions, or bobbing her head—versus "off"—smaller facial expressions, less smiling—the infant's periods of attention changed. When the mother was "on," attention increased. This continued through the twenty-six-week observation period; even though the total time spent gazing at the mother decreased with age, the time looking at the mother when she was "on" did not.

Kaye and Fogel also observed that at the beginning, at the age of six weeks, the mother's facial greetings such as nodding and smiling were rarely effective in eliciting expressive greetings from the infant; however, without the greeting, the infant almost never made any response. By the time the study was completed, at age twenty-six weeks, the infant's spontaneous greetings had become as frequent as those elicited by the mother.

A number of recent studies have shown that face-to-face gazing is one of the most crucial aspects of mother-infant interaction.[45] Apart from its basic function as a setting for interaction, face-to-face interaction enables the infant to regulate the amount of social input at an age when other means are not available. Gazing at faces and particularly at the eyes has also been shown to correlate with the level of physiological arousal. One study, however, implies that, although eye contact is important, when it is extended beyond the period of normal development, it can slow the infant's social growth.[46]

Other researchers indicate that social perception is mirrored in the infant's facial expression. Jeanne Brooks-Gunn and Michael Lewis, for example, showed pictures of parents and strangers (both male and female) to seventy-two infants ages nine to twenty-four months and filmed the infants' facial expression at three- to five-second intervals. Results indicated that infants smile more often and look longer at pictures of parents than those of strangers.[47] Older infants (eighteen to twenty-four months) were more likely to smile at familiar than at unfamiliar faces; younger infants were more likely to smile at strange women than at strange men; there appeared to be no difference in the response to either mother or father. This study infers that even at an early age, even prior to acquisition of verbal communication, infants can display likes and dislikes through nonverbal channels. Jeannette Haviland found that aside from mirroring expression, the type of expression (positive or negative) also influences how we perceive the infant. She found that infants who expressed "negative" emotions (distress, fear, wariness) were more likely to be judged "male," whereas infants who expressed "positive" emotions (laughing, smiling) were more likely to be judged "female."[48]

Physical appearance, both in terms of attraction and clothing, serves an important developmental function in childhood. At least two studies reflect the impact of clothing on children. In one study, Sandford and Jane Weinberg were interested in how others perceived newborns dressed in either blue (masculine) or pink (feminine) gowns.[49] As might be expected, infants dressed in blue were perceived as males and those in pink as females, regardless of the actual sex of the infant. A study by S. Kaiser, M. Rudy, and P. Byfield reinforces the role of clothing on stereotypical judgments. They found that girls tend to associate dresses with traditionally feminine activities and pants with masculine activities, although they found no real association with the behaviors exhibited by the girls in actual play activities.[50]

In a study with potentially far-reaching ramifications, Leonard Berkowitz and Ann Frodi found that physical attraction influenced the degree of punishment a child receives when making mistakes.[51] Their findings indicate that unattractive children receive harsher punishments than do attractive children. This leads to a related question. Do abused or neglected children possess different nonverbal behaviors? Michael Hecht and colleagues suggest that abused and nonabused children do possess different nonverbal behaviors. They observed the kinesic, proxemic, and eye contact behaviors of children aged one to three and found that abused girls were more passive in their nonverbal cues than were abused boys, whereas with the "normal" children, girls were more nonverbally active than were the boys.[52]

Other nonverbal subcodes of interest include proximity, haptics, and olfaction. Some research indicates (1) that infants twelve to twenty-four months seek more proximal interaction from their mothers than from strangers, (2) that older infants initiate more play with strangers (adopt closer distances), (3) that physical proximity decreases and touch decrease between mother and infant as the infant grows older, and (4) that both visual and haptic frequency decreases with age.[53] Finally, perhaps two of the most important initial nonverbal subcodes are touch and olfaction. Touch research indicates that mother-infant bonding is important and plays an important part in the socialization process, although just how important touch is to the process is questionable.[54] Olfaction is one way the infant can identify with its parents. Olfactory memory may play a large part in the bonding between mother and child, although much more information is needed in this area.[55]

E. Z. Tronick has written about emotions in infants. He has indicated that the affect of infants is affected by the emotional experience of dealing with the mother. He concluded that emotions motivate and organize an infant's behavior rather than disrupt it.[56] Davidson and Fox elaborated on infant emotions as compared with hemisphere dominance. Using 35 ten-month-old female infants who were born to right-handed parents, they researched infants' emotions when the mother was in the room and when out of the room. They found that the right region was more active during negative experiences and the left more active during positive experiences. An infant who showed right-region activity during rest was likely to cry during periods of the mother's absence.[57] Fernald found that the mother's "melody" in her voice had a major impact on the behavior of an infant.[58] Legerstee found that infants do nonverbally respond more to humans than to dolls.[59]

Older Children   Nonverbal communication in older children has been examined in much greater detail than that of infants. But there is a large volume of research seeming to indicate that the child has learned most of his nonverbal norms, by about the age of six or seven, certain subcodes seem to change continually. Moreover, there are many theories and ways to analyze this learning. We will take one perspective that postulates a developmental change in the way the child relates to self and others. That perspective has been most closely associated with George H. Mead, and it proposes a three-part developmental orientation: an imitation stage, a play stage, and game stage.[60]

Although Mead's three stages are more closely associated with socialization and *verbal* communication, the discussion of infant nonverbal communication suggests that the same developmental sequence can be found for socialization and nonverbal communication.

At the first stage, **imitation,** the child learns to imitate the communication of adults and those around him or her. During this period, for instance, we can place the infant who is learning through imitation in communicating situations at a very basic level. The second stage, **play,** deals more with self-knowledge. In this stage the child learns to act toward him or herself; also the child learns the norms that are associated with his or her nonverbal communication. At the **game** stage the child is ready to assume several roles, to recognize the nonverbal norms and address them properly, according either to whim or to the needs of his or her audience. It is in the game stage that the child begins to manipulate his or her nonverbal communication.

As with all developmental theories, the stages tend to overlap. The child, for instance, is still imitating well into the teen years. We are continually learning new roles and playing a social ''game'' through them; this is true in the courtship stage of a relationship and on through the parental stages. Hence, although we examine the three stages as rather discrete, they tend to overlap.

Imitation   During the imitation stage, the child begins to expand its repertoire of nonverbal behaviors. Probably the most significant feature at this stage is the acquisition of emblems. It seems that the ability to encode and decode emblems increases with age, up to about age five.[61] The smile, as noted earlier, is acquired quite early, but the interpretation of that smile differs significantly by culture. Irving Alexander and Elisha Babad compared children's smiles, their probability of smiling, and cultural norms as to how adults reacted to the smile. They found that American children with high probabilities of smiling were rated as more adjusted, more attractive, and more affiliative than those with low probabilities of smiling. They did not find a similar difference with an Israeli population.[62] Hence, not only does the imitation stage teach the child what to do, but also what expectations may be associated with the behavior.

There is also evidence to indicate that as early as age two the child begins to notice similarities in physical appearance.[63] Mark Knapp notes that most children before the age of five are able to note distinctions between proper and improper dress.[64] Research on proxemics and touch also infers that during the imitation stage, communication behaviors are being learned. The research of Bretherton and others discussed earlier reported that children seek greater proxemic affiliation as age increases.[65] Recent research indicates that the norms associated with sex and distancing may begin as early as nursery-school age, with boys maintaining greater interaction distances than girls.[66] Finally, John Brownlee and Roger Bakeman found that two-year-olds used different kinds of touch/hitting patterns for different communication purposes. Interestingly enough, however, these patterns seem to disappear with age.[67] It may be that after age two, the child quickly learns the touch norms of his or her culture.

Play   During the play stage, the child begins to learn which nonverbal behaviors are appropriate and which are inappropriate. Probably the most prominent subcodes at this stage are kinesics (emblems and facial expression), physical appearance, and paralanguage. As early as age six, children both know and understand what is physically attractive and unattractive.[68] They seem to base such understanding on body type and stereotyped standards of attractiveness. Some children, for example, after being introduced to dolls such as *Barbie* and *Ken,* associate *Barbie* with sexiness and beauty. Note that both dolls are rather stereotypic of what this culture associates with ''good'' body builds and attractiveness.

In the area of kinesic behaviors, the child begins to understand what the particular emblems and facial expressions stand for. At this stage, the child begins to develop a repertoire of emotional messages.[69] (We consider this in more detail in the next section.) The child at the play stage begins to use the gestures and expressions for particular effect and within the understood meanings associated between children. About this same age, the child begins to understand the vocalizations associated with the same messages.[70]

Game   At the game stage, we have the well-understood norms operating. It is at this stage that most of the nonverbal research cited earlier has been conducted. Now children begin to actively manipulate their nonverbal communications to produce certain expected effects. It is at this stage that they transgress from adult to child to adult.

Affective Communication   There are two basic positions on the acquisition of emotion, although there are many other theories as to how we acquire and interpret emotion.[71] Many people agree with Charles Darwin, who believed that emotions are universal expressions that are inherited.[72] Another perspective theorizes that we develop our emotions. This perspective, proposed by Charlotte Wolff, roughly parallels Mead's three stages of development.[73] (See Table 11.1.)

The first stage is labeled **instinctive.** This phase is found during the period immediately after birth up to about six months. During the instinctive phase, we find such behaviors as crying and smiling. At this stage there is no meaning directly associated with the behavior, the behavior being more instinctive and aimed more at survival and self-awareness than at communication. The second stage is called the **emotional phase.** It is during this phase (from the second week to about two years of age) that the child begins to associate his or her emotional repertoire with basic emotions. At this stage of development, for instance, we find the typical range *of* affection behaviors associated with infants. Early in this period, the child seems to behave at one or the other extreme of emotion. By the end of this stage, the child has developed, as N. G. Blurton Jones demonstrated, some 100-plus expressions of aggression, defensiveness, and escape.[74]

The third stage, the **objective phase,** is characterized by gestures and expressions that are related to thought. This stage begins around six years of age and indicates that the emotional message is now well-integrated into the total communication repertoire of the child and can be used in day-to-day interactions. Judee K. Burgoon and Thomas J. Saine postulate a fourth stage, a ''social interaction phase,'' that overlaps all three of Wolff's phases.[75] They believe that this phase begins with behaviors originating as reflex behaviors evolving into movements with social meaning.[76]

A common gesture among one-year-olds is arm-raising, which is a signal to adults that the child wants to be lifted. By the time the children are two, they laugh and smile and play with other children. In fact, laughter and smiling often occur only in the presence of others. . . By the time a child is three, waving is no longer a sign of general activity but is specifically a departure cue, and crying shifts from being associated with separation to that of reaction to quarrels or falls.

TABLE 11.1   *The Development of Emotional Behaviors*

AGE	EMOTION	TYPICAL BEHAVIORS ASSOCIATED WITH EMOTION
3 months	Rage	Trembling mouth; self-hitting; body rigidity
5 months	Disgust	Downturned, taut mouth; nostril movements
6 months	Passive joy	Relaxed, open mouth; rhythmic movements; opening and closing of fist
7 months	Fear	Tightened lips; startled eyes; recoiling gestures
1 year	Exuberant joy	Heightened activity and muscular tension
2 years	Jealousy	Combination of anger and fear gestures
2 years	Affection	Smiling, caressing, coquettish expressions

Source: J. K. Burgoon and T. J. Saine, *The Unspoken Dialogue: An Introduction to Nonverbal Communication* (Boston: Houghton-Mifflin, 1978). p. 201. Reprinted with permission.

It would appear, then, that the child can be very sensitive to the emotions and needs of others. In a study examining a child's ability to understand and label different kinds of emotions (happiness, sadness, anger, fear, disgust, and surprise), Linda Cameras and Kelvin Allison examined children from preschool to second-grade ages. They found that the child's accuracy in labeling increased with age, but that the verbal label was recognized better than was the facial expression of emotion. They also found that some emotions were easier to recognize (i.e., happiness and sadness) than others (i.e., anger, fear, surprise), and that disgust was the most difficult emotion to identify.[77] As noted earlier, however, children often mistake nonverbal communication or misinterpret it at other stages in their development. Again, this may be due to the learning of their verbal language, a code that is quite complex and specific. Emphasis on this aspect of communication from age two to about six would obviously reduce their attention to the nonverbal messages they receive. They have already mastered the nonverbal, or so they might believe.

Carol K. Sigelman and Robert M. Adams used the naturalistic setting of parks to observe distance and touch behaviors between parents and their children.[78] Consistent with other studies, they found that as the children got older, parents increased their distance and decreased the amount of touch. The presence of other children almost diminished closeness between children and their parents. In their study of gender identity among children, Leslie R. Brody, Deborah H. Hay, and

Elizabeth Vandewater found that both boys and girls six to twelve years old were more hurt and disgusted by the opposite sex than by the same sex. Girls reported more fear than boys, and both sexes were more afraid of boys than girls.[79]

Powell and Steelman studied the spacing of siblings as related to academic performance.[80] They found that on standardized tests, one brother had the same negative effect as having two sisters. Close spacing of siblings also had a detrimental effect. Density of family was more significant to children's scores on tests than was family income.

The amount of haptic behavior has been studied by a number of researchers. They have found that parents gaze more than they touch, but infants touch more than they gaze. There are sex differences in decoding abilities of children. Children had more haptic behavior in a child-care setting than in a laboratory setting. Finally, unpopular children tended to imitate negative responses of their peers.[81]

Nonverbal Communication with the Elderly

An area that is acquiring a new importance is that of **gerontology.** The study of aging and the aged is fast becoming a popular concern due to the increasing age of our population. What we know about how the elderly communicate, both verbally and nonverbally, however, is minimal. It is only in the last fifteen to twenty years that this group has become the target of research; thus, what we know of the elderly and their nonverbal communication is limited. Completing this chapter with a survey of gerontological nonverbal communication seems fitting.

We began this chapter with an examination of the home and then moved to the family, suggesting that this is a natural progression. It would seem that the elderly are an extension of the family, although not quite as integral in the United States as they were years ago. In the end, we all age, some graciously, some not so graciously. As we age, however, some of our nonverbal communication changes, or at least we perceive changes. In part, this may be due to the restricted sensory input that comes with age: hearing loss, movement restrictions, and changes in our physical appearance. How we deal with each is something that will become more important to each of us as we age.

Some researchers believe that as we age the differences in our communication deal with the problem of admitting to communication difficulties. With the onset of sensory problems and other communication difficulties may come irritability, moodiness, and paranoia. This may be due in part to a recognized dependency on others and may create a form of self-imposed isolation or at least the discovery that we are out of the information flow.[82] What we know about the elderly and the process of aging is both limited and general. Perhaps the best way to study the elderly's use of nonverbal communication is to examine it, subcode by subcode. In so doing, we describe what we know of this growing subpopulation and, it is hoped, dispel some of the commonly held misperceptions.

Environment and Space   The elderly's use of space—the environment, territory, and personal space—has not been well researched. Most of the research available is based on student populations or populations of middle-aged adults. What we know about spatial use may be best summarized in general terms. We know very little about environmental preferences. J. Sonnenfeld observes that the young prefer rugged, unfamiliar environments, surroundings that are more exotic.[83] But this research does not infer that the elderly prefer any environment less exotic, less rugged, or more familiar. Due to economic restrictions, the elderly may not be able to seek different surroundings. Yet the move toward the Sunbelt by the elderly would seem to indicate that they, like their younger counterparts, seek different environments.

A perception held by many is that the type of environment influences how the elderly perceive themselves. There seems to be an understood, perhaps guilt-reasoned, perception that when we change an older person's environment drastically—take the person out of his or her home—we induce a feeling of ''institutionalism.'' According to John F. Myers, this perception may not be accurate. He studied both institutionalized and noninstitutionalized elderly and found that (1) the institutionalized perceived themselves no differently, and (2) they were no more ill than were the noninstitutionalized.[84] Although it may seem that when we institutionalize our elderly they appear to look worse, it may be that such a perception is based on our (a younger generation's) perception of what it would be like to be institutionalized.

Research is also scarce in the area of territory and personal space. What we know seems to indicate that the elderly are given more personal space and give each other more space.[85] However, such spatial norms are subject to the same intervening variables mentioned previously, except perhaps relationships between younger and older people.[86] A recent study by M. J. Smith, R. E. Reinheimer, and A. Gabbard-Alley seems to demonstrate that the elderly, at least elderly females, do better on task performances with spatial intrusion or crowding than do younger females. They also found that the elderly exhibited more positive communication behaviors.[87] Furthermore, as part of their study, they examined the problem of loneliness, inferring that part of the reason for increased loneliness may be due to greater privacy being afforded in postretirement periods.[88] Although Smith and associates found that there were higher levels of loneliness among the elderly females they tested, the finding was influenced by educational differences (those with less education reporting more loneliness).

Touch   Very little is known about the effect of touch and the need for touch in the elderly. As Knapp notes:[89]

> . . . The use of touch to communicate emotional and relational messages to the elderly may be crucial—particularly as the reliance on verbal/cognitive messages wanes. Although we seem to give the aged in this country a greater ''license'' to touch others, it is not clear how much others touch them. No doubt the infirmities of age will require more touching, but it may make a big difference whether this increased touching is just ''functional/professional'' or expresses affectionate feelings.

If we were to hypothesize a relationship between touch and the elderly, we would postulate that (1) there is probably *less* touch as we increase in age, regardless of sex; and that (2) even among family members, touch will probably decrease as the age difference increases. Partial explanation may be the increased space provided in conversation and the feeling that we actually may grow old if we touch the elderly. (The skin, with its dry, almost snake-like quality, may be one explanation of this perception.) There is some research indicating that the elderly may actually touch less and want to be touched less because of their sensitivity to touch. According to this body of thought, as we grow older we reduce the number of touch ''spots'' we have, and as the number of touch spots is reduced, our sensitivity to touch decreases.[90] It may be that the elderly touch less and expect less touch due to reduced haptic sensitivity.

Vocalics   The older voice sounds different than the younger voice; how that difference is produced may differ between older males and older females. According to research reported by Barbaranne J. Benjamin, elderly males have greater hypovalving (allowing too much air to pass through the glottis) and less precise articulation than do elderly females.[91] Other changes such as alterations in pitch level, speech rate, and vocal flexibility are not sex-related.[92] Furthermore, research by David W. Addington implies that there are vocal quality differences between older and younger speakers.[93]

Physical Appearance   Our physical appearance changes as we age. Our skin becomes less elastic and dries out. Our hair grays or whitens, dries out, straightens, or falls out. Our bodies tend to soften, to lose their angular perspective. Other than our physical appearance, our clothing choices also seem to change. As Burgoon and Saine note:[94]

> . . . young men wear more varied and extravagant clothing than do older men. This may be partially
> due to the fact that they spend more money on clothes. (Young men supposedly spend twice as much
> money on clothes as do middle-aged men and three times as much as men aged sixty-five to seventy.)

The same probably holds true for women. As a sociological function of age, we are usually forced to reduce the amount of money we spend on making ourselves attractive; we cannot pay as much for our clothing, makeup, and accessories. It may be that young people are more fashion-conscious, but given the changing median age in the United States today, more advertising money will probably appeal to the elderly in the future; hence, fashion may change in their direction.

Kinesics   In the area of kinesics, we would expect that, given the usual frailties of age, the elderly will be less flexible, will be less expressive, and may differ in terms of posture. Although very little research has actually attempted to verify these expectations, common sense and day-to-day observations seem to indicate they are accurate. At least one study, for instance, reports posture differences between young and old females.[95] We may also expect that dependence on kinesic expression will lessen as flexibility and visual acuity decrease.[96]

Chronemics and Olfaction   How the elderly perceive time has not really been examined in any great detail. If we accept Joost Meerloo's notion of clinical time, we may assume that the elderly tend to be oriented toward the past.[97] However, this assumption has not been scientifically tested. Thomas Cottle suggests that time theories in this culture may make age something to deny, stressing instead a present or future orientation. He also infers that there may be a sex difference affecting the way we perceive time. Cottle suggests that we view time as an hour glass, the two large portions being associated with the past and the future and the small middle part (where the sand passes) being the present (see Figure 11.2). Thus, we associate time with the past and future, rather than with what occurs in the present. However, his research has concentrated only on younger subjects.[98] This is one area that needs more research, especially in view of our preoccupation with the present.

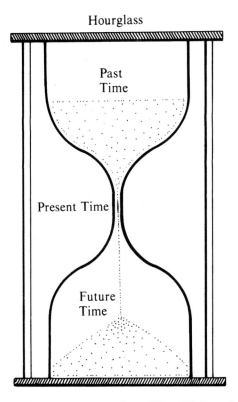

FIGURE 11.2 Cottle's Perception of How We Perceive Time.

What we know about the elderly's olfactory communication is at best minimal. We have stated that the elderly, due to sensory restriction, may be less efficient in smell identification than younger people. It may be that they have more smell memories. The research, however, is at best contradictory. Although olfaction may be influenced by age, this really has not been proved one way or the other.

Review

Nonverbal communication is used at every stage of development, whether or not that development is associated with age or relationship. From the discussion in this section, it should be clear that we are continually learning and relearning what is normative for our nonverbal communications. We should also note that the influence of age on our nonverbal communication is a reciprocal process. As we influence the infant and child, so too is that same infant and child influencing us. The addition of a child can and does change both our lifestyles and our nonverbal expectations. What will happen when that child grows old and becomes a member of the elderly group is a subject that will be explored more as time goes on. At this stage, however, we know relatively little about this period.

☐   **Summary**   ☐

This chapter has examined how our nonverbal communication operates in a context that is very familiar: the family. We began with the home, indicating that it acts as a context for nonverbal communication. We then moved into what we labeled the marriage. We examined how nonverbal communication operates in marriage, how the addition of a child changes our expectations and the practices of nonverbal communication. In this section, we examined some of the developmental literature on the acquisition of nonverbal communication in infancy and childhood. Finally, we described the impact of extreme age on our nonverbal communication. In final review, however, it should be noted that we are really just beginning to understand how our nonverbal communication operates at both extremes: in the infant and in the elderly.

Chapter Twelve

Nonverbal Communication and Occupational Relationships

Key Concepts

Nonverbal Communication on the Job

Relational Messages of Power, Credibility, Leadership

The Nonverbal Interview

Leadership

One of the major contexts in our communication is associated with the occupation we choose to follow for most of our lives, and, as might be expected, nonverbal communication plays a large part in the success we enjoy in that occupation. In this chapter we examine the nonverbal messages associated with the world of work—the job, the occupation. From the perspective of this chapter, an occupation is a general area with which people choose to identify and from which they plan to make a living. Hence, occupations are as general as education, business, and medicine, and they are as specific as cost accounting, elementary education, and cardiovascular surgery. Each occupation also comprises specific jobs, which might include positions as general manager, assembly line worker, nightly news anchor, or third vice-president.

Although there are many occupations that people can choose from, we believe there are some general, nonverbal messages associated with all occupations. We also know and acknowledge that certain jobs within the occupation may differ in their nonverbal needs. This chapter examines the various nonverbal messages associated with the job in general. In so doing, we examine the nonverbal messages associated with certain basic occupational functioning. In particular, we are interested in those nonverbal messages that establish the impressions of self and others and that effectively manage those impressions. We consider how people manipulate others into thinking they are credible, how they create an appropriate communication environment for their duties, and how they build their nonverbal images.

You would think that because most of us spend a great deal of time on the job, there would be volumes of research on the nonverbal aspects of work. This, unfortunately, is not true. Most of the books simply state the obvious: this is what nonverbal communication is (they list the subcodes the authors feel are appropriate and include a number of social science examples for illustration). What we find on the popular market tends to be more prescriptive and is often the result of the "it worked for me once, it'll work for you too" type of reasoning.

Nonverbal Relational Messages

The key to understanding nonverbal communication in any context is an awareness of how the various subcodes operate together—or function—to create messages that are consistent with their desired impact. The nonverbal communication found on the job is different from that found in social situations or in the family; it functions to establish an image or impression relative to someone else's in terms of control and power over the situation. (Recall that affinity was the main nonverbal function in social situations; accuracy and self-presentation were the major functions in the family.)

The relational impact of nonverbal messages may be extremely important on the job, especially a job that requires interaction with others. Your image on the job may be directly affected by such factors as the size of your territory, the furnishings of your office, and your appearance, to name but a few nonverbal cues. Consider, for example, the impact of having to wait on someone *else* for your perceptions of their power, the impact of the layout of your work environment, and the impact of your first impressions of a new boss. Every perception will be heavily influenced by the nonverbal communication associated with each situation.

General Nonverbal Considerations

This section identifies those subcodes we feel are significant and examines them for their general impact on the job. Basically, most of the research has been conducted in the areas of environment and space, kinesics, and physical appearance. Additional material may be found in the spheres of chronemics, haptics, and vocalics, although not much research has been reported in these areas. Perhaps the most important dimensions of nonverbal communication are found in those we perceive, the spatiotemporal, followed closely by those we associate with the body.

Spatiotemporal Dimensions

All jobs take place in space and time. The following section examines the spatiotemporal dimensions and their impact on how we relate to and behave on the job.

Space   The type of environment you work in does several things. First, the environment influences you. How you relate to your environment also affects other people. Both of your authors, for example, were once asked by some friends in the real estate business to look at the physical layout of their office. The office was designed so that several agents could use the space at one time (see Figure 12.1). The supervisor could keep track of what was going on in the office through

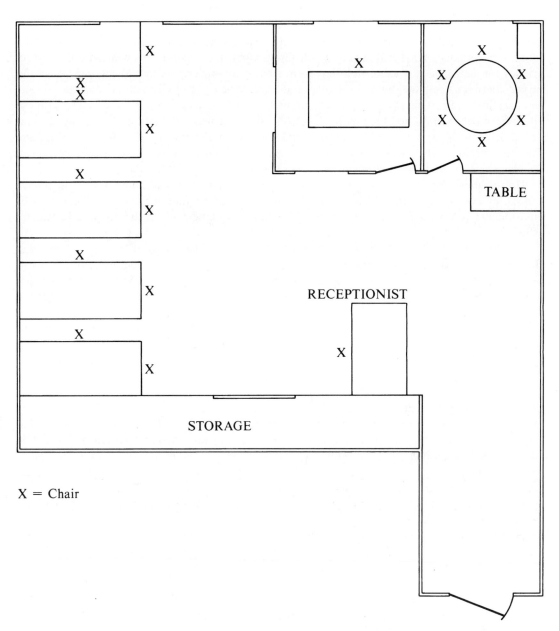

X = Chair

FIGURE 12.1 Layout of Real Estate Office.

two large windows in his office, and next to the supervisor's office was a ''conference'' room for closing deals (where the office soft-drink machine was located). The walls were white, and the office was carpeted. What was wrong? Two things: first, the supervisor's windows allowed no privacy for the agents; the agents felt they were continually under pressure. Second, there was no privacy between agent and buyer in the working area. When you buy something as expensive as a house, there are certain aspects of your situation that must be made clear: features such as salary, children (number and if you plan on having any), and other needs that are not meant for general or public knowledge. Also, having the soft-drink machine in the closing room was inappropriate. The recommendations were simple: (1) have the windows in the supervisor's office curtained, (2) place privacy walls between the desks, and (3) remove the soft-drink machine.

This example may sound rather elementary, but if you visit most real estate offices, insurance offices, or even banks, you will find similar situations. Taking into account the dimensions of environment, how would you rate the real estate office environment before the suggested changes? After?

A second aspect of the environment is where you are located. Michael Korda contends that there are lines of power, of prestige, based on where your office is located. Quite simply, the more windows and space you have, the greater your power and prestige. Thad Sitton points out that some environments are designed to make the user feel powerless and that others are insensitive to the user's needs.[1] Sitton especially targets those messages the schools provide to students and faculty—that they are untrustworthy and powerless. Not all environments, however, indicate insensitivity to the needs of others; modern environmental engineering has attempted to meet the needs of both employees and customers alike. Modern office buildings (such as the Chicago Sears Tower) have been designed with special considerations of such environmental features as noise, comfort, and attractiveness.[2] The way we structure the environment can send various messages, many of which may yield less than satisfactory results.

Finally, we can examine the impact of color in the environment. Have you ever noticed that white is chosen for most of the businesses in which we operate? Why? Two reasons might be offered. First, according to Faber Biren, white is associated with purity and perhaps honesty.[3] Second, white is perceived to be environmentally cooler than other colors, and this can affect mental abilities.[4] Hence, our work environment may suggest an honest business and, at the same time, help control our tempers (as was pointed out in chapter 5, when color and perceived temperature were examined).

Environmentally, we should also examine such features as lighting, together with the general size and architectural design of the buildings in which we work. Research seems to indicate that lighting can increase productivity; such lighting should be bright yet not harsh.[5] Lighting can also be used for effect, to reduce stress, as has been demonstrated by the simple addition of a fish tank in waiting rooms.[6] Something of yourself goes into the type of building in which you work. What we might consider here is size, design, and artifactual additions. From the type of building, we learn how the company perceives itself. One of your authors knows of a company that was located in a suburban house. This company did a little over six million dollars of business a year but had trouble convincing potential clients of its permanence and assets because it did not look like a prosperous business. When the company moved into an office complex, its problems were over.

The same may be true of the Sears Tower or other such buildings. In his memoirs, Albert Speer noted that Adolf Hitler's perception of Berlin was a vision of such a grand style that the buildings would last for 1,000 years.[7] Great buildings are large monuments to the people who build them.

Finally, the environment you are in also tells other people things. Ken Cooper describes some executives whose secretaries are in a separate building.[8] The message of image is obvious: I'm extremely important, so important that I am located elsewhere. In a field study of factory work-places, John Peponis noted that many factories are designed to increase the distance between the powerful and the powerless. His research indicates that, whereas management has offices away from the workplace, the foreman's office is on the shop floor. Additionally, the managerial work-place is structured in such a way as to allow for communication between and among the various managerial levels; the shop foreman's office, on the other hand, has no such connectivity.[9]

Territory   Not only does the location of the office inform us about how the person is perceived— or wants to be perceived—but so too does the arrangement of space and the treatment of space as territory. For instance, consider the door. Not an interesting object, but one that expresses some-thing. What difference is there between an office with an open door and one with a closed door? What is the desire for privacy? Who is perceived as more important, the person with the open door or the one with the closed door? A closed door implies privacy. People who are more important are afforded more privacy. Note, too, that we assume certain things, including privacy, based on the location of the office.

A second feature of spatial use is the placement of objects in the office. The more permanent the type of object (as indicated by its value, its heaviness, and the space it takes up), the more prestige and/or power is indicated. This obviously would also include the size of the office; gen-erally speaking, you can judge prestige and status by the amount of space provided for the person. Just the fact of being in an office may tell you something about that person's status in the orga-nization (Is it shared? How much space? How many plants, decorations, diplomas, etc.?). Figure 12.2 shows how Korda would establish power in two environments, one small and one large.

One aspect of the office is the type of space it comes to represent. Because the office is a territory of sorts, it should fall into one of S. M. Lyman and M. B. Scott's four types of territory.[10] Unfortunately, however, the office tends to be viewed in more than one way. If the office is not shared with anyone else, then the territory should be considered **interactional;** that is, we expect others will enter, but they will have a reason, such as a secretary, for example. However, we tend to treat our offices as extensions of our homes; therefore the office can become a **home territory,** assuming all the privacy and restrictions of the home.

When we enter an office, we tend to treat the other person's territory as if it were home. Unless we are of higher status or power, we are inclined to defer to that person while in his or her office. Even if the door is open, we will probably stop, knock or indicate our presence, and then enter. If the door is closed, we may even pass by. Judee K. Burgoon and Thomas J. Saine describe a situation in which a student and his wife moved into a professor's office (they needed a place to stay and the office was in an old home). After a short period of time, the professor, who usually worked on weekends, felt he was violating *their* (the students') territory.[11] In the same way, we value our office and the privacy it affords; we do not expect others to enter without reason or permission.

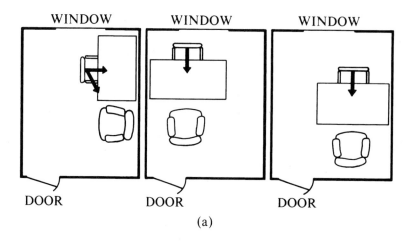

(a)

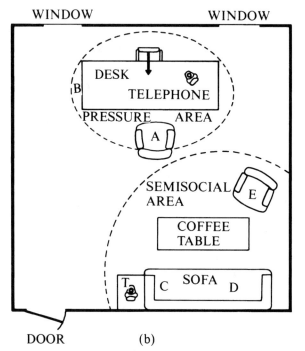

DOOR   (b)

FIGURE 12.2   Office Set Up for Communication and Power.
Source: Michael Korda, *Power! How to Get It, How to Use It* (New York:
Ballantine, 1975), pp. 232–235. Reprinted with permission.

Personal Space   Within the office territory, we have personal space and personal spacing expectations. Normally, on the basis of the arrangement of furniture, we understand how we are to communicate. Figure 12.3 presents two offices, one arranged to encourage communication and the other to restrict communication. The major difference is found in the blocking nature of the desk. In order to reduce the distance between the occupant and the visitor, the occupant can move from behind the desk and sit with the visitor. Where we sit may indicate whether or not we are perceived as conversational and cooperative, or competitive and coactive.[12] (See Figure 12.4.) L. Malandro, L. Barker and D. Barker have analyzed the *shape* of the table and what impressions it communicates to others.[13] They suggest that a round table is equated with equality and unity; however, as noted earlier, there is a particular *spot* from which power radiates in lessening degrees. The square table presents a problem because it sends messages of both equality and power. Because the sides are equally long, power struggles may ensue among equals; hence, unity is reduced. Finally, the rectangular table allows for power positions to be identified (usually at the head—or short side— of the table), factions to be identified, and power struggles established (two equally powerful participants, one at each end of the table).

Malandro, Barker, and Barker's analysis suggests that seat placement may produce role differentiation. That is, your location at a particular table during a meeting or in a working group may help to determine your role in the group. At least two studies suggest that such perceptions may be accurate, at least for those who either fail to contribute or wish to be perceived as noncontributing. In each case, the nonconforming member became isolated from the group.[14]

In a larger space, the location of the seat taken during a training session may yield differing impressions.[15] For instance, sitting in the front of a group is associated with attention to what is being said, but it also indicates a dependence on the instructor. Sitting in the back of the group sends a message of independence and lack of concern. Sitting in the center of the group sends no particular message, although such a preference may indicate a need to avoid distraction.

In general, then, your choice of seating location within a space sends many messages. Some of these messages function to indicate power, unity, and interest. Some of the messages indicate independence, and others indicate subordination. Cooper, for instance, suggests that in order to send an impression of power in group meetings, the person should avoid the table and locate himself or herself away from and above the rest.[16] It may be that elevation is associated with perceptions of dominance and power in the meeting.[17]

A final factor that can be investigated but that has not received attention is the use of the auto as an office. Each year there are hundreds of thousands of people who work out of their cars. What does the car tell us about them? Consider the following: would you buy life insurance from someone who drove a large black automobile? Probably not, but you might if that same automobile were green or red. In a culture supposedly attached to automobiles, this use of territory, both as an office and as home territory, deserves more attention.

Time   In this culture we find time to be very important, especially on the job. We are paid for the time we spend working, sometimes even receiving bonuses for doing more work in a shorter period of time. In this culture, however, we use time in two ways on the job. First, we use time as an indicator of the prominence or prestige of the person we are dealing with. In this regard we

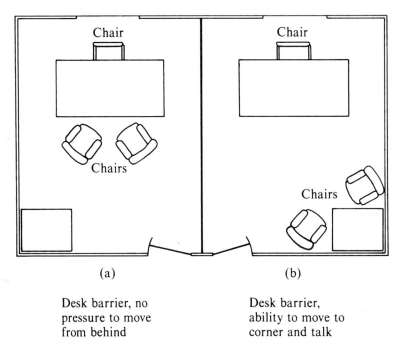

(a)   (b)

Desk barrier, no   Desk barrier,
pressure to move   ability to move to
from behind   corner and talk

FIGURE 12.3   Two Offices with Different Types of Communication structures.

either wait for people (the longer we wait, the more important they are) or keep people waiting for us.[18] Second, the amount of time we spend with someone—customer or coworker—indicates how important he or she is to us.[19]

In this culture we also view time as a message that expresses something about the individual. Leslie Baxter and Jean Ward interviewed secretaries about how they perceived people arriving early, late, and on time for an appointment. They found that people who arrived on time were perceived as being the most competent, composed, and sociable. The prompt person, however, was not rated as dynamic. The late arrivals were rated as more dynamic, but lower in competence, composure, and sociability. The early arriver was rated low to moderate in terms of these variables.[20] In some cultures, however, these results would be quite different.

Touch   Ordinarily we do not think of touch as a nonverbal subcode operating on the job. But there are at least two important messages that touch communicates on the job. One is positive and expresses status and power relationships. The other deals more with sex differences and is probably perceived more negatively. In dealing with status and power, Nancy Henley has described how touch is perceived within superior-subordinate relationships (see Table 12.1). As you may observe, the superior initiates and controls touch.[21] Furthermore, as indicated in the research of J. D. Fisher, M. Rytting, and R. Heslin, simple contact with another person may increase perceptions of credibility.[22]

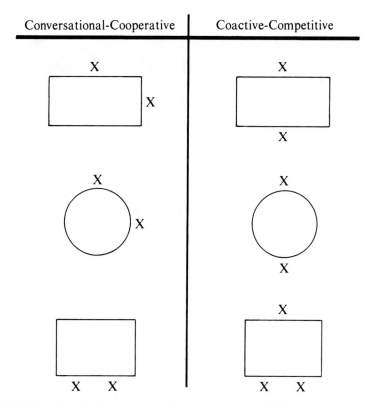

FIGURE 12.4   Seating Arrangements for Cooperative and Competitive Interactions.

There are also negative perceptions based on touch. These are usually considered in the category of ''sexual harassment:'' touch that differs from the ''functional/professional'' touch we may expect on the job. Another negative perception found with touch is *self-touch*. Cooper points out that one of the basic indicators of stress in the business world is based on self-touch. Cooper conjectures that we indicate stress by ''defensive beating.'' In this connection, such self-touch as rubbing the back of our neck, rubbing our forehead, rubbing our eyes, and pulling on our cheeks are seen as signs of stress.[23]

For the most part, we expect a handshake when we meet and when we leave someone, if the meeting pertains to the job. Although this may be an expectation, there are certain types of handshakes that are unexpected, as Gerard Nierenberg and Henry Calero indicate:[24]

> Handshaking customs vary from country to country. . . . The firmness of the typical male handshake in the United States probably originated in contests of strength. . . . Many people consider themselves experts in analyzing character and attitude from a handshake, probably because perspiring palms usually indicate nervousness. The flaccid, or ''dead fish,'' handshake is equally unpopular, although there may be mitigating circumstances . . . in the United States at least there is something vaguely un-American about a flaccid handshake.

TABLE 12.1   Subordinate–Superior Touch by Sex

Superior touches Subordinate		25
Male:Female	1	
Female:Female	3	
Male:Male	16	
Female:Male	5	
Subordinate touches Superior		14
Male:Female	9	
Female:Female	1	
Male:Male	4	
Female:Male	0	
"Equal" touches "Equal"		13
Male:Female	11	
Female:Male	2	

Source: N. M. Henley, *Body Politics: Power, Sex, and Nonverbal Communication* (Englewood Cliffs, NJ: Prentice-Hall, 1977), p. 116. Reprinted with permission.

In general, the type of touch, its location and its duration are conditioned by the environment. Almost everyone has heard or read about stories of bosses and secretaries touching each other. In reality, however, there seems to be a rather strict rule about touch in business: when it is possible that people are present, do not touch unless that touch is in the form of a ritualistic greeting. What types of touches go on behind the closed office door is unknown; but close your door with someone of the opposite sex in the office, and it is probable that others will perceive your touch behavior as less than "functional/professional."

Overt Body Dimensions

Much of what *you* communicate on the job is in the way your body communicates. This approach, commonly labeled "body language" in the popular literature, consists of the kinesic and vocalic dimensions. Most of what we know of these expressions concerns the perceptions of credibility and status on the job. There are also attributions we make, based on these dimensions, that help interpret another person's awareness of you and the way that individual may react to you. Probably the most significant areas of the body are the face (the eyes and total facial expression) and gestures. The total body (posture, tenseness) apparently does not communicate as much as the other body parts. Finally, the voice is the object of perceived credibility and personality.

Kinesic Behaviors   In most business situations, we seem to try to mask our faces. By this we mean that people strive to maintain a noncommital orientation or a positive emotional expression when dealing with others. This would seem to be reasonable. We want others to feel either that we like them or that we want to do business with them; we do not like to be placed in a situation where we are not entirely sure of how the other person perceives us (the ''stone face''). Facial expression is perhaps one of the most important cues on the job. By your facial expression, others can ascertain how well or how bad things are going. Through your face, you express the basic emotions identified by Silvan S. Tompkins:[25]

interest/excitement
enjoyment/joy
surprise/startle
distress/anguish
shame/humiliation
anger/rage
contempt/disgust
fear/terror

Obviously, such emotions and their display are not considered positive indicators on the job. Therefore, we try to deceive others. Significantly, research indicates that we may be better deceivers than we thought, although distortion of *factual* information seems an easier task than concealing or misrepresenting emotional information.[26] On the job, then, we expect that there would be less emotional display because of expectations not to show emotions and because of the idea that it is more difficult to encode emotional deceptions than those dealing with factual information.

Besides encoding and decoding emotional information, the face is important because of eye contact. Direct eye contact, for example, may be interpreted as a sign of credibility.[27] What eye contact and gaze patterns can reveal to us about our relations with others includes the perception of status and power in the relationship, based on who is looked at more often (the higher status/power person), who looks with a steady, direct gaze (again, the higher status/power person), and who does not look at others (for some reason it is the higher status/power person who can avoid all eye contact and get away with it; this, however, is usually observed only when the power or status differential is known).[28] The types of eye contact also affects perceptions of power and self-presentation. There are at least three types of eye contact.[29] Messages of equality are typically found in mutual gaze, or when two people are looking directly at one another (usually in the eyes). A one-sided look occurs when one person looks in the direction of the other's face while the other does not reciprocate the gaze; in this instance, the person gazing possesses more power or influence than the nongazer. Finally, gaze aversion exists when one person intentionally avoids contact with the other; gaze aversion is characterized by an impression of a lack of power and credibility (the perception may be that you are intentionally hiding something or being deceptive).

The smile is also a revealing feature of the face. Some research seems to indicate that simply smiling helps in sales. Other research indicates that smiling people are perceived as being more intelligent than those who do not smile.[30] The smile, however, is also associated with attempted emotional deception.[31] Because in our culture the smile is perceived as a positive and reinforcing display, it should be a predominant facial feature. However, as Cooper points out, the face at rest (the face, he states, that people associate with you and your image on the job) does not ordinarily manifest a smile. Rather, the face at rest is more noncommittal.[32] The smile, then, is one feature we appear to manipulate but also tend to forget about. It is an indicator of positive affect/relations but also of deception.

Gestures and Body Movement   How we elaborate our messages through body movement and gestures provides us with some information about our relation to others at work. Research indicates that mirroring the behaviors of others is a sign of conceding or according status or power to them. Further, the more relaxed the individual is in a situation, the more control this person perceives he or she has over the situation. This feeling usually comes from a knowledge of where the individual is on the organizational ladder.[33] As Burgoon and Saine note, ". . . Watch any business meeting and you'll discover that higher-status people allow arms, legs, and posture to be more relaxed; they are more likely to lean sideways, and they feel free to put their feet up."[34]

When it comes to gestures, we seem to interpret them in several ways. First, there are gestures that are positive and are attributed to confidence, competence, and sincerity. Such gestures as "steepling," and "readiness" are perceived as positive. The majority of the gestures described in the interpretations of popular literature, however, are negative. Nierenberg and Calero list more than 15 negative gestures observed in conversations, compared to only two or three positive gestures.[35] Possibly the work context is such that we seldom furnish positive reinforcement. Competition for the other's job may be one reason; another reason might be fear that giving positive reinforcement would be perceived as weakness in a world where the weak do not survive.

Facing behaviors are also indicative of who has power or status on the job. Obviously, we will defer to those in power. We normally do so by facing that person. This Cooper calls this the "choir effect," with the higher status/power person being faced by his "choir" of underlings.[36] On the job, we normally face that person who has the expertise to do the job; credibility, then, may also be indicated by facing behavior.

One set of kinesic behaviors, adaptors, are perceived negatively. These self-touching gestures are interpreted in two ways: either as indicators of nervousness or as quasi-courtship behaviors. Both, obviously, are perceived negatively on the job. However, the use of illustrators is perceived positively. We expect those who are dynamic or in control to use slightly more animated gestures to accompany their verbal message. Such gestures can also increase message acceptance.[37]

An informative research project carried out by Martin Remland indicates that people in either superior or subordinate positions are evaluated differently, depending upon the perceived status of their actions.[38] Remland posited that a superior will be ranked as more *considerate* when displaying low-status rather than high-status nonverbal behaviors. He also posited that the superior would be rated as more considerate when the subordinate exhibited high-status rather than low-status behaviors. To conduct the research, Remland created the following videotapes of two men:

High-status superior: man was videotaped leaning back in his chair with hands clasped behind the neck; used an "invading" gesture (pointing at subordinate); did not establish eye contact.

High-status subordinate: man rested one arm on his desk and the other on the back of the chair; leaned back with ankle-on-knee leg cross; played with superior's pen at one point; did not look at superior while listening.

Low-status superior: leaned slightly in chair; rested both arms on the desk (close proximity to the desk); gazed at subordinate while subordinate spoke; looked away occasionally while speaking; used a defensive gesture once while speaking (covering face with hands).

Low-status subordinate: leaned slightly forward in chair; faced superior directly; arms positioned on lap and feet on the floor; occasionally looked down while speaking; gazed at superior while superior spoke; nodded head approvingly while listening.

Remland found that people who viewed the videotaped interactions considered the low-status non-verbal communication of the superior as significantly more considerate than people who viewed the high-status nonverbal communication. He also found that the subordinate's nonverbal communication influenced the consideration rankings given to the superior. People who evaluated the superior when he was seen with the high-status subordinate judged him to be more considerate than did people who saw him interact with the low-status subordinate. Remland's findings infer that status behaviors can also influence perceptions of leadership, but that the type of interaction displayed by the subordinate also influences such perceptions.

Vocalics   The degree to which our voice contributes to the way we are perceived on the job is influenced by several factors. As noted in earlier chapters, the rate with which we speak influences perceptions of the speaker. In general, the good speaker uses a conversational, calm, slightly slower, slightly less tense, and lower voice.[39] A speaker with such a voice, as pointed out by Barnett Pearce and Forrest Conklin, is perceived as more trustworthy; is more favorably evaluated; is perceived as more attractive, as more educated, as possessing higher income, as possessing a better job; and is perceived as taller than a speaker using a dynamic voice.[40] Use of a dynamic voice should be reserved for situations in which a perception of dynamism is needed.

More recently, Richard L. Street and Robert M. Brady determined that speech rate affected a listener's perceptions of competence and social attraction.[41] They found that listeners perceived a speaker to be more competent as the speaker's rate of speech increased. They also found that listeners have a strong stereotype about the social attractiveness of speakers: those who spoke with moderate and fast rates were perceived as being more socially attractive than speakers at the slowest rate.

Other than general style, both voice quality and dialect seem to influence judgments about the speaker. As was noted in chapter 8, the major dialect accepted in this culture is the Great American or General American dialect. Those who speak ''without an accent'' may be perceived as more credible than those who speak with a Northeastern or Southern dialect. Based on David W. Addington's research, we should also note that certain voice types are perceived more negatively than others.[42] Who, for example, wants to work with a person who has a nasal voice, with one who is whiny and argumentative, or with a breathy-voiced person on an assignment that requires bold and imaginative thought?

Finally, as a form of nonverbal communication, silences convey messages of power and credibility. The more powerful and credible are able to both initiate and break silences. Those who are less powerful or credible must endure the silence, which is often used as an indication of displeasure or punishment.[43]

Physical Appearance

At one time, this chapter might have begun with an examination of physical appearance. Today, however, there seem to be rather strong stereotypes of what is appropriate and inappropriate in terms of physical appearance on the job. This is probably more true for the white-collar than for the blue-collar worker, but even that seems to be changing quickly. What, or who, is responsible for this change? Most people would probably point to John T. Molloy and his popular books on ''dressing for success.''[44] Before we examine Molloy's contribution to one's appearance on the job, we need to consider the general effect that our physical appearance has on the job.

Body Aspects   We make major attributions based on a person's body size, height, and amount of hair. As mentioned previously, there are probably certain stereotypes that continue on the job. We expect that the larger person will be perceived as more credible, and this same individual will have more power and status in the organization. As noted earlier, a person's physical height is highly correlated with his or her beginning wage.[45] We may also assume that there is a relationship between academic status and height, that the greater the individual's status, the taller he or she is.[46] Cooper sums up the perception of height in the business world in these words:[47]

> Lack of height has always been a sign of inferiority. We can ''fall short'' of a goal, ''think small,'' be ''shortsighted,'' or be ''looked down on.'' Being lower is a sign of servility. In ancient times vanquished soldiers were forced to pass under a chest-high arch of spears in front of the conquering general. Anyone who refused to bow down was allowed to wear the spear home, buried in his chest. Even today we don't like anyone to ''lord over us''. . . . We constantly favor people with a height advantage.

A second physical feature is general somatotype, or body shape. Typically, people perceive endomorphic and ectomorphic body types more negatively than the mesomorphic. Although the research on body type may be somewhat contrived, examination of popular trends infers this culture prefers its males and females to be more mesomorphic. Cooper goes so far as to state:[48]

> Put yourself on a diet to fight the mid-20s and mid-30s metabolism change that seems to catch so many people. Don't let an hour and a half of eating jeopardize the eight hours per day of work you put into being successful. If you don't fit the mold [the mesomorphic, athletic body], try to get there. There is a definite relationship between a sound body and business success.

There are some studies that imply that physical attractiveness may be an asset for some and an encumbrance for others. Although we generally consider attractiveness as an advantage, for people interested in managerial positions, physical attractiveness can be a liability. A study by Madeline Heilman and Lois Saruwatari found that being attractive was an asset for males seeking a managerial position, but it was advantageous for females only if the position was nonmanagerial.[49] Whether this finding represents a general bias in managerial position or is based on the stereotype that attractive women cannot succeed in managerial positions has yet to be ascertained; a clear sexual bias, however, exists at managerial levels. There appears to be a relationship between attractiveness and assertiveness, at least for females. K. Campbell, D. Kleim, and K. Olson examined the relationship between assertiveness and physical attractiveness.[50] They found that more attractive females exhibited more assertive behavior than did less attractive females; they also found that attractive females reported a higher level of personal assertiveness (as measured by a self-expression measure) than did less attractive females. For males, however, there was no significant relationship between attractiveness and assertiveness.

Finally, the amount of hair you have may also affect the way you are perceived. A general rule now is to moderate the amount of cranial hair; if facial hair is to be worn, limit it to a trimmed mustache. It would appear that the short-haired, well-kept individual is perceived as more masculine, mature, wise, and intelligent.[51]

Dress   What are the effects of dress on how a person is perceived? Although we may think that this subject has received much research attention, this is not the case. Besides the work previously cited, little research has actually addressed the question of what clothing does for an individual. Much of what we now read and hear has come from Molloy's *Dress for Success* books. This has produced a stereotype that implies that the well-dressed businessman or businesswoman looks a certain way. This stereotype seems to have become the norm, the thing we expect.

What do we know of how dress communicates on the job? Except for the use of a uniform, very little. As Leonard Bickman found, uniforms convey special meanings.[52] Although we do not, as a rule, expect to wear uniforms on the job, (unless, of course, there is a uniform associated with the job), most jobs have *informal* uniform requirements. Such occupations as bank teller, stock boy or girl, secretary, and even teacher require some kind of informal uniform. We expect people in certain occupations to dress in certain ways; thus we establish an expectation of uniform as normative and not to be deviated from. With the uniform we also find perceptions of similar attitudes and behaviors. Hence, the special garb, whether or not it is a police, fire, or business uniform, implies certain expected behavioral patterns. Most of us have certain ideas of how someone working for IBM dresses; in the same way we also have expectations about other occupations and businesses, expecting their employees to observe certain dress, irrespective of whether there is a dress code.

At least one study has examined the impact of clothing on perceptions of credibility. R. Bassett, A. Stanton-Spicer, and J. Whitehead asked their students to view photographs of two males and two females dressed in high- and low-status clothing. High-status dress for males consisted of a suit, dress shirt, tie, and dress shoes. High-status females wore a dress, heels, stockings, and jewelry. In the low-status conditions, male and female sources wore ''blue-collar'' dress: work jeans and shirts, tennis shoes or boots for males, and inexpensive skirts, blouses, shoes, and no stockings and jewelry for females. Students were then shown each dress condition, after which they rated each on perceived source credibility. Their results indicated that males and females were perceived differently. Whereas high-status males were rated higher in terms of potency than were low-status males, females were not perceived differently. High-status females were rated as being more competent than low-status females, but there was no difference for males. Both males and females in the high-status conditions were perceived as being more competent than those in the low-status condition. And finally, there was no difference between dress conditions in rating for composure.[53]

That these findings are valid in the working world has been corroborated in part in a study carried out by Mary Lynn Damhorst.[54] She had 64 employees of private businesses view four sketches of a male and a female interacting. In one sketch both male and female were dressed in formal business attire; in a second sketch the male and female were dressed less formally. Rather than the dress and suit and tie in the first sketch, the female wore pants and a simple knit or pullover top; the male wore slacks and a knit pullover shirt. In the third and fourth sketches, the male and female wore dissimilar dress (in one the male was formal and the female informal, and vice versa in the other). Damhorst's results are significant in that males and females tended to view the sketches differently. Although both sexes perceived the business suits worn in the sketches as highly informative about the level of managerial position, female respondents assumed that the man had a higher rank than the woman with whom he was interacting. The male respondents were more sensitive to the context of the situation, placing less importance on dress. Moreover, men in business suits interacting with casually dressed women were perceived to be more directive, rewarding, and punishing than when sketched with the formal female/informal male. The men who were dressed casually and interacting with formally dressed women were perceived as occupying nonmanagerial roles and as having ranks equivalent to or lower than those of the women.

Both of these studies imply that the type of clothing you wear has a significant effect on how others perceive your credibility and position. Furthermore, the type of clothing you wear also tells others something about your communication style. Males in business attire are perceived as having a higher rank than females. It may be that the business ''uniform'' is perceived more strongly for males than for females. However, there appears to be a stereotypical ''uniform'' with which people identify in the ''real'' world.

How should we dress in the ''real'' world? If the position requires a uniform, then that uniform will be appropriate. If there is no uniform, then look around to see what others are wearing; you may find that an *informal* uniform policy exists. The relative success of books such as Molloy's indicates that there are uniform policies written nowhere that are known to none but understood by all.

Finally, we consider accessories and artifacts. Molloy recommends that the artifacts and accessories we wear be kept to a minimum.[55] Be smart, be fashion conscious, but do not become a display yourself. Other studies of artifacts include research that reports a difference in perceived credibility between smokers of cigars, pipes, and cigarettes.[56] This study found that the pipe-smoker was perceived as more credible than the other smokers. Finally, your eyeglasses also seem to say something about you. Molloy states that for a position in the business world, you should wear glasses that make you look authoritarian, traditional, and older. For the male, the glasses should be heavy plastic; for female, glasses on the job should be plastic, but contacts should be worn for social occasions.[57]

Review

The importance of nonverbal communication on the job can be demonstrated by our reactions and appearance. From the initial impression we have of the environment to the type of accessories we wear, we are sending and receiving messages. Although there would seem to be many areas in which nonverbal research should be conducted, very little has been done. What we know of the nonverbal communication on the job seems to conform to stereotypic expectations. This is not surprising; we live in a world partially controlled by our nonverbal communication. Like Molloy's influence, once we begin to examine nonverbal communication and report our findings they take on a sort of permanence. This section should have provided you with the material needed to prepare for the needs of the job and, at the same time, provided you with enough information to make fairly accurate predictions about how you are expected to behave and how others want you to act on the job. We now turn to the nonverbal behaviors associated with the job interview; we examine how you can manipulate to the best advantage the nonverbal impression you make.

The Job Interview

In the preceding material, we assumed that you already had a job and could analyze the subcodes in an on-going context. For many, however, this is a false assumption. Probably the most distressing and nerve-racking communication we have is when we are interviewed for a job. Although there are many types of dialogue, the interview we must ''pass'' in order to obtain the job (and perhaps the follow-up interview, if we pass the first) is the most difficult because we are competing against others and must manage our impressions appropriately. For example, in the initial interview, we need to be a little nervous (overconfidence could be perceived wrongly); we must be somewhat submissive, but not too submissive; and we must defer yet be perceived as dynamic. Most of these factors are influenced by the way we control our nonverbal behavior.

Perhaps the most critical feature of the interview is the way we meet the stereotype of what a ''good'' candidate should ''look like.'' In 1964, E. C. Webster examined how judgments are made in the selection interview. He found the following:[58]

- Interviewers have a stereotype of what is ''right'' or ''good,'' and then they match people with these stereotypes.
- Any biases are formed early in the interview, followed closely by either a favorable or an unfavorable decision.
- Interviewers are more influenced by unfavorable impressions than by favorable impressions.

Have these findings changed over the years? Unfortunately, they have changed very little. Today there are even more inflexible stereotypes of what a person should look like for a certain job. We may even find that many interviewers *hire in their own image.* We may also note that decisions to hire seem to be made during the initial interaction, in the first few minutes of the interview. And, finally, because of the large number of applicants for any specific position, interviewers seem more likely to notice negative behaviors that differentiate people than they notice positive behaviors.[59]

A number of researchers have undertaken research to determine which nonverbal cues are most significant in the job interview. Although they do not totally agree, the following list seems to best represent those features you should be prepared for:[60]

- *Paralanguage:* fluency of speech, rate, articulation, loudness
- *Posture:* relaxed, slight backward lean
- *Eye Contact:* increased *mutual* eye contact
- *Personal Appearance:* dressed appropriately for interview
- *Positive Facial Expression and Head Nods*

The factors assume that the difference between two equally qualified applicants may be determined nonverbally.

Kittie W. Watson and Larry R. Smeltzer asked interviewers which nonverbal behaviors were most influential in selecting people for a position, whether or not the importance of nonverbal behaviors changes during the interview, and what nonverbal behaviors job applicants should be most concerned to improve. Their findings indicate that (1) initial impressions are very important, (2) certain nonverbal behaviors are more important than others, and (3) what interviewers look for during the interview changes as the interview progresses.[61]

Watson and Smeltzer found that the two most important nonverbal features were the interviewee's appearance and the amount of eye contact maintained with the interviewer. A third factor that emerged from the study was attention to facial expression and punctuality. Watson and Smeltzer also found that prior to the interview itself, appearance, punctuality, and the handshake were most important. During the first phase of the interview, eye contact, facial expression and gestures were the most influential nonverbal cues. During the rest of the session, eye contact, facial expression, and appearance continued to be important, but interviewers report that eye contact, appearance, and facial expression were remembered most after the interview. Finally, Watson and Smeltzer found that most interviewers felt that interviewees should concentrate on improving eye contact, appearance, and facial expression.

How important are nonverbal cues in the interview? C. L. Bovee and J. V. Thill note that of the top 20 negative factors that may lead to rejection in an employment interview, seven of the top ten factors are nonverbal:[62]

1.   Has poor personal appearance [PHYSICAL APPEARANCE]
2.   Is overbearing, overaggressive, conceited, has a ''superiority complex,'' seems to ''know it all'' [KINESIC, PARALANGUAGE, TOUCH]
3.   Is unable to express self clearly—poor voice, diction, grammar [PARALANGUAGE]
4.   Lacks planning for career—no purpose or goals [CHRONEMIC]
5.   Lacks interest and enthusiasm—passive, indifferent [KINESIC, PARALANGUAGE]
6.   Lacks confidence and poise—nervous, ill at ease [KINESIC, PARALANGUAGE]
7.   Has failed to participate in extracurricular activities
8.   Overemphasizes money—interested only in the best dollar job
9.   Has poor scholastic record—just got by
10. Is unwilling to start at the bottom—expects too much too soon [CHRONEMIC]

This and other research on the interview process suggest that initial impressions are important. Accordingly, the interviewee, in order to maximize his or her chances, should try to most closely manage the first few minutes of the interview. The reason: how the interview turns out will probably be determined from the time the interviewee enters the interview area to somewhere in the first five minutes of interaction. Rounding out this discussion, we have outlined the positive and negative nonverbal behaviors that interviewers seem to look for. *We do not intend this material as a prescription for success in the interview, indeed, the nonverbal cues examined are gleaned from many sources and involve many occupations and interests; they are derived from interviews with professional interviewers and from teaching sections on appropriate nonverbal interviewee behavior in career-planning courses.* Use them as a guide and not a prescription to help in preparing for your interview.

Environmental Factors

Where you are interviewed will undoubtedly influence how you react to the interviewer. If the interview takes place in a ''meat market'' environment, a place where there are many tables and many interviews going on at once, then you should expect to compete with environmental noise and distractions. In this case the interviewer may feel less at ease than if you were being interviewed in his or her office (although professional interviewers know what effects the environment has on the interview and can adjust for them). If you are interviewed in the interviewer's office look around for indicators of who he or she is, what hobbies, interests, and personality factors are indicated by the decor. Based on size of the office, plushness of decor, and so on, you can also obtain some idea of the person's relative position in the organization.

One feature of the interview environment is the arrangement of furniture. Some interviewers prefer to interview applicants across a desk. This presents a barrier between interviewer and interviewee and also heightens that individual's status and power relative to yours. Some interviewers, however, will come out from behind the desk and sit with you. This may be seen as an indication of reduced psychological distance between interviewer and interviewee. Be careful, however, to maintain the appropriate nonverbal behaviors; remember, the desk also tends to hide your legs and feet and what you are doing with them. In any event, after the initial move, most people seem to feel comfortable with the fact that the interviewer has removed the ''power'' symbol.

Sometimes an interviewer will take you to the place where you may be working. This allows him or her to see how you react to your potential new environment, but it sometimes sends the wrong signal. Many times the interviewer will say, ''This will be your office.'' The meaning is, of course, ''if you are selected for the job.'' Most of us, however, perceive it to mean, ''Here is my office, I'll move in tomorrow.'' Take such tours guardedly, but use the occasion to ask job-related questions that may not have been feasible during the formal interview.

One device Cooper tells of is the shortening of one leg on the chair the applicant will sit in.[63] The idea is to see how you react to strange situations. Although this is probably rare, be prepared for anything in the initial interview (to include questions that may not be quite legal—in most cases it's a buyer's market out there).

Chronemic Factors

One critical aspect of the interview is time. We can consider time in two ways. First, we can examine punctuality. It should not be necessary to state that to be late for an interview is the same as not showing up. However, there are those who will arrive late and still expect to be interviewed. Arriving too early can also have negative effects; Baxter and Ward's findings indicate that the prompt person is perceived as most credible.[64] Normally we recommend that you arrive a little early, spend that time composing yourself out of sight of where you will be interviewing, and then ''arrive'' at the designated time.

A second temporal feature concerns the amount of time the interviewer spends with you. Although most interviews are for a predetermined period of time (determined by the interviewer and influenced by a number of factors, including the number of people to be seen, the time of day, and other appointments), the amount of time the interviewer spends with you may be indicative of your chances of being hired. If, as we believe, initial impressions and decisions are formed in the first few minutes, then the interviewer will spend the rest of the interview trying to gain information that justifies such an impression. Since it is usually easier to find negative qualities, the interview that lasts longer *may* be indicative of a favorable decision. We do not recommend, however, that you time your interview and compare it to others' interview times.

Physical Appearance Factors

Although people should by now be aware that their physical appearance is one of their most prominent nonverbal features, many persons seem to forget, or do not care, that most people have stereotypes of what a person should look like. Molloy's influence is just now being felt in regard to its insights concerning "informal" uniforms in the business world. How should you dress? Since most interviewers have a tendency to hire people in their own image (their own preference for uniforms), you do well to dress like the interviewer (appropriately for sex, of course). For either sex, a suit is preferable to something less casual. Remember, you are looking for a job and wish to impress the other person. Even for positions where you would expect to wear something less formal, you should consider dressing properly. As Bovee and Thill note:[65]

> You can impress an interviewer just by the way you look. Pay careful attention to your clothing, grooming . . . because the interviewer will form an opinion of you within the first minute of your meeting. . . . The best policy is to dress conservatively for the interview. Wear the best-quality clothing you can. Avoid flamboyant styles, colors, and prints; the most accepted business colors are dark blue, brown, gray, and maroon. Before you go to the interview, try to find out what others in the company at your target job wear. By dressing like those who work there, you'll fit right in.

Other features that may make a difference in the interview include hygienic aspects. For instance, clean your fingernails (your hands are prominent); get a haircut or style; do not use too much makeup (for females); and wear a watch, a ring (both sexes), and perhaps a necklace (again for females). Lapel flags, pins, and other identifiers may be worn, but remember, they will place you with certain groups. If, for example you are interviewing with a defense contractor, an American flag pin may not harm you. Your shoes should appear conservative (this includes heel height: no more than two inches for either sex), clean, and shined just prior to arrival. Facial hair should be avoided and cranial hair should be short for males, with middle-ear length sideburns at most. Beards are generally undesirable, as are untrimmed mustaches. For females, the hair should be fairly conservative; shoulder length seems best, or shorter. The hair should be styled but should look "natural."

The best way to find out how to dress is to visit an office and observe what people wear on the job for which you will be interviewed. Then when you are being interviewed, dress slightly better than the normal dress observed on the job. Be certain to select clothing that will make you look "good"; this means clothing that presents you as more mesomorphic than endomorphic or ectomorphic. Whether we like it or not, there are stereotypes associated with all body types, and these may influence the interviewer.

Kinesic Factors

When you are interviewed, your gestures, facial expression, and posture will indicate several things. First, through animated (though not extremely animated) gestures, you indicate a comfort level because your gestures match your verbal message. Your body posture should be slightly relaxed; you should sit either slightly back or forward, forward leans indicate an awareness of position, and at the same time, interest. You should place one foot in front of the other, avoid placing both feet under your chair or crossing your legs or ankles (especially for females: do not cross the ankles, unless you intend to take dictation on the job).

One major problem in any interview is what to do with your arms and hands. A trick we have discovered is simply to place your dominant hand (the one you write with) over the other. This will allow you to free the hand you normally gesture with and, at the same time, allow you to touch yourself (hand). If you are seated in a chair with arms, place your elbows on the arms at your side and your hands on your lap (as noted above). Do not grasp the arms with your hands; this induces "white knuckling" behavior, a sign of stress.

As the interview progresses, maintain a pleasant facial expression. Although the face remains pleasant, allow it to move though middle-ranged emotions that indicate such feelings as puzzlement (they will ask you questions that should make you look puzzled), liking, dislike (appropriate, of course to the discussion), and so forth. Maintain appropriate levels of eye contact; do not *stare,* however. One way to judge how you are doing is to observe whether or not the eye contact is being reciprocated. It seems that reciprocated eye contact indicates interest in the interviewee, and may be a positive sign. Be careful not to overdo it, however. (You walk a tight line between appropriate and inappropriate eye contact; you may have to ''play it by ear.'')

Avoid gestures that may appear stressful, including pulling on your clothing, stroking yourself (one reason for the hands on the lap is that this is a natural and conservative way to sit), or using halting and nervous gestures. As in a public speaking situation, you need to gesture throughout the interview. Hopefully, as time passes and you relax, your gestures will become more ''natural.''

Vocalic Factors

Your vocalic cues transmit several messages. First, by the rate, fluency, articulation, and loudness of the voice, you tell the interviewer how relaxed you are. You also give that person an idea of how you relate to others under pressure. Remember, a faster than normal rate is viewed as more credible, so that the pressure of the situation may actually help somewhat by increasing your rate. Be certain, however, that rapidity does not impair your fluency and articulation. Keep the voice at a moderate level, and orchestrate your pitch to indicate interest and affiliation. Second, your voice quality will provide the interviewer with some stereotypical information. Be aware of how you sound, and, if need be, modify the quality of your voice to match the perception you desire. (Review Addington's findings for the stereotypes associated with voice qualities.) Finally, your dialect also tells something about you: where you were brought up, where you are now living, and perhaps also the values you may hold. Be aware of what dialect you have, if any, and the potential perceptions associated with it.

Haptic Factors

There is very little touch in an interview. You should be prepared for an initial handshake, and it should be fairly dry (find a way to wipe your hands just before entering), be of moderate grip, and consist of approximately one and a half shakes. Do not expect a handshake at the end of the interview; you may receive one, but do not extend your hand first. The person in control, the higher status person, will initate touch. If you do receive a handshake at the end of your interview, wipe your hands on your clothing as you get up (just push off with your right hand on your right leg; no one will see it, and you will not have to worry about a ''wet'' handshake). As noted earlier, avoid self-touch.

Olfactory Factors

The way we smell communicates many things about us. We expect those we work with to smell clean. In planning for an interview, make certain that you have bathed and have put on some form of deodorant (preferably an antiperspirant) before interviewing. Since you may also bring with you an odor of what you last ate, chew some gum or use a mouthwash prior to interviewing (remember, the initial interview may begin with a handshake and close proximity). A lingering aroma of cigar, cigarette, and/or pipe smoke informs the interviewer about your smoking habits, and a heavy odor of smoke may indicate nervousness and other chain-smoking types of behavior. Because you can never tell when someone may be allergic to colognes or perfumes, use them in moderation or not at all. In terms of your olfactory communication, it is best to be as conservative as possible; probably the best advice is to smell clean and fresh.

Review

Nonverbal communication is extremely important in the job interview. Those nonverbal cues or behaviors that have been found to be persuasive, to produce positive impressions include: eye contact and smiling; a "pleasant" face; kinesic gestures and a confident, yet not overly aggressive, body orientation; a voice that is fluent and confident (not too loud, yet not too soft); and an appearance that is within the "norms" of the company, yet slightly better than most.

The Performance Appraisal Interview

In addition to the employment interview, most of us find that we are re-evaluated once or twice a year by our superiors. Such interviews are often referred to as **performance appraisal interviews.** In general, these are of two types or a combination of the two types: (1) a review for the purpose of determining salary increases and promotions; and (2) a review for the benefit of the subordinate to determine what, if any, changes need to be made in job performance. Michael Stano has undertaken quite a bit of research on these interviews, and he has found that in addition to the verbal and content aspects of such events, there are also nonverbal elements.[66] Stano especially emphasizes the importance of the setting. According to him, it is best if such interviews are held in neutral places. Most of the effective nonverbal behaviors useful in the employment interview are also important for the performance appraisal interview. Amira Galin and Barbara Benoliel have indicated that dress is important for appraisal interviews, especially because how you dress affects your own behavior and level of confidence.[67]

Nonverbal Interaction in Particular Professions

There have been bits and pieces of research undertaken on particular professions. The teaching-learning environment has probably elicited the most response. Virginia P. Richmond, James C. McCroskey, and Steven K. Payne, for example, have written an entire chapter on the teaching situation.[68] They focus on the importance of immediacy. In regard to dress, for example, they explain that a teacher can get one of two responses, depending on how he or she dresses. One dressed more formally will be perceived as organized, prepared, and knowledgeable; those dressed more casually will be seen as outgoing, honest, fair, receptive, and flexible. They suggest that a teacher dress more formally in the beginning of the class; as the term goes on, the teacher should appear more informal. We suggest, however, that formality should also be the "rule of the day" when giving tests, returning tests, and on the last day of the course. In other words, when the teacher wants to appear authoritative, she or he should dress formally. Such research, in favor of immediacy in the classroom, has been supported by Judith A. Sanders and Richard L. Wiseman.[69]

Judy C. Pearson and Richard West have studied the asking of questions by students in the classroom; they have found some gender differences.[70] Male teachers received more questions than female teachers. When there was a male instructor, female students asked fewer questions than male students. Self-reported masculinity (independence, assertiveness, and task-orientation) was associated with a greater likelihood of question asking. These conclusions are supportive of Deborah Tannen's contention that males operate more overtly in public settings.

As Sommer has noted, those who sit near the front of the class participate more and make better grades than other students. Janet Mercincavage and Charles I. Brooks, however, found that such was not necessarily the case among business majors.[71] They found that, among freshmen only, grades were better among those who sat in the front of the class. Among sophomores and juniors, it made no difference where they sat.

Regarding the chronemic element, L. A. Cinelli and D. J. Ziegler found some interesting results.[72] Students with a Type A personality reported a higher incidence of hassles. However, there was no difference between Type A's and Type B's regarding the intensity of hassles. Perhaps most interestingly, Type A's hassles involved having to wait, having concerns about physical appearance, and having a concern about meeting high standards. Type B subjects were more concerned about owing money and making decisions.

In the legal profession, considerable time and attention is given to nonverbal communication. Law students take courses in courtroom demeanor. Emphasis is placed on the dress of the lawyer, dress of the witnesses, timing, nonverbal intimidation techniques, and the like. According to Ronald J. Matson, such techniques are especially important in choosing jurors.[73]

Richard L. Street and David B. Buller have found that family physicians incorporate much of what is taught about nonverbal communication.[74] They found that physicians generally reciprocated the nonverbal behaviors of patients; physicians were less domineering with patients over 30 years old; physicians were responsive to patients' anxieties; and the patient's sex and education affected the physicians' nonverbal behavior very little.

Leadership and Credibility

Throughout this chapter, we have examined how nonverbal factors affect perceptions of status and power. As you begin to move upward in the organization, your leadership potential will be one factor that may be crucial in your advancement. This section examines those nonverbal behaviors that affect perceptions of credibility and leadership. We believe that this discussion will provide you with the information needed (1) to promote an image associated with leadership and (2) to identify the nonverbal cues that are associated with leadership. How you use them, manipulate them, or simply defer to them, may be important strategies in advancing your career.

Leadership

Surprisingly, not much research has been conducted relative to what nonverbal behaviors are associated with leadership. What we do know, as discussed in earlier chapters, indicates that where you sit, how much eye contact you can control, and perhaps your physical size may contribute to perceptions of leadership. These behaviors, with the exception of eye contact, may be less controllable in a group situation and, therefore, of less value to you than those that deal with your *presentational* behaviors. A number of researchers have stated that several nonverbal behaviors are important in establishing leadership. Albert Mehrabian and Martin Williams infer that facial expression, gesturing, and head nodding are associated with influence.[75] Other researchers affirm that such behaviors are necessary for leadership, but they find that smiling is also an important feature for the leader; smiles and gestures suggest that group members have conferred the approval necessary to emerge as a leader.[76]

Two studies that specifically examined the nonverbal behaviors under the control of the individual reported that gestures are probably most important in determining leadership emergence. J. Regis O'Connor found that mouth movements (the amount of time a person moved his or her mouth), and arm and hand movement were significant predictors of leadership.[77] John E. Baird observed that as many as eight kinesic variables predicted leadership emergence, including gestures with arms and shoulders, head disagreement, eye contact, head agreement, gesticulation of hands and fingers, postural shifts, facial disagreement, and facial agreement. When considered in the absence of other cues, each would be a significant predictor of leadership. However, when considered together, as would be the case in most interactions, only *arm and shoulder gesticulation* significantly differentiated the emerging leader from others.[78] This implies that people perceive someone who is fairly animated, who gestures with the arms and shoulders, as having leadership potential. Gesturing, it would seem, is more important than control of eye contact, although this relationship has not been studied. Gestures may also be closely associated with a leader's credibility.[79]

Credibility

Earlier in this chapter we explained how the environment and other cues can be manipulated to project an image of power and status. We also feel that perceptions of credibility can be manipulated. Dale G. Leathers has identified four factors that may affect a leader's credibility; all deal with either kinesic or vocal cues.[80] Leathers postulates that eye behaviors, gestures, posture, and vocal qualities are useful in establishing a leader's credibility. He also asserts that there are both positive and negative behaviors associated with each set of cues. Many of these cues have been described earlier, but their association with perceptions of credibility indicates that they should be reviewed here.

In terms of eye behavior, Leathers believes that we have a tendency to form a strong cultural stereotype specifying what is positive and negative in how we look at others. He states that positive eye cues include sustaining and maintaining eye contact while talking and listening to others. Negative eye cues include looking down while responding, being ''shifty-eyed,'' blinking excessively or fluttering the eyes, and avoiding eye contact or casting the eyes down and away from the person with whom you are speaking.

Leathers asserts that there are five positive types of gestures that enhance credibility perceptions. First, gestures should be used that add emphasis to points you are making. Second, these gestures should be spontaneous, relaxed, and unrehearsed, rather conversational. Third, gestures should be used to signal that you wish to speak or that you want someone else to speak. Fourth, gestures with the hands and arms should be kept away from the body, thus increasing their persuasive impact. And fifth, gestures should indicate the feelings or emotion.

There are a number of negative gestures; these include defensive, nervous, and lack-of-confidence gestures such as tugging at clothing, lip licking, hand wringing, finger tapping, out-of-context smiling and grimacing, and tentative gestures.

In terms of posture, Leathers suggests that credibility is enhanced when we spread our arms "expansively" in front of ourselves. Rapport will be established by leaning forward in response to a question, whereas responsiveness is indicated by frequent and forceful postural shifts while speaking. Negative postural indicators may include timid and constricted postures, body rigidity, crossed arms and legs, and bodily tension. Because posture and gesture are associated, it is not surprising that positive gestural and postural cues tend to reinforce each other.

Finally, there are a number of vocal cues that affect our perception of a person's credibility. Leathers states that the vocal qualities assigned to credible individuals include conversational style; variation in pitch, rate, and volume (orchestration of the voice); and avoidance of a monotone delivery. Negative vocal qualities include nasalizing, flatness, and/or tenseness of the voice. Leathers reports that *excessive* rate (rapidity of speech) and frequent pauses may undermine perceptions of credibility, implying a lack of confidence and/or competence. He also maintains that although not all nonfluencies are bad, *ahs,* the repetition of words, and stuttering have a negative impact on perceptions of credibility.

The credible leader, then, is one who communicates forcefully, both in terms of kinesic and vocalic cues. These cues can be used to increase your nonverbal repertoire of positive behaviors. They can also be used to discern possible flaws in others' credibility. You must remember, however, that some leaders, leaders by virtue of their position in the organization, do not worry about gesture, posture or voice; they are credible simply because of their position.

A final note on this section involves the increased importance of *sexual harassment* cases in the workplace. Because the number of females in every type of workplace has increased in the past 20 years, more and more focus has been placed on male-female interactions there. Mark Hickson, R. D. Grierson, and Barbara C. Linder have noted, however, that sexual harassment can also be a same-sex offense.[81] In essence, sexual harassment is a case (primarily) where a person in a superior position tries to use his/her influence over a subordinate employee for sexual favors. Such cases do not necessarily involve having sex per se, but they may involve inappropriate touch behavior, gazing, and the like. New employees, in particular, should be on guard for such violators of personal freedom. The researchers have suggested that employees find out the employer's policy. If violations occur, they should be reported. If violations continue, victims should contact appropriate authorities.

□   **Summary**   □

This chapter examined nonverbal communication on the job. It considered both physical and personal cues that a person could use in assessing power, status, credibility, leadership, and other variables on the job. The job interview was examined in terms of nonverbal behaviors that may have an impact on the chances of being hired, or at least of "surviving" the first interview. Finally, we examined what cues may be exhibited in order to create a perception of credibility and, perhaps, of potential as an emergent leader. Because each job may be slightly different, may have different expectations, the suggestions made should be examined carefully and only within the specific work context you are considering. Like most of our nonverbal communication, much of what we perceive may be idiosyncratic. However, there appear to be some rather strong stereotypes within the context of the job; such expectations and norms can be manipulated to your advantage. Knowledge of what is expected and how expectations are reinforced may provide the advantage needed for success on the job.

Chapter Thirteen

The Future of Nonverbal Communication

Key Concepts

What We Know

Future Research

General Overview

From its early beginnings almost 2,500 years ago as merely one of the five canons of rhetoric (*pronuntiatio*), the study of nonverbal communication has come a long way. Unquestionably, the theoretical views of Charles Darwin in the middle of the nineteenth century and the support of such theories through the recent work of Edward O. Wilson in sociobiology have supported the study of nonverbal communication. In addition to the adherence to nurture theory, new fields of study have developed—including anthropology in which both biological and social data enter the study of human beings—and have yielded more and more knowledge about nonverbal communication. Since about 1960, the field we label as speech (or speech communication, or communication) has transformed the study of nonverbal communication from one concerned only with the *prescriptive* gesturing and vocal tone associated with public speaking to an attempt to understand the varieties and eccentricities of nonverbal communication in *all* types of social situations.

Nonverbal communication research has become more enlightening through the use of photographs, films, and videotapes. Voice prints, polygraph machines, and the LOGOPORT have further assisted the development of nonverbal communication research. The "scientific method" of the social scientist has improved with the use of computers for statistics, the addition of new statistical methods (which have in some instances made researchers revise their earlier findings), and the evolution from simplistic data gathering to more sophisticated techniques. Research methods of the qualitative researchers have also changed with the times. Techniques involve more long-term studies, using triangulation techniques to allow for individual bias while protecting the reliability and validity of studies by using multiple researchers and multiple techniques.

The application of nonverbal communication research has seen a major resurgence. Industry has begun to use information based on such nonverbal subcodes as chronemics, physical appearance, and environment and territory in making decisions that affect many. For example, the U.S. Army has used biorhythm information to decide who flies a helicopter when. Commercial transportation companies use similar techniques. Companies with various shifts study chronemics in an attempt to decide who should work when by determining each employee's highest productivity time. The use of clothing studies has changed the business field. Although the research thus far has presented a prescriptive approach, it is likely that future studies will add even more. Proxemic studies are used as a basis for determining sexual harassment charges as well as other aspects in the legal field. The overall study of facial expression, dress, and gestures can be useful to lawyers and students of law in selecting jurors who are likely to be open to one side of the case or the other. The study of gestures in everyday life is useful to those studying drama in order to imitate the gestures of people in real-life situations as well as the various dialects used in daily speech.

Thus, the study of nonverbal communication has changed significantly over the years regarding the theoretical bases of study, the methods used for study, and the applications of research it has produced. Now, from all we have studied, what do we know about nonverbal communication? What do we need to know? Where will nonverbal communication research be in the next 15 years?

What We Know About Nonverbal Communication

At the beginning of this book we examined what we believe to be the major considerations for the study of nonverbal communication. We noted that nonverbal communication, although recognized as important, has not really received the attention that has been directed to verbal communication. It was pointed out that there are a number of diverse opinions as to what constitutes nonverbal communication, and no particular approach is actually more correct than any other. We stated that nonverbal communication operates or functions with the verbal message intentionally or unintentionally to reinforce, contradict, complement, accentuate, regulate, or replace the verbal message. In this connection, we indicated that approximately two-thirds of our total communication is nonverbal in nature. Chapter 3 examined how nonverbal research is carried out and described several ways to conduct research.

In section 2 we examined eight major subcodes, some consisting of one or more "minor" subcodes. We began with the space in which we communicate, indicating that the environment and the territory in which we communicate may be considered our first lines of communication. We then examined the environment to determine its effect on communication, noting that any environment has both perceptual and situational features. How our environment is structured also indicates something about its creator and how others are expected to act and communicate in that setting.

The territories we establish were then examined. Based on this discussion, we inferred that territory consists of areas of space that are marked—possess boundaries—and that certain communications are appropriate based on the access we have to that territory. Personal space, we noted, has no markers and is flexible. Our personal space is treated like a zone around us—larger in some areas and smaller in others. A number of features influence how much personal space we expect from others; these include age, sex, race, intimacy, and formality of interaction. The ultimate violation of personal space is touch, or zero-proxemics. We pointed out that one of the most powerful communication tools we have is touch, but this is also one of the tools we use least. We also examined the impact of violating proxemic and haptic norms and expectations, stating that people may be manipulated and may manipulate others by means of the systematic creation and violation of spatial/touch norms.

Next we examined how the body and its coverings communicate. Physical appearance was defined as body shape, clothing, cosmetics, and accessories. We indicated that because of its power, physical appearance plays a major role in how others perceive us. The effect of this perception is attributable to the fairly strong stereotypes we associate with body shape, hair, skin color and texture, and the clothing people wear. We noted that one's appearance is a major factor in the development of self-image. Finally, we stated that (1) by means of our appearance, we can manipulate others, and in turn, we are manipulated by them; and that (2) we are placed in certain social categories on the basis of our ''uniforms.''

A major nonverbal area deals with communication by the body. In examining the kinesic subcode we looked at several approaches to the study of bodily motion, discussing specific areas of the body and including gesture and facial expression. We then examined the impact of the voice on communication and stereotyping, observing what the voice communicates (in terms of accent, intonation, etc.), what perceptions we have of people based on their vocalizations, and what potential there is for identification through the voice.

We rounded out our study of the various subcodes by describing those based on some type of perceptual ''set.'' These subcodes include the chronemic and olfactory modes of communication associated with internal states. We also noted a third perceptual form of expression: internal nonverbal communication. Chronemics, or our perception of time, was classified in terms of three levels: the impact of time that we acquire through culture and subculture; our psychological orientations toward time; and our biological time orientations, as evidenced by the biorhythm. We then considered how smell affects communication, noting that people differ in their ability to smell, that smell communicates a variety of meanings, and that it is used as a manipulative tool. Finally, we examined internal systems. It was suggested that the telepathic form of communication may be associated with a particular side of the brain. We then reviewed other biofeedback systems to complete our analysis of the areas of emotion, mood state, and deceptive communication.

Section 3 applied what we had covered. In this section we correlated the study of nonverbal communication in three critical contexts: the social situation (initial interaction), the family (both physical and psychological aspects) and home situation, and the job situation. It was pointed out that nonverbal communication plays a large role in our initial interactions with others, including courtship and courtship readiness cues. We then examined how the concepts of the physical and the psychological ''home'' influence our nonverbal communications. In this connection we described how people use nonverbal communication from birth through old age. Finally, we examined nonverbal communication on the job. We described how you can develop or induce perceptions of power, status, and credibility. We also studied the job interview, offered recommendations for improving nonverbal communication during the interview, and discussed potential trouble spots.

Where is the Study of Nonverbal Communication Going?

In the area of theory, Ekman and his colleagues continue to seek support for their nature theory of nonverbal communication. Such research is certainly beneficial in establishing *cultural similarities*. At the same time, the nurture theorists have been assisting us in establishing micro-units of nonverbal behavior, which may be culturally variant or culturally invariant. The functionalists are much more concerned with how nonverbal communication is used than they are with where similarities and differences developed. In this light, the functionalists use the conclusions drawn from both the nature theorists and the nurture theorists to explain behaviors of interest.

Regarding method, technology has been a major factor in the resurgence of nonverbal communication research and study. Film and broadcasting have brought about significant changes. Additionally, devices such as the LOGOPORT and other computer-assisted analysis devices developed in the medical field should assist us in determining similarities and differences in our nonverbal ''internal states'' and external behaviors. Significantly, the relationships between the way communication is processed, both verbally and nonverbally, and the resultant behaviors may provide insight not only into the hows of communication but also into the whys. The study of nonverbal internal states may yield answers as basic as the systems under study.

The area of application is expanding significantly. In the job field, for example, applications are being used in various professions to make services more efficient and productive. As mentioned, transportation companies are looking at chronemics, businesses are looking at environmental engineering, and service companies are looking at making the individual more sensitive to nonverbal cues in general and to specific cues in particular (in sales, leadership, etc.). The medical and health-care professions are looking at proxemics and haptics. The field of psychology is becoming more concerned with kinesic behavior and the relative way in which nonverbal cues are processed by patients.

Yet, there is still more to know. Specifically, we believe that the following represent some significant questions still unanswered.

1.   What is the comparison of internal states and external behavior regarding deception?
2.   Can one's changing external behavior change his or her internal states?
3.   Is nonverbal communication as important to the transmitter (via internal states) as it is to the receiver (as perceived through external behavior)?
4.   Are general solutions to problems of depression, anxiety, conflict, and deception available through the enhanced study of nonverbal communication?
5.   How can we better teach individuals to improve their nonverbal communication for an improved lifestyle?
6.   What impact does nonverbal communication have on our lives as we progress from birth to death?

These are relatively abstract questions, but ultimately the study of small, seemingly insignificant variables may help us understand the larger, more significant questions about who we are and about how we can assist others in understanding who we are.

General Review

To conclude this study of nonverbal communication, we present 16 general statements summarizing the present content and scope of the subject. This list also provides a convenient reference and review.

1.   Nonverbal communication is ''more'' important than verbal communication in face-to-face situations.

2.   Nonverbal communication can be approached in a variety of ways, each offering a slightly different interpretation of the behavior(s) observed.

3.   Nonverbal communication, unlike verbal communication, may only need to be perceived as intentional to be considered communication.

4.   Verbal and nonverbal communication may differ according to which hemisphere is dominant, or which side of the brain receives and interprets the communication.

5.   Kinesics, proxemics, haptics, vocalics, chronemics, olfaction, and physical appearance interact with verbal communication to transmit a message.

6.   Positive messages are commonly associated with forward leans, increased eye contact, relaxed posture, increased touching, and decreased distance; negative messages are transmitted by means of the opposite cues.

7.   Nonverbal communication varies with microcultures, subcultures, cultures, personality, age, sex, and race.

8.   Females are more sensitive to nonverbal cues—except for deception—and transmit more accurate cues to others.

9.   When contradictory messages are sent through verbal and nonverbal channels, most adults consider the nonverbal message more accurate.

10. Social situations provide a setting for determining the quality of relationships through nonverbal cues.

11. Nonverbal cues provide families with a means for achieving better understanding among their members.

12. Nonverbal communication is used differently and is perceived differently at various stages of a relationship.

13. We use nonverbal communication differently at various stages in our lives.

14. In job situations, we should be very careful about nonverbal cues, for they demonstrate power, credibility, assertiveness, and awareness of others.

15. Although we usually assume that nonverbal cues are sincere and spontaneous, they are often manipulated with some particular outcome in mind.

16. We are really just beginning to become aware of our nonverbal potential.

It is hoped that by now you are a better nonverbal communicator. You should be able to understand your nonverbal communication better and should also be more qualified to interpret the research being reported. This book should serve both as a good reference guide in specific contexts and later situations and as a starting point for a lifelong study of communication, whether the emphasis on communication is verbal *or* nonverbal.

REFERENCES

□   □   □

Chapter One

1. A. Mehrabian, *Silent Messages: Implicit Communication of Emotions and Attitudes,* 2d ed. (Belmont, CA: Wadsworth, 1981), 77.
2. R. L. Birdwhistell, *Kinesics and Context: Essays on Body Motion Communication* (Philadelphia: University of Pennsylvania Press, 1970), 158.
3. P. Ekman and W. V. Friesen, "Nonverbal Behavior in Psychotherapy Research," *Psychotherapy* 3 (1968), 181.
4. J. K. Burgoon and T. J. Saine, *The Unspoken Dialogue: An Introduction to Nonverbal Communication* (Boston: Houghton Mifflin, 1978).
5. Some writers have included extrasensory perceptions in their analyses of nonverbal communication. See D. G. Leathers, *Nonverbal Communication Systems* (Boston: Allyn and Bacon, 1976), 169–195. Leathers, however, *deleted* such a chapter from his revision, *Successful Nonverbal Communication: Principles and Applications* (New York: Macmillan, 1986).
6. Leathers, *Nonverbal Communication Systems,* 169–195.
7. E. Sapir, "The Unconscious Patterning of Behavior in Society," in *Selected Writings of Edward Sapir in Language, Culture, and Personality,* ed. E. Mandelbaum (Berkeley, CA: University of California Press, 1949), 556.
8. A. T. Dittman, *Interpersonal Messages of Emotion* (New York: Springer, 1972).
9. See M. F. Roloff and C. R. Berger, "Social Cognition and Communication," in *Social Cognition and Communication,* ed. M. F. Roloff and C. R. Berger (Beverly Hills, CA: Sage Publishers, 1982), 24–26.
10. M. Burgoon and M. Ruffner, *Human Communication* (New York: Holt, Rinehart & Winston, 1978), 15–18.
11. L. A. Malandro, L. L. Barker, and D. Barker, *Nonverbal Communication* 2d ed. (Reading, MA: Addison-Wesley, 1989), 10–12.
12. Burgoon and Saine, *The Unspoken Dialogue.*
13. Mehrabian, *Silent Messages,* 3.
14. D. Druckman, R. M. Rozelle, and J. C. Baxter, *Nonverbal Communication: Survey, Theory, and Research* (Beverly Hills, CA: Sage, 1982).
15. Burgoon and Saine, *The Unspoken Dialogue.*
16. Burgoon and Saine, *The Unspoken Dialogue.*
17. A. T. Dittman, *Interpersonal Messages of Emotion.*
18. Ekman and Friesen, "Nonverbal Behavior."
19. Mehrabian, *Silent Messages.*
20. P. A. Andersen, J. D. Garrison, and J. F. Andersen, Implications of a Neurological Approach for the Study of Nonverbal Communication," *Human Communication Research* 16 (1979), 74–89.
21. M. L. Knapp, *Nonverbal Communication in Human Interaction,* 2d ed., (New York: Holt, Rinehart & Winston, 1978).

22. D. G. Leathers, *Successful Nonverbal Communication.*

23. Burgoon and Saine, *The Unspoken Dialogue.*

24. Malandro, Barker, and Barker, *Nonverbal Communication.*

25. Knapp, *Nonverbal Communication in Human Interaction.*

26. H. J. Jerison, ''Evolution of the Brain,'' in *The Human Brain,* ed. M. C. Wittrock (Englewood Cliffs, NJ: Prentice-Hall, 1977), 39–62.

27. J. Steele, *Prosodia Rationalis* (London: 1779), 51, as reprinted in M. M. Robb, *Oral Interpretation Literature in American Colleges and Universities* (New York: H. W. Wilson Company, 1941), 62. For more information, see P. Fussell, Jr., ''Theory of Prosody in Eighteenth Century England,'' *Connecticut College Monograph No. 5* (New London: Connecticut College, 1954); and P. K. Alkon, ''Joshua Steele and the Melody of Speech,'' *Language and Speech* 2 (1959), 154–174. For a contemporary approach to genetic factors, see P. B. Neubauer and A. Neubauer, *Nature's Thumbprint: The Genetics of Personality* (Reading, MA: Addison-Wesley, 1990).

28. G. Austin, *Chironomia or a Treatise on Rhetorical Delivery,* ed. M. M. Robb and L. Thonssen (Carbondale, IL: Southern Illinois University Press, 1966).

29. J. W. Zorn, ed., *The Essential Delsarte* (Mutuchen, NJ: Scarecrow Press, 1968).

Chapter Two

1. D. Stacks, M. Hickson III, and S. R. Hill, Jr., *Introduction to Communication Theory* (Fort Worth, TX: Harcourt, Brace, and Jovanovich, 1991). p. 5.

2. See, for example, P. Ekman, ''Communication Through Nonverbal Behavior: A Source of Information About an Interpersonal Relationship, in *Affect, Cognition, and Personality,* ed. S. S. Tompkins and C. E. Izard (New York: Springer, 1965); and J. Ruesch and W. Kees, *Nonverbal Communication: Notes on the Visual Perception of Human Relations* (Berkeley, CA: University of California Press, 1956). Both of these

sources provide traditional approaches to the functions of nonverbal communication. Below, we have summarized those findings:

Repetition

One of the major functions of nonverbal communication is to reinforce through redundancy. Through gestures we can reinforce that which we have said. When asked the number of scoops on an ice cream cone, for instance, we might respond, ''three,'' and hold up three fingers as well. Actions that serve a repetitive function help us better understand our messages. In a basketball game, for example, when the referee calls a foul on a player, he moves toward the officials' table, calls out the number of the guilty player, then reinforces that call by holding up the appropriate number of fingers.

Contradiction

Contradiction, on the other hand, tends to negate the verbal message. The best example of contradiction is the vocal message associated with sarcasm. Although the verbal message may be positive, the underlying tone of voice tells a different story. Other contradictory messages may arise out of fear that a particular emotion being felt at the moment is inappropriate. Although you may ''mask'' your face, biting your nails or wringing your hands may negate or contradict the calm facial expression you wear.

Substitution

This function is unique in that it assumes we can create a symbolic meaning out of some nonverbal communication. By substituting, we remove the verbal communication and replace it with the ''appropriate'' nonverbal action. In some cases, such an action becomes symbolic; it becomes an emblem (waving, signaling time out) and can stand by itself. In other cases, we may introduce the action verbally, then substitute that action for the verbal at a later time. In many instances, the nonverbal substitution conveys a stronger message than the verbal. When you really want to show sympathy, simply holding another person often conveys that message far better than the mumbling of some words.

Accentuation

Nonverbal messages that accentuate a verbal message lend emphasis to what is being said. In many cases, we expect such an emphasis to be on the loud, exaggerated side. In most cases, however, such action may backfire. All of us have an image of the drill instructor. This stereotyped person usually violates every nonverbal behavior thinkable (except correctness of uniform, of course), closes to within fractions of inches of people, yells, and generally exhibits "bully" behavior. Most veterans will tell you, however, that this kind of accentuation does not work. The type to watch for is the quiet one, the DI who has it all under control. Many times in lectures, instructors can much better emphasize what they are saying by lowering the voice rather than by yelling.

Complementarity

Complementary nonverbal messages supplement or modify the verbal message. When telling someone you love him or her, holding that person, speaking in a hushed voice, and maintaining eye contact all supplement the verbal message. While being interviewed for a job, both your facial and bodily gestures tend to complement your true internal feelings. As you relax and become accustomed to the other person, so do your expressions; your gestures become more "normal," and your nonverbal communication complements the image of an assured and relaxed person.

Regulation

Finally, nonverbal cues regulate the verbal interaction. Through eye contact, body positioning, vocal pitch, and touch, we can help control the flow of the verbal communication. Simply by looking at someone in a class, instructors can indicate which student they want to answer a question. Typically, the individual who can regulate the interaction is in control, can prevent others from gaining access to the communication, or can allow others to have the "floor." In this culture, for example, there is an alternating timing factor involved with regulation: I speak, you speak, I speak, you speak, and so on. This regulative function, however, may differ in other cultures.

3. D. Tannen, *You Just Don't Understand: Women and Men in Conversation* (New York: Morrow, 1990).
4. R. L. Birdwhistell, "Masculinity and Femininity as Display," In *Foundations of Nonverbal Communication: Readings, Exercises, and Commentary,* ed. A. M. Katz and V. T. Katz (Carbondale: Southern Illnois University Press, 1983), 81–86. See also S. Weitz, "Sex Differences in Nonverbal Communication," *Sex Roles* 2 (1976); D. A. Jenni and M. A. Jenni, "Carrying Behavior in Humans: Analysis of Sex Differences," *Science* 194 (1976), 859–860; and M. Jenni, "Sex Differences in Carrying Behavior," *Perceptual and Motor Skills* 43 (1976), 323–330.
5. The traditional conclusions may be found in B. W. Eakins and R. G. Eakins, *Sex Differences in Human Communication* (Boston: Houghton Mifflin, 1978). The research of Nancy Henley and others has been refuted in a recent critique: J. A. Hall, *Nonverbal Sex Differences: Communication Accuracy and Expressive Style* (Baltimore: The Johns Hopkins Press, 1984). Henley's contentions (that males initiate more "control" touches) is expressly refuted in S. E. Jones and A. E. Yarbrough, "A Naturalistic Study of the Meanings of Touch," *Communication Monographs* 52 (1985), 19–56, at least for general interaction among males and females.
6. Eakins and Eakins, *Sex Differences in Human Communication.* The notion that males *believe* they disclose a great deal is noted in R. J. Cline, "The Effects of Biological Sex and Psychological Gender on Reported and Behavioral Intimacy and Control of Self-Disclosure," *Communication Quarterly* 34 (1986), 41–54. See also R. J. Cline and K. E. Musolf, "Disclosure of Social Exchange: Anticipated Length of Relationships, Sex Roles, and Disclosure Intimacy," *Western Journal of Speech Communication* 49 (1985), 43–56.
7. The conclusions are derived from the studies previously discussed in this text. Two excellent books for describing these differences are: Eakins and Eakins, *Sex Differences in Human Communication;* and N. M. Henley, *Body Politics: Power, Sex,*

and *Nonverbal Communication* (Englewood Cliffs, NJ: Prentice-Hall, 1977). See also J. A. Hall, "Gender, Gender Roles, and Nonverbal Communication Skills," paper presented at the American Psychological Association Convention, Toronto, Canada, 1978; M. La France and C. Mayo, "A Review of Nonverbal Behaviors of Women and Men," *Western Journal of Speech Communication* 43 (1979), 96–107; and C. Kramer, "Women's and Men's Ratings of Their Own and Ideal Speech," *Communication Quarterly* 26 (1978), 2–11. For further discussion of primary and secondary sex differences, see C. Hutt, *Males and Females* (Baltimore: Penguin, 1972); and D. Gelman, J. Carey, E. Gelman, P. Malamud, D. Foote, D. C. Lubenow, and J. Contreras, "Just How the Sexes Differ," *Newsweek* (May 18, 1981), 72–83.

8. L. Powell, S. R. Hill, Jr., and M. Hickson III, "Path Analysis of Attitudinal, Dispositional, and Situational Predictions in Impression Formation," *Psychological Reports* 47 (1980), 327–333.

9. E. Goffman, "Genderisms," *Psychology Today* 21 (1977), 60–63; and E. Goffman, "Gender Advertisements," *Studies in the Anthropology of Visual Communication* 3 (1976), 69–154.

10. E. Goffman, "Gender Advertisements," 127.

11. D. Archer, D. D. Kimes, and M. Barrios, "Face-ism," *Psychology Today* 20 (1976), 65–66.

12. P. A. Andersen, J. D. Garrison, and J. F. Andersen, "Implications of a Neurological Approach for the Study of Nonverbal Communication," *Human Communication Research* 6 (1979), 74–89; D. W. Stacks, "Hemispheric and Evolutionary Use: A Re-Examination of Verbal and Nonverbal Communication and the Brain," paper presented at the annual meeting of the Eastern Communication Association, Hartford, CT, May 1982. See also D. W. Stacks and P. A. Andersen, "Toward a Holistic Neurophysiological Understanding of Intrapersonal Communication," paper presented at the annual meeting of the Speech Communication Association, Boston, MA, November 1987; D. W. Stacks and D. E. Sellers, "Understanding

Intrapersonal Communication: Neurological Processing Implications," in *Intrapersonal Communication Processes: Original Essays,* ed. C. Roberts and K. Watson (Auburn, AL: Spectra Publishers, 1989), pp. 243–267; D. W. Stacks, "Toward a Psychoanalytic-Neurophysiological Interpretation of Nonverbal Communication," *Journal of Communication Therapy* (in press); and D. W. Stacks and P. A. Andersen, "The Modular Mind: Implications for Interpersonal Communication," *Southern Communication Journal 54* (1989), 273–293.

13. R. Buck, "Spontaneous and Symbolic Nonverbal Behavior and the Ontogeny of Communication," in *Development of Nonverbal Behavior in Children,* ed. R. S. Feldman (New York: Springer-Verlag, 1982), 29–62.

14. R. Buck, "Spontaneous and Symbolic Nonverbal Behavior," 29–62; R. Buck, *The Communication of Emotion* (New York: The Guilford Press, 1984); and J. C. Borod, E. Koff, and R. Buck, "The Neuropsychology of Facial Expression: Data From Normal and Brain-Damaged Adults," in *Nonverbal Communication in the Clinical Context,* ed. P. D. Blanck, R. Buck, and R. Rosenthal (University Park, PA: Pennsylvania State University Press, 1986), 196–222.

15. D. W. Stacks, "Toward Establishment of a Preverbal Stage of Communication," *Journal of Communication Therapy* 2 (1983), 39–60.

16. P. MacLean, "The Brain's Generation Gap: Some Human Implications," *Zygon/Journal of Religion and Science* 193 (1972), 137–149.

17. G. Wiseman and L. L. Barker, *Speech— Interpersonal Communication* (New York: Chandler, 1974).

18. P. Watzlawick, J. Beavin, and D. Jackson, *Pragmatics of Human Communication: A Study of Interactional Patterns, Pathologies, and Paradoxes* (New York: Norton, 1967); Burgoon and Saine, *The Unspoken Dialogue.*

Chapter Three

1. D. W. Stacks and J. E. Hocking, *Essentials of Communication Research* (New York: HarperCollins, 1992).

2. D. W. Stacks and M. Hickson III, "Research: A Programmed Approach," *Florida Speech Communication Journal* 2 (1974), 21–25.

3. J. K. Frye, *FIND: Frye's Index to Nonverbal Data* (Duluth, MN: University of Minnesota, 1980); and T. Hore and N. S. Paget, *Nonverbal Behaviour: A Select Annotated Bibliography* (Hawthorn, Victoria, Australia: Australian Council for Educational Research, 1975). See also R. J. Matlon and P. C. Facciola, ed. *Index to Journals in Communication Studies Through 1985* (Annandale, VA: Speech Communication Association, 1987); and D. W. Stacks, *Nonverbal Communication: Theory Assessment, and Instruction: A Selected Annotated Bibliography* (Washington, DC: ERIC Clearinghouse on Reading and Communication Skills, 1982, 1985).

4. T. Kuhn, *The Structure of Scientific Revolutions,* 2d ed. (Chicago: University of Chicago Press, 1970).

5. F. E. X. Dance, ed., *Human Communication Theory: Comparative Essays* (New York: Harper and Row, 1982); E. G. Bormann, *Communication Theory* (New York: Holt, Rinehart and Winston, 1980); B. A. Fisher, *Perspectives on Human Communication* (New York: Macmillan, 1978); and S. W. Littlejohn, *Theories of Human Communication,* 4th ed. (Belmont CA: Wadsworth, 1992).

6. Littlejohn, *Theories of Human Communication,* 77–82.

7. J. K. Burgoon and T. J. Saine, *The Unspoken Dialogue: An Introduction to Nonverbal Communication* (Boston: Houghton Mifflin, 1978), 26–51.

8. W. B. Pearce, V. E. Cronen, and L. M. Harris, "Methodological Considerations in Building Human Communication Theory," in *Human Communication Theory: Comparative Essays,* ed. F. E. X. Dance (New York: Harper and Row, 1982), 1–41.

9. M. Hickson III, L. Powell, S. R. Hill, Jr., G. B. Holt, and H. Flick, "Smoking Artifacts as Indicators of Homophily, Attraction, and Credibility," *Southern Speech Communication Journal* 44 (1979), 191–200.

10. For example, see E. R. Babbie, *Survey Research Methods* (Belmont, CA: Wadsworth, 1973); and A. N. Oppenheim, *Questionnaire Design and Attitude Measurement* (New York: Basic, 1966).

11. E. Berscheid, E. Walster, and G. Bohrnstedt, "Body Image," *Psychology Today* 7 (1973), 119–131.

12. For example, see, L. A. Dexter, *Elite and Specialized Interviewing* (Evanston, IL: Northwestern University Press, 1970); A. Garrett, *Interviewing: Its Principles and Methods* (New York: Family Service Association of America, 1970); and R. W. Budd, R. K. Thorp, and L. Donohew, *Content Analysis of Communications* (New York: Macmillan, 1967).

13. Budd et al., *Content Analysis.*

14. L. Bickman, "Clothes Make the Person," *Psychology Today* 8 (1974), 49–51.

15. D. W. Stacks, "When Reward Fails: An Examination of High Reward and the Violations of Distancing Expectations Model," unpublished manuscript, University of South Alabama, 1983.

16. See Stacks, "When Reward Fails"; and D. W. Stacks and J. K. Burgoon, "The Role of Nonverbal Behaviors as Distractors in Resistance to Persuasion in Interpersonal Contexts," *Central States Speech Journal* 32 (1981), 61–73. See also J. K. Burgoon, D. W. Stacks, and S. A. Burch, "The Role of Interpersonal Rewards and Violations of Distancing Expectations in Achieving Influence," *Communication* 11 (1982), 114–128. This study, although experimental in nature, attempted to create small groups that actually worked as groups; they also found a major difference for subjects who were enrolled in a midwestern versus a southern university.

17. C. M. Rossiter, "Qualitative Methodology in Communication Theory Development" paper presented at the Speech Communication Association Convention, Washington, D.C., 1977; P. Diesing, *Patterns of Discovery in the Social Sciences* (Chicago: Aldine, 1971), 291–303; M. Mead, "Native Languages as Field-Work Tools," *American Anthropologist* 41 (1939), 189–205; D. P. Forcese and S. Richer, *Social Research Methods* (Englewood Cliffs, NJ: Prentice-Hall, 1973), 144–158; and J. Bernstein, "Conversations in Public Places," *Journal of Communication* 26 (1975), 85–95.

18. M. Hickson III, "Communication in Natural Settings: Research Tool for Undergraduates," *Communication Quarterly* 25 (1977), 23–28.

19. A. Mazur, "Interpersonal Spacing on Public Benches in 'Contact' vs. 'Noncontact' Cultures" *Journal of Social Psychology* 101 (1977), 53–58.

20. For example, see M. R. DiMatteo, "Nonverbal Skill and the Physician-Patient Relationship," paper presented at the American Psychological Association Convention, Toronto, 1978; T. Edgar and W. Samter, "Feminist Therapy and Nonverbal Behavior," paper presented at the Eastern Communication Association Convention, Ocean City, MD, 1983; E. Gergerian, "Facial Expression in Mania and Schizophrenia," paper presented at the Eastern Communication Association Convention, Philadelphia, 1979; and D. G. Leathers, "An Examination of Police Interviewers' Beliefs about the Utility and Nature of Nonverbal Indicators of Deception," paper presented at the Speech Communication Association Convention, Louisville, KY, 1982.

21. N. K. Denzin, *The Research Act: A Theoretical Introduction to Sociological Methods* 3d ed. (Englewood Cliffs, NJ: Prentice-Hall, 1989).

22. S. M. Jourard, "An Exploratory Study of Body-Accessibility," *British Journal of Social and Clinical Psychology* 5 (1966), 221–231; and S. M. Jourard and J. E. Rubin, "Self-Disclosure and Touching: A Study of Two Modes of Interpersonal Encounter and Their Inter-Relation," *Journal of Humanistic Psychology* 8 (1968), 39–48.

23. L. B. Rosenfeld, S. Kartus, and C. Ray, "Body Accessibility Revisited," *Journal of Communication* 26 (1976), 27–30.

24. S. E. Jones and A. E. Yarbrough, "A Naturalistic Study of the Meaning of Touch," *Communication Monographs* 52 (1985), 19–56; and S. E. Jones, "Problems of Validity in Questionnaire Studies of Nonverbal Behavior: Jourard's Tactile Body-Accessibility Scale," *Southern Communication Journal* 56 (1991), 83–95. See also: D. K. Fromme, W. E. Jaynes, D. K. Taylor, E. G. Hanold, J. R. Daniell, J. Richard, and M. L. Fromme, "Nonverbal Behavior and Attitudes Toward Touch, *Journal of Nonverbal Behavior* 13 (1989), 3–14.

Chapter Four

1. S. Weitz, ed., *Nonverbal Communication: Readings with Commentary* (New York: Oxford University Press, 1974), 203; and S. Thayer, "Touch: Frontier of Intimacy." *Journal of Nonverbal Behavior* 10 (1986), 7–11.

2. R. Adler and N. Towne, *Looking Out/ Looking In* (San Francisco: Rinehart Press, 1975), 225–226.

3. A. Montagu, *Touching: The Human Significance of the Skin* (New York: Perennial Library, 1971), 82.

4. J. L. Despert, "Emotional Aspects of Speech and Language Development," *International Journal of Psychiatry and Neurology* 105 (1941), 193–222; and J. Bowlby, *Maternal Care and Mental Health* (Geneva: World Health Organization, 1961).

5. M. H. Hollender, "Prostitution, the Body, and Human Relatedness," *International Journal of Psychoanalysis* 42 (1961), 403–413; and M. H. Hollender, "The Need or Wish to be Held," *Archives of General Psychiatry* 22 (1970), 445–453.

6. C. P. Malmquist, T. J. Kiresuk, and R. M. Spano, "Personality Characteristics of Women with Repeated Illegitimacies: Descriptive Aspects," *Journal of Orthopsychiatry* 36 (1966), 467–484; and N. M. Henley, *Body Politics: Power, Sex, and Nonverbal Communication* (Englewood Cliffs, NJ: Prentice-Hall, 1977).

7. M. Sanfilipo and N. Stein, "Depression and the Wish to be Held," *Journal of Abnormal Psychology* 41 (1985), 3–9. For more information on self touch, see F. Barroso, "Self-Touching and Attentional Processes: The Role of Task Difficulty, Selection Stage, and Sex Differences," *Journal of Nonverbal Behavior* 10 (1986), 51–64; and S. Goldberg and R. Rosenthal, "Self-Touching Behavior in the Job Interview: Antecedents and Consequences," *Journal of Nonverbal Behavior* 10 (1986), 65–90. Foot touching, for example, was found to be positive in the job interview situation.

8. H. F. Harlow and R. R. Zimmerman, "The Development of Affectional Responses in Infant Monkeys," *Proceedings, American Philosophical Society* 102 (1958), 501–509.

9. W. H. Thorpe, "The Lower Vertebrates and the Invertebrates," in *Nonverbal Communication,* ed. R. A. Hinde (Cambridge: Cambridge University Press, 1972), 128; and N. Tinbergen, *Social Behavior in Animals* (London: Methuen, 1953).

10. Thorpe, "The Lower Vertebrates," 128; and P. Pliner, L. Krames, and T. Alloway, eds. *Nonverbal Communication* (New York: Plenum, 1974).

11. F. S. Hammett, "Studies of the Thyroid Apparatus: I," *American Journal of Physiology* 56 (1921), 196–204; and F. S. Hammett, "Studies in the Thyroid Apparatus, V," *Endocrinology* 8 (1922), 221–229.

12. L. A. Malandro, L. L. Barker and D. Barker, *Nonverbal Communication* 2d ed. (Reading, MA: Addison-Wesley, 1989), 206.

13. M. E. Lamb, "Paternal Influences on Early Socio-Emotional Development," *Journal of Child Psychology* 23 (1982), 185–190; M. E. Lamb, "The Bonding Phenomenon: Misinterpretations and Their Implications," *Journal of Pediatrics* 101 (1982), 555–557; and M. E. Lamb, "Early Contact and Maternal-Infant Bonding: One Decade Later," *Pediatrics* 70 (1982), 763–768.

14. V. S. Clay, "The Effect of Culture on Mother-Child Tactile Communication," Ph.D. Diss., Columbia University, 1966.

15. L. K. Frank, "Tactile Communication," *Genetic Psychology Monographs* 56 (1957), 209–255.

16. D. Morris, *Intimate Behavior* (New York: Random House, 1971).

17. Morris, *Intimate Behavior,* 31.

18. J. K. Burgoon and T. J. Saine, *The Unspoken Dialogue: An Introduction to Nonverbal Communication* (Boston: Houghton Mifflin, 1978), 66–68.

19. See Despert, "Emotional Aspects of Speech," Bowlby, *Maternal Care and Mental Health;* and P. L. J. Rogels, E. Roelen, and J. M. Van Meel, "The Function of Self-Touchings, Posture Shifts, and Motor Discharges in Children from 3 to 6 Years of Age," *Perceptual and Motor Skills* 70 (1990), 1169-1178.

20. J. L. Prescott, "Body Pleasure and the Origins of Violence," *The Futurist* 9 (1975), 64–74.

21. S. M. Jourard, "An Empirical Study of Body Accessibility," *British Journal of Social and Clinical Psychology* 5, (1966), 221–231; and S. M. Jourard, *Disclosing Man to Himself* (Princeton, NJ: Van Nostrand, 1968).

22. L. T. K. Haung, R. Phares, and M. H. Hollender, "The Wish to be Held," *Archives of General Psychiatry* 33 (1976), 41–43.

23. M. Argyle, *Bodily Communication* (New York: International Universities Press, 1975).

24. R. Heslin, "Steps Toward a Taxonomy of Touching," paper presented at the Western Psychological Association Convention, Chicago, 1974.

25. Heslin, "Steps Toward a Taxonomy of Touching," 3–4; and S. Thayer, "Touch Encounters," *Psychology Today* 22 (1988), 31-36.

26. M. Goldman, O. Kiyohara, and D. A. Pfanners, "Interpersonal Touch, Social Labelling, and the Foot-in-the-Door Effect," *Journal of Social Psychology* 125 (1985), 143–147. Similar results were found in M. L. Patterson, J. L. Powell, and M. G. Lenihan, "Touch, Compliance and Interpersonal Effect," *Journal of Nonverbal Behavior* 10 (1986), 41–50.

27. A. Anastasi, *Differential Psychology* (New York: Macmillan, 1958); A. Mehrabian, "Some Determinants of Affiliation and Conformity," *Psychological Reports* 27 (1970), 19–29; and A. Mehrabian, "Verbal and Nonverbal Interaction of Strangers in a Waiting Situation," *Journal of Experimental Research in Psychology* 5 (1971), 127–138.

28. T. Nguyen, R. Heslin, and M. L. Nguyen, "The Meaning of Four Modes of Touch as a Function of Sex and Body Area," paper presented at the Central States Speech Association Convention, 1974; T. Nguyen, R. Heslin, and M. L. Nguyen, "The Meaning of Touch: Sex Differences," *Journal of Communication* 25 (1975), 93–103; M. L. Nguyen, R. Heslin, and T. Nguyen, "The Meaning of Touch: Sex and Marital Status Differences," *Representative Research in Social Psychology* 7 (1976), 13–18.

29. A. Mehrabian, *Silent Messages* (Belmont, CA: Wadsworth, 1971), 1.

30. E. Berscheid and E. H. Walster, *Interpersonal Attraction* (Reading, MA: Addison-Wesley, 1969); and T.L. Huston, ed., *Foundations of Interpersonal Attraction* (New York: Academic Press, 1974).

31. V. P. Richmond, J. S. Gorham, and J. C. McCroskey, ''The Relationship Between Selected Immediacy Behaviors and Cognitive Learning,'' in *Communication Yearbook 10,* ed. M. McLaughlin (Beverly Hills, CA: Sage, 1987); and Patterson, Powell, and Lenihan, ''Touch, Compliance, and Interpersonal Affect,'' 41–50.

32. K. Stolte and P. G. Friedman, ''Patients' Perceptions of Touch During Labor,'' *Journal of Applied Communications Research* 8 (1980), 10–21.

33. D. R. Maines, ''Tactile Relationships in the Subway Affected by Racial, Sexual, and Crowded Situations,'' *Environmental Psychology and Nonverbal Behavior* 2 (1977), 100–107.

34. S. E. Jones, ''Sex Differences in Tactile Communication,'' *Western Journal of Speech Communication* 50 (1986), 227–241; and C. M. Rinck, F. N. Willis, Jr., and L. M. Dean, ''Interpersonal Touch Among Residents of Homes for the Elderly,'' *Journal of Communication* 30 (1980), 44–47.

35. D. Storrs and C. L. Kleinke, ''Evaluation of High and Equal Status Male and Female Touchers,'' *Journal of Nonverbal Behavior* 14 (1990), 87–95.

36. P. A. Andersen and K. Keibowitz, ''The Development and Nature of the Construct Touch Avoidance,'' *Environmental Psychology and Nonverbal Behavior* 3 (1978), 89–106.

37. J. D. Fisher, M. Rytting, and R. Heslin, ''Hands Touching Hands: Affective and Evaluative Effects of an Interpersonal Touch,'' *Sociometry* 39 (1976), 416–421.

38. D. W. Stacks, C. Browning, S. Browning, L. Busby, A. Carrol, M. Devery, D. Flowers, K. Graham, P. Henderson, K. Kendrick, N. Kozoroski, D. Leverett, J. Milne, E. Turnipseed, M. K. Walker, L. Walters, K. Weaver, and L. Wiedeimer, ''Hands Touching Hands: An Examination of the Ritualistic Handshake on Attitude and Credibility,'' unpublished paper, The University of South Alabama.

39. B. E. Pressner, ''The Therapeutic Implications of Touch During Articulation Therapy,'' Master's Thesis, University of Florida, 1978.

40. D. Morris, ''Please Touch is Message of Morris,'' in *With Words Unspoken: The Nonverbal Experience,* ed. L. B. Rosenfeld and J. M. Civikly (New York: Holt, Rinehart & Winston, 1976), 129–131.

41. See also M. Pisano, S. M. Wall, and A. Foster, ''Perceptions of Nonreciprocal Touch in Romantic Relationships,'' *Journal of Nonverbal Behavior* 10 (1986), 29–40; and P. A. Andersen and K. K. Sull, ''Out of Touch, Out of Reach: Predispositions as Predictors of Interpersonal Distance,'' *Western Journal of Speech Communication* 49 (1985), 57–72.

42. M. Clynes, ''Human Emotion Communication by Touch: A Modified Replication of an Experiment,'' *Perceptual and Motor Skills* 66 (1988), 419–424; and S. J. Trussoni, A. O'Malley, and A. Barton, ''Human Emotion Communication by Touch: A Modified Replication of an Experiment by Manfred Clynes,'' *Perceptual and Motor Skills* 66 (1988), 419–424.

Chapter Five

1. E. T. Hall, *The Hidden Dimension* (Garden City, NY: Anchor Books, 1966), 1.

2. The study of lining up is interesting. For example, see B. Schwartz, *Queuing and Waiting: Studies in the Social Organization of Access and Delay* (Chicago: University of Chicago Press, 1975).

3. J. J. Edney, ''Human Territories,'' *Environment and Behavior* 8 (1976), 31–47.

4. E. T. Hall, ''Proxemics,'' *Current Anthropology* 9 (1968), 83–95, 106–108.

5. M. Argyle and J. Dean, ''Eye Contact, Distance, and Affiliation,'' *Sociometry* 28 (1965), 289–304.

6. M. Dosey and M. Meisels, ''Personal Space and Self-Protection,'' *Journal of Personality and Social Psychology* 11 (1969), 93–97.

7. M. J. Horowitz, D. F. Duff, and L. O. Strattan, ''Body Buffer Zones,'' *Archives of General Psychology* 11 (1964), 651–656.

8. L. A. Hayduk, "Personal Space: An Evaluative and Orienting Overview," *Psychological Bulletin* 85 (1978), 117–134.

9. M. Argyle and J. Dean "Eye Contact," 289–304; J. C. Baxter and B. F. Deanovich, "Anxiety Arousing Effects of Inappropriate Crowding," *Journal of Consulting and Clinical Psychology* 35 (1970), 174–178; N. Felipe and R. Sommer, "Invasions of Personal Space," *Social Problems* 14 (1966), 206–214; H. Garfinkel, "Studies in the Routine Grounds of Everyday Activities," *Social Problems* 11 (1964), 225–250; G. N. Goldberg, C. A. Kiesler, and B. E. Collins, "Visual Behavior and Face-to-Face Distance During Interaction," *Sociometry* 37 (1974), 43–53; M. J. Horowitz, D. F. Duff, and L. O. Stratton, "Body Buffer Zones"; K. A. Krail and G. Leventhal, "The Sex Variable in the Invasion of Personal Space," *Sociometry* 39 (1976), 170–173; G. McBride, M. G. King, and J. W. James, "Social Proximity Effects on Galvanic Skin Responses in Adult Humans," *Journal of Psychology* 61 (1965), 153–157; A. Mehrabian, "Relationship of Attitude to Seated Posture, Orientation, and Distance," *Journal of Personality and Social Psychology* 10 (1968), 26–30; R. D. Middlemist, E. S. Knowles, and C. F. Mather, "Personal Space Invasions in the Lavatory: Suggestive Evidence for Arousal," *Journal of Personality and Social Psychology* 33 (1976), 541–546; M. L. Patterson, S. Mullins, and J. Romano, "Compensatory Reactions to Spatial Invasion," *Sociometry* 34 (1971), 114–121; M. L. Patterson and L. B. Sechrest, "Interpersonal Distance and Impression Management," *Journal of Personality* 38 (1970), 161–166; R. Sommer, *Personal Space: The Behavioral Basis of Design* (Englewood Cliffs, NJ: Prentice-Hall, 1969).

10. S. Albert and J. M. Dabbs, "Physical Distance and Persuasion," *Journal of Personality and Social Psychology* 15 (1970), 265–270; J. K. Burgoon, "Further Explication and an Initial Test of the Theory of Violations of Personal Space Expectations," *Human Communication Research* 4 (1978), 129–142; J. K. Burgoon, D. W. Stacks, and W. G. Woodall, "A Communicative Model of Violations of Distancing Expectations: Further Tests and a Critique," *Western Journal of Speech Communication* 43 (1979), 153–167; P. H. Garner, "The Effects of Invasions of Personal Space on Interpersonal Communication," Masters thesis, Illinois State University, 1972; A. Mehrabian and M. Williams, "Nonverbal Concomitants of Perceived and Intended Persuasiveness," *Journal of Personality and Social Psychology* 13 (1969), 37–58; M. Riess, "Proxemic Determinants of Perceived Communicator Characteristics and Attitude Change," Ph.D. Diss., University of Florida, 1977; T. J. Rosegrant and J. C. McCroskey, "The Effects of Race and Sex on Proxemic Behavior in an Interview Setting," *Southern Speech Communication Journal* 40 (1975), 408–420; D. W. Stacks and J. K. Burgoon, "The Effects of Violating Spatial Distance Expectations in Small Groups," paper presented at the Southern Speech Communication Association Convention, Biloxi, MS, April 1979.

11. Felipe and Sommer, "Invasions of Personal Space"; Krail and Leventhal, "The Sex Variable"; S. M. S. Ahmed, "Invasion of Personal Space: A Study of Departure Times as Affected by Sex of the Intruder, Sex of the Subject, and Saliency Condition," *Perceptual and Motor Skills* 49 (1979), 85–86.

12. E. C. O'Neal, J. Schultz, and T. E. Christenson, "The Menstrual Cycle and Personal Space," *Journal of Nonverbal Behavior* 11 (1987), 26–32.

13. Burgoon, "Further Explication and an Initial Test"; J. K. Burgoon and S. B. Jones, "Toward a Theory of Personal Space Expectations and their Violations," *Human Communication Research* 2 (1976), 131–146.

14. G. H. Tennis and J. M. Dabbs, Jr., "Sex, Setting and Personal Space: First Grade Through College," *Sociometry* 38 (1975), 385–394.

15. L. M. Dean, J. M. La Rocco, and F. N. Willis, "Invasion of Personal Space as a Function of Age, Sex and Race," *Psychological Reports* 58 (1976), 959–964.

16. J. R. Aiello and T. C. Aiello, "The Development of Personal Space: Proxemic Behavior of Children 6 through 16," *Human Ecology* 2 (1974), 177–189.

17. See R. M. Lerner, "The Development of Personal Space Schemata Toward Body Build," *Journal of Psychology* 84 (1973), 229–235; and D. M. Pedersen, "Developmental Trends in Personal Space," *Journal of Psychology* 83 (1973), 3–9; J. Lomranz, A. Shapira, N. Choresa, and G. Yitzchak, "Children's Personal Space as a Function of Age and Sex," *Developmental Psychology* 11 (1975), 541–545.

18. S. E. Jones and J. R. Aiello, "Proxemic Behavior of Black and White First-, Third-, and Fifth-Grade Children," *Journal of Personality and Social Psychology* 25 (1973), 21–27.

19. Tennis and Dabbs, "Sex, Sitting and Personal Space."

20. F. N. Willis, "Initial Speaking Distances as a Function of the Speaker's Relationship," *Psychonomic Science* 5 (1966), 221–222.

21. Rosegrant and McCroskey, "The Effects of Race and Sex on Proxemic Behavior."

22. J. D. Fisher and D. Byrne, "Too Close for Comfort: Sex Differences in Response to Invasions of Personal Space," *Journal of Personality and Social Psychology* 32 (1975), 15–21; D. M. Pedersen and A. B. Heaston, "The Effects of Sex of Subject, Sex of Approaching Person, and Angle of Approach on Personal Space," *Journal of Psychology* 82 (1972), 277–286.

23. D. M. Pedersen, "Developmental Trends in Personal Space," *Journal of Psychology* 83 (1973), 3–9; R. J. Pellergrini and J. Empey, "Interpersonal Spatial Orientation in Dyads," *Journal of Psychology* 76 (1970), 67–70; D. R. Thomas, "Interaction Distances in Same-Sex and Mixed-Sex Groups," *Perceptual and Motor Skills* 36 (1976), 15–18; A. J. Wolfgang, "Exploration of Attitudes via Physical Interpersonal Distance Toward the Obese, Drug Users, Homosexuals, Police, and Other Marginal Figures," *Journal of Clinical Psychology* 27 (1971), 510–512; J. R. Aiello and R. E. Cooper, "The Use of Personal Space as a Function of Social Affect," *American Psychological Association, Annals Convention Proceedings* 7 (1972), 207–208; S. J. Beck and T. H. Ollendick, "Personal Space, Sex of Experimenter, and Locus of Control in Normal and Delinquent Adolescents," *Psychological Reports* 36

(1975), 383; R. Shuter, "The Alternative Situation: A Small Group Study of Environmental Influence on Sex-Role Interaction Style," *Today's Speech* 23 (1975), 45–50; M. Giesen and H. A. McClaren, "Discussion, Distance, and Sex: Changes in Impressions and Attraction During Small Group Interaction," *Sociometry* 39 (1976), 60–70; A. Palmer and R. Bailey, "Sex Differences and the Statistics of Crowd Fluids," *Behavioral Science* 20 (1975), 223–227. One study that is an exception (but in terms of spatial violation) is Krail and Leventhal, "The Sex Variable."

24. Pedersen and Heaston, "The Effects of Sex of Subject."

25. M. Hendricks and R. Bootzin, "Race and Sex as Stimuli for Negative Affect and Physical Avoidance," *Journal of Social Psychology* 98 (1976), 111–120.

26. R. M. Tipton, K. G. Bailey, and J. P. Obenchain, "Invasion of Male's Personal Space by Feminists and Nonfeminists," *Psychological Reports* 37 (1975), 99–102.

27. G. Banziger and R. Simmons, "Emotion, Attractiveness, and Interpersonal Space," *Journal of Social Psychology* 124 (1984), 255–256.

28. See Burgoon, "Further Explication and an Initial Test"; Burgoon and Jones, "Toward a Theory of Personal Space Expectations"; and J. K. Burgoon, D. W. Stacks, and W. G. Woodall, "Personal Space Expectations and Reward as Predictors of Recall, Credibility, and Attraction," paper presented at the Speech Communication Association Convention, Washington, D.C., 1977.

29. E. T. Hall, *The Silent Language* (Garden City, NY: Doubleday, 1959); O. M. Watson, *Proxemic Behavior: A Cross-Cultural Study* (The Hague: Mouton, 1970); O. M. Watson and T. D. Graves, "Quantitative Research in Proxemic Behavior," *American Anthropologist* 68 (1966), 971–985.

30. R. F. Forston and C. U. Larson, "The Dynamics of Space: An Experimental Study in Proxemic Behavior Among Latin Americans," *Journal of Communication* 18 (1968), 109–116; S. Jones, "A Comparative Proxemic Analysis of Dyadic Interaction in Selected Subcultures of New York City," *Journal of Social Psychology* 84 (1971), 34–44; and A. Mazur, "Interpersonal

Spacing on Public Benches in 'Contact' vs. 'Noncontact' Cultures,'' *Journal of Social Psychology* 101 (1977), 53–58.

31. R. Shuter, ''Proxemics and Tactility in Latin America,'' *Journal of Communication* 26 (1976), 46–76; J. C. Baxter, ''Interpersonal Spacing in Natural Settings,'' *Sociometry* 33 (1970), 444–456; D. B. Roger and E. E. Schalekamp, ''Body-Buffer Zone and Violence: A Cross-Cultural Study,'' *Journal of Social Psychology* 98 (1976), 153–158.

32. J. F. Hansen, ''The Proxemics of Danish Daily Life,'' *Studies in Anthropology of Visual Communication* 3 (1976), 52–61; E. T. Hall with E. Hall, ''How Cultures Collide,'' *Psychology Today* 10 (1976), 66–74 and 97.

33. Baxter, ''Interpersonal Spacing.''

34. J. Lorenz, ''Cultural Variations in Personal Space,'' *Journal of Social Psychology* 99 (1976), 21–27.

35. Roger and Schalekamp, ''Body-Buffer Zone and Violence.''

36. D. Engelbretsen and D. Fullmer, ''Cross-Cultural Differences in Territoriality: Interaction Distances of Native Japanese, Hawaii Japanese, and American Caucasians,'' *Journal of Cross-Cultural Psychology* 1 (1970), 261–269.

37. R. Shuter, ''Proxemics and Tactility.''

38. R. Shuter, ''A Field Study of Nonverbal Communication.''

39. Mazur, ''Interpersonal Spacing on Public Benches.''

40. Forsten and Larson, ''The Dynamics of Space.''

41. S. Jones, ''A Comparative Proxemic Analysis.''

42. J. C. Baxter, ''Interpersonal Spacing.''

43. S. E. Jones and J. R. Aiello, ''The Acquisition of Proxemic Norms of Behavior: A Study of the Lower-Class Black and Middle-Class White Children at Three Grade Levels,'' unpublished paper, 1972; Jones and Aiello, ''Proxemic Behavior,'' 21–27.

44. E. A. Bauer, ''Personal Space: A Study of Blacks and Whites,'' *Sociometry* 36 (1973), 402–408.

45. Rosegrant and McCroskey, ''The Effects of Race and Sex on Proxemics Behavior,'' 408. For additional material on race and personal space, see P. R. Connolly, ''The Perception of Personal Space Among Black

and White Americans,'' *Central States Speech Journal* 26 (1975), 21–28; and B. M. Erbe, ''Race and Socioeconomic Segregation,'' *American Sociological Review* 40 (1975), 801–812.

46. J. K. Burgoon, D. W. Stacks, and W. G. Woodall, ''Personal Space Expectations and Reward''; Burgoon, Stacks, and Woodall, ''A Communicative Model.''

47. D. F. Lott and R. Sommer, ''Seating Arrangement and Status,'' *Journal of Personality and Social Psychology* 7 (1967), 90–94; A. Mehrabian, ''Relationship of Attitude to Seated Posture, Orientation, and Distance,'' *Journal of Personality and Social Psychology* 10 (1968), 26–30; A. Mehrabian and M. Willams, ''Nonverbal Concomitants of Perceived and Intended Persuasiveness,'' *Journal of Personality and Social Psychology* 13 (1969), 37–58.

48. See W. Leipold, ''Psychological Distance in Dyadic Interviews,'' Diss., University of North Dakota, 1963; M. L. Patterson and D. S. Holmes, ''Social Interaction Correlates of the MPI Extroversion-Introversion Scale,'' *American Psychologist* 21 (1966), 724–745; J. L. Williams, ''Personal Space and Its Relation to Extroversion-Introversion,'' Masters Thesis, University of Alberta, 1963.

49. J. Fast, *Body Language* (New York: M. Evans, 1970); Horowitz, Duff, and Stratton, ''Body Buffer Zones.''

50. A. M. Hildreth, L. R. Derogatis, and K. McClusker, ''Body Buffer Zone and Violence: A Reassessment and Confirmation,'' *American Journal of Psychiatry* 127 (1971), 77–81; Roger and Schalekamp ''Body-Buffer Zone and Violence''; R. Fisher, ''Social Schema of Normal and Disturbed Children,'' *Journal of Educational Psychology* 58 (1967), 58–92.

51. See A. R. Allgeier and D. Byrne, ''Attraction Toward the Opposite Sex as a Determinant of Physical Proximity,'' *Journal of Social Psychology* 90 (1973), 213–219; M. G. King. ''Interpersonal Relations in Preschool Children and Average Approach Distance,'' *Journal of Genetic Psychology* 108 (1966), 109–116; R. Kleck, P. L. Buck, W. L. Goller, R. S. London, J. R. Pfieffer, and D. P. Vukcevic,

"Effect of Stigmatization Conditions on the Use of Personal Space," *Psychological Reports* 23 (1968), 111–118; R. M. Lerner; D. F. Lott, and R. Sommer, "Seating Arrangement and Status," *Journal of Personality and Social Psychology* 7 (1967), 90–94; Mehrabian, "Relationship of Attitude to Seated Posture"; G. A. Norum, J. K. Gergen, S. Peele, and J. van Ryneveld, "Reactions to Receiving Expected and Unexpected Help From a Person Who Violates or Does Not Violate a Norm," *Journal of Experimental Psychology* 13 (1977), 397–402; Patterson and Sechrest, "Interpersonal Distance and Impression Formation," unpublished manuscript, Northwestern University, 1972.

52. See D. J. A. Edwards, "Approaching the Unfamiliar: A Study of Human Interaction Distances," *Journal of Behavioral Science* 1 (1972), 249–250; K. B. Little, "Personal Space," *Journal of Experimental Social Psychology* 1 (1965), 237–247; N. Russo, "Connotation of Seating Arrangements," *Cornell Journal of Social Relations* 2 (1967), 37–44; Willis, "Initial Speaking Distances."

53. E. Goffman, *Stigma: Notes on the Management of Spoiled Identity* (Englewood Cliffs, NJ: Prentice-Hall, 1963), 3; and L. Conigliaro, S. Cullerton, K. Flynn, and S. Rueder, "Stigmatizing Artifacts and Their Effect on Personal Space," *Psychological Reports* 65 (1989), 897–898.

54. M. E. Worthington, "Personal Space as a Function of the Stigma Effect," *Environment and Behavior* 6 (1974), 289–294; T. W. Mallenby, "Personal Space—Direct Measurement Techniques with Hard of Hearing Students," *Environment and Behavior* 6 (1974), 117–121; B. A. Barrios, L. C. Corbitt, J. P. Estes, and J. S. Topping, "Effect of a Social Stigma on Interpersonal Distance," *Psychological Record* 26 (1976), 343–348.

55. J. K. Heston and P. Garner, "A Study of Personal Space and Desk Arrangement in a Learning Environment," paper presented at the International Communication Association Convention, Atlanta, 1972.

56. M. Cook, "Experiments in Orientation and Proxemics," *Human Relations* 23 (1970), 61–76; G. T. Lang, L. G. Calhoun, and J. W. Selby, "Personality Characteristics Related to Cross-Situational Consistency of Interpersonal Distance," *Journal of Personality Assessment* 41 (1977), 274–278; G. A. Norum, N. J. Russo, and R. Sommer, "Seating Patterns and Group Task," *Psychology in the Schools* 4 (1967), 240.

57. Cook, "Experiments in Orientation and Proxemics."

58. M. Riess and P. Rosenfeld, "Seating Preference as Nonverbal Communication: A Self-Presentational Analysis," *Journal of Applied Communications Research* 8 (1980), 22–28.

59. See H. Gardin, K. J. Kaplan, I. J. Firestone, and G. A. Cowen, "Proxemic Effects of Cooperation, Attitude, and Approach-Avoidance in a Prisoner's Dilemma Game," *Journal of Personality and Social Psychology* 27 (1973), 13–18; A. P. Hare and R. F. Bales, "Seating Position and Small Group Interaction," *Sociometry* 26 (1963), 480–486; G. Hearn, "Leadership and the Spatial Factor in Small Groups," *Journal of Abnormal and Social Psychology* 54 (1957), 269–272; L. T. Howells and S. W. Becker, "Seating Arrangement and Leadership Emergence," *Journal of Abnormal and Social Psychology* 64 (1962), 148–150; A. Kendon, "Some Functions of Gaze Direction in Social Interaction," *Acta Psychologica* 26 (1976), 22–63; A. Mehrabian and S. Diamond, "Effects of Furniture Arrangement, Props, and Personality on Social Interaction," *Journal of Personality and Social Psychology* 20 (1971), 18–30; N. Russo, "Connotations of Seating Arrangements"; and F. L. Stodtbeck and L. H. Hook, "The Social Dimensions of a Twelve Man Jury Table," *Sociometry* 24 (1961), 397–415.

60. J. J. Edney and N. L. Jordan-Edney, "Territorial Spacing on a Beach," *Sociometry* 37 (1974), 92–104.

61. Burgoon and Jones, "Toward a Theory of Personal Space Expectations."

62. Leathers, *Nonverbal Communication Systems*, 61.

63. Burgoon, "Further Explication and an Initial Test"; Burgoon and Jones, "Toward a Theory of Personal Space Expectations"; Burgoon, Stacks, and Woodall, "Personal Space Expectations"; Burgoon, Stacks, and Woodall, "A Communicative Model"; D. W. Stacks and J. K. Burgoon, "The Role

of Nonverbal Behaviors as Distractors in Resistance to Persuasion in Interpersonal Contexts," *Central States Speech Journal* 32 (1981), 61–73; J. K. Burgoon, D. W. Stacks, and S. A. Burch, "The Role of Interpersonal Rewards and Violations of Distancing Expectations in Achieving Influence," *Communication* 11 (1982), 114–128; D. W. Stacks, "The Role of Interpersonal Influence as Mediated by Proxemic Behaviors," *Proceedings: ABCA Southeast Regional Meeting* (1982), 13–26; D. W. Stacks, "Violations and Persuasion," paper presented at the Eastern Communication Association Convention, Ocean City, MD 1980; D. W. Stacks, "A Further Test of the Distractive Impact of Violating Interpersonal Distancing Expectations on Small Group Persuasion," paper presented at the Southern Speech Communication Association Convention, Birmingham, AL, 1980; J. K. Burgoon and L. Aho, "Three Field Experiments on the Effects of Violations of Conversational Distance," *Communication Monographs* 49 (1982), 71–88.

64. See Burgoon "Further Explication and an Initial Test"; Burgoon, Stacks, and Woodall, "A Communicative Model"; Stacks and Burgoon, "The Effects of Violating"; Stacks and Burgoon, "The Role of Nonverbal Behaviors"; Burgoon, Stacks, and Burch, "The Role of Interpersonal Rewards"; Stacks, "Violations"; Stacks, "The Role of Interpersonal Influence"; Stacks, "A Further Test"; J. K. Burgoon and J. B. Walther, "Nonverbal Expectancies and the Evaluative Consequences of Violations," *Human Communication Research* 17 (1990), 232–265; A. Rustemili, "The Effects of Personal Space Invasion on Impressions and Decisions," *Journal of Psychology* 122 (1988), 113–118; D. B. Buller, "Communication Apprehension and Reaction to Proxemic Violations," *Journal of Nonverbal Behavior* 11 (1988), 13–25; and B. A. LePoire, "Orientation and Defensive Reactions as Alternatives to Arousal in Theories of Nonverbal Reactions to Changes in Immediacy," *Southern Communication Journal* 56 (1991), 138–145.

65. Goffman, *Relations in Public,* 44–49.

66. A major research investigation of the use of gaze and the eyes can be found in M. Argyle and M. Cook, *Gaze and Mutual Gaze* (Cambridge: Cambridge University Press, 1976).

67. D. T. Kendrick and S. W. MacFarlane, "Ambient Temperature and Horn Honking," *Environment and Behavior* 18 (1986), 179–191. For other violations, see L. A. Jason and R. Jung, "Stimulus Control Techniques to Handicapped-Designated Parking Spaces," *Environment and Behavior* 16 (1984), 675–686; and S. Milgram, H. J. Liberty, R. Toledo, and J. Wackenhut, "Response to Intrusion Into Waiting Lines," *Journal of Personality and Social Psychology* 61 (1986), 683–689.

68. Goffman, *Relations in Public,* 47.

69. Hall, *The Hidden Dimension,* 7.

70. S. M. Lyman and M. B. Scott, "Territoriality: A Neglected Sociological Dimension," *Social Problems* 15 (1967), 237–241.

71. For example; see E. S. Knowles, "Boundaries Around Social Space: Dyadic Responses to an Invasion," *Environment and Behavior* 4 (1972), 437–445; R. S. Sobel and N. Liffith, "Determinants of Nonstationary Personal Space Invasion," *Journal of Social Psychology* 97 (1974), 39–45.

72. J. B. Calhoun, "Population Density and Social Pathology," *Scientific American* 206 (1962), 130–146; and J. B. Calhoun, "The Study of Wild Animals under Controlled Conditions," *Annals of the New York Academy of Sciences* 51 (1950), 113–122.

73. A. S. Parkes and H. M. Bruce, "Olfactory Stimuli in Mammalian Reproduction," *Science* 134 (1961), 1049–1054.

74. Calhoun, "Population Density;" Calhoun, "The Study of Wild Animals."

75. J. J. Christian, "The Pathology of Overpopulation," *Military Medicine* 128 (1963), 571–603; J. J. Christian and D. E. Davis, "Social and Endocrine Factors are Integrated in the Regulation of Growth of Mammalian Populations," *Science* 146 (1964), 1550–1560; J. J. Christian with V. Flyger and D. E. Davis, "Phenomena Associated with Population Density," *Proceedings National Academy of Science* 47 (1961), 428–449; and J. J. Christian, with

V. Flyger and D. E. Davis, "Factors in Mass Morality of a Herd of Sika Deer (*Cervus nippon*)," *Chesapeake Science* 47 (1961), 79–95.

76. G. McCain, V. C. Cox, and P. B. Paulus, "The Relationship Between Illness Complaints and the Degree of Crowding in a Prison Environment," *Environment and Behavior* 8 (1976), 283–289.

77. D. A. D'Atri, "Psycho-physiological Responses to Crowding," *Environment and Behavior* 7 (1975), 237–251.

78. J. Bonta, "Prison Crowding: Searching for the Functional Approach," *American Psychologist* 41 (1986), 99–101.

79. I. Altman, "An Ecological Approach to the Functioning of Social Groups," in *Individual and Group Behavior in Isolation and Confinement,* ed. J. G. Rasmussen (Chicago: Aldin Press, 1973), 241–269; I. Altman, *The Environment and Social Behavior: Privacy, Personal Space, Territoriality, and Crowding* (Monterey, CA: Brooks/Cole, 1975); I. Altman and W. W. Haythorn "The Ecology of Isolated Groups," *Behavioral Science* 12 (1967), 169–182; I. Altman, R. A. Nelson, and E. E. Lett, "The Ecology of Home Environments," *Man-Made Systems* 2 (1972), 189–191; I. Altman, D. A. Taylor, and L. Wheeler, "Ecological Aspects of Group Behavior in Isolation," *Journal of Applied Social Psychology* 1 (1971), 76–100.

80. C. Hunt and M. J. Vaizey, "Differential Effects of Group Density on Social Behavior," *Nature* 209 (1966), 1371–1372. See also Z. Solomon and R. Behbenisty, "The Role of Proximity, Immediacy, and Expectancy in Frontline Treatment of Combat Stress Reaction Among Israelis in the Lebanon War," *American Journal of Pychiatry* 143 (1986), 613–617.

81. E. Goffman, *Relations in Public: Microstudies of the Public Order* (New York: Harper Colophon Books, 1971), 31.

82. Goffman, "Relations in Public," 31.

83. Goffman, "Relations in Public," 35.

84. R. W. Belk, "My Possessions, Myself," *Psychology Today* 22 (1988), 51–52.

85. Goffman, "Relations in Public," 29–41.

86. Goffman, "Relations in Public," 41–42.

87. R. Ardrey, *The Territorial Imperative: A Personal Inquiry into the Animal Origins of Property and Nations* (New York: Dell Publishing Company, 1966), 3.

88. L. B. Rosenfeld and J. M. Civikly, *With Words Unspoken: The Nonverbal Experience* (New York: Holt, Rinehart, and Winston, 1976), 148.

89. J. Edney, "Human Territoriality," *Psychological Bulletin* 81 (1974), 959–975.

90. J. L. Freedman, "The Crowd: Maybe Not So Madding After All," *Psychology Today* 4 (1971), 58–61, 86. Quotation on p. 61.

91. F. O'Brien, "A Crowding Index for Finite Populations," *Perceptual and Motor Skills* 70 (1990), 3–11.

92. E. P. Willems and D. E. Campbell, "One Path Through the Cafeteria," *Environment and Behavior* 8 (1976), 125–140.

93. C. Bagley, "Urban Crowding and the Murder Rate in Bombay, India," *Perceptual and Motor Skills* 69 (1989), 1241–1242.

94. M. K. Fried and V. J. DeFazlo, "Territoriality and Boundary Conflicts in the Subway," *Psychiatry* 37 (1974), 47–58.

95. A. Booth and J. N. Edwards, "Crowding and Family Relations," *American Sociological Review* 41 (1976), 308–321.

96. J. N. Edwards and A. Booth, "Crowding and Human Sexual Behavior," *Social Forces* 55 (1977), 791–808. See also F. V. Wenz, "Household Crowding, Loneliness, and Suicide Ideation," *Psychology: A Quarterly Journal of Human Behavior* 21 (1984), 25–28.

97. M. L. Knapp, *Nonverbal Communication in Human Interaction,* 2d ed. (New York: Holt, Rinehart, and Winston, 1978), 87–89.

98. J. K. Burgoon and T. J. Saine, *The Unspoken Dialogue: An Introduction to Nonverbal Communication* (Boston: Houghton-Mifflin, 1978), 103–115.

99. E. T. Hall, "Proxemics: The Study of Man's Spatial Relations," in *Intercultural Communication: A Reader,* ed. L. A. Samovar and R. E. Porter (Belmont, CA: Wadsworth, 1972), 210–217.

100. Hall, "Proxemics," 210.

101. Hall, "Proxemics," 210.

102. A. H. Maslow and N. L. Mintz, "Effects of Esthetic Surroundings: I. Initial Effects of Three Esthetic Conditions Upon Perceiving 'Energy' and 'Well-Being' in Faces,"

Journal of Psychology 41 (1956), 247–254. See also N. L. Mintz, ''Effects of Esthetic Surroundings: II. Prolonged and Repeated Experience in a 'Beautiful' and 'Ugly' Room,'' *Journal of Psychology* 41 (1956), 459–466.

103. J. T. Kitchens, T. P. Herron, R. R. Behnke, and M. J. Beatty, ''Environmental Esthetics and Interpersonal Attraction,'' *Western Journal of Speech Communication* 41 (1977), 126–130.

104. L. B. Wexner, ''The Degree to Which Colors (Hues) Are Associated with Mood-Tones,'' *Journal of Applied Psychology* 38 (1954), 432–435. See also D. C. Murray and H. L. Deabler, ''Colors and Mood-Tones,'' *Journal of Applied Psychology* 41 (1957), 279–283. A popular test of the association between color preference and personality has been developed by Max Luscher, *The Luscher Color Test,* trans. and ed. I. Scott (New York: Pocket Books, 1971).

105. R. O. Sommer, *Personal Space* (Englewood Cliffs, NJ: Prentice-Hall, 1969), 110–119.

106. See R. S. Adams and B. Biddle, *Realities of Teaching: Explorations with Video Tape* (New York: Holt, Rinehart, and Winston, 1970); and D. Becher, R. Sommer, J. Bee, and B. Osley, ''College Classroom Ecology,'' *Sociometry* 36 (1973), 514–525.

107. T. High and E. Sundstrom, ''Room Flexibility and Space Use in a Dormitory,'' *Environment and Behavior* 9 (1977), 81–90.

108. W. Griffitt, ''Environment Effects of Interpersonal Affective Behavior: Ambient Effective Temperature and Attraction,'' *Journal of Personality and Social Psychology* 15 (1970), 240–244.

109. E. Huntington, *Civilization and Climate* (New Haven: Yale University Press, 1915); and D. McClelland, *The Achieving Society* (New York: Van Nostrand Reinhold, 1961).

110. M. Korda, *Power! How to Get It, How to Use It* (New York: Ballantine Books, 1975); and K. Cooper, *Nonverbal Communication for Business Success* (New York: AMACOM, 1980).

111. D. N. Freeman, D. Roach, and K. Gladney, ''The Nonverbal Persuasive Influence of the Supermarket in Food Purchasing Behavior,'' paper presented at the Southern Speech Communication Association Convention, Birmingham, AL, 1980.

Chapter Six

1. C. R. Berger and J. J. Calabrese, ''Some Explorations in Initial Interactions and Beyond: Toward a Developmental Theory of Interpersonal Communication,'' *Human Communication Research* 1 (1975), 99–112.

2. J. G. Martin, ''Racial Ethnocentrism and Judgement of Beauty,'' *Journal of Social Psychology* 63 (1964), 59–63.

3. A. H. Illife, ''A Study of Preference in Feminine Beauty,'' *British Journal of Psychology* 61 (1960), 267–273; and Martin, ''Racial Ethnocentrism.''

4. Illife, ''A Study of Preference''; and W. E. Henley, ''The Effect of Attire, Location and Sex on Aiding Behavior: A Similarity Explanation, *Journal of Nonverbal Behavior* 6 (1981), 3–11.

5. J. E. Singer, ''The Use of Manipulative Strategies: Machiavellianism and Attractiveness,'' *Sociometry* 27 (1964), 128–151.

6. J. E. Singer and P. F. Lamb, ''Social Concern, Body Size, and Birth Order,'' *Journal of Social Psychology* 68 (1966), 143–151.

7. J. Mills and E. Aronson, ''Opinion Change as a Function of the Communicator's Attractiveness and Desire to Influence,'' *Journal of Personality and Social Psychology* 1 (1965), 73–77.

8. R. N. Widgery and B. Webster, ''The Effects of Physical Attractiveness Upon Perceived Initial Credibility,'' *Michigan Speech Journal* 4 (1969), 9–15; and R. Eiland and D. Richardson, ''The Influence of Race, Sex, and Age on Judgments of Emotion Portrayed in Photographs,'' *Communication Monographs* 43 (1976), 167–175; H. S. Friedman, R. E. Riggio, and D. F. Casella, ''Nonverbal Skill, Personal Charisma, and Initial Attraction,'' *Personality and Social Psychology Bulletin* 14 (1988), 203–211; S. M. Kalick, ''Physical Attractiveness as a Status Cue,'' *Journal of Experimental Social Psychology* 24 (1988), 469–489; K. G. De Bono and R. J. Harnish, ''Source Expertise, Source Attractiveness, and the Processing of Persuasive Information: A Function Approach,'' *Journal of Personality and Social Psychology* 55 (1988), 541–550;

K. E. O'Grady, "Physical Attractiveness, Need for Approval, Social Self-Esteem and Maladjustment," *Journal of Social and Clinical Psychology* 8 (1989), 62–69; W. R. Zakahi and R. L. Duran, "Physical Attractiveness as a Contributing Factor to Loneliness: An Exploratory Study," *Psychological Reports* 63 (1988), 747–751; and M. Rubin and R. Sabatelli, "Nonverbal Expressiveness and Physical Attractiveness as Mediators of Interpersonal Perceptions," *Journal of Nonverbal Behavior* 10 (1986), 120–133.

9. H. T. Ries, J. Nezlek, and L. Wheeler, "Physical Attractiveness in Social Interaction," *Journal of Personality and Social Psychology* 38 (1980), 604–617; P. Kenealy, N. Frude, and W. Shaw, "Influence of Children's Physical Attractiveness on Teacher Expectations," *Journal of Social Psychology* 128 (1988), 373–383; and S. T. Romano and J. E. Bordieri, "Physical Attractiveness Stereotypes and Students' Perceptions of College Professors," *Psychological Reports* 64 (1989), 1099–1102.

10. K. K. Dion and E. Berscheid, "Physical Attractiveness and Evaluation of Children's Transgressions," *Journal of Personality and Social Psychology* 30 (1972), 207–213.

11. D. Bar-Tal and L. Saxe, "Physical Attractiveness and Its Relationships to Sex-Role Stereotyping," *Sex Roles* 2 (1976), 123–133.

12. M. M. Clifford and E. H. Walster, "The Effect of Physical Attractiveness in Teacher Expectation," *Sociological Education* 46 (1973), 248–258.

13. S. J. Marwit, "Students' Race, Physical Attractiveness, and Teachers' Judgements of Transgressions: Follow-up and Clarification," *Psychological Reports* 50 (1982), 242.

14. R. Felson, "Physical Attractiveness and Perceptions of Deviance," *Journal of Social Psychology* 114 (1981), 85–90.

15. J. May, "What Tips Tippers to Tip," *Psychology Today* (1980), 98–99.

16. D. A. Infante, A. S. Rancer, L. L. Pierce, and W. J. Osborne, "Effects of physical attractiveness and Likeableness of First Name on Impressions Formed of Journalists," *Journal of Applied Communications Research* 8 (1980), 1–9.

17. J. M. Dabbs, Jr., and N. A. Stokes III, "Beauty is Power: The Use of Space on the Sidewalk," *Sociometry* 38 (1975), 551–557.

18. J. K. Burgoon and S. B. Jones, "Toward a Theory of Personal Space Expectations and Their Violations," *Human Communication Research* 2 (1976), 131–146; see also J. K. Burgoon, "Nonverbal Violations of Expectations," in *Nonverbal Interaction,* ed. J. M. Weimann and R. P. Harrison (Beverly Hills, CA: Sage Publications, 1983), 77–111; and J. K. Burgoon, D. W. Stacks, and S. A. Burch, "The Role of Interpersonal Rewards and Violations of Distancing Expectations in Achieving Influence in Small Groups," *Communication* 11 (1982), 114–128.

19. D. W. Stacks, "When Reward Fails: An Examination of High Reward and the Violations of Distancing Expectations Model," unpublished manuscript, University of South Alabama, 1983.

20. K. Debevac, T. J. Madden, and J. B. Kernan, "Physical Attractiveness, Message Evaluation, Compliance: A Structural Examination," *Psychological Reports* 58 (1986), 503–508.

21. M. E. Heilman and M. H. Stopeck, "Being Attractive, Advantage or Disadvantage? Performance-Based Evaluations and Recommended Personnel Actions as a Function of Appearance, Sex, and Job Type," *Organizational Behavior and Human Decision Processes* 35 (1985), 202–215.

22. N. L. Kerr, H. C. B. Raymond, R. J. MacCoun, and H. Rathborn, "Effects of Victim Attractiveness, Care, and Disfigurement on the Judgments of American and British Mock Jurors," *British Journal of Social Psychology* 24 (1985), 54–58.

23. C. Austad, C. Bugglin, G. L. Burns, A. Farina, and E. H. Fisher, "Role of Physical Attractiveness in the Readjustment of Discharged Psychiatric Patients," *Journal of Abnormal Psychology* 95 (1985), 139–143.

24. M. R. Cunningham, "Measuring the Physical in Physical Attractiveness: Quasi-Experiments on the Sociobiology of Female Facial Beauty," *Journal of Personality and Social Psychology* 50 (1986), 925–935; and C. F. Keating, "Gender and the

Physiognomy of Dominance and Attractiveness,'' *Social Psychology Quarterly* 48 (1985), 61–70.

25. M. L. Knapp, *Nonverbal Communication in Human Interaction,* 2d ed. (New York: Holt, Rinehart and Winston, 1978), 159–160.

26. B. W. Eakins and R. G. Eakins, *Sex Differences in Human Communication* (Boston: Houghton-Mifflin Company, 1978), 166.

27. G. Wilson and D. Nias, ''Beauty Can't Be Beat,'' *Psychology Today* (1976), 98.

28. R. F. Guy, B. A. Rankin, and M. J. Norvell, ''The Relation of Sex Role Stereotyping to Body Image,'' *Journal of Psychology* 105 (1980), 167–174.

29. Wilson and Nias, ''Beauty Can't Be Beat.''

30. E. Walster, V. Aronson, D. Abrahams, and L. Rohmann, ''Importance of Physical Attractiveness in Dating Behavior,'' *Journal of Personality and Social Psychology* 4 (1966), 508–516.

31. R. C. Bailey and T. S. Schreiber, ''Congruency of Physical Attractiveness Perception and Liking,'' *Journal of Social Psychology* 115 (1981), 285–286.

32. R. H. Stretch and C. R. Figby, ''Beauty and the Beast: Predictors of Interpersonal Attraction in a Dating Experiment,'' *Psychology* 17 (1980), 35–44.

33. J. L. Peterson and C. Miller, ''Physical Attractiveness and Marriage Adjustment in Older American Couples,'' *Journal of Psychology* 105 (1980), 247–252.

34. R. M. Jones and G. R. Adams, ''Assessing the Importance of Physical Attractiveness Across the Life-Span,'' *Journal of Social Psychology* 118 (1982), 131–132.

35. E. D. Tanke, ''Dimensions of the Physical Attractiveness Stereotype: A Factor/Analytic Study,'' *Journal of Psychology* 110 (1982), 63–74.

36. J. C. Finkelstein and L. A. Walker, ''Evaluation Apprehension as a Mediator of Responses to Pupil-Size Cues,'' *Personality and Social Psychology Bulletin* 2 (1976), 474–477.

37. E. H. Hess and J. M. Polt, ''Pupil Size as Related to Interest Value of Visual Stimuli,'' *Science* 132 (1960), 349–350; M. P. Janisse and W. S. Peavler, ''Pupillary Research Today: Emotion in the Eye,'' *Psychology Today* 7 (1974), 60–73; E. Hess, ''The Role of Pupil Size in Communication,'' *Scientific American* 222 (1975), 110–119; and J. Beatty, ''Activation and Attention in the Human Brain,'' in *The Human Brain,* ed. M. C. Wittrock et al. (Englewood Cliffs, NJ: Prentice-Hall, 1977), 63–85.

38. For example, see, A. King, ''The Eye in Advertising,'' *Journal of Applied Communications Research* 2 (1974), 1–12.

39. C. Kleine and R. Staneski, ''First Impressions of Female Bust Size, *The Journal of Social Psychology* 110 (1980), 123–134.

40. S. Feiman and G. W. Gill, ''Sex Differences on Physical Attractiveness Preferences,'' *The Journal of Social Psychology* 105 (1978), 43–52.

41. Martin, ''Racial Ethnocentrism.''

42. J. B. Cortes and F. M. Gatti, ''Physique and Self-Description of Temperament,'' *Journal of Consulting Psychology* 29 (1965), 434.

43. Knapp, *Nonverbal Communication,* 164.

44. J. K. Burgoon and T. J. Saine, *The Unspoken Dialogue: An Introduction to Nonverbal Communication* (Boston: Houghton-Mifflin, 1978), 79.

45. D. P. Millar and F. E. Millar, *Messages and Myths* (New York: Alfred Publishing, 1976).

46. J. Karris, ''Prejudice Against Obese Renters,'' *Journal of Social Psychology* 101, (1977), 159–160; M. B. Harris, S. Waschull and L. Walters, ''Feeling Fat: Motivations, Knowledge, and Attitudes of Overweight Women and Men,'' *Psychological Reports* 67 (1990), 1191–1202; L. Waddell-Kral and C. D. Thomas, ''Body Attitudes and Eating Behaviors of Female Clothing Sales Personnel,'' *Psychological Reports* 67 (1990), 451–456; P. Pliner and S. Chaiken, ''Eating, Social Motives, and Self-Presentation in Women and Men,'' *Journal of Experimental Social Psychology* 26 (1990), 240–254; and A. B. Heilbrun and N. Witt, ''Distorted Body Image as a Risk Factor in Anorexia Nervosa: Replication and Clarification,'' *Psychological Reports* 66 (1990), 407–416.

47. D. Elman, ''Physical Characteristics and the Perception of Masculine Traits,'' *Journal of Social Psychology* 103, (1977) 157–158.

48. E. Lechelt, ''Occupational Affiliation and Ratings of Physical Height and Personal Esteem,'' *Psychological Reports* 36 (1975), 943–946.

49. N. M. Henley, *Body Politics: Power, Sex, and Nonverbal Communication* (Englewood Cliffs, NJ: Prentice-Hall, 1977).

50. Knapp, *Nonverbal Communication* 167.

51. W. H. Sheldon, *Atlas of Man: A Guide for Somatyping the Adult Male at All Ages* (New York: Harper and Row, 1954); W. H. Sheldon, *The Varieties of Human Physique* (New York: Harper and Row, 1940); W. H. Sheldon, *The Varieties of Temperament* (New York: Harper and Row, 1942). For other treatments, see Burgoon and Saine, *The Unspoken Dialogue,* 76–77; and Knapp, *Nonverbal Communication,* 162–165.

52. D. Lester, "Ectomorphy and Suicide," *Journal of Social Psychology* 113 (1981), 135–136.

53. Guy, Rankin, and Norvell, "The Relation of Sex Role Stereotyping to Body Image."

54. S. Fisher and S. Cleveland, *Body Image and Personality* (New York: Dover Publications, 1968), x.

55. Fisher and Cleveland, xi.

56. Fisher and Cleveland, xii.

57. Fisher and Cleveland, 3–8.

58. E. Berscheid, E. Walster, and G. Bohrnstedt, "Body Image," *Psychology Today* (1973), 119–131.

59. R. Lerner and B. Brackney, "The Importance of Inner and Outer Body Parts on Attitudes in the Self Concept of Late Adolescents," *Sex Roles* 2 (1976).

60. Kleine and Staneski, "First Impressions of Female Bust Size."

61. W. Lucker, W. Beane, and R. L. Helmreich, "The Strength of the Halo Effect in Physical Attractiveness Research," *Journal of Psychology* 107 (1981), 69–76.

62. J. F. Higdon, "Roles of Power, Sex, and Inadequate Attractiveness in Paranoid Women," *Psychological Reports* 50 (1982), 399–402.

63. Berscheid, Walster, and Bohrnstedt, "Body Image."

64. T. F. Cash, B. A. Winstead, and L. H. Janda, "The Great American Shape-Up," *Psychology Today* 20 (1986), 30–37.

65. T. F. Cash, S. W. Noles, and B. A. Winstead, "Body Image, Physical Attractiveness, and Depression," *Journal of Consulting and Clinical Psychology* 53 (1985), 88–94.

66. T. F. Cash and G. K. Green, "Body Weight and Body Image Among College Women: Perception, Cognition, and Affect," *Journal of Personality Assessment* 50 (1986), 290–300; P. Rozin and A. Fallon, "Body Image, Attitudes Toward Weight, and Misperceptions of Figure Preferences of the Opposite Sex: A Comparison of Men and Women in Two Generations," *Journal of Abnormal Psychology* 97 (1988), 342–345; A. B. Heilburn, Jr., and L. Friedberg, "Distorted Body Image in Normal College Women: Possible Implications for the Development of Anorexia Nervosa," *Journal of Clinical Psychology* 46 (1990), 398–401; D. A. Brodie, P. D. Slade, and H. Rose, "Reliability Measures in Distorting Body-Image," *Perceptual and Motor Skills* 69 (1989), 723–732; T. F. Cash, B. Counts, J. Hangen, and C. E. Huffins, "How Much Do You Weigh?: Determinants of Validity of Self-Reported Body Weight," *Perceptual and Motor Skills* 69 (1989), 248–250; and P. H. Silverstone, "Low Self-Esteem in Eating Disordered Patients in the Absence of Depression," *Psychological Reports* 67 (1990), 276–278.

67. J. K. Thompson, "Larger Than Life," *Psychology Today* 20 (1986), 39–44.

68. A. Rothenberg, "Eating Disorder as a Modern Obsessive-Compulsive Syndrome," *Psychiatry* 49 (1986), 45–52.

69. R. L. Dicker and V. R. Syracuse, *Consultation with a Plastic Surgeon* (Chicago: Nelson-Hall, 1976), 1.

70. N. J. Knorr, M. T. Edgerton, and J. E. Hoopes, "The 'Insatiable' Cosmetic Surgery Patient," *Plastic and Reconstructive Surgery* 40 (1967), 285.

71. M. T. Edgerton and N. J. Knorr, "Motivational Patterns of Patients Seeking Cosmetic (Esthetic) Surgery," *Plastic and Reconstructive Surgery* 48 (1971), 553–554.

72. D. G. Leathers, *Nonverbal Communication Systems* (Boston: Allyn and Bacon, 1976), 107.

73. Leathers, *Nonverbal Communication Systems,* 107.

74. M. T. Edgerton, W. E. Jacobson, and E. Meyer, "Surgical-Psychiatric Study of Transsexual Patients Seeking Plastic (Cosmetic) Surgery: Ninety-Eight Consecutive Patients with Minimal Deformity," *British Journal of Plastic*

Surgery 13 (1960), 144; and A. C. Hamburger, "Beauty Quest," *Psychology Today* 22 (1988), 29–32.

75. E. Goffman, *Stigma: Notes on the Management of Spoiled Identity* (Englewood Cliffs, NJ: Prentice-Hall, 1963).

76. Goffman, *Stigma*, 8, 20, 44, and 73.

77. M. E. Worthington, "Personal Space as a Function of the Stigma Effect," *Environment and Behavior* 8 (1974), 289–294.

78. B. A. Barrios, L. C. Corbitt, J. P. Estes, and J. S. Topping, "Effect of a Social Stigma on Interpersonal Distance," *Psychological Record* 26 (1976), 343–348; and M. Young, M. M. Henderson, and D. Marx, "Attitudes of Nursing Students Toward Patients with AIDS," *Psychological Reports* 67 (1990), 491–497.

79. Worthington, "Personal Space as a Function"; S. Kanekar, D. Mayundar, and M. B. Kolsawalla, "Perception of an Aggressor and His Victim as a Function of Physical Attractiveness and Retaliation," *Journal of Social Psychology* 113 (1981), 289–290; and L. Wispe and J. Kiecolt, "Victim Attractiveness and Nonhelping," *Journal of Social Psychology* 112 (1980), 67–74.

80. S. R. Deitz and L. E. Byrnes, "Attribution of Responsibility for Sexual Assault: The Influence of Observer Empathy and Defendent Occupation and Attractiveness," *Journal of Psychology* 108 (1981), 17–30.

81. S. Kanekar and M. B. Kilsawalla, "Responsibility of a Rape Victim in Relation to Her Respectability, Attractiveness, and Provocativeness," *Journal of Social Psychology* 112 (1980), 153–154.

82. J. E. Hocking, B. A. Walker, and E. L. Fink, "Physical Attractiveness and Judgements of Morality Following an 'Immoral' Act," *Psychological Report* 48 (1982), 111–116.

83. Stacks, "When Reward Fails."

84. K. Peterson and J. C. Curran, "Trait Attribution as a Function of Hair Length and Correlates of Subject Preferences for Hair Style," *Journal of Psychology* 93 (1976), 331–339.

85. *Placement Manual* (Gainesville, Florida: University of Florida, Fall 1976), 22–23.

86. Burgoon and Saine, *The Unspoken Dialogue*, 155.

87. J. T. Molloy, *The Woman's Dress for Success Book* (New York: Warner Books, 1978).

88. D. G. Freedman, "The Survival Value of the Beard," *Psychology Today* 3 (1969), 36–39; and W. E. Addison, "Beardedness as a Factor in Perceived Masculinity," *Perceptual and Motor Skills* 68 (1989), 921–922.

89. R. J. Pelligrini, "Impressions of a Male Personality as a Function of Beardedness," *Psychology* 10 (1973), 29–33.

90. W. Thourlby, *You Are What You Wear* (New York: New American Library, 1978), 143–151.

91. Burgoon and Saine, *The Unspoken Dialogue,* 77.

92. Knapp, *Nonverbal Communication* 174.

93. W. McKeachie, "Lipstick as a Determiner of First Impressions on Personality: An Experiment for the General Psychology Course," *Journal of Social Psychology* 36 (1952), 241–244.

94. Knapp, *Nonverbal Communication* 174.

95. P. N. Hamid, "Some Effects of Dress Cues on Observational Accuracy, A Perceptual Estimate, and Impression Formation," *Journal of Social Psychology* 86 (1972), 279–289.

96. M. Hickson III, L. Powell, and M. L. Sandoz, "The Effects of Eye Color on Credibility, Attraction, and Homophyly," *Communication Research Reports* 4 (1987), 20–23.

97. Molloy, *The Woman's Dress for Success Book,* 85–86.

98. E. Mathes and S. B. Kempher, "Clothing as a Nonverbal Communicator of Sexual Attitudes and Behavior," *Perceptual and Motor Skills* 43 (1976), 495–498.

99. J. Fowles, "Why We Wear Clothes," *ETC.: A Review of General Semantics* 21, (1974), 343; and J. C. Flugel, *The Psychology of Clothes* (London: Hogarth Press, 1950).

100. H. Freed, "Nudity and Nakedness," *Sexual Behavior* 3 (1973), 3–5.

101. J. Schwartz, "Men's Clothing and the Negro," *Phylon* 24 (1963), 224–231.

102. J. Kelly, "Dress as Non-Verbal Communication," paper presented at the Annual Conference of the American Association for Public Opinion Research, 1969.

103. W. Thourlby, *You Are What You Wear.*

104. N. Gittelson, ''What Your Clothes Say About You,'' *McCalls* 102 (1975), 23.

105. J. H. Fortenberry, J. Maclean, P. Morris, and M. O'Connell, ''Mode of Dress as a Perceptual Cue to Deference,'' *The Journal of Social Psychology* 104 (1978).

106. Hensley, ''The Effect of Attire.''

107. M. Walker, S. Harriman, and S. Costello, ''The Influence of Appearance on Compliance with a Request,'' *Journal of Social Psychology* 112 (1980), 159–160.

108. L. R. Aiken, ''The Relationship of Dress to Selected Measures of Personality in Undergraduate Women,'' *Journal of Social Psychology* 59 (1963), 119–128.

109. M. L. Rosencrantz, ''Clothing Symbolism,'' *Journal of Home Economics* 54 (1962), 18–22.

110. T. F. Hoult, ''Experimental Measurement of Clothing as a Factor in Some Social Ratings of Selected American Men,'' *American Sociological Review* 19 (1954), 326–327.

111. L. Bickman, ''Social Roles and Uniforms: Clothes Make the Person,'' *Psychology Today* 7 (1974), 48–51.

112. M. Lefkowitz, R. R. Blake, and J. S. Mouton, ''Status of Actors in Pedestrian Violation of Traffic Signals,'' *Journal of Abnormal and Social Psychology* 51 (1955), 704–706.

113. B. M. Huddleston and J. H. Huddleston, ''An Experimental Test of Perceptions Regarding Credibility of Judicial Decisions: The Cult of the Robe,'' in Proceedings: *Current Trends in Nonverbal Communication: A Multidisciplinary Approach,* (Arkansas State University, Jonesboro, AR, 1986), 72–87.

114. J. T. Molloy, *The New Dress for Success Book* (New York: Warner Books, 1988); J. T. Molloy, *Dress for Success* (New York: Warner, 1975); and V. P. Richmond, J. C. McCroskey, and S. K. Payne, *Nonverbal Behavior in Interpersonal Relations,* 2d ed. (Englewood Cliffs, NJ: Prentice-Hall, 1991).

115. Molloy, *The Woman's Dress for Success Book.*

116. K. W. Watson and L. R. Smeltzer, ''Perceptions of Nonverbal Communication During the Selection Interview,'' *The ABCA Bulletin* (1982), 30–34.

117. M. R. Solomon, ''Dress for Effect,'' *Psychology Today* 19 (1986), 20–22, 26–28.

118. Knapp, *Nonverbal Communication* 180.

119. Molloy, *The Woman's Dress for Success Book,* 91.

120. P. N. Hamid, ''Style of Dress as a Perceptual Cue in Impression Formation,'' *Perceptual and Motor Skills* 26 (1968) 904–906.

121. P. N. Hamid, ''Some Effects of Dress Cues on Observational Accuracy.''

122. K. Beattie et al., ''Eyeglasses as Nonverbal Credibility Indicators,'' unpublished manuscript, Mississippi State University, 1975.

123. R. Levy and A. P. Poll, ''Through a Glass, Darkly,'' *Dun's Review* (1976), 77–78.

124. Molloy, *The New Dress for Success Book,* 199–200.

125. Molloy, *The Woman's Dress for Success Book,* 89.

126. M. Hickson III, L. Powell, S. R. Hill, Jr., G. B. Holt, and H. Flick, ''Smoking Artifacts as Indicators of Homophily, Attraction, and Credibility,'' *Southern Speech Communication Journal* 44 (1979), 191–200.

Chapter Seven

1. R. L. Birdwhistell, *Kinesics and Context: Essays on Body Motion Communication* (Philadelphia: University of Pennsylvania Press, 1970); R. L. Birdwhistell, ''Kinesics and Communication,'' in *Explorations in Communication: An Anthology,* ed. E. Carpenter and M. McLuhan (Boston: Beacon Press, 1960), 54–64; R. L. Birdwhistell, ''Some Body Motion Elements Accompanying Spoken American English,'' in *Communication: Concepts and Perspectives,* ed. L. Thayer (Washington: Spartan, 1967), 53–76; and R. L. Birdwhistell, ''The Language of the Body: The Natural Environment of Words,'' in *Human Communication: Theoretical Explorations,* ed. A. Silverstein (New York: John Wiley and Sons, 1974), 203–220.

2. Birdwhistell, *Kinesics and Context.*

3. Birdwhistell, *Kinesics and Context.*

4. K. R. Johnson, ''Black Kinesics: Some Non-verbal Communication Patterns in the Black Culture,'' in *Intercultural Communication: A Reader,* ed. L. A. Samovar and R. E. Porter (Belmont, CA: Wadsworth, 1972), 181–189.

5. Johnson, "Black Kinesics," 185.
6. D. Morris, P. Collett, P. Marsh, and M. O'Shaughnessy, *Gestures: Their Origins and Distribution* (New York: Stein and Day, 1979). See also R. Shuter, "A Field Study of Nonverbal Communication in Germany, Italy, and the United States," *Communication Monographs* 44 (1977), 298–305.
7. Birdwhistell, *Kinesics and Context,* 81.
8. Birdwhistell, *Kinesics and Context,* 78.
9. Birdwhistell, *Kinesics and Context,* 81.
10. R. G. Barker, "The Social Interrelatedness of Strangers and Acquaintances," *Sociometry* 5 (1942), 176–179
11. D. Morris, *Manwatching: A Field Guide to Human Behavior* (New York: Henry N. Abrams, 1977), 10–23.
12. Morris, *Manwatching,* 11.
13. Morris, *Manwatching,* 13.
14. Morris, *Manwatching,* 17.
15. Morris, *Manwatching,* 18.
16. E. T. Hall, *Beyond Culture* (Garden City, NY: Anchor, 1976), 76.
17. Morris, *Manwatching,* 21–23.
18. A. Meharabian, *Silent Messages: Implicit Communication of Emotions and Attitudes,* (Belmont, CA: Wadsworth, 1981), 5–8; and A. Meharabian, *Nonverbal Communication.* (Chicago: Aldine-Atherton, 1972).
19. M. L. Knapp, *Nonverbal Communication in Human Interaction,* 2d ed. (New York: Holt, Rinehart, and Winston, 1978), 221.
20. N. M. Henley, *Body Politics: Power, Sex, and Nonverbal Communication* (Englewood Cliffs, NJ: Prentice-Hall, 1972).
21. E. G. Goffman, "Gender Advertisement," *Studies in Anthropology of Visual Communication* 3 (1976), 65–154.
22. M. Argyle and M. Williams, "Observer or Observee? A Reversible Perspective in Person Perception," *Sociometry* 39 (1976), 170–173.
23. V. P. Richmond, J. C. McCroskey, and S. K. Payne, *Nonverbal Behavior in Interpersonal Relations,* 2d ed. (Englewood Cliffs, NJ: Prentice-Hall, 1991), pp. 204–228.
24. R. G. Powell and B. Harville, "The Effects of Teacher Immediacy and Clarity on Instructional Outcomes: An Intercultural Assessment," *Communication Education* 39 (1990), 369–379; and J. A. Sanders and R. L. Wiseman, "The Effects of Verbal and Nonverbal Teacher Immediacy on Perceived Cognitive, Affective, and Behavioral Learning in the Multicultural Classroom, *Communication Education* 39 (1990), 341–353.
25. P. Kearney, T. G. Plax, V. R. Smith, and G. Sorensen, "Effects of Teacher Immediacy and Strategy on College Student Resistance to On-Task Demands," *Communication Education* 37 (1988), 54–67.
26. J. K. Burgoon and D. A. Newton, "Applying a Social Meaning Model to Relational Message Interpretations of Conversational Involvement: Comparing Observer and Participant Perspectives," *Southern Communication Journal* 56 (1991), 96–113; and B. A. Le Poire, "Orientation and Defensive Reactions as Alternatives to Arousal in Theories of Nonverbal Reactions to Changes in Immediacy," *Southern Communication Journal* 56 (1991), 138–146.
27. J. Ruesch and W. Kees, *Nonverbal Communication: Notes on the Visual Perception of Human Relations* (Berkeley, CA: University of California Press, 1956), 189.
28. P. Ekman and W. V. Friesen, "The Repertoire of Nonverbal Behavior: Categories, Origins, Usage, and Codings," *Semiotica* 1 (1969), 49–98.
29. P. Ekman, "Movements and Precise Meanings," *Journal of Communication* 26 (1976), 14–26.
30. Morris et al., *Gestures,* 79–160.
31. A. A. Cohen, "The Communicative Functions of Hand Gestures," *Journal of Communication* 27 (1977), 54–63.
32. A. Kendon and A. Ferber, "A Description of Some Human Greetings," in *Comparative Ecology and Behavior of Primates,* ed. R. P. Michael and J. H. Crook (London: Academic Press, 1973).
33. S. Duncan, "Some Signals and Rules for Taking Speaking Turns in Conversations," *Journal of Personality and Social Psychology* 23 (1972), 283–292; S. Duncan, "Interaction Units During Speaking Turns in Face-to-Face Conversations," in *Organization of Behavior in Face-to-Face Interaction,* ed. A. Kenden, R. Harns, and M. Key (The Hague: Mouton, 1975); S. Duncan, "Speaking Terms: Studies of Structure and Individual Differences," in *Nonverbal Interaction,* ed. J. M. Wiemann and R. P. Harrison (Beverly Hills, CA: Sage Publication, 1983).

34. J. M. Weimann and M. L. Knapp, "Turn-Taking in Conversations," *Journal of Communication* 25 (1975), 75–92.

35. Weimann and Knapp, "Turn-Taking in Conversation."

36. Duncan, "Some Signals and Rules," 283–292.

37. J. K. Burgoon and T. J. Saine, *The Unspoken Dialogue: An Introduction to Nonverbal Communication* (Boston: Houghton Mifflin 1978), 232.

38. P. Ekman and W. V. Friesen, "Constants Across Cultures in the Face and Emotion," *Journal of Personality and Social Psychology* 17 (1971), 124–129; P. Ekman, K. A. Brattesani, M. O'Sullivan, and W. V. Friesen, "Does Image Size Affect Judgments of the Face?" *Journal of Nonverbal Behavior* 4 (1979), 57–71; P. Ekman and H. Oster, "Facial Expression of Emotion," *Annual Review of Psychology* 30 (1979), 527–554; H. Oster and P. Ekman, "Facial Behavior in Child Development," in *Minnesota Symposia on Child Psychology,* vol 11, ed. W. A. Collins (Hillsdale, NJ: Lawrence Erlbaum, 1978); 231–276; P. Ekman, "Facial Signs: Facts, Fantasies, and Possibilities," in *Sight, Sound and Sense,* ed. T. Sebeok (Bloomington: Indiana University Press, 1978), 124–156; P. Ekman, "Biological and Cultural Contributions to Body and Facial Movement," in *The Anthropology of the Body,* ed. J. Blacking (London: Academic Press, 1977), 29–84; J. C. Hager and P. Ekman, "Long-Distance Transmission of Facial Affect Signals," *Ethology and Sociobiology* 1 (1979), 77–82; P. Ekman, "Assymetry in Facial Expression," *Science* 209 (1980), 833–834; J. C. Hager and P. Ekman, "Methodological Problems in Tourangeau and Ellsworth's Study of Facial Expression and Experience of Emotion," *Journal of Personality and Social Psychology* 40 (1981), 358–362; P. Ekman, G. Roper, and J. C. Hager, "Deliberate Facial Movement," *Child Development* 51 (1980), 886–891; P. Ekman, W. V. Friesen, and S. Ancoli, "Facial Signs of Emotional Experience," *Journal of Personality and Social Psychology* 39 (1980), 1125–1134; P. Ekman, J. C. Hager, and W. V. Friesen, "The Symmetry of Emotional and Deliberate Facial Actions,"

Psychophysiology 18 (1981), 101–106; P. Ekman, "Face Muscles Talk Every Language," *Psychology Today* 9 (1975), 35–39; P. Ekman, W. V. Friesen, M. O'Sullivan, and K. Scherer, "Relative Importance of Face, Body and Speech in Judgments of Personality and Space," *Journal of Personality and Social Psychology* 38 (1980), 270–277; and J. McDermott, "Face to Face, It's the Expression That Bears the Message," *Smithsonian* 12 1986, 113–116, 118, 120, 122–123.

39. P. Ekman and W. V. Friesen, *Unmasking the Face: A Guide to Recognizing Emotion for Facial Clues* (Englewood Cliffs, NJ: Prentice-Hall, 1975).

40. D. G. Leathers and T. H. Emigh, "Decoding Facial Expressions: A New Test with Decoding Norms," *The Quarterly Journal of Speech* 66 (1980), 418–436.

41. Ekman and Friesen, *Unmasking the Face.*

42. J. D. Boucher and P. Ekman, "Facial Areas and Emotional Information," *Journal of Communication* 25 (1975), 22.

43. Ekman and Friesen, *Unmasking the Face,* 63, 47.

44. Boucher and Ekman, "Facial Areas and Emotional Information," 22; and Ekman and Friesen, *Unmasking the Face,* 78–80, 97.

45. Ekman and Friesen, *Unmasking the Face,* 34–36.

46. Ekman and Friesen, *Unmasking the Face,* 66–67.

47. Ekman and Friesen, *Unmasking the Face,* 126.

48. Ekman and Friesen, *Unmasking the Face,* 112.

49. R. P. Harrison, *Beyond Words: An Introduction to Nonverbal Communication* (Englewood Cliffs, NJ: Prentice Hall, 1974), 120; R. P. Harrison, "Nonverbal Communication," in *Handbook of Communication,* ed. I. de Sola Pool, F. W. Frey, W. Schramm, N. MacCroby, and E. B. Parker (Chicago: Rand McNally, 1973), 93–115; R. P. Harrison, "The Face in Face-to-Face Interaction," in *Explorations in Interpersonal Communication,* ed. G. R. Miller (Beverly Hills, CA: Sage Publications, 1976), 217–235; and R. P. Harrison, "Nonverbal Behavior: An

Approach to Human Communication,'' in *Approaches to Human Communication,* ed. R. W. Budd and B. D. Ruben (New York: Spartan, 1972), 253–268.

50. P. Ekman and W. V. Friesen, ''A New Pan-Cultural Facial Expression of Emotion,'' *Motivation and Emotion* 10 (1986), 159–168.

51. P. Ekman and W. V. Friesen, ''Is the Startle Reaction an Emotion?'' *Journal of Personality and Social Psychology* 49 (1985), 1416–1426.

52. P. Ekman, ''Facial Expression and Nerve Name Surgery,'' *Disorders of the Facial Nerve* (New York: Raven Press, 1982), 363–368.

53. M. Biaggio, ''Sex Differences in Behavioral Reactions to Provocation of Anger,'' *Psychological Reports* 64 (1989), 23–26; J. S. Tucker and R. E. Riggio, ''The Role of Social Skills in Encoding Posed and Spontaneous Facial Expressions,'' *Journal of Nonverbal Behavior* 12 (1988), 87–97; R. M. Akert and A. T. Panter, ''Extraversion and the Ability to Decode Nonverbal Communication, *Personality and Individual Differences* 9 (1988), 965–972. Women's superior encoding and decoding was supported by N. G. Rotter and G. S. Rotter, ''Sex Differences in the Encoding and Decoding of Negative Facial Emotions,'' *Journal of Nonverbal Behavior* 12 (1988), 139–148.

54. T. Hill, P. Lewicki, M. Czyzewska, and G. Schuller, ''The Role of Learned Intentional Encoding Rules in the Perception of Faces: Effects of Nonconscious Self-Perpetuation of a Bias,'' *Journal of Experimental Social Psychology* 26 (1990), 350–371.

55. A. Makaremi, ''Anger Reactions of Iranian Adolescents.'' *Psychological Reports* 67 (1990), 259–262; D. Matsumoto, ''Cultural Influences on Facial Expressions of Emotion,'' *Southern Communication Journal* 56 (1991), 128–137; D. Matsumoto, ''Face, Culture, and Judgements of Anger and Fear: Do the Eyes Have It?'' *Journal of Nonverbal Behavior* 13 (1989), 171–188; S. Sogon and M. Matsutani, ''Identification of Emotion From Body Movements: A Cross-Cultural Study of Americans and Japanese,'' *Psychological Reports* 65 (1989), 35–46; M. A. Hoots and F. T. McAndrew, ''Decoding of Gestures by Kindergarten, First-, and Third-Grade

Children,'' *Journal of Genetic Psychology* 150 (1988), 117–118; C. Saarni, ''Children's Understanding of the Interpersonal Consequences of Dissemblance of Nonverbal Emotional-Expressive Behavior,'' *Journal of Nonverbal Behavior* 12 (1988), 275–293; and E. Z. Tronick, ''Emotions and Emotional Communication in Infants,'' *American Psychologist* 44 (1989), 112–119.

56. P. J. Lang, M. M. Bradley, and B. N. Cuthbert, ''Emotion, Attention, and the Startle Reflex,'' *Psychological Review* 97 (1990), 377–395; M. Margalit, ''Ethnic Differences in Expressions of Shame Feeling by Mothers of Severely Handicapped Children,'' paper presented at the Annual Congress of the Israel Psychological Association, Jerusalem, 1977; W. F. Sharkey and L. Stafford, ''Responses to Embarrassment,'' *Human Communication Research* 17 (1990), 315–342; and S. A. Shields, M. E. Mallory, and A. Simon, ''The Experience and Symptoms of Blushing,'' *Journal of Nonverbal Behavior* 14 (1990), 171–186.

57. A. Orthony and T. J. Turner, ''What's Basic About Basic Emotions?'' *Psychological Review* 97 (1990), 315–331.

58. C. L. Ridgeway, J. Berger, and L. Smith, ''Nonverbal Cues and Status: An Expectation States Approach,'' *American Journal of Sociology* 90 (1985), 995–978.

59. N. M. Henley, *Body Politics.*

60. Mehrabian, *Nonverbal Communication.*

61. M. H. Bond and D. Shiraishi, ''The Effect of Body Lean and Status of an Interviewer on the Non-Verbal Behavior of Japanese Interviewers,'' *International Journal of Psychology* 9 (1974), 117–128.

62. A. Mehrabian and M. Williams, ''Nonverbal Concomitants of Perceived and Intended Persuasiveness,'' *Journal of Personality and Social Psychology* 13 (1969), 37–58; G. Breed and M. Porter, ''Eye Contact, Attitudes and Attitude Change Among Males,'' *Journal of Genetic Psychology* 120–122 (1972), 211–217; M. B. LaCrosse, ''Nonverbal Behavior and Perceived Counselor Attractiveness and Persuasiveness,'' *Journal of Counseling Psychology* 22 (1975), 563–566; H. McGinley, R. LeFevre, and P. McGinley, ''The Influence of a Communicator's Body

Position on Opinion Change in Others,'' *Journal of Personality and Social Psychology* 31 (1975), 686–690; H. S. Friedman and R. E. Riggo, ''Effect of Individual Differences in Nonverbal Expressiveness a Transmission of Emotion,'' *Journal of Nonverbal Behavior* 6 (1981), 96–104.

63. R. Ho and S. Mitchell, ''Students' Nonverbal Reaction to Tutor's Warm/Cold Nonverbal Behavior,'' *Journal of Social Psychology* 114 (1982), 121–130; C. Kleinke, ''Interaction Between Gaze and Legitimacy of Request on Compliance in a Field Setting,'' *Journal of Nonverbal Behavior* 5 (1980), 3–12.

64. B. Schwartz, A. Tesser, and E. Powell, ''Dominance Cues in Nonverbal Behavior,'' *Social Psychology Quarterly* 45 (1982), 114–120.

65. K. Cooper, *Nonverbal Communication for Business Success* (New York: AMACOMM, 1979).

66. V. Hadar, F. Steiner, and F. C. Rose, ''Head Movements During Listening Turns in Conversation,'' *Journal of Nonverbal Behavior* 9 (1985), 214–221.

67. A. E. Scheflen, ''Quasi-Courtship Behavior in Psychotherapy,'' *Psychiatry* 28 (1965), 245–257.

68. Scheflen, ''Quasi-Courtship,'' 255.

69. D. S. Berry and L. Z. McArthur, ''Perceiving Character in Faces: The Impact of Age-Related Craniofacial Changes on Social Pereption,'' *Psychological Bulletin* 100 (1986), 3–18.

70. R. M. Sabatilli and M. Rubin, ''Nonverbal Expressiveness as Mediators of Interpersonal Perceptions,'' *Journal of Nonverbal Behavior* 10 (1986), 120–133.

71. S. Goldberg and R. Rosenthal, ''Self-Touching Behavior in the Job Interview: Antecedents and Consequences,'' *Journal of Nonverbal Behavior* 10 (1986), 65–80.

72. S. Friedman and A. Mehrabian, ''An Analysis of Fidgeting and Associated Individual Differences,'' *Journal of Personality* 84 (1986), 406–429.

73. P. Ekman ''Would a Child Lie?'' *Psychology Today* 23 (1989), 62–65.

74. D. D. Winter, C. Widell, G. Truitt, and J. George-Falvy, ''Empirical Studies of Posture-Gesture Mergers,'' *Journal of Nonverbal Behavior* 13 (1989), 207–223.

75. J. O. Greene, H. D. O'Hair, M. J. Cody, and C. Yen, ''Planning and Control of Behavior During Deception,'' *Human Communication Research* 11 (1985), 335–364.

76. M. Zucherman, R. Driver, and N. S. Guadango, ''Effects of Segmentation Patterns on the Perception of Deception,'' *Journal of Nonverbal Behavior* 9 (1985), 160–168.

77. D. O'Hair, M. J. Cody, and R. R. Behnke, ''Communication Apprehension and Vocal Stress as Indices of Deception,'' *Western Journal of Speech Communication* 49 (1985), 286–300. See also J. B. Stiff and G. R. Miller, ''Come to Think of It . . . Interrogative Probes, Deceptive Communication, and Deception Detection,'' *Human Communication Research* 12 (1986), 339–357.

78. M. A. deTurck and G. R. Miller, ''Deception and Arousal: Isolating the Behavioral Correlates of Deception,'' *Human Communication Research* 12 (1985), 181–201; and D. G. Leathers, *Successful Nonverbal Communication: Principles and Applications* (New York: Macmillan, 1986), 171–181. See also M. L. Knapp and M. E. Comadena, ''Telling It Like It Isn't: A Review of Theory and Research on Deceptive Communications,'' *Human Communication Research* 5 (1979), 270–285; and A. A. Harrison, M. Hwalek, D. F. Raney, and J. G. Fritz, ''Cues to Deception in the Interview Situation,'' *Social Psychology* 41 (1978), 156–161.

79. P. Ekman, *Telling Lies: Clues to Deceit in the Marketplace, Politics, and Marriage* (New York: Norton, 1985).

80. C. F. Bond, Jr., A. Omar, A. Mahmoud, and R. N. Bonser, ''Lie Detection Across Cultures,'' *Journal of Nonverbal Behavior* 14 (1990), 189–203; D. B. Buller, J. Comstock, R. K. Aune, and K. D. Strzyzewski, ''The Effect of Probing on Deceivers and Truthtellers,'' *Journal of Nonverbal Behavior* 13 (1989), 155–170; D. B. Buller and R. K. Aune, ''Nonverbal Cues to Deception Among Intimates, Friends, and Strangers,'' *Journal of Nonverbal Behavior* 11 (1987), 269–289; K. Hurd and P. Noller, ''Decoding Deception: A Look at the Process,'' *Journal of Nonverbal Behavior* 12 (1988), 217–232; G. E. Littlepage, J. Maddox, and M. A.

Pineault, "Recognition of Descrepant Nonverbal Messages and Detection of Deception," *Perceptual and Motor Skills* 60 (1985), 119–124; M. O'Sullivan, P. Ekman, and W. V. Friesen, "The Effect of Comparisons on Detecting Deception," *Journal of Nonverbal Behavior* 12 (1988), 203–213; J. B. Stiff, G. R. Miller, C. Sleight, P. Mongeau, R. Garlick, and R. Rogan, "Explanations for Visual Cue Primacy in Judgements of Honesty," *Journal of Personality and Social Psychology* 56 (1989), 555–564; and J. B. Stiff, J. L. Hole, R. Garlick and R. G. Rogan, "Effect of Cue Congruence and Social Normative Influences on Individual Judgements of Honesty and Deceit," *Southern Communication Journal* 55 (1990), 206–229.

81. A. Mehrabian, "Nonverbal Betrayal of Feeling," *Journal of Experimental Research in Personality* 5 (1971), 64–73.

82. B. M. DePaulo, M. Zuckerman, and R. Rosenthal, "Detecting Deception: Modality Effects," in *Review of Personality and Social Psychology* (vol. 1), ed. L. Wheeler (Beverly Hills, CA: Sage Publications, 1980); L. A. Streeter, R. M. Krauss, V. Geller, C. Olsen, and W. Apple, "Pitch Changes During Attempted Deception," *Journal of Personality and Social Psychology* 35 (1977), 345–350.

83. J. B. Stiff and G. R. Miller, "Come to Think of It . . . Interrogative Probes, Deceptive Communication and Deception Detection," *Human Communication Research* 12 (1986), 339–357.

84. M. A. deTurck and G. R. Miller, 181–201.

85. J. O. Greene, H. D. O'Hair, M. C. Cody, and C. Yen, 335–364.

86. D. O'Hair, M. J. Cody, and R. B. Behnke, 286–300.

87. See Stiff and Miller, "Come to Think of It . . ."; and J. E. Hocking, "Detecting Deceptive Communication from Verbal, Visual, and Paralinguistic Cues: An Exploratory Experiment," Ph.D. Diss., Michigan State University, 1976; J. E. Hocking, J. E. Bauchner, G. R. Miller, and E. P. Kaminski, "Detecting Deceptive Communication from Verbal, Visual, and Paralinguistic Cues," *Human Communication Research* 6 (1979), 33–46; M. Knapp, R. Hart, and H. Dennis, "An Exploration of Deception as a Communication Construct," *Human Communication Research* 1 (1974), 15–29; J. E. Bauchner, E. A. Kaplan, and G. R. Miller, "Detecting Deception: The Relationship of Available Information to Judgmental Accuracy in Initial Encounters," *Human Communication Research* 6 (1980), 253–264.

88. K. R. Johnson, "Black Kinesics," 181–189.

89. G. Michael and F. N. Willis, Jr., "The Development of Gestures as a Function of Social Class, Education, and Sex," *Psychological Record* 18 (1968), 515–519.

90. H. A. Bosmajian, *The Rhetoric of Nonverbal Communication: Readings* (Glenview, IL: Scott, Foresman and Co., 1971).

91. "Culturegram: Kingdom of Saudi Arabia," *Culturegram,* (Provo, UT: Brigham Young University, 1982); "Culturegram: The Commonwealth of Puerto Rico," *Culturegram* (Provo, UT: Brigham Young University, 1981); "Culturegram: China (People's Republic)," *Culturegram,* (Provo, UT: Brigham Young University, 1981); "Culturegram: Italy," *Culturegram,* (Provo, UT: Brigham Young University, 1981).

92. "Culturegram: Western Canada and Ontario," *Culturegram,* (Provo, UT: Brigham Young University, 1981).

93. L. W. Richardson, *The Dynamics of Sex and Gender* (Boston; Houghton Mifflin, 1981), 26.

94. Richardson, *The Dynamics of Sex,* 174–177.

95. Birdwhistell, *Kinesics and Context,* 45.

96. Henley, *Body Politics,* 138.

97. M. Argyle, M. Lalljee, and M. Cook, "The Effects of Visibility on Interaction in a Dyad," *Human Relations* 21 (1968), 3–17; P. C. Ellsworth and L. M. Ludwig, "Visual Behavior in Social Interaction," *Journal of Communication* 22 (1972), 375–403; R. Exline, "Exploration in the Process of Person Perception: Visual Interaction in Relation to Competition, Sex, and the Need for Affiliation," *Journal of Personality* 31 (1963), 1–20.

98. G. Kirouac and F. Y. Dore, "Acuracy of the Judgment of Facial Expression of Emotions as a Function of Sex and Level of Education," *Journal of Nonverbal Behavior* 9 (1985), 3–7; R. F. Stanners, D. M. Byrd, and R. Gabriel, "The Time It Takes to Identify Facial Expressions: Effects of Age,

Gender of Subject, Sex of Sender, and Type of Expression," *Journal of Nonverbal Behavior* 9 (1985), 201–211; V. Callan and C. Gallios, "Decoding Emotional Messages: Influences of Ethnicity, Sex, Message Type, and Channel," *Journal of Personality and Social Psychology* 51 (1986), 755–762; S. Palchoudhury and M. K. Mandal, "Perceptual Skills in Decoding Facial Affect," *Perceptual and Motor Skills* 60 (1985), 96–98; and J. A. Hall, *Nonverbal Sex Differences: Communication Accuracy and Expressive Style* (Baltimore: Johns Hopkins University Press, 1984).

99. B. B. Bhattacharya and M. K. Mandal, "Recognition of Facial Affect in Depression," *Perceptual and Motor Skills* 61 (1985), 13–14.

100. A. Weisel, "Deafness and Perception of Nonverbal Expression of Emotion," *Perceptual and Motor Skills* 61 (1985), 515–523.

101. A. Halberstadt, "Family Socialization of Emotional Expression and Nonverbal Communication Styles and Skills," *Journal of Personality and Social Psychology* 51 (1986), 827–836; See also P. Bull and E. Connelly, "Body Movement and Emphasis in Speech," *Journal of Nonverbal Behavior* 9 (1985), 169–187.

102. Exline, "Exploration in the Process of Person Perception," 11.

103. Henley, *Body Politics,* 151.

104. Henley, *Body Politics,* 152.

105. D. W. Stacks and F. W. Stacks, "Getting on Board for the CME," *Tri-Lakes Division News U.S.C.G. Auxillary* 3 (1982), 5–7.

106. Duncan, "Some Signals."

107. Henley, *Body Politics,* 159.

108. S. A. Beebe, "Eye Contact: A Nonverbal Determinant of Speaker Credibility," *Speech Teacher* 23 (1974), 21–25.

109. P. C. Ellsworth and J. M. Carlsmith, "Effect of Eye Contact and Verbal Content on Affective Response to a Dyadic Interaction," *Journal of Personality and Social Psychology* 10 (1968), 15–24.

110. A. Abele, "Functions of Gaze in Social Interaction: Communicating and Monitoring," *Journal of Nonverbal Behavior* 10 (1986), 83–101.

111. C. L. Kleinke, "Gaze and Eye Contact: A Research Review," *Psychological Bulletin* 100 (1986), 78–100.

112. J. K. Burgoon, V. Manusov, P. Mineo, and J. L. Hale, "Effects of Gaze on Hiring, Credibility, Attraction and Relational Message Interpretation," *Journal of Nonverbal Behavior* 9 (1985), 133–146.

113. J. K. Burgoon, D. A. Coker, and R. A. Coker, "Communicative Effects of Gaze Behavior: A Test of Two Contrasting Explanations," *Human Communication Research* 12 (1986), 495–524.

114. A. Mulac, L. B. Studley, J. M. Wiemann, and J. J. Bradac, "Male/Female Gaze in Same-Sex and Mixed-Sex Dyads," *Human Communication Research* 13 (1987), 323–343.

115. A. S. King. "The Eye in Advertising," *Journal of Applied Communications Research* 1 (1973), 1–12; and M. P. Wilbur and J. Roberts-Wilbur, "Lateral Eye-Movement Responses to Visual Stimuli," *Perceptual and Motor Skills* 61 (1985), 167–177.

116. J. Korn, *The Studio* (New York: Time-Life Books, 1971), 130.

117. E. H. Hess, telephone conversation with the authors, February 13, 1985, as published in *Experimetelle unt Angewandte Psychologie* 26 (1979), 436–447.

118. B. Ambler, "Information Reduction, Internal Transformation, and Task Difficulty," *Bulletin of Psychonomic Science* 10 (1977), 43–46.

119. I. Heilville, "Deception and Pupil Size," *Journal of Clinical Psychology* 32 (1976), 675–676.

120. M. Hickson III and S. R. Hill, Jr., *The Progress of Communication* (Mississippi State University, MS: Communication Applications, 1980), 14.

121. W. Weiten and C. Etaugh, "Lateral Movement as a Function of Cognitive Mode, Question Sequence, and Sex of Subject," *Perceptual and Motor Skills* 38 (1974), 439–444.

122. R. Gur and R. Gur, "Defense Mechanisms, Psychosomatic Symptomatology and Conjugate Lateral Eye Movements," *Journal of Consulting and Clinical Psychology* 43 (1975), 416–420.

Chapter Eight

1. See R. L. Birdwhistell, *Kinesics and Context: Essays on Body Motion Communication* (Philadelphia: University of Pennsylvania Press, 1970).
2. J. K. Burgoon and T. J. Saine, *The Unspoken Dialogue: An Introduction to Nonverbal Communication* (Boston: Houghton-Mifflin, 1978), 80–81.
3. R. G. Harper, A. N. Wiens, and J. D. Matarazzo, *Nonverbal Communication: The State of the Art* (New York: John Wiley Interscience, 1976), 22–23.
4. G. L. Trager, "Paralanguage: A First Approximation," *Studies in Linguistics* 2 (1958), 1–10.
5. Harper, Wiens, and Matarazzo, *Nonverbal Communication,* 21.
6. Hans-Peter Krueger, "Nonverbal Characteristics of Verbal Behavior: A Biological Approach to Personality and Syntality," *Proceedings: Conference on Current Trends in Nonverbal Communication: A Multidisciplinary Approach* Jonesboro, AR: Arkansas State University, (1986), 121–168.
7. Krueger, "Nonverbal Characteristics of Normal Behavior," 8.
8. P. Heinberg, *Voice Training for Speaking and Reading Aloud* (New York: The Ronald Press Company, 1964).
9. L. A. Malandro, L. L. Barker, and D. Barker, *Nonverbal Communication* 2d ed. (Reading, MA: Addison-Wesley, 1989).
10. D. W. Addington, "The Relationship of Selected Vocal Characteristics to Personality Perception," *Speech Monographs* 35 (1968), 492–503.
11. See C. Kramer, "Perceptions of Female and Male Speech," *Language and Speech* 20 (1977), 151–161; C. Kramer, "Women's and Men's Ratings of Their Own and Idealized Speech," *Communication Quarterly* 26 (1978), 2–11; and H. Giles, J. Scholes, and L. Young, "Stereotypes of Male and Female Speech: A British Study," *Central States Speech Journal* 34 (1983), 255–256.
12. Kramer, "Perceptions of Female and Male Speech."
13. Kramer, "Women's and Men's Ratings."
14. Giles, Scholes, and Young, "Stereotypes of Male and Female Speech."
15. M. Zuckerman, H. Hodgins, and M. Miyake, "The Vocal Attractiveness Stereotype: Replication and Elaboration," *Journal of Nonverbal Behavior* 14 (1990), 97–112; D. S. Berry, "Vocal Attractiveness and Babyishness: Effects on Stranger, Self, and Friend Impressions," *Journal of Nonverbal Behavior* 14 (1990), 141–153; and S. Naidoo and G. Pillay, "Personal Constructs of Fluency: A Study Comparing Stutterers and Nonstutterers," *Psychological Reports* 66 (1990), 375–378.
16. S. Weitz, *Nonverbal Communication: Readings With Commentary,* 2d ed. (New York: Oxford University Press, 1979), 227.
17. Weitz, *Nonverbal Communication,* 227.
18. A. R. Reich, K. L. Moll, and J. F. Curtis, "Effects of Selected Vocal Disguises Upon Spectrographic Speaker Identification," *Journal of the Acoustical Society of America* 60 (1976), 919–925.
19. F. McGehee, "The Reliability of the Identification of the Human Voice," *Journal of General Psychology* 17 (1937), 249–271.
20. Such advertisements have been placed in *Playboy,* airline sales magazines (aimed at the executive), as well as *Esquire* and other distribution media.
21. E. Winograd, N. H. Kerr, and M. J. Spence, "Voice Recognition: Effects of Orienting Task and the Blind Versus Sighted Listeners," *American Journal of Psychology* 97 (1984), 57–69.
22. C. K. Thomas, *An Introduction to the Phonetics of American English* (New York: The Ronald Press Co., 1958).
23. M. L. Knapp, *Nonverbal Communication in Human Interactions,* 2d. ed. (New York: Holt, Rinehart, and Winston, 1978).
24. Burgoon and Saine, *The Unspoken Dialogue,* 182–183.
25. A. Mulac, "Assessment and Application of the Revised Speech Dialect Attitudinal Scale," *Communication Monographs* 43 (1976), 238–245.
26. M. Jensen and L. B. Rosenfeld, "Influence of Mode of Presentation, Ethnicity, and Social Class on Teachers' Evaluations of Students," *Journal of Educational*

Psychology 66 (1974), 540–547; see also F. Williams, "The Psychological Correlates of Speech Characteristics: On Sounding "Disadvantaged'," *Journal of Speech and Hearing Research* 13 (1970), 472–488.

27. H. Giles, "Communication Effectiveness as a Function of Accented Speech," *Speech Monographs* 40 (1970), 330–331.

28. See J. K. Burgoon, "A Communication Model of Personal Space Violations: Explication and an Initial Test," *Human Communication Research* 4 (1978), 129–142.

29. N. J. Lass and L. A. Harvey, "An Investigation of Speaker Photograph Identification," *Journal of the Acoustical Society of America* 59 (1976), 1232–1236.

30. G. F. Mahl, "Disturbances and Silences in the Patients' Speech in Psychology," *Journal of Abnormal Social Psychology* 53 (1956), 1–15.

31. See D. S. Boomer, "Speech Dyfluencies and Body Movement in Interviews," *Journal of Nervous and Mental Disease* 136 (1963), 263–266; S. V. Kasl and G. F. Mahl, "The Relationship of Disturbances and Hesitations in Spontaneous Speech to Anxiety," *Journal of Personality and Social Psychology* 1 (1965), 425–433; M. S. Krause and M. Pilisuk, "Anxiety in Verbal Behavior: A Validation Study," *Journal of Consulting Psychology* 25 (1961), 414–429; Mahl "Disturbances and Silences''; D. M. Panek and B. Martin, "The Relationship Between GSR and Speech Disturbances in Psychotherapy," *Journal of Abnormal and Social Psychology* 58 (1959), 402–405; B. Pope, T. Blass, A. W. Siegman, and J. Raher, "Anxiety and Depression in Speech," *Journal of Consulting and Clinical Psychology* 35 (1970), 128–133; A. W. Siegman and B. Pope, "Effects of Question Specificity and Anxiety-Producing Messages on Verbal Fluency in the Initial Interview," *Journal of Personality and Social Psychology* 2 (1965), 522–530; A. W. Siegman and B. Pope, *Studies in Dyadic Communication* (New York: Pergamon Press, 1972).

32. S. J. Beckman, "Sex Differences in Nonverbal Behavior," cited in Harper, Wiens, and Matarazzo, *Nonverbal Communication,* 46.

33. R. Dauterive and J. D. Ragsdale, "Relationship Between Age, Sex, and Hesitation Phenomena in Young Children," *Southern Speech Communication Journal* 52 (1986), 22–34.

34. See D. A. Coker and J. K. Burgoon, "The Nature of Conversational Involvement and Nonverbal Encoding Patterns," *Human Communication Research* 14 (1987), 463–494; and J. O. Greene, "Speech Preparation Processes and Verbal Fluency," *Human Communication Research* 11 (1984), 61–84.

35. L. A. Hosman and J. W. Wright II. "The Effects of Hedges and Hesitations on Impression Formation in a Simulated Courtroom Context," *Western Journal of Speech Communication* 51 (1987), 173–188; and E. J. Clemmer and N. M. Carrocci, "Effects of Experience on Radio Language Performance," *Communication Monographs* 51 (1984), 116–139.

36. Hosman and Wright, "The Effects of Hedges and Hesitations."

37. See Harper, Wiens, and Matarazzo, *Nonverbal Communication,* 46–51.

38. M. L. Ray and E. J. Webb, "Speech Duration Effects in the Kennedy News Conference," *Science* 153 (1966), 899–901.

39. K. B. McComb and F. M. Jablin, "Verbal Correlates of Interviewer Empathic Listening and Employment Interview Outcomes," *Communication Monographs* 51 (1984), 353–371; and R. L. Street, Jr., and T. L. Murphy, "Interpersonal Orientation and Speech Behavior," *Communication Monographs* 54 (1987), 42–62.

40. M. Booth-Butterfield and F. Jordan, "Communication Adaptation Among Racially Homogeneous and Heterogenous Groups," unpublished paper, Department of Speech Communication, West Virginia University, *Southern Speech Communication Journal* (in press).

41. Beckman, "Sex Differences."

42. J. Bernard, *The Sex Game: Communication Between the Sexes* (New York: Atheneum Press, 1973); C. Kramer, "Women's Speech: Separate But Unequal," *The Quarterly Journal of Speech* 60 (1974), 14–24; J. E. Baird, "Sex Differences in Group Communication: A Review of Relevant Research," *The Quarterly Journal*

of Speech 62 (1976), 179–192; D. W. Zimmerman and C. West, "Sex Roles: Interruptions and Silences in Conversation," in *Language and Sex: Difference and Dominance,* ed. B. Thorne and N. Henley (Rowling, MA: Newbury House, 1975).

43. See C. W. Kennedy and C. T. Camden, "A New Look at Interruptions," *Western Journal of Speech Communication* 47 (1983), 45–58; K. Dindia, "The Effects of Sex of Subject and Sex of Partner on Interruptions," *Human Communication Research* 13 (1987), 345–371.

44. Dindia, "The Effects of Sex."

45. Kennedy and Camden, "A New Look at Interruptions."

46. Zimmerman and West, "Sex Roles"; C. West, "Against Our Wills: Male Interruptions of Females in Cross-Sex Conversation," *Annals of the New York Academy of Sciences* 327 (1979), 81–97.

47. F. Strodbeck, R. James, and C. Hawkings, "Social Status in Jury Deliberations," in *Interpersonal Behavior in Small Groups,* ed. R. A. Ofshe (Englewood Cliffs, NJ: Prentice-Hall, 1973); M. S. Walker, "The Sex of the Speaker as a Sociolinguistic Variable," in *Language and Sex: Difference and Dominance,* ed. B. Thorne and N. Henley (Rowley, MA: Newbury House, 1975); Baird, "Sex Differences"; M. Argyle, M. Lallijee, and M. Cook, "The Effects of Visibility and Introduction in a Dyad," *Human Relations* 21 (1968), 3–17. Kramer, "Women's Speech."

48. N. Henley and J. Freeman, "The Sexual Politics of Interpersonal Behavior," in *Women: A Feminist Perspective,* ed. J. Freeman (Palo Alto, CA: Mayfield Publishing, 1975); J. Courtwright, F. Millar, and L. E. Rogers-Millar, "Domineeringness and Dominance: Replication and Expansion," *Communication Monographs* 46 (1979), 179–192; Zimmerman and West, "Sex Roles."

49. R. L. Street, Jr., R. M. Brady, and R. Lee, "Evaluative Responses to Communicators: The Effects of Speech Rate, Sex, and Interaction Content," *Western Journal of Speech Communication* 48 (1984), 14–27; see also P. H. Bradley, "Sex, Competence, and Opinion Deviation: An Expectation Status Approach," *Communication Monographs* 47 (1980), 101–110.

50. R. L. Street, Jr., "Speech Convergence and Speech Evaluation in Fact-Finding Interviews," *Human Communication Research* 11 (1984), 139–169.

51. G. Ray, "Vocally Cued Personality Prototypes: An Implicit Personality Theory Approach," *Communication Monographs* 53 (1986), 266–276.

52. S. Duncan, "Some Signals and Rules for Taking Turns in Conversations," *Journal of Personality and Social Psychology* 23 (1972), 283–292; S. Duncan, "Interaction Units During Speaking Turns in Face-to-Face Conversations," in *Organization of Behavior in Face-to-Face Interaction,* ed. A. Kendon, R. Harns, and M. Key (The Hugue: Monton, 1975); M. L. Knapp, R. Hart, and G. Schulman, "The Rhetoric of Goodbye: Verbal and Nonverbal Correlates of Leave-Taking," *Speech Monographs* 40 (1973), 182–198; J. M. Wiemann and M. L Knapp, "Turn-Taking in Conversations," *Journal of Communication* 25 (1975), 75–92.

53. T. J. Saine, "Synchronous and Concatenous Behavior: Two Models of Rule-Violation in Conversational Interaction," paper presented at the Southeastern Psychological Association, New Orleans, 1976.

54. S. Jaffe and S. Feldstein, *Rhythms of Dialogue* (New York: Academic Press, 1970); Wiemann and Knapp, "Turn-Taking in Conversations."

55. Duncan, "Some Signals."

56. Duncan, "Some Signals," 185.

57. Wiemann and Knapp, "Turn-Taking in Conversations."

58. T. Bruneau, "Communicative Silences: Forms and Functions," *Journal of Communication* 23 (1973), 17–46.

59. See P. A. Andersen, J. F. Andersen, and S. M. Mayton, "The Development of Nonverbal Communication in the Classroom: Teachers' Perceptions of Students in Grades K–12," *Western Journal of Speech Communication* 49 (1985), 188–203.

60. Street and Murphy, "Interpersonal Orientation and Speech Behavior."

61. Street and Murphy, "Interpersonal Orientation and Speech Behavior," 58.

62. Coker and Burgoon, "The Nature of Conversational Involvement."

63. M. L. McLaughlin and M. J. Cody, "Awkward Silences: Behavioral Antecedents and Consequences of the Conversational Lapse," *Human Communication Research* 8 (1982), 299–316; see also M. L. McLaughlin, *Conversation: How Talk is Organized* (Beverly Hills, CA: Sage Publications, 1984).

64. K. Dindia, "Antecedents and Consequences of Awkward Silence: A Replication Using Revised Lag Sequential Analysis," *Human Communication Research* 13 (1986), 108–125.

65. Krueger, "Nonverbal Characteristics of Verbal Behavior," 18.

66. O. Robbins, S. Devoe, and M. Wiener, "Social Patterns of Turn-Taking: Nonverbal Regulators," *Journal of Communication* 28 (1978), 38–46.

67. See J. F. Andersen, P. A. Andersen, M. A. Murphy, and N. Wendt-Wasco, "Teachers' Reports of Students' Nonverbal Communication in the Classroom: A Developmental Study in Grades K–12," *Communication Education* 34 (1985), 292–307; D. B. Buller and J. K. Burgoon, "The Effects of Vocalics and Nonverbal Sensitivity on Compliance: A Replication and Extension," *Human Communication Research* 13 (1986), 126–144; J. K. Burgoon, M. Pfau, T. Birk, and V. Manusov, "Nonverbal Communication and Perceptions Associated with Reticence: Replications and Classroom Implications," *Communication Education* 36 (1987), 117–130; Coker and Burgoon, "The Nature of Conversational Involvement"; Dindia, "Antecedents and Consequences of Awkward Silence"; Dindia, "The Effects of Sex of Subject and Sex of Partner on Interruptions"; Krueger, "Nonverbal Characteristics of Verbal Behavior"; Ray, "Vocally Cued Personality Prototypes"; Street, "Speech Convergence and Speech Evaluation"; Street and Murphy, "Interpersonal Orientation and Speech Behavior"; and W. G. Woodall and J. K. Burgoon, "Talking Fast and Changing Attitudes: A Critique and Clarification," *Journal of Nonverbal Behavior* 8 (1985), 126–141.

68. Burgoon, Pfau, Birk, and Manusov, "Nonverbal Communication Performance and Perceptions Associated with Reticence."

69. Woodall and Burgoon, "Talking Fast and Changing Attitudes"; see also A. Mehrabian and M. Williams, "Nonverbal Concomitants of Perceived and Intended Persuasiveness," *Journal of Personality and Social Psychology* 13 (1969), 37–58; and N. Miller, G. Maruyama, R. Beaber, and K. Valone, "Speech of Speech and Persuasion," *Journal of Personality and Social Psychology* 34 (1976), 615–624.

70. J. A. Hall, "Voice Tone and Persuasion," *Journal of Personality and Social Psychology* 36 (1980), 924–934.

71. Buller and Burgoon, "The Effects of Vocalics and Nonverbal Sensitivity on Compliance," 139–140.

72. K. R. Scherer, "Acoustic Concomitants of Emotional Dimensions: Judging Affect from Synthesized Tone Sequences," in S. Weitz, *Nonverbal Communication: Readings With Commentary,* 2d ed. (New York: Oxford University Press, 1979), 249–253.

73. Burgoon and Saine, *The Unspoken Dialogue,* 205.

Chapter Nine

1. See L. A. Malandro, L. L. Barker, and D. Barker, *Nonverbal Communication* 2d ed. (Reading, MA: Addison-Wesley, 1989), 325–336.

2. N. J. Lass, M. E. Tekieli, and M. P. Eye, "A Comparative Study of Two Procedures for Assessment of Oral Tactile Perception," *Central States Speech Journal* 62 (1971), 21–26; and N. J. Lass, R. R. Bell, J. C. Simcoe, N. J. McClung, and W. E. Park, "Assessment of Oral Tactile Perception: Some Methodological Considerations," *Central States Speech Journal* 23 (1972), 165–173.

3. M. Cox, "A Question of Taste," *Omni* 11 (February, 1989), 43–46; 78–81.

4. For example, see P. Byers, "Biological Rhythms as Information Channels in Interpersonal Communication Behavior," In *Nonverbal Communication: Readings With Commentary,* 2d. ed. S. Weitz (New York: Oxford University Press, 1979), 398–418;

L. L. Lane, "Communicative Behavior and Behavior and Biological Rhythms," *Speech Teacher* 20 (1971), 16–19.

5. A Montagu, *Touching: The Human Significance of the Skin* (New York: Harper and Row, 1971).

6. For example, see R. A. Hinde, ed., *Nonverbal Communication* (Cambridge University Press, 1975).

7. For example, see A. S. Parks and H. M. Bruce, "Olfactory Stimuli in Mammalian Reproduction," *Science* 134 (1961), 1049–1054; Byers, "Biological Rhythms"; Wiener, "Human Exocrinology."

8. R. Dumas and A. Morgan, "EEG Asymmetry as a Function of Occupation, Task, and Task Difficulty," *Neuropsychologia* 13 (1975), 220.

9. Dumas and Morgan, "EEG Asymmetry."

10. See K. W. Watson and L. L. Barker, "An Investigation of Lateralized Alpha Activity of Oral Interpreters While Listening to Varied Oral Messages," *Southern Speech Communication Journal* 45 (1980), 173–186.

11. M. Bushsbaum and P. Fedio, "Visual Information and Evoked Responses from the Left and Right Hemispheres," *Electroencephalography and Clinical Neurophysiology* 26 (1969), 266–272.

12. A. Morgan, P. McDonald, and H. MacDonald, "Differences in Bilateral Alpha Activity as a Function of Experimental Task with a Note on Lateral Eye Movements and Hypnotizability," *Neuropsychologia* 9 (1971), 459–469; G. McKee, B. Humphrey, and D. McAdam, "Scaled Lateralization of Alpha Activity During Linguistic and Musical Tasks," *Psychophysiology* 10 (1973), 441–443; K. Robbias and D. McAdam, "Interhemispheric Alpha Symmetry and Imagery Mode," *Brain and Language* 1 (1974), 189–193; D. Galin and R. Ellis, "Asymmetry in Evoked Potentials as an Index of Lateralized Cognitive Processes: Relation to EEG Alpha Asymmetry," *Neuropsychologia* 13 (1975), 45–50.

13. Interview with W. H. Moore, Department of Speech Communication, Auburn University, May 1975.

14. Edward T. Hall, *The Dance of Life: The Other Dimension of Time* (New York: Anchor Books, 1984), 178.

15. Hall, *The Dance of Life,* 180.

16. See William S. Condon, "Method of Micro-Analysis of Sound Films of Behavior," *Behavior Research Methods and Instrumentation* 2 (1970), 51–54; and William S. Condon and W. D. Ogston, "Speech and Body Motion Synchrony of Speaker-Hearer," in *Perception of Language,* ed. D. L. Horton and J. J. Jenkins (Columbus, OH: Charles E. Merrill Press, 1971).

17. Hall, *The Dance of Life,* 181.

18. Condon, "Method of Micro-Analysis"; and Condon and Ogston, "Speech and Body Motion Synchrony of Speaker-Hearer."

19. See P. Weintraub, "Scentimental Journeys," *Omni* 8 (1986), 48–52, 114–116.

20. S. Schachter, "The Interaction of Cognitive and Physiological Determinants of Emotional State," in *Advances in Experimental Social Psychology, Vol. 1,* ed. L. Berkowitz (New York: Academic Press, 1964), 49–80.

21. Schachter, "The Interaction of Cognitive and Physiological Determinants, 50–51.

22. H. Wiener, "Human Exocrinology: The Olfactory Component of Nonverbal Communication," in *Nonverbal Communication Studies with Commentary,* 2d ed., ed. S. Weitz (New York: Oxford University Press, 1979), 338–345.

23. Byers, "Biological Rhythms," 398–418.

24. D. Lombardi, "A Model of the Process of Recogniton of Nonverbal Leakage from Deception Clues," unpublished manuscript, University of Florida, 1976.

25. P. Ekman, "Mistakes While Deceiving," *Annals of the New York Academy of Sciences* 364 (1981), 269–278; see also P. Ekman and W. V. Friesen, *Unmasking the Face* (Englewood Cliffs, NJ: Prentice-Hall, 1975).

26. P. Ekman and W. V. Friesen, "Felt, False, and Miserable Smiles," *Journal of Nonverbal Behavior* 6 (1982), 238–252.

27. P. Ekman, "Facial Expression and Facial Nerve Surgery," in *Disorders of the Facial Nerve,* ed. P. Ekman (New York: Raven Press, 1982), 363–368.

28. Byers, "Biological Rhythms," 398–418.

29. Byers, "Biological Rhythms," 415.

30. D. G. Leathers, *Nonverbal Communication Systems* (Boston: Allyn and Bacon, 1976), 155.

31. W. S. Cain, "Educating Your Nose," *Psychology Today* 15 (1981), 48–56.
32. T. Engen, "Why the Aroma Lingers On," *Psychology Today* 14 (1980), 138.
33. Engen, "Why the Aroma Lingers On."
34. Cain, "Educating Your Nose."
35. For a discussion of the phenomenon, see H. Wiener, "Human Exocrinology: The Olfactory Component of Nonverbal Communication," in *Nonverbal Communication: Readings with Commentary,* 2d ed., ed. S. Weitz (New York: Oxford University Press, 1979), 338–345.
36. Wiener, "Human Exocrinology."
37. R. L. Doty, M. Ford, G. Preti, and G. R. Huggins, "Changes in the Intensity and Pleasantness of Human Vagina Odors During the Menstrual Cycle," *Science* 190 (1975), 1316–1318.
38. J.J. Cowley, A. L. Johnson, and B. Brooksbank, "The Effects of Two Odorous Compounds on Performance in an Assessment-of-People Test," *Psychoneuroendocrinology* 2 (1977), 159–172.
39. E. E. Filsinger, J. J. Braun, and W. C. Monte, "An Examination of the Effects of Putative Pheromones on Human Judgments," *Ethology and Sociobiology* 6 (1985), 227–236.
40. M. K. McClintock, "Menstrual Synchrony and Suppression," *Nature* 229 (1971), 244–245.
41. Wiener, "Human Exocrinology," 341.
42. L. A. Gottschalk, "Phatic Circulating Biochemical Reflections of Transient Mental Content," in *Psychochemical Research in Man: Methods, Strategy, and Theory,* eds. A. J. Mandell and M. P. Mandell (New York: Academic Press, 1969), 357–378.
43. Wiener, "Human Exocrinology."
44. F. Orlandi, D. Serra, and G. Sotgiu, "Electric Stimulation of Olfactory Mucosa: A New Test for the Study of Hypothalmic Functionality," *Hormone Research* 4 (1973), 141–152.
45. K. Smith and J. O. Sines, "Demonstration of a Specific Odor in the Sweat of Schizophrenic Patients," *Archives of General Psychiatry* 2 (1960), 184–188.
46. Wiener, "Human Exocrinology," 341.
47. A. Hoffer and H. Osmond, "Olfactory Changes in Schizophrenia," *American Journal of Psychiatry* (1962), 72–75.
48. R. Porter and J. Moore, cited in "Newsline," *Psychology Today* 16 (1982), 19.
49. For example, see T. Engen and L. P. Lipsitt, "Decrement and Recovery of Response to Olfactory Stimuli in the Human Neonate," *Journal of Comparative and Physiological Psychology* 56 (1963), 75–77; L. P. Lipsitt, T. Engen, and H. Kaye, "Developmental Changes in the Olfactory Threshold of the Neonate," *Child Development* 34 (1963), 371–376; Porter and Moore, "Newsline."
50. Porter and Moore, "Newsline."
51. Cain, "Educating Your Nose," 51.
52. R. W. Moncrieff, *Odour Preferences,* (New York: Wiley, 1966).
53. Cain, "Educating Your Nose," 52.
54. A. V. Gilbert and C. J. Wysocki, "The Smell Survey: Its Results," *National Geographic,* 172 (1987), 514–525.
55. Gilbert and Wysocki, "The Smell Survey," p. 514.
56. B. Gibbons, "The Intimate Sense of SMELL," *National Geographic* 170 (1986), 348–351.
57. R. C. Erb, *The Common Scents of Smell: How the Nose Knows and What It All Knows* (Cleveland: World Publishing, 1968).
58. R. Winter, *The Smell Book: Scents, Sex, and Society* (New York: J. P. Lippincott, 1976).
59. W. B. Key, *Media Sexploitation* (Englewood Cliffs, NJ: Prentice-Hall, 1976).
60. Key, *Media Sexploitation.*
61. Winter, *The Smell Book.*
62. T. Luka, E. S. Berner, and C. Kanakis, "Diagnosis by Smell?" *Journal of Medical Education* 52 (1977), 349–350.
63. Winter, *The Smell Book.*
64. Winter, *The Smell Book.*
65. Key, *Media Sexploitation,* 78.
66. Erb, *The Common Scents of Smell,* 81.
67. Gilbert and Wysocki, "The Smell Survey," 524.
68. L. A. Malandro, L. Barker, and D. Barker, *Nonverbal Communication* 2d ed. (Reading, MA: Addison-Wesley, 1989), 317.
69. D. C. Rubin, E. G. Groth, and D. J. Goldsmith, "Olfactory Cuing and Autobiographical Memory," *American*

Journal of Psychology 97 (1984), 493–505; and G. J. F. Smets and C. J. Overbeeke, "Scent and Sound of Vision: Expressing Scent or Sound as Visual Forms," *Perceptual and Motor Skills* 69 (1989), 227–333.

70. E. T. Hall, *The Silent Language* (Garden City, NY: Doubleday, 1959), 26.
71. E. T. Hall, *The Dance of Life: The Other Dimension of Time* 13 (New York: Doubleday, 1984). Reprinted with permission.
72. Our discussion of Hall's time mandala is taken from Hall's *The Dance of Life.*
73. Hall, *The Dance of Life,* 206. Reprinted with permission.
74. Tom Bruneau, "The Structure of Chronemics," paper presented at the conference on Current Trends in Nonverbal Communication: A Multidisciplinary Approach, Arkansas State University, April 1986. Used with permission.
75. Bruneau, "The Structure of Chronemics," 2. Used with permission.
76. Bruneau, "The Structure of Chronemics," 5. Used with permission.
77. Bruneau, "The Structure of Chronemics," 13. Used with permission.
78. Bruneau, "The Structure of Chronemics," 17. Used with permission.
79. Bruneau, "The Structure of Chronemics," 23. Used with permission.
80. Bruneau, "The Structure of Chronemics," 26. Used with permission.
81. E. T. Hall, *Beyond Culture* (Garden City, NY: Doubleday, 1976).
82. E. Goffman, *Frame Analysis* (New York: Harper and Row, 1974).
83. J. Horton, "Time and Cool People," in *Intercultural Communication: A Reader,* 2d ed., eds. L. A. Samovar and R. E. Porter (Belmont, CA: Wadsworth Publishing, 1976), 84–94.
84. J. K. Burgoon and T. J. Saine, *The Unspoken Dialogue: An Introduction to Nonverbal Communication* (Boston: Houghton-Mifflin, 1978), 131.
85. Burgoon and Saine, *The Unspoken Dialogue.*
86. Burgoon and Saine, *The Unspoken Dialogue,* 102.
87. Burgoon and Saine, *The Unspoken Dialogue,* 101–104; Hall, *Silent Language.*

88. J. Meerloo, "The Time Sense in Psychiatry," in *The Voice of Time,* ed. J. T. Fraser (New York: Braziller, 1966).
89. T. J. Cottle, *Perceiving Time: A Psychological Investigation With Men and Women* (New York: John Wiley & Sons, 1976).
90. Meerloo, "The Time Sense."
91. Cottle, *Perceiving Time,* 171.
92. Cottle, *Perceiving Time,* 182.
93. Cottle, *Perceiving Time,* 185.
94. Burgoon and Saine, *The Unspoken Dialogue,* 103.
95. L. Baxter and J. Ward, cited in "Newsline," *Psychology Today* 8 (1975), 28.
96. T. J. Bruneau, "Communicative Silences: Forms and Functions," *Journal of Communication* 23 (1973), 32–39.
97. A. R. Perry, K. M. Kane, K. J. Bernesser, and P. T. Spicker, "Type A Behavior, Competitive Achievement-Striving, and Cheating Among College Students," *Psychological Reports* 66 (1990), 449–465.
98. L. A. Cinelli and D. J. Ziegler, "Cognitive Appraisal of Daily Hassles in College Students Showing Type A or Type B Behavior Patterns," *Psychological Reports* 67 (1990), 83–88; and G. A. Fine, "Organizational Time: Temporal Demands and the Experience of Work in Restaurant," *Social Forces* 69 (1990), 95–114.
99. A. N. Nicholson, P. A. Smith, B. M. Stone, A. R. Bradwell and J. H. Coote, "Altitude Insomnia: Studies During an Expedition to the Himalayas," *Sleep* 11 (1988), 354–361.
100. R. Levine, "The Pace of Life," *Psychology Today* (October, 1989), 42–46.

Chapter Ten

1. See C. R. Berger and R. L. Calabrese, "Some Explorations in Initial Interaction and Beyond: Toward a Developmental Theory of Interpersonal Communication," *Human Communication Research* 1 (1975), 99–112.
2. D. Bar-Tal and L. Saxe, "Perceptives of Similarity and Disimilarity of Attractive Couples and Individuals," *Journal of Personality and Social Psychology* 33 (1976), 772–781.

3. Eakins and Eakins, *Sex Differences,* 166.

4. C. L. Muelenhard, "Verbal and Nonverbal Cues that Convey Interest in Dating," *Behavior Therapy* 17 (1986), 404–419; M. A. Benassi, "Effects of Romantic Love on Perceptions of Stranger's Physical Attractiveness," *Psychological Reports* 56 (1985), 355–358; and R. Abloff and J. Hewitt, "Attraction to Men and Women Varying in Self-Esteem," *Psychological Reports* 56 (1985), 615–618. Another study found that physical appearance of counselors was important to clients. See B. S. Conway, L. V. Paradise, and J. Zwieg, "Effects of Expert and Referent Influence, Physical Attractiveness, and Gender on Perceptions of Counselors Attributes," *Journal of Counseling Psychology* 3 (1986), 16–22.

5. M. A. Benassi, "Effects of Romantic Love on Perception of Strangers' Physical Attractiveness," *Psychological Reports* 56 (1985), 355–358.

6. J. Donovan, E. Hill, and W. R. Jankowiak, "Gender, Sexual Orientation, and Truth of Consensus in Studies of Physical Attractiveness," *Journal of Sex Research* 26 (1988), 264–271.

7. R. E. Rainville and S. G. Gallagher, "Vulnerability and Heterosexual Attraction," *Sex Roles* 23 (1990), 25–31.

8. S. Brownlow and L. A. Zebowitz, "Facial Appearance, Gender, and Credibility in Television Commercials," *Journal of Nonverbal Behavior* 14 (1990), 51–60.

9. A. Furnham and S. Radley, "Sex Differences in Perception of Male and Female Body Shapes," *Personality and Individual Differences* 10 (1989), 633–642.

10. J. H. Dunkle and P. L. Francis, "The Role of Facial Masculinity/Femininity in the Attribution of Homosexuality," *Sex Roles* 23 (1990), 157–168. See also: F. Pratto and J. A. Bargh, "Stereotyping Based on Apparently Individuating Information: Trait and Global Components of Sex Stereotypes Under Attention Overload," *Journal of Experimental Social Psychology* 27 (1991), 26–47; G. Sawin, "How Could I Be Wrong About Her?" *Etc.* 41 (1989), 375–377; A. Feingold, "Matching for Attractiveness in Romantic Partners and Same-Sex Friends: A Meta-Analysis and Theoretical Critique," *Psychological Bulletin* 104 (1988), 226–235; M. R. Laner, "Competitive vs. Noncompetitive Styles: Which is Most Valued in Courtship?" *Sex Roles* 20 (1989), 165–172; H. S. Friedman, R. E. Riggio, and D. F. Casella, "Nonverbal Skill, Personal Charisma, and Initial Attraction," *Personality and Social Psychology Bulletin* 14 (1988), 203–211; S. Brown, P. L. Francis, and J. P. Lombardo, "Sex-Role and Opposite Sex: Interpersonal Attraction," *Perceptual and Motor Skills* 58 (1988), 855–859; and I. G. Bruscke and B. Raymond, "What Women Think and What Men Think: Perceptions of Abuse and Kindness in Dating Relationships," *Psychological Reports* 67 (1990), 115–128.

11. L. A. Malandro, L. L. Barker, and D. Barker, *Nonverbal Communication* 2d ed. (Reading, MA: Addison-Wesley, 1989), 61.

12. D. Morris, *Intimate Behaviour* (New York: Random House, 1971), 63.

13. J. T. Molloy, *The Woman's Dress for Success Book* (Chicago: Follett, 1977), 21.

14. Molloy, *The Woman's Dress for Success Book,* 148–166.

15. L. Birnback, ed., *The Official Preppy Handbook* (New York: Workman, 1980); and R. Schoenstein, *The I-Hate-Preppies Handbook: A Guide for the Rest of Us* (New York: Simon and Schuster, 1981).

16. Morris, *Intimate Behavior,* 74–79.

17. See D. G. Walsh and J. Hewitt, "Giving Men the Come-On: Effect of Eye Contact and Smiling in a Bar Environment," *Perceptual and Motor Skills* 61 (1985), 873–874; J. S. St. Lawrence, D. J. Hansen, T. F. Cutts, D. A. Tisdelle, J. D. Irish, "Situational Context: Effects of Perceptions of Assertive and Unassertive Behavior," *Behavior Therapy* 16 (1985), 51–62; H. L. Wagner, C. J. MacDonald, and A. S. R. Manstead, "Communication of Individual Emotions by Spontaneous Facial Expressions," *Journal of Personality and Social Psychology* 50 (1986), 737–741; A. P. Jurich and C. J. Polson, "Nonverbal Assessment of Anxiety as a Function of Intimacy of Sexual Attitude Questions," *Psychological Reports* 57 (1985), 1247–1253; J. C. Horn, "Measuring Man by the Company He Keeps," *Psychology Today* 20 (1986), 12; and J. Laird and J. Lewis,

''Looking and Loving: The Effects of Mutual Gaze on Feelings of Romantic Love,'' *Journal of Research in Personality* 23 (1989), 145–161.

18. Morris, *Intimate Behavior,* 77.

19. L. Tieffer, ''The Kiss,'' *Human Nature* 1 (1978), 28.

20. C. Ford and F. Beach, *Patterns of Sexual Behavior* (New York: Harper and Row, 1951).

21. Tieffer, ''The Kiss,'' 37.

22. Tieffer, ''The Kiss,'' 30.

23. Tieffer, ''The Kiss,'' 34.

24. Tieffer, ''The Kiss,'' 35–36.

25. Tieffer, ''The Kiss,'' 36.

26. Morris, *Intimate Behaviour,* 77.

27. Diagram Group, *Man's Body: An Owner's Manual* (New York: Bantam, 1976); see also Diagram Group, *Woman's Body: An Owner's Manual* (New York: Bantam, 1977).

28. Morris, *Intimate Behavior,* 78; see also J. H. Williams, *Psychology of Women: Behavior in a Biosocial Context* (New York: W. W. Norton, 1977), 219–233; and S. Hite, *The Hite Report: A Nationwide Study of Female Sexuality* (New York: Dell, 1976). See also S. Hite, *The Hite Report on Male Sexuality* (New York: Knopf, 1981).

29. A. Mehrabian, *Public Places and Private Spaces: The Psychology of Work, Play, and Living Environments* (New York: Basic, 1976).

30. Mehrabian, *Public Places,* 205.

31. Mehrabian, *Public Places,* 218.

32. D. A. D'Atri, ''Psychophysiological Responses to Crowding,'' *Environment and Behavior* 7 (1975), 237–252; and L. Wheeler, ''Toward A Theory of Behavioral Contagion,'' *Psychological Review* 73 (1966), 179–192; Mehrabian, *Public Places,* 231; and R. Sommer, *Personal Space: The Behavioral Basis of Design* (Englewood Cliffs, NJ: Prentice-Hall, 1969), 120.

33. Sommer, *Personal Space,* 122.

34. Mehrabian, *Public Places,* 255.

35. A. Booth and E. Hess, ''Cross-Sex Friendship,'' *Journal of Marriage and Family* (1974), 44. See also G. M. Phillips and J. T. Wood, *Communication and Human Relationships: The Study of Interpersonal Communication* (New York: Macmillan, 1983), 243–246.

36. J. Haley, *Strategies of Psychotherapy* (New York: Grune and Stratton, 1963), 11. See also P. Watzlawick, J. H. Beavin, and D. D. Jackson, *Pragmatics of Human Communication: A Study of Interactional Patterns, Pathologies, and Paradoxes* (New York: W. W. Norton, 1967), 67–70.

37. L. Tiger, ''Sex-Specific Friendship,'' in *The Compact,* ed. E. Leyton (Canada: University of Newfoundland Press, 1974), 44.

38. A. Booth, ''Sex and Social Participation,'' *American Sociological Review* 37 (1972), 186–187.

39. R. R. Bell, *Worlds of Friendship* (Beverly Hills, CA: Sage, 1981), 79.

40. Bell, *Worlds of Friendship,* 79.

41. H. Goldberg, *The New Male: From Self-Destruction to Self-Care* (New York: Signet, 1979), 35–38.

42. M. E. McGill, *The 40-to-60 Year-Old Male* (New York: Simon and Schuster, 1980), 43.

43. McGill, *The 40-to-60 Year-Old Male,* 71.

44. McGill, *The 40-to-60 Year-Old Male,* 99.

45. McGill, *The 40-to-60 Year-Old Male,* 96.

46. J. Money, *Love and Love Sickness: The Science of Sex, Gender Difference, and Pair Bonding* (Baltimore: Johns Hopkins University, 1980), 123. See also S. Hite, *The Hite Report: A Nationwide Study of Female Sexuality,* 507–524. Although some contend that females go through greater depression than men during menopause, this contention has been contested by E. S. Gomberg and V. Franks, *Gender and Disordered Behavior: Sex Differences in Psychopathology* (New York: Brunner/Mazel, 1979), 403–405.

47. F. N. Willis, ''Initial Speaking Distance as a Function of the Speaker's Relationship,'' *Psychonomic Science* 5 (1966), 221–222.

Chapter Eleven

1. See J. K. Burgoon and T. J. Saine, *The Unspoken Dialogue: An Introduction to Nonverbal Communication* (Boston: Houghton-Mifflin, 1978); H. M. Proshansky, W. H. Ittelson, and L. G. Rivlin eds., *Environmental Psychology: Man and His Physical Setting* (New York: Holt, Rinehart and Winston, 1970).

2. T. High and E. Sundstrom, "Room Flexibility and Space Use in a Dormitory," *Environment and Behavior* 9 (1977), 81–90.
3. S. M. Lyman and M. B. Scott, "Territoriality: A Neglected Sociological Dimension," *Social Problems* 15 (1967), 236–249.
4. J. E. Nash, "The Family Camps Out: A Study in Nonverbal Communication," *Semiotica* 39 (1982), 331–341.
5. J. K. Burgoon, "Privacy," in *Communication Yearbook 6,* ed. M. Burgoon (Beverly Hills, CA: Sage Publications, 1983).
6. For example, see Proshansky, Ittelson, and Rivlin, *Environmental Psychology.*
7. I. Altman and W. W. Haythorn, "The Ecology of Isolated Groups," *Behavioral Science* 12 (1967), 169–182; I. Altman, R. A. Nelson, and E. E. Lett, "The Ecology of Home Environments," *Man-Made Systems* 2 (1972), 189–191.
8. J. B. Roebuck and M. Hickson III, *The Southern Redneck: A Phenomenological Class Study* (New York: Praeger, 1982), 117.
9. N. P. Hamid and A. G. Newport, "Effect of Colour on Physical Strength and Mood in Children," *Perceptual and Motor Skills* 69 (1989), 179–185.
10. For example, see G. McCain, V. C. Cox, and P. B. Paulus, "The Relationship Between Illness Complaints and the Degree of Crowding in a Prison Environment," *Environment and Behavior* 8 (1976), 283–289; D. A. D'Atri, "Psychophysiological Responses to Crowding," *Environment and Behavior* 7 (1975), 237–251; and C. Hunt and M. J. Vaizey, "Differential Effects of Group Density on Social Behavior," *Nature* 209 (1966), 1371–1372.
11. J. L. Freeman, "The Crowd, Not So Madding After All," *Psychology Today* 4 (1971), 58–61, 86.
12. For example, see M. Argyle, *Bodily Communication* (New York: International Universities Press, 1975); R. Heslin, "Steps Toward a Taxonomy of Touching," paper presented at the Western Psychological Association Convention, Chicago, 1974; A. Mehrabian, "Some Determinants of Affiliation and Conformity," *Psychological Reports* 27 (1970), 19–29; and A. Anastasi, *Differential Psychology* (New York: Macmillian, 1958).

13. T. Nguyen, R. Heslin, and M. L. Nguyen, "The Meaning of Four Modes of Touch as a Function of Sex and Body Area," paper presented at the Central States Speech Association Convention, 1974; T. Nguyen, R. Heslin, and M. L. Nguyen, "The Meaning of Touch: Sex Differences," *Journal of Communication* 25 (1975), 93–103; M. L. Nguyen, R. Heslin, and T. Nguyen, "The Meaning of Touch: Sex and Marital Status Differences," *Representative Research in Social Psychology* 7 (1976), 13–18.
14. D. Morris, *Intimate Behavior* (New York: Random House, 1971).
15. See A. Mehrabian, "Some Determinants of Affiliation"; G. Birchler, R. Weiss, and J. Vincent, "Multi-method Analysis of Social Reinforcement Exchange Between Maritally Distressed and Nondistressed Spouse and Stranger Dyads," *Journal of Personality and Social Psychology* 31 (1975), 349–360; and E. G. Beier, "Nonverbal Communication: How We Send Emotional Messages," *Psychology Today* 8 (1974), 52–59.
16. J. L. Prescott, "Body Pleasure and the Origins of Violence," *The Futurist* 9 (1975), 64–74.
17. R. Porter and J. Moore, cited in "Newsline," *Psychology Today* 16 (1982), 19.
18. See, for example, P. J. Salem and R. D. Gratz, "Computers, Pac-Man, and the New Identity Crisis: Communication Relationships in a New Era," paper presented at the Southern Speech Communication Convention, Orlando, FL, 1983.
19. See J. T. Molloy, *Dress for Success* (New York: Warner Books, 1975); and J. T. Molloy, *The Woman's Dress for Success Book* (New York: Warner Books, 1978).
20. See A. L. Sillars, "The Semantics of Family Relationships," paper presented at the Family Communication Conference, Northwestern University, 1984, cited in L. H. Turner, "Communication Patterns in Marital Conflict: An Examination of Conceptual Models," paper presented at the International Communication Association Convention, New Orleans, LA, 1988.
21. Turner, "Communication Patterns."
22. Turner, "Communication Patterns," 3.

23. Proshansky, Ittelson, and Rivlin, *Environmental Psychology,* 328–331.
24. Student paper, University of South Alabama, Mobile, Alabama, 1983.
25. Birchler, Weiss, and Vincent, "Multimethod Analysis of Social Reinforcement"; Beier, "Nonverbal Communication."
26. J. M. Gottman, "Consistency of Nonverbal Affect and Affect Reciprocity in Marital Interaction," *Journal of Consulting and Clinical Psychology* 48 (1980), 711–717.
27. J. M. Gottman and A. Porterfield, "Communicative Competence in the Nonverbal Behavior of Married Couples," *Journal of Marriage and the Family* 43 (1981), 454–464.
28. P. Noller, "Misunderstandings in Marital Communication: A Study of Couples' Nonverbal Communication," *Journal of Personality and Social Psychology* 39 (1980), 1135–1148.
29. P. Noller and C. Gallois, "Sending Emotional Messages in Marriage: Non-Verbal Behavior, Sex, and Communication Clarity," *British Journal of Social Psychology* 25 (1986), 287–297.
30. R. Buck, D. A. Kenny, and R. Sabatelli, "A Social Relations Analysis of Nonverbal Communication Accuracy in Married Couples," *Journal of Personality* 3 (1986), 513–527.
31. Gottman, "Consistency of Nonverbal Affect"; Gottman and Porterfield, "Communicative Competence," 454–464; Noller, "Misunderstandings in Marital Communication."
32. J. Swain, G. M. Stephenson, and M. E. Dewey, "Seeing a Stranger: Does Eye-Contact Reflect Intimacy?" *Semiotica* 42 (1982), 2–4, 107–108.
33. T. J. Saine, "Synchronous and Concatenous Behavior: Two Models of Rule-Violation in Conversational Interaction," paper presented at the Southeastern Psychological Association Convention, New Orleans, 1976.
34. Burgoon and Saine, *The Unspoken Dialogue,* 179.
35. T. J. Cottle, *Perceiving Time: A Psychological Investigation With Men and Women* (New York: John Wiley and Sons, 1976).
36. M. L. Lewis, "Communication Rules and Work Motivation Patterns as Predicators of Marital Satisfaction," paper presented at the Southern Speech Communication Convention, Orlando, FL 1983.
37. B. Murstein and P. Christy, "Physical Attractiveness and Marriage Adjustment in Middle-Aged Couples," *Journal of Personality and Social Psychology* 34 (1976), 537–542.
38. Murstein and Christy, "Physical Attractiveness."
39. J. C. Pearson, *Gender and Communication* (Dubuque, IA: Wm. C. Brown Company Publishers, 1985).
40. J. E. Bates, "Effects of Children's Nonverbal Behavior upon Adults," *Child Development* 47 (1976), 1079–1088.
41. P. J. Mohan, "Child Raising Attitudes, Family Size, and the Value of Children," *Journal of Psychology* 107 (1981), 97–104.
42. See D. W. Stacks, "Toward a Preverbal Stage of Communication," *Journal of Communication Therapy* 2 (1983), 39–60.
43. For example, see R. L. Fantz, "The Origin of Form Perception," *Scientific American* 204 (1961), 66.
44. K. Kaye and A. Fogel, "The Temporal Structure of Face-to-Face Communication Between Mothers and Infants," *Developmental Psychology* 16 (1980), 454–464.
45. See J. Berger and C. C. Cunningham, "The Development of Eye Contact Between Mothers and Normal Versus Downs Syndrome Infants," *Developmental Psychology* 17 (1981), 678–689.
46. Berger and Cunningham, "The Development of Eye Contact."
47. J. Brooks-Gunn and M. Lewis, "Infant Social Perception: Responses to Pictures of Parents and Strangers," *Developmental Psychology* 17 (1981), 647–649.
48. J. M. Haviland, "Sex-related Pragmatics in Infants' Nonverbal Communication," *Journal of Communication* 27 (1977), 80–84.
49. S. Weinberg and J. Weinberg, "The Influence of Clothing on Perceptions of Infant Sex Roles," *Journal of Applied Communications Research* 8 (1980), 111–119.
50. S. Kaiser, M. Rudy, and P. Byfield, "The Role of Clothing in Sex-Role Socialization: Person Perceptions Versus Overt Behavior," *Child Study Journal* 15 (1985), 83–98.

51. L. Berkowitz and A. Frodi, ''Reactions to a Child's Mistakes as Affected by His/Her Looks and Speech,'' *Social Psychology Quarterly* 42 (1979), 420–425.

52. M. Hecht, S. H. Foster, D. J. Dunn, J. K. Williams, D. R. Anderson, and D. Pulbratek, ''Nonverbal Behavior of Young Abused and Neglected Children,'' *Communication Education* 35 (1985), 134–142.

53. For example, see I. Bretherton, U. Stolberg, and M. Kreye, ''Engaging Strangers in Proximal Interaction: Infants' Social Development,'' *Developmental Psychology* 17 (1981), 746–755; and A. Clarke-Stewart and C. Hervey, ''Longitudinal Relations in Repeated Observations of Mother-Child Interaction from 1 to 2½ Years,'' *Developmental Psychology* 17 (1981), 127–145.

54. See chapter 2, this text; Prescott, ''Body Pleasure,'' 64–74; Porter and Moore, ''Newsline''; L. A. Malandro and L. L. Barker, *Nonverbal Communication* (Reading, MA: Addison-Wesley, 1983), 317–319; and M. E. Lamb, ''Parental Influences on Early Socioemotional Development,'' *Journal of Child Psychology and Psychiatry* 23 (1982), 185–192; M. E. Lamb, ''The Bonding Phenomenon: Misinterpretations and Their Implications,'' *Journal of Pediatrics,* 101 (1982), 555–557; and M. E. Lamb, ''Early Contact and Maternal-Infant Bonding: One Decade Later,'' *Pediatrics* 70 (1982), 763–768.

55. See R. Porter and J. Moore, ''Newsline,'' 19.

56. E. Z. Tronick, ''Emotions and Emotional Communication in Infants,'' *American Psychologist* 44 (1989), 112–119.

57. R. J. Davison and N. A. Fox, ''Frontal Brain Asymmetry Predicts Infants' Responses to Maternal Separation,'' *Journal of Abnormal Psychology* 20 (1989), 127–131.

58. A. Fernald, ''Intonation and Communicative Intent in Mothers' Speech to Infants: Is the Melody the Message?'' *Child Development* 6 (1989), 1497–1510.

59. M. Legerstee, ''The Development of Infants' Responses to People and a Doll: Implications for Research in Communication,'' *Infant Behavior and Development* 10 (1987), 81–95.

60. M. L. Hickson III, ''Toward a Biosocial Theory of Human Communication,'' Master's thesis, Mississippi State University, 1981.

61. See G. Michael and F. N. Willis, ''The Development of Gestures as a Function of Social Class, Education, and Sex,'' *Psychological Record* 18 (1965), 515–519; G. Michael and F. N. Willis, ''The Development of Gestures in Three Subcultural Groups,'' *Journal of Social Psychology* 79 (1969), 35–41; and L. Kumin and M. Lazar, ''Gestural Communication in Preschool Children,'' *Perceptual and Motor Skills* 38 (1974), 708–710.

62. I. Alexander and E. Y. Babad. ''Returning the Smile of a Stranger: Within-culture and Cross-culture Comparisons of Israeli and American Children,'' *Genetic Psychological Monographs* 103 (1981), 31–77.

63. C. Golomb, ''Evolution of the Human Figure in a Three Dimensional Medium,'' *Developmental Psychology* 6 (1972), 385–391.

64. M. L. Knapp, *Nonverbal Communication in Human Interaction,* 2nd ed. (New York: Holt, Reinhart and Winston, 1978).

65. Bretherton et al., ''Engaging Strangers.''

66. P. Gifford and J. Price, ''Personal Space in Nursery School Children,'' *Canadian Journal of Behavioral Science* 11 (1979), 318–326.

67. J. R. Brownlee and R. Bakeman, ''Hitting in the Toddler-Peer Interaction,'' *Child Development* 52 (1981), 1076–1079.

68. N. Cavior and D. A. Lombardi, ''Developmental Aspects of Judgments of Physical Attractiveness in Children,'' *Developmental Psychology* 8 (1973), 67–71; and K. K. Dion, ''Physical Attractiveness and Evaluations of Children's Transgressions,'' *Journal of Personality and Social Psychology* 24 (1972), 207–213.

69. L. Dimitrovsky, ''The Ability to Identify the Emotional Meaning of Vocal Expression at Successive Age Levels,'' in *The Communication of Emotional Meaning,* ed. J. R. Davitz (New York: McGraw-Hill, 1964), 69–86.

70. A. Fenster and A. M. Goldstein, ''The Emotional World of Children 'Vis-a-Vis' the Emotional World of Adults: An Examination of Vocal Communication,'' *Journal of Communication* 21 (1971), 353–362.

71. For example, see C. E. Izard, *Human Emotions* (New York: Plenum Press, 1977); and R. J. Trotter, ''Baby Face,'' *Psychology Today* 17 (1983), 14–20.

72. C. Darwin, *The Expression of the Emotions in Man and Animals* (Chicago: University of Chicago Press, 1965).

73. C. Wolff, *A Psychology of Gesture* (New York: Arno Press, 1972).

74. N. G. Blurton Jones, ''Non-Verbal Communication in Children,'' in *Non-Verbal Communication,* ed. R. A. Hines (Cambridge: Cambridge University Press, 1972), 271–295.

75. Burgoon and Saine, *The Unspoken Dialogue,* 200.

76. Burgoon and Saine, *The Unspoken Dialogue,* 200.

77. L. Cameras and K. Allison, ''Children's Understanding of Emotional Facial Expressions and Verbal Labels,'' *Journal of Nonverbal Behavior* 9 (1985), 84–93.

78. C. K. Sigelman and R. M. Adams, ''Family Interactions in Public: Parent-Child Distance and Touching,'' *Journal of Nonverbal Behavior* 14 (1990), 63–75.

79. L. R. Brody, D. H. Hay, and E. Vandewater, ''Gender, Gender Role Identity, and Children's Reported Feelings Toward the Same and Opposite Sex,'' *Sex Roles* 23 (1990), 363–387.

80. B. Powell and L. C. Steelman, ''Beyond Sibship Size: Sibling Density, Sex Composition, and Educational Outcomes,'' *Social Forces* 69 (1990), 181–206.

81. C. J. Peery and L. A. Roggman, ''Parent-Infant Social Play in Brief Encounters: Early Gender Differences,'' *Child Study Journal* 19 (1989), 65–79; L. Beck and R. S. Feldman, ''Enhancing Children's Decoding of Facial Expression,'' *Journal of Nonverbal Behavior* 13 (1989), 269–277; A. Baxter and T. A. Walden, ''The Effect of Context and Age on Social Referencing,'' *Child Development* 60 (1989), 1511–1518; and S. Nowicki and C. Oxenford, ''The Relationship of Hostile Communication Styles to Popularity in Preadolescent Children,'' *Journal of Genetic Psychology* 150 (1988), 39–44.

82. C. E. Kennedy, *Human Development: The Adult Years and Aging* (New York: Macmillan, 1978); and M. J. Smith, R. E. Reinheimer, and A. Gabbard-Alley, ''Crowding, Task Performance, and Communicative Interaction in Old Age,'' *Human Communication Research* 7 (1981), 259–272.

83. J. Sonnenfeld, ''Variable Values in Space and Landscape: An Inquiry into the Nature of Environmental Necessity,'' *Journal of Social Issues* 22 (1966), 71–82.

84. J. F. Myers, ''Institutionalization and Sick Role Identification Among the Elderly,'' *American Sociological Review* 43 (1978), 508–521.

85. Burgoon and Saine, *The Unspoken Dialogue,* 94, 150.

86. Burgoon and Saine, *The Unspoken Dialogue,* 94, 150.

87. Smith, Reinheimer, and Gabbard-Alley, ''Crowding, Task Performance''; and I. Altman, *The Environment and Social Behavior* (Monterey, CA: Brooks/Cole, 1975).

88. Smith, Reinheimer, and Gabbard-Alley; P. D. Ryan, S. M. M. Tainsh, V. Kolodny, B. L. Lendrum, and R. H. Fisher, ''Noise-Making Amongst the Elderly in Long-Term Care,'' *The Gerontologist* 28 (1988), 369–371; D. Fromm and A. L. Holland, ''Functional Communication in Alzheimer's Disease,'' *Journal of Speech and Hearing Disorders* 54 (1989), 535–540; M. D. Shulman and E. Mandel, ''Communication Training of Relatives and Friends of Institutionalized Elderly Persons,'' *The Gerontologist* 28 (1988), 797–800; and D. O'Hair, J. Allman, and L. A. Gibson, ''Nonverbal Communication and Aging,'' *Southern Communication Journal* 45 (1990), 147–160.

89. Knapp, *Nonverbal Communication,* 245–246.

90. H. Ronger, ''Altersveränderungen des Berührungs-sinnes. I. Druchpunktschwellen und Bruckpunktfrequenz,'' *Acta Physiologia Scandinavia* 6 (1943), 343–352; and S. Axelrod and L. D. Cohen, ''Senescence and Embedded-Figure Performance in Vision and Touch,'' *Perceptual and Psychophysiology* 12 (1961), 283–288.

91. B. J. Benjamin, ''Sex Differences in the Older Voice,'' paper presented at the Southern Speech Communication Association Convention, Hot Springs, AK, 1982.

92. Burgoon and Saine, *The Unspoken Dialogue;* R. E. McGlone and H. Hollien, "Vocal Pitch Characteristics of Aged Women," *Journal of Speech and Hearing Research* 6 (1963), 164–170; and E. D. Mysak, "Pitch and Duration Characteristics of Older Males," *Journal of Speech and Hearing Research* 2 (1959), 46–54.

93. D. W. Addington, "The Relationship of Selected Vocal Characteristics to Personality Perception," *Speech Monographs* 35 (1968), 492–503.

94. Burgoon and Saine, *The Unspoken Dialogue,* 149.

95. B. R. Hasselkus, "Variation of Postural Sway Related to Aging in Women," Master's thesis, University of Wisconsin-Madison, 1974.

96. B. Anderson and E. Palmore, "Longitudinal Evaluation of Ocular Function," in *Normal Aging,* ed. E. Palmore (Durham, NC: Duke University Press, 1974), 24–32; and E. A. Lovelace and J. E. Aikens, "Vision, Kinesthesis, and Control of Hand Movement by Young and Old Adults," *Perceptual and Motor Skills* 70 (1990), 1131–1137.

97. J. Meerloo, "The Time Sense in Psychiatry," in *The Voices of Time,* ed. T. Fraser (New York: Braziller, 1966).

98. Cottle, *Perceiving Time,* 111–119.

Chapter Twelve

1. M. Korda, *Power! How to Get it, How to Use it* (New York: Ballentine, 1975); T. Sitton, "Inside School Spaces: Rethinking the Hidden Dimensions," *Urban Environment* 15 (1980), 65–82.

2. W. V. Schmidt and M. E. Dorsey, "Office Design: The Spatial Dimension of Organizational Communication and Reflector of Communication Climate," paper presented at the Southern Speech Communication Association Convention, Houston, TX, April 1986.

3. F. Biren, *Selling Color to People* (Secaucus, NJ: Lyle Stuart, University Books, 1956).

4. See J. K. Burgoon and T. J. Saine, *The Unspoken Dialogue: An Introduction to Nonverbal Communication* (Boston: Houghton-Mifflin, 1978), 109, 274–275.

5. Burgoon and Saine, *The Unspoken Dialogue,* 109.

6. C. Block, "Design to Dispel Fear of Oral Surgery," *Dental Surgery: The Journal of Dental Practice* 4 (1975), 85–89.

7. A. Speer, *Inside the Third Reich,* trans. R. Winston and C. Winston (New York: Macmillan, 1970), 50–71, 102–116, 132–159.

8. K. Cooper, *Nonverbal Communication for Business Success* (New York: AMACOM, 1979).

9. J. Peponis, "The Spacial Culture of Factories," *Human Relations* 38 (1985), 357–390.

10. S. M. Lyman and M. B. Scott, "Territoriality: A Neglected Sociological Dimension," *Social Problems* 15 (1967), 236–249.

11. For example, see Burgoon and Saine, *The Unspoken Dialogue,* 92.

12. M. Cook, "Experiments on Orientation and Proxemics," *Human Relations* 23 (1970), 61–76.

13. L. A. Malandro, L. L. Barker, and D. Barker, *Nonverbal Communication* 2d ed. (Reading, MA: Addison-Wesley, 1989), 194–195.

14. See D. B. Roger and R. L. Reid, "Role Differentiation and Seating Arrangements: A Further Study," *British Journal of Social Psychology* 21 (1982), 23–29; and M. Riess and P. Rosenfeld, "Seating Preferences as Nonverbal Communication: A Self-Presentational Analysis," *Journal of Applied Communications Research* 8 (1980), 22–28.

15. J. C. MacPherson, "Environments and Interaction in Row and Column Classrooms," *Environment and Behavior* 16 (1984), 481–502.

16. Cooper, *NVC for Business Success.*

17. For more on this concept, see B. Schwartz, A. Tesser, and E. Powell, "Dominance Cues in Nonverbal Behavior," *Social Psychology Quarterly* 45 (1982), 114–120.

18. For example, see Cooper, *Nonverbal Communication;* E. T. Hall, *The Silent Language* (Greenwich, CT: Fawcett, 1966); E. T. Hall, *The Hidden Dimension* (Garden City, NY: Anchor Books, 1966); and Burgoon and Saine, *The Unspoken Dialogue,* 185.

19. Burgoon and Saine, *The Unspoken Dialogue,* 98–104, 185.

20. L. Baxter and J. Ward, cited in "Newsline," *Psychology Today* 8 (1975), 28.

21. N. M. Henley, *Body Politics: Power, Sex, and Nonverbal Communication* (Englewood Cliffs, NJ: Prentice-Hall, 1977), 94–123.

22. J. D. Fisher, M. Rytting, and R. Heslin, "Hands Touching Hands: Affective and Evaluative Effects of an Interpersonal Touch," *Sociometry* 39 (1976), 416–421.

23. Cooper, *Nonverbal Communication,* 98–99.

24. G. I. Nierenberg and H. H. Calero, *How to Read a Person Like a Book* (New York: Pocket Books, 1973).

25. S. S. Tompkins, *Affect, Imagery, Consciousness* (New York: Springer, 1962).

26. M. E. Comadena, "Nonverbal Correlates of Deception: A Contextual Analysis," paper presented at the Speech Communication Association Convention, Louisville, KY, 1982.

27. Burgoon and Saine, *The Unspoken Dialogue,* 180.

28. B. E. Collins and H. Guetzkow, *A Social Psychology of Group Processes for Decision-Making* (New York: John Wiley 1964); G. Hearn, "Leadership and the Spatial Factor in Small Groups," *Journal of Abnormal and Social Psychology* 54 (1957), 269–272; A Mehrabian, "Significance of Posture and Position in the Communication of Attitudes and Status Relationships," *Psychological Bulletin* 71 (1969), 365; and R. M. Weisbred, "Looking Behavior in a Discussion Group," cited by M. Argyle and A. Kendon, "The Experimental Analysis of Social Performance," in *Advances in Experimental Social Psychology,* ed. L. Berkowitz (New York: Academic Press, 1967), 55–98.

29. See R. G. Harper, A. N. Wiens, and J. D. Matarazzo, *Nonverbal Communication: The State of the Art* (New York: John Wiley, 1978), 77–118, 171–245; and M. von Cranach, "The Role of Orienting Behavior in Human Interaction," in *Behavior and Environment: The Use of Space by Animals and Men,* ed. A. H. Esser (New York: Plenum, 1971), 217–237.

30. J. Timnick, "How You Can Learn to be Likeable, Confident, Socially Successful for Only the Cost of Your Present Education," *Psychology Today* 16 (1982), 42–49; D. J.

Moore, "To Trust, Perchance to Buy," *Psychology Today* 16 (1982), 50–54; and L. Lau, "The Effect of Smiling on Person Perception," *Journal of Social Psychology* 117 (1982), 63–67.

31. Comadena, "Nonverbal Correlates of Deception."

32. Cooper, *Nonverbal Communication,* 197.

33. R. S. Mach, "Postural Carriage and Congruency as Nonverbal Indicators of Status Differentials and Interpersonal Attraction," Ph.D. Diss., University of Colorado, 1972; A. Mehrabian and M. Williams, "Nonverbal Concomitants of Perceived and Intended Persuasiveness," *Journal of Personality and Social Psychology* 13 (1969), 37–58; and E. Goffman, *Encounters* (New York: Bobbs-Merrill, 1961).

34. Burgoon and Saine, *The Unspoken Dialogue,* 182.

35. Nierenberg and Calero, *How to Read a Person Like a Book.*

36. Cooper, *Nonverbal Communication,* 18–21.

37. H. McGinley, R. LeFevre, and P. McGinley, "The Influence of a Communicator's Body Position on Opinion Change in Others," *Journal of Personality and Social Psychology* 31 (1965), 686–690.

38. M. S. Remland, "Leadership Impressions and Nonverbal Communication in a Superior-Subordinate Interaction," *Communication Quarterly* 32 (1984), 41–48.

39. W. B. Pearce and B. J. Brommel, "Vocalic Communication in Persuasion," *Quarterly Journal of Speech* 58 (1972), 298–306; W. B. Pearce and F. Conklin, "Nonverbal Vocalic Communication and Perception of Speaker," *Speech Monographs* 38 (1971), 235–241; and Moore, "To Trust."

40. Pearce and Conklin, "Nonverbal Vocalic Communication."

41. R. L. Street, Jr., and R. M. Brady, "Speech Rate Acceptance Ranges as a Function of Evaluative Domain, Listener Speech Rate, and Communication Context," *Communication Monographs* 49 (1982), 290–308.

42. D. W. Addington, "The Effect of Vocal Variations on Ratings of Source Credibility," *Speech Monographs* 38 (1971), 242–247.

43. See Burgoon and Saine, *The Unspoken Dialogue,* 185; T. Bruneau, "Communicative Silences: Forms and Functions," *Journal of Communication* 23 (1973), 17–46.

44. J. T. Molloy, *Dress for Success* (New York: Warner Books, (1975); and J. T. Molloy, *The Woman's Dress for Success Book* (Chicago: Follett, 1977).

45. M. L. Knapp, *Nonverbal Communication in Human Interaction,* 2d ed. (New York: Holt, Rinehart, and Winston, 1978), 167.

46. P. R. Wilson, "Perceptual Distortion of Height as a Function of Ascribed Academic Status," *Journal of Social Psychology* 74 (1968), 97–102.

47. Cooper, *Nonverbal Communication,* 21–22.

48. Cooper, *Nonverbal Communication,* 55–56.

49. M. E. Heilman and L. R. Saruwatari, "When Beauty is Beastly: The Effects of Appearance and Sex on Evaluations of Job Applicants for Managerial and Non-managerial Jobs." *Organizational Behavior and Human Performance* 23 (1979), 360–372.

50. K. E. Campbell, D. M. Kleim, and K. Olson, "Gender, Physical Attractiveness, and Assertiveness," *Journal of Social Psychology* 125 (1986), 697–698.

51. P. A. Andersen, T. A. Jenson, and L. B. King, "The Effects of Homophilous Hair and Dress Styles on Credibility and Comprehension," paper presented at the International Communication Association Convention, Atlanta, 1972; K. Peterson and J. C. Curran, "Trait Attribution as a Function of Hair Length and Correlates of Subjects' Preferences for Hair Style," *Journal of Psychology* 93 (1976), 331–339; and Cooper, *Nonverbal Communication,* 81–83.

52. L. Bickman, "Social Roles and Uniforms: Clothes Make the Person," *Psychology Today* 7 (1974), 49–51; L. Bickman, "The Effect of Social Status on the Honesty of Others," *Journal of Social Psychology* 85 (1971), 87–92; L. Bickman, "The Social Power of a Uniform," *Journal of Applied Social Psychology* 4 (1974), 47–61; and W. E. Hensley, "The Effects of Attire, Location, and Sex on Aiding Behavior: A Similarity Explanation," *Journal of Nonverbal Behavior* 6 (1981), 3–11.

53. R. E. Bassett, A. Q. Stanton-Spicer, and J. L. Whitehead, "Effects of Attire and Judgments of Credibility," *Central States Speech Journal* 30 (1979), 282–285.

54. M. L. Damhorst, "Influences of Context Upon the Use of Nonverbal Symbols," paper presented at the Speech Communication Association Convention, Louisville, KY, 1982.

55. Molloy, *The Woman's Dress for Success Book,* 91.

56. M. L. Hickson, L. Powell, S. R. Hill, Jr., G. B. Holt, and H. Flick, "Smoking Artifacts as Indicators of Homophily, Attraction, and Credibility," *Southern Speech Communication Journal* 44 (1979), 191–200.

57. Molloy, *Dress for Success,* 123; and Molloy, *The Woman's Dress for Success Book,* 89.

58. E. C. Webster, ed., *Decision-Making in the Employment Interview* (Montreal: McGill University Industrial Relations Center, 1964).

59. For example, see B. M. Springbett, "Effect on Decision of Order in Which Interviewer Receives Information," in *Decision-Making in the Employment Interview,* ed. E. C. Webster (Montreal: McGill University Industrial Relations Center, 1964), 16–26; P. C. Smith, S. Mitchel, and J. Rollo, "Influence of Varying Sources of Information on Judgments of Interviews," *Psychological Reports* 34 (1974), 683–688; M. M. O'Kanes and H. Tschirgi, "Impact of the Face-to-Face Interview on Prior Judgment of Candidate," *Perceptual and Motor Skills* 46 (1978), 322; and D. M. Young, E. G. Beier, and S. Beier, "Beyond Words: Influences of Nonverbal Behavior of Female Job Applicants in the Job Interview," *Personnel and Guidance Journal* 57 (1979), 346–350.

60. For example, see J. R. Barbee and E. C. Keil, "Experimental Techniques of Job Interview Training for the Disadvantaged: Videotape Feedback, Behavior Modification, and Microcounseling," *Journal of Applied Psychology* 58 (1973), 209–214; P. Ekman, "Body Position, Facial Expression, and Verbal Behavior During Interviews," *Journal of Abnormal and Social Psychology* 68 (1964), 295–301; A. Mehrabian and S. Friar, "Encoding of Attitude by Seated

Communicator Via Posture Cues," *Journal of Consulting and Clinical Psychology* 33 (1969), 330–336; R. V. Exline and L. C. Winters, "Affective Relationships and Mutual Glances in Dyads," in *Affect, Cognition, and Personality,* eds. P. Tompkins and C. E. Izard (New York: Springer, 1965); Mehrabian and Williams, "Nonverbal Concomitants"; P. V. Washburn and M. D. Hakel, "Visual Cues and Verbal Content as Influences on Impressions After Simulated Employment Interviews," *Journal of Applied Psychology* 58 (1973), 137–141; Young, Beier, and Beier, "Beyond Words"; A. G. Miller, "The Role of Physical Attractiveness in Impression Formation," *Psychonomic Science* 24 (1970), 241–243; R. L. Dipboye, H. L. Fromkin, and K. Wiback, "Relative Importance of Applicant Sex, Attractiveness, and Scholastic Standing in Evaluation of Job Resumes," *Journal of Applied Psychology* 60 (1975), 39–43; S. L. Cohen and K. A. Bunker, "Subtle Effects on Sex-Role Stereotype on Recruiter Hiring Decisions," *Journal of Applied Psychology* 60 (1975), 566–572; R. L. Dipboye, R. D. Arvey, and D. E. Terpstra, "Sex and Physical Attractiveness of Raters and Applicants as Determiners of Resume Evaluations," *Journal of Applied Psychology* 62 (1977), 288–294; M. Z. Sincoff, "Favorable Impression Characteristics of the Recruiting Interview," *Personnel Psychology* 31 (1978), 495–504; and J. G. Hollandsworth, R. Kazelskis, J. Stevens, and M. E. Dressel, "Relative Contributions of Verbal, Articulative, and Nonverbal Communication to Employment Decisions in the Job Interview Setting," *Personnel Psychology* 32 (1979), 359–367.

61. K. W. Watson and L. R. Smeltzer, "Perceptions of Nonverbal Communication During the Selection Interview," *ABCA Bulletin* 45 (1982), 30–34.

62. C. L. Bovee and J. V. Thill, *Business Communication Today* (New York: Random House, 1983), 358–359.

63. Cooper, *Nonverbal Communication.*

64. Baxter and Ward, "Newsline."

65. Bovee and Thill, *Business Communication Today,* 359.

66. M. Stano, "The Performance Appraisal Interview: Guidelines for Academic Department Chairs," in *Effective Communication for Academic Chairs,* ed. by M. Hickson III and D. W. Stacks (Albany: State University of New York Press, 1992), 107–120.

67. A. Galin and B. Benoliel, "Does the Way You Dress Affect Your Performance?" *Personnel* 67 (1990), 49–52; and K. P. DeMeuse, "A Review of the Effects of Non-verbal Cues on the Performance Appraisal Process," *Journal of Occupational Psychology* 60 (1987), 207–226.

68. V. P. Richmond, J. C. McCroskey, and S. K. Payne, *Nonverbal Behavior in Interpersonal Relations,* 2d ed. (Englewood Cliffs, NJ: Prentice-Hall, 1991), 268–290.

69. J. A. Sanders and R. L. Wiseman, "The Effects of Verbal and Nonverbal Teacher Immediacy on Perceived Cognitive, Affective, and Behavioral Learning in the Multicultural Classroom," *Communication Education* 39 (1990), 341–353.

70. J. C. Pearson and R. West, "An Initial Investigation of the Effects of Gender on Student Questions in the Classroom: Developing a Descriptive Base," *Communication Education* 40 (1991), 22–32.

71. J. E. Mercincavage and C. I. Brooks, "Differences in Achievement Motivation of College Business Majors as a Function of Year in College and Classroom Seating Position," *Psychological Reports* 66 (1990), 632–634.

72. L. A. Cinelli and D. J. Ziegler, "Cognitive Appraisal of Daily Hassles in College Students Showing Type A and Type B Behavior Patterns," *Psychological Reports* 67 (1990), 83–88. See also: S. R. St. J. Neill, "Children's Reported Responses to Teachers' and Non-Teachers' Nonverbal Communication," *Educational Research* 31 (1989), 71–74; and A. A. Badini and R. Rosenthal, "Visual Cues, Student Sex, Material Taught, and the Magnitude of Teacher Expectancy Effects," *Communication Education* 38 (1989), 162–166.

73. R. J. Matlon, *Communication in the Legal Process* (New York; Holt, Rinehart, and Winston, 1988); and T. A. Mauet, *Fundamentals of Trial Techniques,* 2d ed. (Boston: Little, Brown, 1988).

74. R. L. Street, Jr., and D. B. Buller, "Patients' Characteristics Affecting Physician-Patient Nonverbal Communication," *Human Communication Research* 15 (1988), 60–90. See also A. Vrugt, "Negative Attitudes, Nonverbal Behavior and Self-Fulfilling Prophecy in Simulated Therapy Interviews," *Journal of Nonverbal Behavior* 14 (1990), 77–86.

75. Meharabian and Williams, "Nonverbal Concomitants."

76. For example, see M. Shaw, *Group Dynamics: The Psychology of Small Group Behavior,* 3d ed. (New York: McGraw-Hill, 1981); H. Rosenfeld, "Instrumental Affiliative Functions of Facial and Gestural Expressions," *Journal of Personality and Social Psychology* 4 (1966), 65–72; and R. Stogdill, "Personal Factors Associated with Leadership: A Survey of the Literature," *Journal of Psychology* 25 (1948), 35–71.

77. J. O'Connor, "The Relationship of Kinesic and Verbal Communication to Leadership Perception in Small Group Discussions" Ph.D. diss., Indiana University, 1971.

78. J. E. Baird, Jr., "Some Nonverbal Elements of Leadership Emergence," *Southern Speech Communication Journal* 42 (1977), 352–361.

79. Burgoon and Saine, *The Unspoken Dialogue,* 181–182.

80. D. G. Leathers, "The Role of Nonverbal Factors in Shaping Perceptions of Leadership," seminar presented at the University of Southern Mississippi, Hattiesburg, MS, 1982. See also D. G. Leathers, *Successful Nonverbal Communication* (New York: Macmillan, 1986).

81. M. Hickson III, R. D. Grierson, and B. C. Linder, "A Communication Perspective on Sexual Harassment; Affiliative Nonverbal Behaviors in Asynchronous Relationships," *Communication Quarterly* 39 (1991), 111–118; and M. Hickson III, R. D. Grierson, and B. C. Linder, "A Communication Model of Sexual Harassment," *Association for Communication Administration Bulletin* 74 (1990), 22–33.

Glossary

□   □   □

accentuation A function of nonverbal communication as it relates to verbal communication; accentuation lends emphasis to what is said.

accessories Objects worn in plain view that indicate group membership or that serve to enhance one's appearance.

action language All kinesic movements not used as signals (Ruesch and Kees).

activity Informal time dimension of what is done in a given period of time.

adaptors Gestures learned early in life that relate to the touching of the body or objects (Ekman and Friesen).

additions Devices worn beneath the clothing or hidden from view that accentuate, hide, or correct the appearance.

aesthetic feeling A generalized positive to negative feeling based on reactions to an environment.

affect blends Expressions that show two or more emotions at the same time.

affect displays Gestures that reflect the emotional state of the person (Ekman and Friesen).

allokine Smallest unit in the structure-centered approach to kinesics; cultural variation of a kine (Birdwhistell).

alpha wave A biofeedback state associated with a relaxed or rested state.

analogical information. Continuous, infinite, and natural units of information.

anthropological roots An approach to nonverbal communication based on anthropological and zoological thought.

appeals to invitations Gestures inviting others to engage in quasi-courtship behaviors (Schlefen).

approach The way a person sees that which is around him or her.

articulation Clearness and control of the voice in oral communication.

atomistic time A discontinuous and egocentric view of time.

backchanneling Kinesic behaviors that confirm the other person or suppress the taking of a turn.

baseline date An understanding of a subject's (person's) actions and behaviors prior to study, analysis, or manipulation.

baton An illustrator that emphasizes words or sentences in oral communication (Ekman and Friesen).

behavior Any action or reaction by a person.

behavioral sink A result of high density, yielding deviant and nonsocial behaviors.

biofeedback systems Perceptual state consisting of feedback from brain waves, the skin, muscles, heart rate, and blood pressure.

biological time orientation A natural time orientation based on internal (endogenous) rhythms.

biorhythm A biological time orientation suggesting an internal human clock based on cycles the person is on.

body image The way a person views his or her body, including attitudes and feelings.

body territory The space immediately surrounding us, marked by the skin and clothing (Lyman and Scott).

chronemics The study of how we use and structure time.

circadian rhythm   Internal time clock of forty-eight hours divided into two twenty-four hour cycles.

clinical time   A personal life span between birth and death—both conscious and unconscious (Meerloo).

cocooning   A withdrawing into oneself; creating a personal territorial behavior.

code material   Type of information processed in communication.

communication   An interactive process whereby people seek to induce change through the sending and receiving of messages by means of a commonly understood code system.

complementary relationship   A relationship whereby two people are exchanging different types of behavior.

complementation   A function of nonverbal communication as it relates to verbal communication, supplementing and/or modifying the verbal message.

condition   A grouping of participants in a research study, providing for a particular manipulation based on an independent variable.

context   The background against which communication occurs.

contradiction   A function of nonverbal communication as it relates to verbal communication, negating the verbal message.

conversation preserve   Involves who can summon others into offices or areas to talk and when we can be summoned to talk; one of Goffman's territories of the self.

co-orientation   Degree of liking and attraction in an interaction or relationship.

courtship readiness cues   Physiological changes in people as they prepare to engage in quasi-courtship behaviors (Schlefen).

CPT   Colored People's Time; a time orientation.

crowding   A psychological reaction to decreased space and increased density.

cumulative structure   An approach to kinesics; see *meaning-centered*.

deception clue   An expression or gesture that indicates a person is engaged in deception but that does not reveal the content of the deception.

deictic movement   Illustrator that indicates where objects are (Ekman and Friesen).

density   The number of people in a given territory or space.

dependent variable   The variable in research in comparison with which we judge the effects of the independent variable(s).

digital information   Arbitrary, discrete, and finite bits of information.

duration   How long a sound is made in oral communication (paralanguage); informal time dimension relating to how long something lasts (chronemics).

dynamic environments   Space that changes as people change.

ectomorph   A body type typified as tall, frail, and thin.

elocutionary system   A system of expressions and gestures relating to the content of the oral message.

emblematic movement   Illustrators that serve as temporary emblems during the flow of conversations (Ekman and Friesen).

emblems   Gestures with direct verbal translations (Ekman and Friesen).

emotional biorhythm cycle   A twenty-eight day cycle dealing with emotional reactions and the nervous system.

emotional phase   Acquisition phase during which feelings or sensations combine to form an emotional repertoire in children (found between two weeks and two years of age).

endomorph   A body type typified as soft, plump, short, and round.

environment   An area you attempt to structure so as to create a mood or a response.

exohormone   An odor secreted by an organism which alters the behavior of others; for example, a pheromone.

explicit communication   Verbal cues definable by rules of syntax and a dictionary meaning (Mehrabian).

family   An extension of the physical home; a psychological home consisting of three stages beyond social interaction: the marriage, the children, and the elderly.

fantasy   Thoughts of possible intimacy originating from social interaction; imagination.

field experiment   Research that attempts to exert some control over the variables of interest but that is conducted in a "natural" setting, which allows for a more realistic test of the hypotheses.

field study   Research with little or no control, except for the objectivity of the researcher.

fixed-feature environments   An environment with a particular architectural arrangement based on specific cultural configurations.

formal time   A time system that represents the way a culture views, expresses, and teaches time as a perceived entity.

future time orientation A projection to the future based on analysis of today (Meerloo).

game stage A developmental stage at which a child has well-understood nonverbal norms operating (Mead).

gender Learned sexual characteristics; tertiary sexual differences; sex.

genderism Stereotypes based on common gender differences.

gerontology The study of aging and the aged.

gestaltist time A continuous and historiocentric view of time.

great/general American dialect Major dialect found in native North American speakers: perceived as the most credible of the three major dialects (Great/General, Northeastern, Southern).

haptics The study of touch and touching; also known as *zero-proxemics*.

hauley time White person's time (in Hawaii); a time frame.

hemisphere One of two major parts of the human brain responsible for communication.

hemispheric style The way each of the brain's hemispheres processes communication.

home A physical place, a barrier behind which we can hide from the world and an environment we sometimes use to express ourselves both publically and privately; a place of residence.

home territory The physical territory to which an individual lays claim, marked by legal and physical barriers (Lyman and Scott).

hypothesis A statement that predicts relationships between variables based on some theoretical perspective.

ideographs Illustrators that represent the thought processes (Ekman and Friesen).

illustrators Gestures that support what is being said orally; cannot stand alone and must accompany or follow the oral message (Ekman and Friesen).

imitation stage A developmental stage at which a child begins to expand his or her repertoire of nonverbal behaviors (Mead).

implicit communication Vague and informal explanations of the significance of nonverbal behaviors (Mehrabian).

independent variable The variable that is manipulated in research.

informal time Based on practice and takes on a more psychological time orientation.

information preserve Territories that contain facts about the self we wish to control; one of Goffman's territories of the self.

instinctive emotional phase Acquisition phase in which emotions are instinctive (birth to six months of age).

intellectual biorhythm cycle A thirty-three day cycle dealing with cognitive activity and intellectual ability.

intentionality A concern as to whether a message (verbal or nonverbal) has been consciously sent (or received) by a communicator.

interactional territory An area, mobile or fixed, that is restricted in terms of accessibility by someone (Lyman and Scott).

intimate space A distance zone measuring from touching to about eighteen inches between interactants (Hall).

kine Combinations of allokines in the structure-centered approach to kinesics, still below meaningful analysis (Birdwhistell).

kineme A combination of kines in the structure-centered approach to kinesics that creates the first meaningful level of analysis (Birdwhistell).

kinemorpheme Sequential movements in the structure-centered approach to kinesics, consisting of kineme combinations (Birdwhistell).

kinesics The study of body movement and facial expression.

kinetographs Illustrators that represent some form of bodily action (Ekman and Friesen).

laboratory research "Experimental" approach by means of which the researcher attempts to understand behavior under controlled conditions.

lateralized alpha wave A biofeedback state associated with a task or a problem-solving activity.

leakage An expression "accidentally" revealing information the person wished to conceal.

left hemisphere The abstract, logical, and analytic side of the brain, best suited for the processing of verbal communication.

licensed touchers People who are allowed to touch others, usually regulated by some legal or authoritative body (e.g., nurses, doctors, hair dressers/barbers).

linguistic analogy Language analogy as equated to the study of kinesics; see *structure-centered approach*.

literature review A method of critical research that involves collecting and verifying information and sources.

loudness Intensity of the voice.

machismo A role in which a person is perceived as a "real man," when males are viewed as independent and females as dependent.

markers Signs that denote ownership of a territory.

matching hypothesis A proposition that people choose partners considered to be in the same category of physical appearance.

meaning-centered approach to kinesics Approach to the study of kinesics that stresses meaning of movement over structure. Associated with Ekman and Friesen.

Mehrabian's functional approach Approach to the study of kinesics that categorizes behavior into functional groups: liking, power, and responsiveness.

mesomorph A body type typified as properly proportioned, athletic, trim, muscular, and average in height.

metamessage A message about how to communicate in a given context or environment.

mid-life crisis Refers to a rapid and substantial change in personality and behavior in people between forty and sixty years of age.

mirroring The matching of another's behaviors without conscious knowledge of the behavior.

Morris' derivation system Approach to the study of kinesics based on the assumption that human behavior is not free flowing; instead, it is said to be divided into a series of separate events, each with its special rules and rhythms.

natural endowment That which a person possesses about his or her body, and which is relatively fixed.

Neomammalian brain Most recent brain, comprising the neocortex, which is responsible for symbols, signs, rules, and language.

neurophysiological approach An approach to the study of nonverbal communication based on how people process verbal and nonverbal information in the brain.

nonverbal communication A process whereby people, through the intentional or unintentional manipulation of normative actions and expectations, express experiences, feelings, and attitudes in order to relate to and control themselves, others, and their environments.

norm Those behaviors we take for granted or that are expected of us in communicating with others.

normative expectations Expectations of behavior that over a period of time, become the norms that govern our behavioral and communication patterns.

object language Intentional and nonintentional displays of material things (Ruesch and Kees).

objective emotional phase Acquisition phase in which emotions are related to thought and gesture (six years of age and up).

olfaction The study of how we use and perceive odors.

olfactory deja vu The association of odor with location that is generalized but not matched with new stimulus.

olfactory (odor) memory One of the oldest and most direct of the senses; a sensation that is vague and half-understood but accompanied by strong emotions.

olfactory signature A ''smell print'' or identification based on some odor that classifies people, places, or things.

Paleomammalian brain Middle brain responsible for emotive and imaginistic interpretations; more nonverbal.

parakinesic phenomena Those physiological features that influence kinesic expression (intensity, duration, and range of expression) (Birdwhistell).

paralanguage The study of how we say the words we speak; includes sociological (dialect) and physiological characteristics (vocal production) of oral communication; the communication potential of the voice.

paravocal communication The study of paralanguage as content-free speech.

past time orientation Time viewed as a cycle in which experiences are relived (Meerloo).

pauses Silences within or between a turn.

perceptual system A state that is not quite as obvious to us as are other states and that is found just below conscious recognition.

personal space (1) An invisible space immediately surrounding the person, a body buffer zone, micro-space; (2) a distance zone measuring from eighteen inches to about four feet between interactants (Hall); (3) Goffman's equivalent of body territory, includes touch, one of the territories of the self.

pheromone A substance that serves as a sexual attractant; an exohormone.

physical appearance The impression people have of others based on the body, personal aesthetics, clothing, body adaptors, and additions.

physical biorhythm cycle A twenty-three day cycle dealing with endurance, energy strength, and coordination.

pictograph Illustrators that represent shapes or objects in space (Ekman and Friesen).

pitch Range of voice during conversation.

plastic surgery A means of altering natural endowments, either by areas of aesthetic or reconstructive surgery.

play stage A developmental stage during which a child begins to learn which nonverbal behaviors are appropriate and which are inappropriate (Mead).

positional cue Kinesic cues that exclude some persons from an interaction while including another person in quasi-courtship behavior (Schlefen).

possessional territory Objects that we view as our own; one of Goffman's territories of the self.

power In relationships, indicates who is dominant.

preening behavior Preparation for quasi-courtship, including adjustments of clothing and primping (Schlefen).

present time orientation A time orientation of the "here and now;" a time of the immediate (Meerloo).

pronunciation Clearness and control of sound; the rhythm and rate of speech.

proxeme A unit of space, measured as "inner" and "outer," in Hall's spatial zones.

proxemics The interrelated observations and theories of our use of space as a specialized elaboration of culture; usually divided into territory and personal space.

psychological home The family: an extension of the physical home.

psychological roots Approach to the study of nonverbal communication based on psychological orientation.

psychological time orientation Personal or individual time orientations.

public space A distance of ten feet or more between people (Hall).

public territory An area people may enter freely; an area open to people with a legitimate use for that space (Lyman and Scott).

punctuality Informal time dimension relating to how prompt or "on time" we are, or how we synchronize with others.

quasi-courtship behavior Schlefen's model of kinesic behavior, according to which both sexes note one another's sexual interest.

R-complex brain Oldest brain; instinctive behaviors; sensory-motor actions, including sexual drive, territoriality, aggression, and so forth.

REM Rapid eye movement.

regularity Rate of speech, including stress in the voice.

regulation A function of nonverbal communication as it relates to verbal communication; regulates who speaks when and, sometimes, where.

regulators Gestures that indicate when to talk or when to allow others to talk (Ekman and Friesen).

reodorize Changing an odor from one smell to another.

repetition A function of nonverbal communication as it relates to verbal communication, reinforcing the verbal message.

rhythmic movement Illustrators that represent the timing of an event or occurrence (Ekman and Friesen).

right hemisphere The spontaneous, unconscious, and holistic side of the brain, best suited for the processing of nonverbal communication.

semifixed environment Space in which people can increase or decrease their interactions with others and provide some control over others.

sequencing Structuring of an interaction in a "my turn, your turn . . ." format.

sex differences Biological or sociological differences in how people communicate based on their sex; may be primary, secondary, or tertiary.

sheath The territory of the skin and its coverings (clothing); one of Goffman's territories of the self.

sign The natural representation of an event or act.

sign language Kinesic system including all forms of codification in which words, numbers, and punctuation signs are supplanted by gestures. (Ruesch and Kees)

silence The lack of sound.

similarity hypothesis A proposition positing a tendency to like those who do not distort our own view of ourselves (self-image) or who do not disparage our own level of attraction.

smell adaptation An occurrence when an odor becomes part of your environment or general background.

social cognition An awareness of others that is associated with some behavior.

social interaction emotional phase   Overlaps the instinctive, emotional, and objective emotional phases during which a child's behaviors evolve from reflexive movements to movements with social meaning.

social space   A distance zone measuring from four feet to ten feet between interactants (Hall).

spatial movements   Illustrators that represent spatial relationships (Ekman and Friesen).

spatiotemporal   Refers to an awareness of time and place.

speech disturbances   Nonfluencies, speech rates, and latency of response, characterizes the voice during conversation.

stall   A well-bounded space used by one person at a time; one of Goffman's territories of the self.

stigma   The possession of an attribute that makes one different from others in the category of people available, and of a less desirable kind.

structure-centered approach to kinesics   Approach to kinesics that stresses structure of movement over meaning; associated with Birdwhistell.

subject   Someone chosen to participate in a research project.

substitution   A function of nonverbal communication as it relates to verbal communication; creates a symbolic nonverbal behavior.

survey research   A method of collecting data in the field with a carefully worked out questionnaire pretested so that it does not bias the results.

symbol   Something that represents an abstraction; a symbol that takes the place of the referent.

symmetrical relationship   A friendship in which two people exchange the same type of behavior.

technical time   A precise way of measuring the relationship between a variable and time.

telepathic system   Perceptive communication at the level of vibrations or biofeedback from internal states.

territoriality   Laying claim to an area and defending it against members of the same species.

territories of the self   Goffman's eight territories that humans possess.

territory   A fixed space bounded by markers.

theoretical perspective   A way of viewing the phenomena under study.

time frames   Expectations of time that differ among and between cultures and subcultures.

time-line orientation   An analytic view of time, according to which time is seen as a systematic progression of past and projected future (Meerloo).

turn   (1) Goffman's temporal element in space that relates to space and time, a territory of the self; (2) the time you speak or have the "floor" in a conversation.

turn-maintaining cue   Paralanguage cue that keeps your turn from ending ("maintaining the floor").

turn-suppressing cue   Paralanguage cue that enables one person to maintain control of the interaction.

turn-taking cue   Paralanguage cue that allows the other person to take his or her turn.

turn-yielding cue   Paralanguage cue that indicates you wish to yield your turn in the interaction.

types of touch   Classification of touch based on interpersonal relationships (Heslin); or what touch communicates as attitude, regulation, or meaningless messages (Argyle).

use space   Space claimed by people within their line of vision, or as instrumental in performing a function; one of Goffman's territories of the self.

violation of expectations   A systematic study of the effect of violating norms and expectations of nonverbal subcodes.

vocalics   Similar to paralanguage.

vocalizations   Specific features of the voice that characterize the voice at specific points in time.

vocal characterizers   Vocalization as nonverbal sounds, such as laughing, crying, whimpering, and so forth.

vocal segregates   Nonwords that are used to fill pauses, or words and phrases used as meaningless fillers.

voice print   An analysis based on the uniqueness of the voice; similar to the finger print.

voice qualities   Modifications of the voice: includes pitch range, vocal lip control, glottis control, pitch control, articulation control, tempo control, resonance, rhythm control.

voice set   Background against which the voice is to be judged.

voice types   Certain voice qualities that stereotype people one way or another.

zero-proxemics   Study of the effects of touch, also called *haptics*.

Author Index

Subject Index

□   □   □

A

Accents, 146–49
Accessories, 106–107, 246
Activity (time), 182
Adaptors, 117–18
Advertising, 21, 89, 134, 172–73, 174. *See also* Marketing
Aesthetics (room design), 78–79
Affect blends, 120
Affect displays, 118, 120
Affective communication, 223–25
Affective information, 18–19, 125, 159
Age. *See also* Children; Elderly; Infants
    filters, 24
    personal space, 61–62
    same-sex relationships, 202–203
Aggression, 74
AIDS, 96, 198
Allokine, 112
Alpha waves, 163
Analogical codes, 23
Anger, 118
Animal studies, 46, 70–71, 74
Apprehension (communication), 127, 129
Approaches to nonverbal communication, 8–11
Arms-akimbo position, 113
Articulation, 138
Ascribed communication, 7
Atomism, 186
Attitude, 53–54

B

Backchanneling, 117
Biofeedback systems, 162–64
Body
    alterations, 97–102
    image, 92–95
    occupational relationships, 242–43, 244
    orientation, 113–14
    overt communication, 13
    shape, 89–92, 149
    territory, 69
    vocal expressiveness, 149
Body buffer zone, 60
Brain, 22–24, 135–36, 163

C

Catharsis, 19
Child abuse, 221
Children
    family relationship, 218–25
    personal space, 61–62, 72
    physical attractiveness, 86
    tactile development, 47–48
    weight and personality, 91
Chronemics culture, 181–84
    elderly, 227
    home, 213
    job interviews, 249
    marriage, 217
    occupation, 237–38
    perceptions of time, 175
    psychological orientations, 184–87
    significance of time, 187–88
    social interactions, 198–99, 202
    structure of time, 176–81
Class (socioeconomic), 130, 156, 173. *See also* Status
Classrooms, 80
Clinical time, 184
Clothing, 102–106, 196, 221, 245–46, 250
Cocooning, 72, 211
Coding methods, 115
Cognitive information, 18, 125, 159
Color, 78, 79–80
Communication, defined, 5
Communication attempt, 7
Conditions (experimental), 31
Contempt, 120
Context, 23–24, 36, 111